Anne Henderson AM is Deputy Director of The Sydney Institute, editor of *The Sydney Papers Online*. She is the author of *From All Corners: Six Migrant Stories* (Allen & Unwin, 1993), *Educating Johannah: A Year in Year 12* (Allen & Unwin, 1995), *Mary MacKillop's Sisters: A Life Unveiled* (Harper-Collins, 1997), *Getting Even: Women MPs on Life, Power and Politics* (Harper-Collins, 1999*), The Killing of Sister Irene McCormack* (HarperCollins, 2002) and *An Angel in The Court – The Life of Major Joyce Harmer* (HarperCollins, 2005), *Enid Lyons – Leading Lady to A Nation* (Pluto Press 2008), *Joseph Lyons – The People's Prime Minister* (University of NSW Press, 2011) and *Menzies At War* (University of NSW Press, 2014) which was shortlisted for the 2015 Prime Minister's Award for Australian History. Among her essays of note are the biographical chapter on Prime Minister Joe Lyons for *Australian Prime Ministers* edited by Michelle Grattan (New Holland, 2000) and for the UK's *New Dictionary of National Biography* (OUP, 2004).

ENID LYONS –
LEADING LADY TO A NATION

Anne Henderson

Jeparit Press

Published by Jeparit Press, 2018

PO Box 7257
Redland Bay QLD 4165
sales@connorcourt.com
www.connorcourt.com

ISBN: 9781925826050

Cover design by Shireen Nolan

Printed in Australia

Jeparit Press was established in 2017 as an imprint of Connor Court Publishing Pty Ltd, in association with the Menzies Research Centre, dedicated to publishing enduring works of Australian political philosophy and history. The imprint is edited by Nick Cater.

Menzies Research Centre
R.G. Menzies House
1 Macquarie St. Barton, ACT 2600
www.menziesrc.org

For my late mother Gwen and her five great-grandchildren:
Hannah, Naomi, Xavier, Tobias and Molly

CONTENTS

Introduction   ix

Foreword   xvii

1. Dear Joe   1

2. The Family   9

3. The Family Closet   21

4. Return to Emu Bay   37

5. The Teacher   51

6. Bride and Groom   63

7. A Political Spouse   83

8. Hobart   101

9. The Heart of the Matter   113

10. A Sea Change   129

11. The Break   141

12. All for Australia   159

13. First Lady   177

14. Not Just a Pretty Face   199

15. Putting it over the Natives   215

16. Saying Goodbye   235

17. Paying the Piper   253

18. Joining the Carrion Crows   273

19. Leading Lady of the House   287

20. That Other Life   307

21. The Lyons Legacy   327

Postscript: 'Home Hill'   341

The Children of Dame Enid Lyons   343

Acknowledgements and a Note on Sources   345

Bibliography   349

Index   353

INTRODUCTION

At 8 pm on the evening of Wednesday 29 September 1943, a small female figure rose in the House of Representatives to make her first speech there. Enid Lyons, widow of Prime Minister Joseph Lyons and mother of twelve, was about to become a national icon as the first woman to stand and speak in Australia's house of the people.

Her words struck a number of chords, but her voice would have been familiar to many thousands of Australians. As first lady in the 1930s at the Lodge and in the year following her husband's death in April 1939, Enid Lyons had often broadcast to the nation at a time when radio was the new electronic device invading Australian homes.

Enid's unpretentious yet deftly modulated voice had long been added to by a dramatic quality learned from amateur stage performances in her teens and her mother Eliza's enforced elocution lessons. Well before her rise in public life, Joe Lyons had recognised that his wife's presence on a political platform was one of his most cherished assets. He would call her forward on the campaign trail to add a few words to pull in the votes, especially from women.

On their two trips abroad, both to Europe and the United Kingdom and one to the United States and Canada, Enid captured attention in the press with her speechmaking, even being paid twenty guineas herself to write a half page article in the *Daily Mail* – headed "A Prime Minister's Wife on The Joys of a Large Family". Keith Murdoch published her reports of their travels in his Australian newspapers. She became a curiosity – Lady Astor just *had* to have her visit.

Michael Collins Persse, a fellow Australian who dined with Enid at Lord and Lady Gowrie's London home, described her accurately as "intelligent rather than intellectual, good at conversation, affable and motherly". Such was the Lyons phenomenon with the media, Joe Lyons made the cover of *Time* on 8 July 1935 to coincide with their arrival in New York and later Washington. They spent a night with the King and Queen at Windsor Castle and another with Franklin D Roosevelt at the White House.

At the state election of 1925, when Joe Lyons was Labor's Tasmanian premier, Enid had stood as a Labor candidate in the electorate of Denison to draw votes away from an independent female candidate. Assumed to have no chance of winning, she came within a handful of votes to capturing a seat in Tasmania's House of Assembly. Her thespian qualities and warm personality, along with her ability to communicate ideas – something Joe had taught her early in his mentoring – drew much personal support.

Elected as the United Australia Party Member for Darwin in northern Tasmania in August 1943, Enid Lyons was no stranger to Canberra. Her election that year broke records not only for her win as the first woman to gain a seat in the House of Representatives. Enid had also won Darwin for the UAP opposition, against all odds – the 1943 election result was a huge landslide for the Curtin Labor government.

Sheila Lacey (nee Lyons), Enid's eldest daughter, in an interview for *The Mercury* in March 1990 described family life for the Lyons tribe as politics "breakfast, dinner and tea for us before we were old enough to know anything". This is a reflection of the life Enid Lyons accepted on marrying Joe Lyons in April 1915 when she was still only seventeen and Joe eighteen years her senior, as well as being Tasmanian Treasurer, Minister for Railways and Minister for Education.

The romance between Joe and Enid had blossomed after Enid's mother, a member of the Labor Party and friend of Joe Lyons, had introduced her daughters to her parliamentary associates on a visit to

Hobart while the girls were studying at teachers' college there. Enid was just fifteen. Joe and Enid began corresponding and occasionally meeting at Parliament House in the evening, after which Joe would accompany the girls home. They became engaged on 1 October 1914.

The union of Joe Lyons and Enid Burnell, its timing, its success and its many contexts, says as much about Australia as the characters of Joe and Enid. It was an era laced with sectarian divisions between Catholic and Protestant, tensions that would only increase during the war years about to begin. The Burnells were Methodist and the Lyons Catholic. Joe Lyons saw no reason for Enid to give up her religion to marry him, but Eliza Burnell believed it was important for a couple to hold the same faith for the good of their marriage.

Father Tom O'Donnell, Catholic priest at Stanley and a good friend of Joe, agreed to give Enid instruction for a Catholic conversion at his presbytery just a couple of months before their marriage. The conversion had its own uniqueness. O'Donnell, who did not impress Enid, was called away. At the presbytery, Eliza urged her daughter to read the Catholic texts. In the end, it was Methodist Eliza who converted Enid to the Catholic faith.

On the eve of Enid and Eliza's departure for O'Donnell's presbytery, the Burnell family's Methodist preacher had pleaded with Enid not to give up the "faith of your father". Enid also recorded that her grandmother had "disowned" her mother for allowing her to marry a Catholic. And she had had no pre-wedding parties due to the similar disapproval of her Methodist girlfriends.

In spite of such a beginning, Joe and Enid Lyons and their large Catholic family would become central to Australians of all backgrounds during the harsh years of the Great Depression. It took no spin doctors to fashion Joe and Enid into salt-of-the earth family folk. They caught the popular imagination and were a comforting and unifying symbol for many who sought solace in those years. Enid became something of a mother to the nation with Joe writing to her at one point, "you don't know what a place you have in the hearts of the people of Australia, nor how interestedly and sympathetically the women are looking toward you just now".

On Good Friday, 7 April 1939, Enid Lyons sat by Joe's bedside at St Vincent's Hospital in Sydney and watched him die. Her youngest child Janice was just five and not yet at school. At a time of no superannuation for MPs, there would be a bitter debate in parliament over what, if any, allowance this former first lady to the nation should be given. Years later, Enid would watch with growing emotion debate in a parliamentary vote on John Curtin's widow Elsie's allowance, behind which Enid would throw her support. Her own allowance broke new ground and was not so easily won.

Enid Lyons had faced years of family upheaval and at times acute distress. Joe's death, however, almost crippled her. And, yet, within a few years, Enid Lyons had picked up the pieces of her life and taken up the challenge to stand for parliament when the sitting member for Darwin retired. Standing against a string of candidates for the seat – including two others from her own United Australia Party (forerunner of the Liberal Party of Australia) – after a week of counting preferences, Enid Lyons was declared the winner.

As an accomplished public speaker, Enid Lyons believed that a winning speech should make its audience laugh within the first five minutes. Her maiden speech was no disappointment. After commencing with serious reflection on the historic nature of the moment, Enid moved seamlessly into elaborate metaphor comparing herself to a new broom in a cupboard of somewhat alarmed old brooms but assuring her male colleagues that she had "very sound views on brooms, and sweeping" and that "this particular new broom knows that she has a very great deal to learn from the occupants of, I dare not say, this particular cupboard".

Thus, her well-modulated words rung out in the chamber, moving between great public issues of the day from war and peace, jobs and life for returned service men, progress after the war, issues from population growth to social service, all interlaced with her personal and female experience as a wife and mother. This softly edged voice was immediately recognised as vastly different in perspective and approach from other speeches so often given in this national forum. Here was a woman's touch, not intimidated by the masculine world she had entered and not afraid to speak openly of her homely life and the opportunities that experience opened for political insight.

She spoke of the need for public housing, and for population growth which she said she had pondered on "not with my feet upon the mantle-piece, but knee deep in shawls and feeding bottles". She spoke up for a child endowment system rather than a basic wage calculated around a man, his wife and his three children – "how many thousands of men in this country have no children at all" while others had "families of six and seven and eight". She added, "Let the man's wages be a direct charge on industry, but the children should be a charge on the whole community."

Without mentioning her late husband by name, Enid paid homage to him as being revered for his focus in government on the "problems of human values and human hearts and human feelings". And, in conclusion, she nailed her colours to a higher authority saying, "the duty of every government, whether in this country or any other, is to see that no man, because of the condition of his life, shall ever need lose his vision of the city of God".

Little wonder that Robert Menzies once commented that Enid Lyons could move listeners to tears over the condition of a railway track. And in spite of her reflection in her maiden speech that as a woman in parliament she would work shoulder to shoulder with male colleagues "not as a woman but as a citizen", the acclaim her speech received, both privately and in the press, signified her presence as a burst of light on a stale corner of the polis. No surprise that aging former prime minister Billy Hughes called her a bird of paradise among the carrion crows.

It was Enid Lyons' burden in her later years that she was all too often regarded as the energy and mind behind her husband Joe's success in politics. This is a misguided view given that his own efforts long before they met showed an ambitious political mind in Joe Lyons himself. In fact, a lot of Enid Lyons' achievements in public life she owed to her husband's initiative and his mentoring in their early married life. He pushed her on to the stage when she herself admitted her nerves were against it. His confidence in her drove her on as much as hers in him took them both to the heights.

Looking back on her life's meanderings, Enid reflected in an interview with Ruth Brown in November 1969 that, "My story has run on so many different lines. Nothing would surprise me now." And so much of that life was Enid accepting and taking up rather than seeking challenges. It was what her mother Eliza called throwing one's cap over a windmill. The challenges came, and Enid vaulted them – one by one. Babies came, one after the other, none planned; house moves came as Joe rose in state politics and then in federal politics – she juggled and kept pace.

Years of train journeys and ferry crossings of Bass Strait took their toll. Enid was often near nervous collapse, at other times suffered depression. She was hospitalised on a number of occasions apart from her babies' births. Her mother Eliza, sister-in-law Mavis Lyons and (later) her older children were a constant support at the home base. But, in all of it, Enid and Joe lived by a fundamental belief in divine providence so that facing their difficulties was part of their life as Christians.

Then Joe was gone, and Enid needed to earn her living as well as keep occupied. After a few quieter years at her beloved Home Hill in Devonport, making gardens and decorating rooms, she let her daughter Enid convince her to stand for parliament. Another chapter of her life opened. At the election of April 1951, Enid stepped aside after a bout of ill health.

In retirement, Enid wrote three books and, for some years, wrote two syndicated newspaper columns a week. All the while keeping the wolf from the door while building a public profile as a wise and entertaining personality. Enid had a number of broadcasting contracts. She served for almost a decade on the board of the ABC. She even took up an offer to write an agony aunt page for the *Woman's Day and Home* magazine. The offers came to her and she followed their lead.

Till the end she could move an audience with her words. Senator Jocelyn Newman recalled that she asked Dame Enid Lyons to open an event for International Women's Day in 1976 – Enid was then aged 78. "She spoke for quite a while, standing" said Newman, "and she was old … she could take you from one minute of laughing with her and the next minute to having a few tears. So, I looked around, wondering how it was going in a mixed group, and the men were weeping too."

FOREWORD

This year marks the seventy-fifth anniversary of the occasion of the first speech of the first female member of the House of Representatives. On 29 September 1943, the newly-elected Tasmanian MP told the chamber that "the problems of government were not problems of blue books, not problems of statistics, but problems of human values and human hearts and human feelings." As a wife, mother, and now an elected official, the new Member for Darwin brought a warm and insightful understanding of human nature to the realm of politics.

Enid Muriel Burnell, or Dame Enid Lyons as she would later become, was born on 9 July 1897 in the modest timber settlement of Leesville. While training for a career in teaching, she met and then married Joseph Aloysius Lyons on 29 April 1915. As Anne Henderson observes, their marriage of thirty-four years would prove to be a "true political match". Ever supportive of her husband, Enid Lyons would be remembered for her powerful influence as a close confidante to Joe Lyons, seeing him rise from a Tasmanian state Cabinet Minister to Premier in 1923, and eventually to Prime Minister of Australia from 1932 to 1939.

As First Lady to Prime Minister Lyons, Enid became one of the most recognised Prime Minister's spouses to occupy The Lodge, writing newspaper articles, making radio broadcasts, and giving open-air speeches. Indeed, so compelling was her public speaking that Henderson notes that "her ability to move an audience was extraordinary". Gifted with the common touch, her homely analogies and turns-of-phrase resonated with households across the country as she addressed the major issues of the day. At the same time as projecting a traditional family image – Australia's first couple – they typified a contemporary partnership.

Rightly characterised by Henderson as "Australia's first modern political woman", Lyons is revered for her trailblazing contribution to Australian politics, in her own right, as both the first woman elected to the House of Representatives and the first woman to serve in federal Cabinet. At the 1943 federal election, she won the Tasmanian seat of Darwin to enter the House of Representatives as its first female member. As a member of the United Australia Party and then the succeeding Liberal Party, she served in Parliament for eight years before her retirement from politics in 1951. During her term, Lyons was elevated to Vice-President of the Executive Council in the Menzies Government from 1949 to 1951, becoming the nation's first female member of the federal Cabinet.

Throughout her long and distinguished career in Australian public life, Enid Lyons stood out as a woman of strong character and high principles. Her commitment to advancing the status of women in Australian public life was unwavering. As early as 1932, she had encouraged women to stand for Parliament when she addressed an opening session of the Australian Women's National League. Committed to both the primacy of the family and advancement of women, as exemplified in her own personal and public life, she affirmed family life to be the underpinning of a moral society while women of all backgrounds had a natural right to equality. Like Robert Menzies, she espoused a Liberal creed of ordered liberty, individual initiative, enterprise and service to the community that drew on Australia's early pioneering spirit.

In this excellent biography of Dame Enid Lyons, Anne Henderson provides a rich and holistic portrait of this remarkable Australian woman with the narrative of her personal life skilfully interwoven with her public achievements. In these pages, readers will encounter the free-spirited girl growing up in rural Tasmania, the supportive wife and devoted mother, the charming and publicly engaged First Lady, the trailblazing female parliamentarian and the dignified, elder stateswoman of Australian politics. I am delighted to commend Ms Henderson's book as both an invaluable contribution to Australia's political history and as an inspiring life-story for Australian women and men from all walks of life.

The Hon Julie Bishop MP
Minister for Foreign Affairs
Canberra
July 2018

'Home Hill', circa 1916, built on the orchard Joe Lyons gave his bride-to-be in 1915; later extended, it was Enid Lyons' home for most of her life and is today a National Trust museum in Devonport, Tasmania.

CHAPTER 1

DEAR JOE

At 11 am on 7 April 1939, Good Friday, the leader of the Country Party and Deputy Prime Minister Sir Earle Page made a radio broadcast to all states of the Commonwealth of Australia. His statement stopped a nation. Prime Minister Joe Lyons had died, at 10.40 am, after fighting hard to beat a series of heart attacks over almost two days. For twenty-four hours, newspapers and radio had reported his battle to survive which was remarkable, amazing his doctors. But in the end, at just fifty-nine, Joe Lyons became Australia's first prime minister to die in office, a fortnight within reach of toppling Billy Hughes as the longest serving Australian prime minister.

Keeping vigil at Sydney's St Vincent's Hospital in the last hours of Joe Lyons' life was his wife Enid, so much younger at forty-one and yet a woman who had accumulated vast experience in her years married to Joe – their twenty-fourth wedding anniversary was just three weeks away. They'd parted in Melbourne, on Tuesday evening, he for the journey back to The Lodge and later Sydney, she to their children at "Home Hill", the Devonport home they built on an orchard Joe had given his bride as a wedding present. Some of their older children would arrive home from boarding school later that week. The family would be together at Easter – as they were every Christmas. These monuments in the Christian calendar meant not just church going as a family. They were also the rare occasions in the public life of a Prime Minister that might be interrupted for private celebrations.

1

The Tuesday before Joe Lyons died, Dame Enid Lyons took the night ferry across Bass Strait. Joe caught the train to Canberra via Goulburn. Prime Minister Lyons was to open the Easter Show in Sydney and then rejoin his family in time for Easter Sunday. But Lyons had collapsed with chest pains after collecting his son Kevin from St Patrick's College in Goulburn, en route to Sydney. By the end of that week, Joe and Enid would abruptly end their married life as they had lived it – parted by the distances between Australia's major cities, before air travel became the norm.

"I had never felt the isolation of the island as I felt it then," Enid would write in her memoirs. Bad weather had made the Bass Strait crossing so rough Enid left the ship that morning at Burnie, its first port of call, intending to travel the rest of the way to Devonport by car. But, at her sister Annie's house in Burnie, Enid had received the phone call telling her of Joe's collapse.

The news was a jolt, although the true seriousness of Joe's collapse was not immediately clear. Enid was needed, and quickly. However, to retrace her steps and then some with the added journey to Sydney was impossible under two days. The only plane from northern Tasmania to the mainland would leave Launceston, some four hours drive away, before she could be there. The ferry from Devonport would not return to Melbourne until that evening and the train journey from Melbourne to Sydney would take another twelve hours, but only if she made the morning connection. If she didn't, she wouldn't be in Sydney before Friday morning.

Joe and Enid Lyons were no strangers to stress, trauma and life threatening experiences. Candidly, in her speeches, Enid had often argued that women, those closest to the crises of the ordinary person, should enter the public arena wherever possible; she'd illustrate the virtues of resilience, hope, sacrifice, even ingenuity telling stories of home life that could inspire the most hardened listener.

Religious faith, a belief that their God would reward their strength of conviction, had taken Joe and Enid through many a sorrow. Eleven of the Lyons' twelve children would live to adulthood, although Barry, birth number nine for Enid, was found to be an achrondroplastic. Barry would never grow to full height and there would be many attempts to correct his deformity. Enid later wrote that Barry's condition had tempered the attitudes of others in the family towards those with disabilities, while Barry himself had succeeded "intellectually and morally – even materially – no less a citizen of stature than any of his kin". With Garnet, however, it had been different. Born seventh in the line-up, Garnet died at ten months – of pneumonia. The tragedy left Enid bereft – long after, with tears in her eyes, she wrote of her desolation at thinking her children would grow up and he would not be among them.

Joe and Enid had escaped death themselves. In 1935, aboard the *Niagara* just three hours out of Victoria, British Columbia and heading for Australia they collided with another vessel and had to be brought back to shore. In the 1920s, while Premier of Tasmania, Joe survived a serious car accident that would lead to one passenger's death and leave him with a permanent limp. There were accidents with the children, sickness and, on one occasion, their daughter Kathleen had fallen off the bonnet of the car Joe was driving at Home Hill resulting in injuries which took months to mend. Over years, Enid herself had been taken to hospital numerous times, sometimes for very serious ailments.

Then, unconquerable, there were the political machinations, all freely chosen by anyone entering a political career with the ambition to lead. But Joe had complicated his career, almost uniquely. In the sectarian 1930s, Catholic Joe Lyons had left Labor to join the very non-Catholic conservatives. With the backing of a handful of businessmen and a much younger, and likewise ambitious, Robert Menzies, he had spearheaded the formation of the United Australia Party in 1931. That most pragmatic of political alliances. Lyons' move had resulted in triumph, and made him the most popular and successful leader in Australian politics after Billy Hughes, Australia's wartime leader from 1915-18 and another to leave Labor to head a new conservative party. Like Hughes, Joe Lyons was the people's prime minister. But his move from Labor to the conservatives had left him very much an isolated figure should his luck diminish.

Federal politics delivered Joe and Enid a few years respite while they stood as Australia's first couple against the effects of the depression of the early 1930s. Joe Lyons, the man known throughout the world's financial capitals as the one who had resisted radical Labor to uphold international standards on borrowing. Shunned by the noisier corners of Labor, he'd left the party he had joined so young and felt so much part of − all with deep misgivings. But he'd found a way through nonetheless. And for three glorious federal elections he'd triumphed in spite of those who said he was a traitor, a sell out merchant. The conservatives loved it.

But, by 1938, war was threatening again in Europe. The Munich Agreement, signed in September 1938, had handed the Czech Sudetenland to Hitler; Czechoslovakia had not even been invited to the Munich meeting. British Prime Minister Neville Chamberlain, whom the Lyons couple had befriended during their trip to London in 1937, returned to England waving a white piece of paper and proclaiming "peace in our time". After visiting Germany in 1938, even Robert Menzies had advised Lyons that Hitler was not a threat. But the rumblings suggesting war was close continued and Lyons, along with many of his opponents in Cabinet and among the Opposition, were frozen like rabbits in a glare of lights. Government was in free fall. The egos in Cabinet had begun to jostle for the top job.

It had got beyond endurance for Joe and Enid Lyons. Until that weekend in Melbourne, just passed, they wanted out. In 1938, Enid had taken the younger children away from The Lodge and back to local schools in Devonport while they waited for an appropriate successor to show his hand. But the UAP was not convinced. No successor could be assured – and Joe and Enid were a proven team at election time. They must stay on.

On the weekend of 1-2 April 1939, Enid had left her younger children in the care of her adult daughters, Sheila and Enid, in Devonport and gone to Melbourne for a two hour Sunday meeting with UAP president Sir Robert Knox and Ernest Willis. The pressure on the couple had been strong; for these UAP officials, Joe was the only one. Knox and Willis knew Enid must agree as much as Joe – if she had not, there would be no deal. But Lyons must stay on. Robert Menzies was not acceptable, too remote from the voters.

So, now, what had it all been for? Joe lay semi conscious in a hospital bed far from Enid as she desperately tried to find a quicker way to Sydney. Was he close to death? The doctors still seemed to believe that he was strong enough to pull through, with rest and hospitalisation. Enid could not be sure. As she would write in her memoirs, public life had strangled their private time so thoroughly over recent years that she had not even looked back to watch the train pull out of Spencer Street Station as Joe left for Canberra that Tuesday evening.

The next phone call Enid took brought some relief. A plane from Broken Hill Proprietary Limited had been found available and would be sent to bring Enid across Bass Strait, in time for her to catch the overnight train to Sydney from Melbourne. Enid arrived at Sydney's Central that Thursday morning and went straight to Joe's bedside.

Enid recalled much later how unreal the journey to Sydney became. Flooded with memories of the many trips she and Joe had made together on that same train, their crossings of Bass Strait, the first within days of their marriage. From the age of seventeen, she had absorbed Joe's political life. They had honeymooned in Sydney while Joe attended a Premiers' Conference, on the way spending three days in Melbourne where they dined privately with Prime Minister

Andrew Fisher and his wife. How affected she had been to discover the ease she had felt in the presence of such important public figures. That this had largely been because of the kindness of her hosts was not lost on Enid, such diplomacy and good manners being a trait she would soon adopt in her own lengthy public life.

At St Vincent's Hospital, Enid found the Prime Minister's office had invaded significantly. Telephonists were frantic, the switch board open and lit up with calls. Prime ministerial staff would soon take over a table to work on the piles of telegrams. Her husband was suffering, she was told, from coronary occlusions caused by a small clot stopping the flow of blood to his heart. But he was still conscious and the doctors thought he might pull through after a good rest in hospital.

Enid sat by Joe's bed. They even shared a joke. A nun rustled in occasionally to check on the couple, clad in white from head to toe, the small oval of a fresh face almost all there was to be seen of her body or shape, as assuring as an angel. Joe needed toiletries and pyjamas, so Enid left him for a while to drop into David Jones department store and bring some back. By the time she returned to the Commonwealth car, Joe had suffered three seizures and the doctors had pronounced his condition critical. Deputy Prime Minister Page was informed and within hours half the Cabinet had visited the hospital. Joe's former driver, Ray Tracey, kept vigil outside. By the evening, Joe had shown signs of improvement, his pulse had risen and he could speak with Enid a little. Within minutes he had slipped into a deep sleep. Enid refused to leave Joe's bedside and the night closed in, humid and oppressive.

> Through the night in his room, I watched, I prayed, saw the daylight filling the windows at last but I knew it was hopeless, and the doctor arrived, about 6 o'clock I should think, and suddenly there was a gush of blood from his mouth and that was very dreadful. The doctor said to me, "He's gone." But two minutes later, he was breathing again.

Enid had by now called the priest, Father Hudson. Soon after, their son Kevin arrived with his sister Kathleen, aged 18, who had travelled to Sydney directly behind her father not knowing he had collapsed in the car ahead of her. Again Joe managed to recover long enough to speak a few words to his wife.

The nuns gathered around the bed, praying, and Enid clung to Joe's hand with her eyes closed. By 8.30am, Dr Diethelm issued a statement that the Prime Minister might die at any time. Ministers had begun arriving in Sydney by train from Melbourne. Just after 10.30 am, the Reverend Mother's lilting voice broke the silence of the hospital room, "Look child, look! He knows you!" And with one last gaze at his wife, Joe was gone. Around 11am, Dame Enid and her two children left the hospital room and the tributes began pouring in.

This was not how they had planned it. Although they'd tried to extricate themselves from public service and seen the day delayed again and again, they'd still imagined there would be years left to enjoy a normal family life. Over more than two decades, they'd allowed their private and domestic world to take a back seat, their large family evolving around separations, relocations and adjustments, all accepted as part of the job. They'd known heights few would ever experience; by 1939, Enid could count among her personal acquaintances the wives of some of the most famous leaders of the Western world. Not bad, after a couple of decades, for a teenager from northern Tasmania whose father worked in saw mills and whose mother was a postmistress. She'd married up, a darling man twice her age. He too had come from humble circumstances – State Treasurer in 1915 but printer's devil at the age of ten. This was no ordinary story.

As Enid buried Joe, in spite of all the pomp and grandeur of a State funeral, her world began to crumble. The black dog of break down would envelop her for weeks. And yet, in time, she would start again and become Australia's only stateswoman and a maker of history.

Enid (left) with her sister Nellie, c. 1900.

CHAPTER 2

THE FAMILY

Enid Burnell or Dame Enid Lyons, as she would become, was born into an outpost of colonial society at Leesville, Duck River, in the British settled colony of Tasmania on 9 July 1897, and given the name Enid Muriel. This modest outpost, now known as Smithton, is situated in the far corner of north western Tasmania, and is still today remote, scenic and relatively untouched by development. Enid was born in a small cottage near Lees Mill, a timber workers camp, and her birth was not registered until a month later on 12 August.

At the time of Enid's birth, her father William Burnell was a sawyer at Lees Mill in the Duck River timber industry. His wife, Eliza (nee Taggett), was a pretty woman of Cornish stock, with a small frame, fine bones and a head of thick brown hair. The Burnells were itinerants, moving with William's employment as so many of the newly settled did at the time, finding work where it was most plentiful; depots with the continent's rapidly expanding rail network, tin mining and timber cutting from plentiful native forests where cleared land soon became valuable for farming.

The Burnell-Taggett line was solid British and reflected the immigrant experience prevalent in the colonies soon to become the Commonwealth of Australia. In this century when religion was a mark of character, a majority of settlers were Protestant, Anglophile and on the make from a very lowly position in the Anglo pecking order. The significant other section of the population was of Irish

9

Catholic origins, similarly working off their impoverished beginnings, albeit mostly from lower down the social order. Family histories from this time quite commonly included the black sheep of a respectable household who might find a new beginning in this far flung English world. Or the struggling immigrant facing the loss of a first family from the ordeals at sea or the cruelty of life on the land. Second marriages were frequent as the graveyards filled with mothers and infants cut off from medical help. Orphans were brought up by relatives or in cold hearted institutions. And, in a society that relied on good name for survival, scandals were quickly hidden in the record with future generations hearing a version of the truth or none at all.

The Taggetts

On the Taggett side of family history, Eliza (Taggett) Burnell would pass down the story of her father Harry, the son of Henry Taggett, a schoolmaster in Devonshire who had fallen in love with the daughter of the local squire, Major Seton (Indian Civil Service), whom he had married. The squire, angry with his only daughter for defying his wishes and marrying a humble and penniless school teacher, cut her off. The couple escaped to Cornwall where Henry became schoolmaster at the village of Redruth Highway. Enid Burnell later wrote of how her mother would retell the story with a romantic relish that fascinated her. So much so, that on her visit to London as Prime Minister's wife in 1935, she had the story checked through Somerset House. It was found to be largely correct.

Following the birth of her fourth child, Henry Taggett's wife developed consumption and Henry sought financial help for medical treatment from the Seton family only to have his requests ignored. Later he managed to see his wife's brother at the Savoy Hotel in London, on leave from India, and made a similar plea for help. The brother told him that he no longer had a sister. Within a few years

Harry's wife was dead. One of her sons was Eliza (Taggett) Burnell's father, Harry. Reared by a schoolmaster and with a mother from the gentry, Harry turned his back on learning and is said to have become a miner. The folklore of his middle class origins remained however; as an adult around colonial mining towns he was nicknamed "Gentleman Harry" because of his ability to retain his manners and bearing after a few drinks. In the 1840s Harry was thought to have migrated to South Australia.

In Kate White's well researched *A Political Love Story: Joe and Enid Lyons*, the accepted version of the history of Harry Taggett has him setting out for Australia alone, leaving behind a wife and two children whom he hoped to bring to the colony after he had established himself. The story was that after he had worked in the South Australian mines at Burra or Kapunda for some years, he sent money to his wife and children for their passage to Australia. On their arrival at Port Melbourne, Harry's wife died suddenly on board the ship and her two children were left in the care of other passengers. Harry, arriving a day or two late at the wharf, so the anecdote went, found the children had disappeared. From South Australia, Harry would have had to travel hundreds of kilometres to get to the dock in Melbourne; the passengers would have searched in vain for the children's father and the captain would have broken the sad news to Harry on his arrival, of his wife's death. It was all very tragic – except, it was not what happened. As passed down the generations, the story had been invented at some point in Harry's life to avoid explaining a more complicated reality.

From archival digging on the part of a descendant of Harry's eldest daughter from his first marriage, Lavinia, a truer record has since emerged. Harry, or Henry Taggett as his travel documents record, married Eliza Frances in December 1849 in Redruth, Cornwall. By 1852, when the couple emigrated to Victoria, they had two children – Lavinia and William Henry. They travelled on a ship chartered by the Port Phillip and Colonial Mining Company. Aboard also were Harry's sister Matilda and her family. It was the height of the Victorian gold rushes and Harry had decided to try his luck on the goldfields, like thousands of others. He took up prospecting at Forest Creek (now part of Castlemaine) about 119 kilometres north west of Melbourne. By 1852, there were some 25,000 people in the diggings around Forest Creek; for a while it was the administrative centre for the entire Victorian goldfields. Here, in November 1853, Eliza gave birth to a third child, a daughter they named Elizabeth Jane. Then, on 16 February 1854, Eliza died and the suspicion was that she may have committed suicide – she had drowned. This is not hard to contemplate. Life in these overcrowded shanty towns of canvas tents was rude and rough – hardly the future expected of a young woman reared in domesticated Cornwall.

There was a coronial enquiry into Eliza Taggett's drowning, with an open finding. Harry, devastated, took off. He left his three young children with his dead wife's brother, Henry Francis, who lived at near-by Daylesford. It appears that was the last contact Harry had with the children of his first marriage. Over a decade later, Harry remarried. His second wife was Louisa Orchard and their first child, born 11 October 1869, was given the name Eliza after Harry's first wife. It is highly doubtful Louisa was ever told the truth of Harry's first marriage – the story he concocted of his children's disappearance meant he could start again, free of the burden of extra mouths to feed. At her marriage to Smith McCracken, from Belfast, Lavinia Taggett was given away by her uncle and guardian Henry Francis.

For Harry Taggett, life never became any easier, in spite of his relaxed Saturday evenings, striding off to the pub to drink with his mates. Enid Lyons recalls her mother telling her that he was "six feet tall and strikingly handsome, black-haired and wearing a carefully trimmed Vandyke beard" with the "courtliness of a Spanish grandee", a foreign trait often found in Cornwall where Spanish sailors had come ashore after the sinking of the Armada in the reign of Elizabeth I. But Harry's drinking would become his curse. It would also explain Eliza Burnell's life long horror of alcohol and both her mother's and her own strict adherence to the Methodist church, a strong presence in the mining towns dotting Australia at the time. At the height of the copper boom in South Australia, in the nineteenth century, the mining town of Mootna had sixteen Methodist churches, one built to hold more than twelve hundred people. Methodism was popular among the Cornish and Welsh who settled many areas where Eliza and her family lived, and where many a miner sought solace after a hard week at the bar of a public house. Eliza's intolerance of alcohol was what her daughter Enid would regard as a "near-phobia of hers". With the drink and a miner's complaint or consumption, Harry's health deteriorated rapidly and he died at Murray Bridge, apparently after a coughing fit, on 31 May 1878.

In a column Enid wrote for *The Sun* newspaper, she would record a story her mother had told her of how impoverished the family was after Harry died and the scars it left:

> When my mother was orphaned at the age of nine, she was put into deep mourning, in the fashion of the day, and long after the cheap black was rusty, she had to wear it because there was no money to replace it. One day, in a Sunday school group, the child of well-to-do parents took her friend by the arm and said, 'Come away from that shabby little thing!' It hurt my mother as few things in the whole of her life hurt her, and I can feel the pain of it still for her sake.

At this young age, Eliza was forced to become the day-to-day carer for her siblings, the youngest just eighteen months, while her mother Louisa made what money she could with her portable sewing machine, going into the homes of the small and diminishing copper mining town of Kanmantoo in South Australia. With a couple of tiny rented cottages to live in, Louisa also took responsibility for her

13

great aunt Honor who became Eliza's only adult companion in her mother's long absences. Carrying the baby, Eliza would take all the children with her to school. At home, this child mother cooked family meals in a camp oven heated over hot coals, carried water half a mile and washed the family laundry by hand. Her life would instill in her adaptability, tenacity and fearless courage that in time would rear a daughter who could take her place with dignity anywhere.

In the mid 1880s, Eliza's widowed mother Louisa applied for and won a contract to cater meals for the men working on the central western railway line in the Maranoa District of Queensland. She packed up the family's scant belongings and took her children on a grueling sea journey of 2500 kilometres from South Australia to Brisbane, then a further 1200 kilometres west by train to Charleville and finally the last thirty kilometres by horse and cart south to Angellala. There in the heat and dust, Louisa, a feisty little red headed woman, made hundreds of meals for gangers while Eliza and her sister Matilda cared for their young brothers Mark and Henry, their other brother Joseph (between Matilda and Eliza) having died. It was at Angellala that Eliza became friendly with William Burnell.

The Burnells

Born in Devonshire in January 1863, William Burnell had lived in Cardiff, Wales, from the age of four – his father Charles was a sawyer. At seventeen and musically gifted, William had migrated to Australia by working his passage on board ship as an entertainer and steward. His family remembers him claiming to have been a choir boy at Cardiff cathedral and to have won a gold medal in a musical contest at sixteen. He had taught himself the violin and was a wonderful accordion player. But, in South Australia and later Queensland, he worked as a sawyer in the family tradition. Over time, William Burnell developed a widespread reputation for sharpening saws – even in retirement he was known for being a miracle worker with a bent or blunt saw.

William's parents, Charles and Elizabeth Burnell, also arrived in Australia around 1880, migrating to northern Tasmania where in time they took up a small farm off Seabrooke Road, Somerset, a farming district nestled on the lower slopes of Mount Hicks, rising from the main road about six kilometres beyond Burnie's western fringe. They were followed by Frank Burnell, William's brother, who settled close to his parents some time in the 1880s. Charles Burnell knew nothing about farming and the farm, like many such small hinterland farms in Tasmania, was never prosperous. Enid wrote decades later of the Burnell farmhouse as Elizabeth Burnell's "treasure-house of her unfulfilled dreams". As an immigrant from England Enid recalled how she "worked from morning till night, year after year, until she could no longer work and she lay down to die". Inside she kept the windows covered to protect her ornaments and furnishings from the sun – "her room was always in twilight," Enid wrote, but "the sash was always raised an inch or two and the air was always sweet with lavender".

In Queensland, William and Eliza became close while at the gangers camp at Angellala, where he was cutting sleepers for newly laid tracks and Eliza helping to raise her younger siblings while her mother catered for hungry rail workers. They had much in common with their fringe existences around gang workers camps and mining. Eliza, born on the eastern side of the Adelaide Hills to parents who were new chums had taken to William, himself a new chum with loads of stories to tell and songs to sing of the old country. And their family backgrounds, from Cornwall and Devonshire, had much overlap. William had a lively, at times fanciful and racy wit. One family joke he told was that he had won Eliza in a bet. Early photos show him to have been good looking with a strong muscular build. For Eliza, in that tough and isolated world, he no doubt attracted her

15

as having the trappings of a man of the world. William had a brash confidence that belied his humble status as itinerant worker.

Eliza Taggett married William Burnell in the residence of a Presbyterian minister, the Rev James Stewart, at Fortitude Valley, Brisbane, on 13 June 1888. Eliza was eighteen and William twenty-six. William gave his address at that time as Thompson Estate, Wooloongabba. As work ran out on the railway networks in Queensland, Eliza and William moved from Queensland to Burringbar, south of the New South Wales border. They were living at Burringbar when Eliza gave birth to Nellie, in February 1894, their first child, nearly six years after their marriage. Eliza would eventually give birth to four children, Nell, Enid, Annie (November 1899) and Bertram (November 1904).

Soon after Nell's birth, with William's parents in Tasmania and a child to rear, it wasn't surprising to find that the Burnells' next move was to northern Tasmania where work for sawyers was plentiful. The Burnells were a close family. Kate White records that William and Eliza first rented a house at Chasm Creek on the Ulverstone side of Burnie where Eliza spent weeks at a time alone with baby Nellie while William was off at camps cutting timber. She would have also spent time with her in-laws at Somerset. For a short time, Eliza moved closer to William's work and lived with the timber cutters at Glance Creek near Stowport, in heavily forested and hilly country remote from towns. It is not known for how long or why she made this move. When Nell was three, the family had moved again, this time to Duck River to live at a camp connected with Lees Mill. Here, lacking female friends or company, Eliza would spend her time through 1897, caring for Nell and growing month by month with her second child, Enid, until her birth in July.

Married life for Eliza was another sort of mixed blessing. After the responsibilities foisted on her at such a young age following Harry's death, it was not surprising she grew to be a woman of strict codes and habits; she could be very exacting and, much later as the Cooee postmistress in northern Tasmania, held to strong religious beliefs. She could enjoy a pleasure and laugh at good times, but she had little sense of the ironic. Her children would recall how she could make them feel guilty just for enjoying their father William's sense of fun and mischief; he was full of the sort of pranks that delight young ones. William Burnell was a show off, a regular clown – not something to be frowned on by those aged ten or younger, however much it might frustrate their mother.

William was easy going and unambitious, very much a contrast to Eliza who was focused and determined to improve her lot. William had no religious belief, and his saucy mockery of the church in time would encourage Eliza to advise Enid that religious harmony was important for any couple contemplating marriage. William is described by Enid Lyons as having been "something of a swashbuckler", and was certainly by all accounts a charmer. This no doubt had caught young Eliza off guard as she fell in love with him. With the familiarity of married life, she soon became irritated by his histrionics. And she would despair at his less than sober habits, and his regular nights at the bar with his mates. But he had, no doubt, much of her own father about him – the dark good looks, the genial manner, the artful entertainer. He was a natural musician of the folksy kind, could sing tenor or bass, loved music and dance and a rollicking good time. As Enid described him, he tended to be overly dramatic, and "many a sober gathering was shattered by his picturesque images and piquant turns of phrase". This ability to shatter genteel gatherings with baser good humour continued till long after Enid was the wife of a Prime Minister, regardless of who had come to dinner.

In truth, the Burnell match was an incongruous one but, in an age where separation and divorce were not a ready choice for ill matched partners, the answer was to grin and bear it. Married life for Eliza Burnell had barely lifted her, materially, beyond what she had known as a youngster growing up with her widowed mother. William found work where he could and they moved as he did, often living in remote settlements around saw mill camps. Eliza, in spite of her disappointment in William, developed a hard won independence out of her itinerant life, becoming adept at makeshift remedies and familiar with the gregarious nature of life on the road. They could move and set up house at any moment, thrown in with a new community of strangers and having to earn their place in the group on their talents alone. Years later, Enid would describe her mother's hardened experience as the result of "being condemned to spend so many years of her life in small male-dominated communities where a woman was regarded solely as an adjunct to man's happiness". Out of this, Eliza developed a steely hunger for self improvement, both socially and intellectually.

By the end of the 1890s, it was as the mother of two young daughters that Eliza Burnell began to make extra efforts to improve the status of her family. Around 1897, she dabbled in spiritualism. Most accounts of Eliza and William Burnell's experiments with spiritualism take on a quaint sense of the idiotic. However, in the nineteenth century, beginning in the USA, spiritualism had become linked with radical movements for reform, from the abolition of slavery to women's rights. Many followers were liberal Christians and connected by beliefs in matters that varied from temperance and vegetarianism to dress reform.

Spiritualism was a belief for middle class radicals; connecting with spirits of the dead was seen as a liberating involvement. Australia's second Prime Minister and founding father of the constitution, Alfred Deakin, was a follower of spiritualism; it was extremely fashionable in the latter part of the nineteenth century. At Duck River, Eliza and William would conduct séances with two other timber workers until, when Eliza was three months off giving birth to Enid, during one séance she suffered a violent seizure and was thrown to the floor.

It was to be their last and Enid records that stories went about the neighbourhood suggesting the Burnell infant would be born with "either horns or hooves". It did, however, seem to leave its mark. Enid Lyons gives a lengthy account in her memoirs of how a fortune teller read her palm in Melbourne prior to Joe's break with Labor and his momentous win in the 1931 election. What the fortune teller foretold, in the colourful way of all fortune tellers, convinced Enid looking back that this had been a sign of what was to come. In spite of her solid Catholic faith throughout her life from 1915, Enid would continue to believe she could be "read".

After her brush with spiritualism, Eliza began a rudimentary education by making the best of people she met in the timber settlements where many were drifters from countries across the globe. While somewhat prim in her manners, Eliza was at the same time personally adventurous and quite devoid of fear or inhibitions. Her growing thirst for knowledge had begun early in her adulthood; she would seek out those who could discuss the issues of the day. She admitted freely that men held the key to the power and knowledge she wanted. The word "man" for Eliza meant a not just male but also significant in the community. Her instincts were not unlike many of her better educated contemporaries, such as the supporters of the Women's Suffrage League in South Australia where temperance groups and church groups had joined in radical action. Eliza's Methodist associations also encouraged self improvement, through discussion at church gatherings each week and in the emphasis on individuals presenting themselves well in public, at meetings and the like. It gave its followers not only the desire to make an impact on the wider community but also the skills to make that impact. This tradition would underpin both Eliza and Enid's success as women in public affairs.

When Enid was three, the family moved back to the Stowport area, undulating, pretty country but still heavily forested. Fifteen kilometres from Burnie, it was a tight knit community where the locals depended on each other in the absence of many services. It was here Annie was born and Bertram some five years later. After Bert arrived, the Burnells moved to a house and shop they had built on land at Cooee, a few kilometres west of Burnie and acquired by Eliza through a "loan" sometime around 1900. Little has been known of how a woman with barely any income managed to achieve such a transaction. But, from this point on and particularly from Eliza's efforts and contacts, the Burnells seem to have steadily prospered – and this in spite of William having spells of sickness and unemployment.

To understand why this might have been possible, another account of Enid Lyons' family has come to light, hidden as a dark secret for over a century.

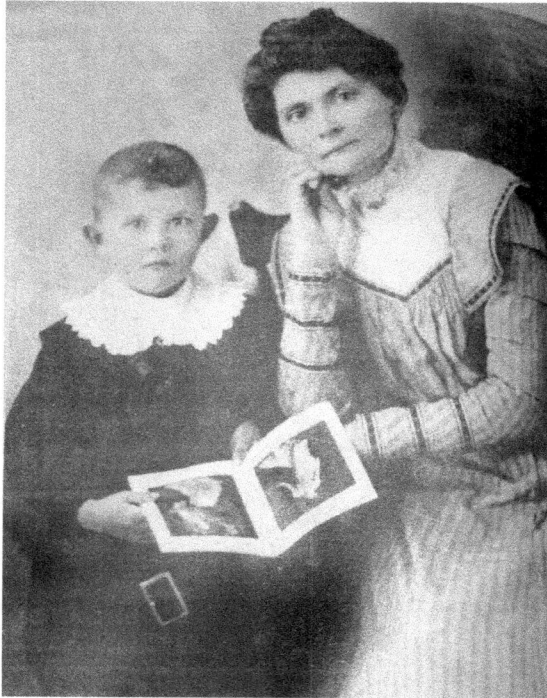

Eliza Burnell, Enid's mother, with Enid's brother Bert (c. 1910).

CHAPTER 3

THE FAMILY CLOSET

Family history is not always reliable. Especially in a colonial world, at the end of the known universe where adventure and desperation go hand in hand, in communities that are gutsy, gritty backdrops for the dispossessed to make good. Anecdotes passed on to cover potential scandals or misdemeanors have often become accepted truth or folklore. And this may well have been the case with the history of Enid Burnell Lyons with a story that has come to light and which may explain many of the gaps in Enid Lyons' heritage. It is colourful, even dramatic.

William Burnell, it would now appear, never believed he had fathered Enid – his second daughter. The family view, as she grew, was that Enid's heavier build made her more of a Burnell than a Taggett in appearance. In fact, a close inspection of family photos reveals that the young Enid looked unlike her mother, her father or her siblings. In Kate White's *A Political Love Story*, the reason given for the late registration of Enid's birth is the isolation of the Mill settlement from the nearest town. This may have been so, although a more intriguing set of circumstances may also have contributed to the delay. It has now been revealed that Eileen Natal Joyce and her sister Agnes, daughters of prominent Burnie businessman Aloysius James Joyce, witnessed an incident in 1896 that confirmed William Burnell believed their brother had conceived a child with Eliza Burnell – the child that would become Enid Burnell.

Until William secured employment at Duck River, the Burnells had lived with separations at various stages while William worked at hinterland locations and Eliza stayed with Nellie in more secure accommodation. Of her parents' marriage, Enid Lyons would write much later that, for William Burnell, "the yoke of matrimony rode uneasily on his sturdy shoulders". From the time of their move to Duck River at the end of 1896, the Burnells would live close to William's employment, except when he lost regular work in Burnie around 1914. It was almost as if they did not trust themselves any longer to those earlier separations.

Before Enid was born in 1897 and while William was away, it is not known to what extent Eliza spent time on the older Burnells' farm at Somerset for visits, but there would have been occasions when she would have taken Nellie there and stayed, if only to provide her and her baby with some relief from the loneliness of life while William was away. In Enid Lyons' memoir *So We Take Comfort*, she tells of William and Eliza's fortnightly Sunday visits, during the winter of 1904, to the Burnell grandparents (over thirty kilometres there and another thirty kilometres back with three young children in a buggy) when William's mother was dying of cancer and Eliza was expecting her fourth child. Here Eliza worked all day, preparing meals for the week and cleaning the house for her sick mother-in-law. William and Eliza and the older Burnells were always in close contact.

The Joyces

One of the best known families of the Burnie district at the end of the nineteenth century was the Joyce family, descendants of Henry Joyce and his wife Mary who had settled in Hobart from Dublin, Ireland in 1833. Mary (nee Poole) was Henry's second wife and her father was a Captain Poole of the British Army in Dublin. At the time of Henry and Mary's arrival in Hobart they had just one infant son and it is possible, as a mixed marriage, emigration to the fledgling colony had been an attractive option for the Irish couple. As a Catholic, Henry Joyce was not typical of most Irish settlers in the colony. He had migrated with money to invest and, by the 1890s, the Joyces were among the prominent families of Tasmania.

The fifth child of Henry and Mary's nine children was Aloysius James, born in 1844. As a grown man, he had invested in property at Deloraine. Later, the family moved to Branxholm where Joyce bought the Branxholm Hotel and built the village around it. The Tasmanian government used one of Joyce's cottages for the local school. After Branxholm, the Joyces moved to Burnie, where Aloysius James Joyce became a property owner in a number of locations on the north coast and, by 1900, controlled the Emu Bay Butter Factory and the Brookside Bacon Factory. He took an old rifle with him in his buggy as he collected rents from his tenants, to protect himself from

Left: Aloysius Joyce (seated) with his wife Elizabeth and son William around 1907, with sister Eileen Natal Joyce and brother Doug behind him. Right: Enid Burnell, aged 12, with her sister Nellie and William Burnell whom they called "Farvie".

bushrangers. Aloysius James was a great believer in the cash economy and his total wealth was never disclosed.

Aloysius James Joyce had married Clara Gregory in 1867. They would have fourteen children, although this never prevented Clara from enjoying her independence. Her daughter Eileen Natal's searing memory of her mother was watching her ride off on her horse. Clara's fourth child and second son was Aloysius junior. He was born in 1873 and named after his father. It would be Aloysius junior whose life would mysteriously entwine the Burnell and Joyce families and be the cause of a secretly stored upset between them, a secret William, Eliza and Aloysius Joyce senior hoped to bury in time and memory.

Aloysius Joyce junior preferred mining to farming and eventually found himself in Zeehan, sometime after his sixteenth birthday. He studied at the Zeehan mining school and achieved a first class certificate in engine driving, mining surveying and mineralogy. In his account for *Those Were the Days*, edited by Arthur Reid, Aloysius Joyce (junior) recalls that pay for competent miners was never more than eight shillings a day. He tried tributing – or working a site for commission – but found he needed too much equipment to make it profitable.

In his short recollection of his life and times adventuring, Aloysius Joyce (junior) jumps the years between 1886 and 1897 with little detail. From his account, it might be thought that he spent all his time before 1897 (when he would leave Tasmania) in Zeehan. But this was not so. Joyce family anecdotes often referred to "Uncle Aly" working on his father's farms. Perhaps he came home as the 1890s depression hit the mining industry or maybe he needed to get out of Zeehan. But one of his younger siblings, Eileen Natal Joyce (born in 1884 on Christmas Day) told her sister Agnes' grand daughter, in 1946, that her brother Aloysius, aged 23, was working his father's farm at Somerset in 1896. Their father had land in many locations.

Eliza and Aloysius

In 1946, Eileen Natal Joyce related the following story to her grand niece. At some point in late 1896, as a girl of about 13, Eileen Natal and her older sister Agnes overheard a heated exchange between their father and William Burnell A man had called at the Joyce estate home and the girls could hear what was being said from outside the door. It was William Burnell and, for a man of his background to have called at the Joyce family home, this was itself a most unusual occurrence. Burnell's appearance there would have excited particular interest in the servants who let him in. In the room where Burnell eventually met old Joyce, the voices were raised to such an extent that Eileen and Agnes (aged 18) went to listen outside the door.

William Burnell was accusing their brother Aloysius of having had a relationship with William's wife Eliza and saying that Eliza was carrying Aloysius' child, due in the middle of 1897.

The Burnell farm, belonging to William's father Charles, was in Somerset. In this rustic and provincial society, the Burnells and Aloysius Joyce (junior) would have been known to each other. But no record remains of the nature of the growing relationship between Eliza Burnell and Aloysius Joyce, although Eileen Natal spoke of Eliza Burnell knowing Aloysius and often taking him scones and biscuits, as he worked through the day perhaps for a small payment as she did later in Stowport.

Eliza Burnell was desperate to improve her lot by acquiring interesting friends who could pass on to her the benefits of their knowledge. With just formal education to the fifth grade, she saw opportunity in engaging with local personalities, men who had the breadth of experience and reading. In her socially and intellectually starved marital existence, Eliza often reached out to some of the more exotic or educated locals for conversation and friendship, not least as a way of broadening her limited education. In Stowport, she would have them eat at her home adding conversation and knowledge to conversation at dinner. In the language of the day, Eliza was something of a small time social climber. So it would not be unexpected that a member of the Joyce family working in the district would have interested her.

Eliza and Aloysius seem to have become close friends; they certainly incurred the belief that there had been a flirtation, even something more serious. A photo of Aloysius with his extended family in Western Australia, a decade later, shows him to have been a disarmingly handsome chap with a fine moustache. As to Eliza's likelihood of straying from the marital bed, no doubt she had reason to suspect William himself was a bit of a philanderer and with their long separations this may have been her breaking point.

In the Joyce parlour, William's arguments and evidence about the relationship between his wife and Joyce's son must have been persuasive. Old Joyce certainly found Burnell credible. As retold by Eileen Natal, she and Agnes heard their father responding with assurances his son would not remain in the area and that, if Burnell was happy to bring the child up as his own, old Aloysius would see that the child was provided for.

As Eileen Natal and her sister Agnes heard it, this was the agreement reached in order to save face on both sides. Old Joyce was an obsessive Catholic. He was one of the Burnie Catholic parish's most generous donors and on his death in 1926 he would leave various of his children parcels of money to have Masses said for the repose of their parents' souls. Confronted with the accusation against his son in regard to Eliza Burnell, he also knew that any breath of scandal would have crossed the neighbourhood like a bushfire. To keep a lid on the matter, it was going to cost him. And he was scornful of the fact that he would eventually have to make some financial compensation. None of this is surprising for the times. Extra marital relationships in "good" households were simply covered up, with the children of those relationships absorbed into the regular families of the married women involved, as deals were made. Queen Victoria's heir, the Prince of Wales at the time, was a master at it. Eileen Natal Joyce remembered that her father scoffed at the outcome of his meeting with William Burnell, muttering how he'd put a "beggar on horseback", not realising his daughters knew exactly what he meant.

William Burnell, however, does not seem to have made much financial gain for himself out of whatever deal was arranged. He continued to work as a sawyer for many years, and the family suffered financially when he could not find work. And old Joyce was not prepared to put his hand in his pocket immediately, even if he was more than ready to cut his son off at that point. After all, the baby had not yet been born. Anything might still happen.

Joyce senior was not only steeped in Catholicism, he was also a dictatorial patriarch; he changed his two eldest children's names, from Mary and Joseph, when his first set of twins was born in 1875. The twins then became Mary and Joseph and the older children were renamed as Grace and Clarence. He would cut off any of his children if they made an unacceptable marriage – only to take them back if the marriage ended. His daughter Agnes, who had heard William Burnell accuse Aloysius junior, would marry John Apps in April 1904. The Apps' family was Church of England and John Apps had been brought up by his older sister and her husband, after the Apps parents had died in their early thirties in Swansea, leaving a young family. Apps was not what old Joyce wanted in a son-in-law – he was the wrong religion and had little money – but Agnes had refused earlier suitors and he didn't want her left on his hands. When John died in a mining accident in 1910 on the west coast, old Joyce reclaimed his daughter and supported her until she remarried the much older Thomas O'Brien. As one of his church's most respected benefactors, he also arranged for Father Hayes at the Catholic parish in Burnie to give John Apps a Catholic burial.

The jigsaw comes together

After the upset over William Burnell's visit to the Joyce estate, Aloysius Joyce (junior) seems to have returned to Zeehan for a while before leaving for Sydney with forty pounds in his pocket. From Sydney, he purchased a passage on the *SS Warrimoo*, leaving in August 1897, and headed for Vancouver and the Klondike, Canada's gold rush of the 1890s. The Burnells, in late 1896 or early 1897, relocated to Lees Mill in remote Duck River. Aloysius Joyce (junior) would return to Australia in 1901 and be met at the Devonport ferry by his father who drove him home for Christmas lunch. Soon after, he enlisted as a private in the Tasmanian First Battalion (Horse) that left for the Boer War in February 1902.

With his demobbing, later in 1902, Aloysius worked in mining in South Africa for a time until he realised the risks. He then returned to Burnie and set up a profitable book selling and newsagency business with his sister Agnes. This wasn't to last, in spite of its success. Agnes, his business partner and sister, married on 3 April 1904 (Easter Sunday) and left for the west coast. Then, on 12 April, Aloysius married Elizabeth Borradale and the couple immediately left Tasmania for Sydney. Aloysius and Elizabeth's sudden departure from Burnie was undoubtedly because of Elizabeth's advanced pregnancy at the time of the marriage, something Aloysius' father would have cursed yet again. Aloysius junior had form.

Elizabeth and Aloysius' son, William James, would be born just three months later, on 21 July 1904. The cover up of the premarital pregnancy was so successful, William James would spend more than half his life (until he had to produce a birth certificate for insurance) believing he had been born in January 1905. After his son's birth, Aloysius Joyce headed for a new frontier, taking his family to Kalgoorlie in Western Australia where he linked up with his brother Jack. For some years he ran a grocery business there. He later became a partner in Joyce and Watkins, a skin and hide export business run from Fremantle, and prospered.

The story of William Burnell's accusation against Aloysius Joyce (junior) might have been unreliable, but for the messenger. Eileen Natal Joyce was a forthright and honest person. And very much of the old school in her discretion and good manners. At an early age she had entered a convent in Ascot Vale, Melbourne, but left soon after because of a cranky novice mistress. All her life, Eileen was an independent and forceful lady and, after her experience with the convent, no church goer. Eventually she became a real estate agent, like her father, and became one of Burnie's pioneers, playing an important part in the development of Brooklyn where the family had first established themselves in the Emu Bay area.

When Eileen Natal Joyce passed on the secret she had carried all those years to Agnes' grand daughter, she was known by locals for her straight talking and integrity. She knew what she had heard that day so many years before. Her ears had not tricked her. Agnes, moreover, had heard it too. Perhaps it was Eileen Joyce's way of passing on the facts before she died. She was a stickler for the truth and it might have nagged at her that Enid and her descendents would never have a chance know their background if she did not at some stage pass it on. It would not disappear with her going.

Aloysius Joyce (junior) died in 1946 and this may have left Eileen Natal feeling she could safely tell what she knew. It seems her sister Agnes had already whispered some of the story to her own daughter Kathleen as both Kathleen and Agnes, by the 1940s living in Hobart, were shocked to learn Eileen had disclosed the scandal to a girl of sixteen. They did not dispute the facts of the story, but such details were not for the ears of one so young. Eileen was telling her grand niece a family scandal that no one should hear. But Eileen couldn't stay silent as she watched Dame Enid Lyons become increasingly a household name. So the story survived and was subsequently passed on to writer Kate White in the 1980s. White thought it had credibility; it seemed to bring a family puzzle together. But she lacked another piece of the puzzle that has since come to light. On the Lyons side.

Peter Lyons, Joe and Enid Lyons' second youngest child, recalls that he was about 13 or 14 when he overheard a "blazing verbal row" at Home Hill between his mother, Enid Lyons, and her father whom the Lyons children all called "Farvie". "I was hiding behind a hedge and saw and heard it all," Peter Lyons wrote in an email in 2007. "At one stage he [Farvie] accused Mum of not being his daughter and she replied, 'You only have to look at me.' Indeed I can still recall they looked like two peas in a pod. Both shortish, thickset and both extremely angry. Mum was mortified when she found out later that I had been a witness, but for my part I loved it. No doubt the Irish in me." And he added, in a further email, "My ears certainly heard the 'discussion' right; that was one of the reasons why Mum was so distressed."

Dame Enid's reaction in this encounter is also telling. Her response, on hearing her father accuse her of not being his child, was not shock. It was as if she had heard it before, maybe in a drunken rave from her father or other sober but bad tempered moment. Maybe she had always thought this story, like others, was just to spite his wife as only he could. Yet, by the time Peter Lyons overheard this row between his grandfather and mother, Eliza Burnell had been dead some four years or more. It is inconceivable that a father would say something so extraordinary to a daughter just to spite a wife who, by that stage, was no longer alive.

A paternity test is impossible now; a DNA test between the families would need the agreement of one of Enid Lyons' children because of the advanced distance in the generations – but a match still might be made. Without this, however, the truth can never be absolutely proved. Kate White records that Eliza recognised in Enid something special from the moment she was born. This may have been a case of the family record reading history backwards or could well have reflected the fact that Eliza knew her baby Enid had a genetic connection to a wealthy and respectable family, and a man she still loved.

For whatever reason, William Burnell seems not to have accepted that Enid was his biological child – although nothing he did in rearing her would suggest she was not his own. Enid even wrote to Joe Lyons, during their courtship, that she was her father's pet and he would deny her nothing. Certainly Enid believed she was a Burnell in features. The fact that she was heavy in build made her not unlike family photos of Burnell relatives, although they are dark where she was fair. An early photo of Enid (aged twelve), her sister Nell and William Burnell, however, does not support the belief that Enid looked like her father. William and Enid both were heavily built in their mature years but in this photo it is Nellie and William who are strikingly alike, and William is not as heavily built as he later became (probably from his drinking). Enid, on the other hand, looks nothing like either her sister or William. This difference in looks is remarkable.

Meanwhile, Agnes Joyce's daughter, Kathleen Apps, looked strikingly like Enid Burnell Lyons – with Aloysius as Enid's biological father, Kathleen and Enid would have been first cousins. At one stage, when both Kathleen and Enid Lyons lived in New Town, Hobart, Kathleen would often be mistaken for Enid in the street. But, one might say, what if it was William Burnell who fathered Kathleen with Agnes? Not possible. Kathleen was born exactly ten months after her parents, John and Agnes Apps, married. And since they had set up house at Linda Valley (far west coast) after their marriage, there was no possibility of William and Agnes having any social contact whatsoever. Until she married, Agnes Joyce, sixteen years younger than William Burnell, lived under the watchful eye of her parents. She may not have married the man her father preferred but her chances of being alone with any suitor were extremely limited while she lived with her father. And, finally, Enid did not resemble William in appearance, as the photo of her (aged 12), with Nell and William shows. Her looks come from another source. Apart from that, there must have been some reason for William to carry his doubts about Enid's paternity, even after half a century, even after his own wife had died.

Cooee

The story takes on an interesting twist a few years after Enid's birth. By the early 1900s, Eliza Burnell had purchased half an acre of land (two roods) at Cooee, close to the sea a few kilometres west of Burnie on the main road to Wynyard. Here, in a couple of years, Eliza would build a house with an adjoining shop and a dance hall for William who for years would register himself as "hall proprietor" on the Post Office register. The project in Cooee was Eliza's alone and, extraordinary for the time, this mother of three (in time four), who earned at best a tiny amount of pocket money each week doing laundry and feeding men from a saw mill, was said to have convinced a Mr Edward Tracey (a Burnie businessman) that he should loan her the money to buy the land. This is explained in Kate White's *A Political Love Story* by reference to Eliza's outstanding personality and determination and her ability to persuade the businessman she was worth the risk. The source for this information seems to be a profile piece on Eliza Burnell in the Burnie *Advocate* (24 October 1981) by Iris Milutinovic, a distant cousin of Eliza Burnell.

The story, however, does not stand up to scrutiny. At the time of the original purchase in 1901, the Burnells had barely returned to the Emu Bay district from Duck River. Eliza was hardly known in the neighbourhood. How indeed did she become acquainted with a Burnie businessman of Mr Tracey's standing at this time? Impossible, without someone of note in the district making the introduction. Someone like Aloysius Joyce. Moreover, it is beyond belief that a woman, of little personal income, could secure a property loan of this kind in 1901. As well, within a couple of years, Eliza would build on the land not only a house and shop, but also a multipurpose hall. The first land transaction alone cost £30, and at a time when workers' wages were around £2 a week, out of which there would be precious little for extras. Had such a transaction been so easy for one so financially limited, most working Australians of the day would have been little capitalists with large tracts of land. The fact is they weren't.

But there is another possibility. Aloysius Joyce senior was a wealthy man. Whatever the propriety of the conception, he had accepted that Enid Burnell was his grand daughter. And he had an agreement with William Burnell, according to Eileen Natal Joyce, that he would take care of the child's financial future. It was not unusual for wealthy individuals in these sorts of situations to operate through a third party who would make the required arrangements. Through the businessman who gave Eliza the "loan", no doubt old Joyce secured the money or made over the land as part of his obligation to the child he believed to be his grand daughter. Iris Milutinovic records that the original transaction was undertaken entirely by Eliza Burnell. William had nothing to do with it.

There is only one Mr Tracey listed in the Tasmanian Post Office Directory in northern Tasmania at the time, an Edward Tracey who was a Burnie farmer, and no doubt knew Aloysius Joyce, another investor and farmer of the district. The land Eliza Burnell "bought" came from a parcel of land purchased by an Andrew Morris, yet another local farmer, in 1887 and 1894. The documents also show that while Eliza Burnell was the sole purchaser on 20 May 1901 of the original £30 half acre of land, on 12 June 1901 a further loan of £125 (with interest) was agreed to by Edward Tracey to Eliza Burnell with William as the second party. William did not sign the deed – just Eliza. On 24 October 1905, Tracey agreed to a further £175 loan (with interest). These loans were discharged on 14 February 1920, despite William's periods of unemployment and his never earning more than a working man's wage when employed. Eliza's post office and tea rooms would also not have made great amounts of money. As recorded by Enid, the family income while she lived at home was never comfortable. When Nellie and Enid had a chance to become trainee teachers as teenagers, it was only with Eliza's zealous thrift that she found the extra money needed for them to go to Hobart.

Postscript

There was to be an interesting postscript to this story of the connection between the Burnells and the Joyce family – one that has never surfaced before, even privately. Enid did eventually meet Aloysius Joyce, thanks to his sister Eileen. It was decades after Enid's birth and happened in Burnie, at a time when Enid was known across the world as Dame Enid Lyons. We'll never know if Enid had any idea of the implications, but Eileen Joyce was the go-between for the meeting in this instance. Somehow, perhaps after Eliza had died in January 1941, Aloysius sought to meet the woman he believed was his biological daughter. Enid was by then a widow and had her financial difficulties. In the Joyce way, Aloysius might have wanted to offer Enid financial help or opportunity. Whatever the case, Eileen organised a meeting in her office between Enid Lyons and Aloysius Joyce, who had come all the way to Burnie from Western Australia, no small distance in those days.

It is significant that Dame Enid Lyons went to Eileen Joyce's office in Burnie for this meeting with Aloysius Joyce, a man she did not know. Did he introduce himself as an old friend of her mother? William was not involved. As Enid's biological father, Aloysius would have made Enid part Irish, something that could well explain the romantic and sentimental in much of her writing and broadcasting as a public figure, and the many times people thought she was "Irish".

The record of the meeting is brief – and has lain undetected in

National Library archives for years. Among the many telegrams and letters congratulating Enid Lyons on her triumph as the new Member for Darwin in 1943, and first woman to take a seat in Australia's House of Representatives, there are hardly any from Western Australia. Yet there is one from Aloysius Joyce in Fremantle which reads, "CONGRATULATIONS ON YOUR VICTORY AND SINCERE GOOD WISHES FOR YOUR FUTURE SUCCESS STOP LONG TIME SINCE WE MET IN EILEENS OFFICE BURNIE ALOYSIUS JOYCE". And, after Joe's death in 1939, among the hundreds of condolence messages to Enid there is another telegram from Aloysius Joyce and his wife at the time. Joyce followed Enid's progress from a distance for many years.

Enid always thought she took after William because of her plump body from an early age. As a small child she walked three kilometres to Stowport school and back again, an agonising journey for a heavy little girl, so much so that decades later Enid Lyons would write of it in sharply remembered detail. Her boots never fitted her wider than average feet. But Enid's feet were certainly not from William's genes. He had small and narrow dancing feet, as can be seen in the photo taken of him and his daughters when Enid was twelve.

It would be her natural grace in public, her pretty face and striking blue eyes that would be Enid's fortune, although growing up with William as her father eventually did reflect his influence. Her thespian streak and sense of the dramatic had a lot to do with William's influence, likewise her quick wit and sense of humour. Although reading Aloysius Joyce's accounts of his adventures, Enid's humour has more in common with the Joyce's Irish sense of the ironic than William's coarser sense of the absurd. From her mother, Enid would gain more considered attributes – an appreciation of the value of education, a strong moral sensibility, the skills of mannerly behaviour and, in time, the opportunity and strategy to capture the heart of a mature and significant public figure as her love and husband. Eventually, she

Raising funds for the Red Cross in Hobart, 1915, Enid Lyons became a pageant's Queen of the Public Service, with a young Errol Flynn as her page boy (far right).

would walk the family beyond respectable homemakers and into the public glare of national and international recognition.

In 1901, with the purchase of land at Cooee which awaited future development and with William back working at the Glance Creek mill, Eliza was determined on a path to social mobility. So while she frowned and drew her lips together at William's largesse and nonsense with his young daughters, playing tunes and tricks with his accordion, Eliza read avidly and looked about for interesting locals who might come for dinner and share their knowledge, as she planned her buildings by the sea. No matter that the marriage was between a couple whose emotions for each other had frosted over. The children might register her disapproval at William and find his drinking a burden. But, at Stowport in 1901, they were settled as a family in a proper local community, and Eliza's table could readily become her classroom. The disadvantaged destiny she had known would not be her children's – not if she could help it.

CHAPTER 4

RETURN TO EMU BAY

A new century dawned. Golden haired toddler Enid Burnell was oblivious to developments taking place that would shape her future so dramatically. On New Year's Day 1901, Australia became a nation. Just over a fortnight later, a federal election was called for 29 March but Queen Victoria's death, on 19 January, probably resonated more with the Burnells and their Lees Mill neighbours than the first ever federal election campaign. And this in spite of a 94 per cent "Yes" vote for Federation in Tasmania from the slight majority of those eligible who did vote. As an itinerant, Enid's father would not have qualified to vote until the Commonwealth was proclaimed bringing adult male suffrage to all states; Enid's more politically astute mother would have to wait till 1902 to gain the right to vote. Grandfather Charles Burnell was a registered voter, from 1881, as a farmer and landowner.

In Hobart, the long sandstone building housing the State Parliament was hung with festoons, buntings and garlands, and huge banners proclaiming the new Australian Commonwealth, all giving it the appearance of a giant wedding cake. It was in this year of Federation that the Burnells moved to live at Stowport, fifteen kilometres south of Burnie where William returned to work at the Glance Creek Mill.

Enid Burnell was born into a world of bullock drays, where the forests of northern Tasmania rang out with the sounds of virgin timber being harvested with axes and hand saws, where, every so often, the creak, crack and thud of a falling giant would bring work to a stop, where great logs were hauled out from the dusty, bark strewn floors of disappearing thickets letting the sharpness of light flood in. It was back breaking work, clearing land for profit. Timber and tin mining had saved the settlement of Burnie or Emu Bay district when farming there at first proved impossible. Timber left the docks around the clock, shipped to rapidly growing Melbourne and Adelaide. Tin from the Mount Bischoff mines was hauled along a 75 kilometre tramway, at first by horses and later a steam train, to be loaded at the Emu Bay port. In the 1890s, the train line to Zeehan brought silver to the port for export. In 1901, the rail link from Launceston came. The Van Diemen's Land Company dominated development with its investments, right up to the turn of the century. Before long, though, farms would dot the hills and valleys Enid had known as the forests of her childhood, and with them come the pretty patchwork landscape to be found beyond Burnie today.

Writing some sixty years later, Enid would recall how the virgin bush of her childhood was full of "sassafras, musk and wattle and a hundred flowering shrubs and vines" but where the "hungry mill was slowly eating its way". These were the native forests of northern Tasmania, providing a meal ticket for workers and their families, and a steady profit for investors. As for many children in forest industries, Enid was enchanted by the beauty of her natural surroundings, writing of "a little clearing like a fairy balloon in an enchanted wood … [where] light was a soft green dimness as though the little clearing were a cavern under the sea". She absorbed William's understanding of the forest and its majestic specimens, with all the appreciation woodsmen have. But she also accepted the forester's way, just as farm children do the food cycle as they watch a herd being loaded into trucks for sale at the cattle yards. Forests were beautiful places but they were also there to be milled for the family income, and survival.

Among its small and barely growing population of 1500, in 1901,

Burnie could boast of many an adventurer, visitor from the old country and any number of eccentrics. Provincial society suited Eliza. In such communities, the pecking order will be diluted somewhat as people of many classes are thrown together. While the oddities were tolerated, and the familiar worker families from the Mill not encouraged ("[those] whose wives and families lived nearby and who in consequence we seldom saw," wrote Enid), many others came to call, bringing a richness of background and experience.

Enid wrote of William entertaining a visitor from England, showing him the bush. And her mother, who developed a unique strategy for exploiting whatever breeding or education might be found among men who had travelled far to work in the knockabout environment of Stowport and Glance Creek Mill. Men like Aloysius Joyce (junior), who had lived tough in rugged Canadian gold towns as the infant Enid grew to walk and talk. In all such frontier settlements, there were men seeking the freedom of the road; the global adventurer, some escaping personal or political troubles. Eliza Burnell offered her services of laundering and mending to a select few, for their best clothing – linen shirts, stiff white collars, socks that needed darning – sitting after dinner in her rocking chair beside the big hearth in the kitchen. She prepared meals that were delivered, again to a select few, or shared at the Burnell table. These Eliza called her "boarders" and made tiny pockets of cash. The men provided entertaining conversation, what Eliza saw as a way to broaden and educate the family.

Among those Enid recalled was a Mr Beck, an accountant from Denmark. He spoke three languages and gave Enid her first copy of Hans Christian Andersen's *Fairy Tales*. He introduced Eliza to Schopenhauer and suggested young Enid would like a copy of *Vanity Fair*. Another was a Russian Finn, a big man with fair hair and Enid's favourite. She would sit on his knee and listen to his stories of the places he'd come from. Their local Methodist preacher came to dinner as well as a family of Theosophists, people who believed there was a universal truth in all religions. The Burnell table was a regular discussion circle for politics, religion and philosophy presided over, like a happy Victorian family, by the figure of William Burnell. He enjoyed the chance to chin wag, but it was Eliza who was chief director.

This was an era when self improvement for those of basic education came with the Mechanics Institute libraries and the fledgling workers groups fed by tracts emanating from better educated middle class radicals such as the Fabian Society which had sprung up in Australia – established in the 1890s by Fabians from Britain. Some of them had connections with Anglican and Methodist churches but had transformed Christian principles into a more secular program for social reform; they agitated for the election of members of parliament who supported the working man and the dispossessed. All of this was meat for Eliza's mind. Whether she ever read the *Pioneer*, a journal that published prominent Fabians, or *Fabian Essays in Socialism* which became available in Australia in 1891 is not known. But she did read pamphlets sent from England and articles in journals written by leading socialists of the day. Ideas permeating from such publications would have also been rife among the mining and working communities of Eliza's dinner guests.

Not invited to the Burnell table, however, were the colourful others; men like Jimmy and Tommy Tye living up the road on a small impoverished selection of land, one round and merry faced, the other lean and glum. Or small and dark George Leech, the mill's bullocky who carried a whip with an eight foot handle and a twelve foot lash which he cracked while sending forth a volley of colourful language over the team's shoulders. There was Bill Bugg, the tailor-out or benchman at the mill who had managed to ride fifteen kilometres after suffering a severe accident, as well as ordinary mill workers like Jack Mollison and Charlie Dickson and their wives and children, or Charlie Vo Kong from Hong Kong working the district with his cart selling goods at the door. None of these came to dinner at the Burnell home.

Eliza was as tough as cast iron, with what Enid once called a character of steel; she could rise to a crisis at any given moment. Enid writes of her calmly applying a tourniquet to a heavily bleeding axeman who had sliced open his leg with the blade of his razor sharp axe. She later washed and dressed his leg using a clean sheet torn into bandages. Enid, aged five, claims to have watched it all, simply curious and with not an ounce of fear. But Eliza knew the boundaries she wanted to draw for her children; and she chose their company carefully. Life in Australian timber depots and hinterland fringes made her well aware of the limited opportunities and consequent impoverishment there would be for those, especially girls, who lacked both formal education and induction into the world of good manners. On occasion, the Burnell girls were allowed playmates at their home but never permitted to visit other children's houses by themselves.

Nonetheless, Enid's memoir records, in intricate detail, the character and appearance of many of the district's lesser orders, which suggests her mother's attempts to sanitise her daughters' experience of roughneck Stowport failed. Meanwhile, at the Stowport public school, another kind of melting pot met the Burnell girls. Eliza could do little to prevent rough and smooth integrating here – twenty-five children aged six to fourteen, from mixed family backgrounds and all in their Blundstone boots. And as Enid recalled her childhood, it was the walk to school, nearly four kilometres there and the same back, she remembered best in her education – learning such things as "when the year's first lambs appear in the paddocks; the season to be specially wary of snakes; the colour of blackberry leaves in autumn and the storm warning of seagulls inland from the sea; the shape of all the native trees and the variations of their folliage".

Nell, Nin and Nan, as William called his daughters, happily straddled both the aspirational environs their mother worked her fingers red to provide them with, as well as the raw frontier of the road and mill beyond their cosy cottage. And, as much as Eliza refused to see it, they benefited hugely from rubbing up against the rugged tumble of the outside world. Had their mother succeeded, Enid might have grown into an insufferable snob rather than the well rounded woman she became. Enid Lyons never forgot her roots. She could mix with high and low, and always with respect – it was the mark of an accomplished politician. She could thank William for much of that, as well. Rogue and "ne'er do well" might be Eileen Joyce's view of William, but his geniality and frankness, albeit with course edges and times he collected his children from school the worse for drink, left its trace on Enid, never affronted by her closeness to simple folk and humble circumstance.

For while Eliza was painfully polite to Mr Vo Kong at the cottage gate but never asked him in for refreshments, it was William who took Enid to visit the elderly Tye brothers where she was shocked at the grime of their womanless indoors and where Tommy's trousers appeared to be held up by nothing more than the unwashed stiffness of many years constant wear. And when her father built a shed for his new buggy and laid a dance floor on it, Jimmy Tye was part of William's musical backdrop, described by Enid with "his head thrown so far back that his thin grey beard pointed to the sky, gently rocking from side to side … breaking his heart as he played." Eliza kept her table with propriety and by selection, but William opened his shed for a dance night to neighbours, without discrimination.

Enid's sister Nell was the real scholar and scored the nickname "Clever Buck" for her efforts at school. In their one teacher Stowport classroom of six separate grades, studious Nell was a target for jibes from boys distinguished by what Enid called "the herd instinct of anonymity" – or a tendency to "avoid, as far as was humanly possible, any display of intelligence that could distinguish one above the other". Enid, on the other hand, moved through her primary years, happily undistinguished although her first term's report card in fifth grade shows that she was often placed first in her class. In her earlier memoir "My Life", published by *Woman's Day* in 1949, Enid described her school teacher at Stowport public school as "a lady for whom I have always entertained the liveliest gratitude". Enid would refer to the lessons in social behaviour from that lady teacher as "dicta [which] have come to my mind in difficult situations since the days of my childhood".

Enid loved the stage from an early age, and the excitement of concerts. Her one outstanding moment at school seems to have been at a school concert when, among a line-up on stage of five tiny tots, she rocked her dolly so dramatically she stole the show. These concerts were makeshift occasions but, as a child, Enid found them "great events", recalling how she was in them, "even before I became an actual member of the school, because I could sing and apparently had sufficient histrionic ability, I was soloist in the cantata." The mothers provided the stage curtain which consisted of what Enid described as "varied collection of draperies from several different homes strung together on a rope". Her childhood pride in the "bright blue cretonne generously strewn with enormous yellow sun flowers and bright green leaves" that her mother provided had her recall decades later how "all the gorgeous theatres and opera houses from Melbourne to Milan have never given me half the delight that I knew as I peeped".

Enid's self effacing good humour revealed she could not remember ever being given a nickname, but that "later during my term at college I was to build up a fairly solid reputation for conceit". Eliza's constant drilling in good manners may not have helped this conceit, although who in similar circumstances would blame her? Basic primary schooling was well established by then in every Australian state – free and compulsory. Eliza's girls were urged to study hard in order to make best use of the public benefits on offer. Since secondary schooling was not provided by the State, Eliza was determined they would get a further education by application to the government run teacher training college where they could matriculate. She saved assiduously and pushed them to acquire all the attributes of well bred young ladies of the time. Money might be tight and every penny carefully allocated but some investments could be had quite cheaply with extra effort. It also had drawbacks. Eliza would pounce if she heard slang, believing it directly linked to slovenly morals. But Enid found William's slacker and more imaginative phrases entertaining and seductive when compared to Eliza's stiff and pretentious approach to language. In *So We Take Comfort* Enid wrote that Eliza's "overweening pride in her children's modest achievements" was the "one great blot on my mother's escutcheon as a parent" even if it did bring her to "the notice of my future husband".

As Eliza and William became stable and settled residents in Stowport and eventually Cooee, Eliza became prominent in her local Burnie community, not least of all through the Methodist Church. When the Methodist authorities decided on holding a competition in music and elocution, Eliza felt one of her children must enter and was ready to put in hours of practice and training. Enid became the chosen one; Nell was too shy and Annie too young. Mother and daughter practised for weeks; lines of poems, prose and the diction and pronunciation required. But, having succeeded in one of the sections, Enid then found she was forced to enter "every concert promoted in the district for years to come". Likewise, to be pushed forward and made to recite during Eliza's social gatherings, so much so that Enid would recall how she became "an integral part of the hospitality of the home".

Ironically, this was how Joe Lyons first laid eyes on Enid when his sister Adeline, a dressmaker by trade and a friend of Eliza Burnell at the local Workers Political League, took him to the Burnell home during a Christmas holiday break. Enid was just eleven and made to recite for her mother's guests, a practice she admitted made her frightfully nervous. As an adult, Enid would always say she did not remember Joe that day, but Joe would recall her being "a lovely kid". From the first, it was Eliza who took to Joe, and Enid would look back with some amusement on how Joe had been her mother's friend when he began courting her.

The Burnells' move to Cooee around the end of 1904, following Eliza's mysterious acquisition of both money and land, would set the family up as locals of reasonable note. The Burnell shop and adjoining house, built on the half acre Eliza had acquired a year or so earlier, was three kilometres west of Burnie. Some time after, William added a building that would become the local hall, where he held weekly dances and in time a monthly ball. Eliza provided all the refreshments. The shop became the local (unofficial) post office and Eliza the postmistress; in time she ran a teashop and small general store. The shop/house building still stands, double fronted shop windows and door between jutting beyond the almost equally wide entrance to the private quarters, behind a picket fence, on what is now the corner of the Bass Highway and Burnell Street.

Cooee is a coastal strip along the main Burnie road heading further west, where dwellings cling to a narrow stretch of flat land between the wide expanse of Bass Strait and the hills behind it. It is now an outer suburb of Burnie and unremarkable. Eliza had was keen on Cooee, which Enid explained as coming from her mother's love of the sea and Cornish blood. In her memoirs, Enid writes of the sea of Bass Strait, which was a "stone's throw" from the house on the northern side of the main road tucked in behind Cooee Point, as an ever present element of her earliest sense of childhood – "the sight of it when the winter gales were blowing or when the sun was pouring diamonds on it from somewhere in the sky; the sound of it as I lay in bed after my mother had kissed me goodnight and taken away the candle. My mother and the sea! Always my mother and the sea!"

On stormy evenings, sitting in some sheltered spot, Eliza and Enid would watch the waves surge over low mounds of rock scattered along the shore. On better days and in summer, they collected driftwood and shells; in one of Enid's enduring images of her mother Eliza is dragging a piece of driftwood over grass, her hair wind-blown against the backdrop of the sea, her eyes bright with pleasure.

Living at Cooee meant being closer to the Burnell farm at Somerset; William's mother Elizabeth was very ill in the winter of 1904 and died in 1905, and this may have affected the move. Charles Burnell needed help and the trek from Stowport to Somerset had been unendurable as Eliza neared Bertram's birth. Grandfather would need looking after more than ever with his wife gone. In time, however, Charles Burnell arranged for his deceased wife's widowed sister Emma to migrate to Tasmania with her daughter. Charles and Emma subsequently married. William's brother Frank also lived in the area. Enid writes of Burnell cousins saving her, at the age of four, when she slipped, just thirty feet from the wheel or wooden boxing, into the stream of a water-driven saw mill. Two cousins pulled her out. The Burnells were a close knit lot.

The Burnell girls now attended Burnie public school. Walking there and home again each day, the hills of Stowport had become the sea while mobs of cattle on the road moved to and from the sale yards at Cooee where there were weekly sales. They would run for it if a steer did a bolt and often avoided the mobs by climbing fences and tracing the shoreline where they threw stones at the waves. Their world was quietly expanding. When Eliza couldn't afford the train fares for Nell and Enid to spend a day at an Australian industries exhibition in Launceston, the headmaster issued them with complimentary tickets. In spite of Eliza's hurt pride at having to accept charity, Nell and Enid could not contain their excitement, even when they almost missed the train's departure from Burnie at 6 am.

They might have been going to another country on the six hour journey to Launceston. "We saw marvellous things," wrote Enid.

Burnie might have been a metropolis but Launceston was a real city. They watched brooches, made with gold wire and glass, being etched and they bought Eliza a glass with her name on it. They saw fairy floss for the first time. They discovered ice cream – "never before had we tasted anything so delicious". And in their ignorance they bought six iced cones to take home only to see them melt and have to eat it all themselves long before the train was due to leave. With just a few shillings of pocket money, they managed to take away little presents for all the family – which would be not only a lesson in bargain hunting but also in the wonders of industrialisation and mass production which could make such exciting manufactured goods affordable.

Enid Lyons would straddle two very different eras. In her forties she would make regular radio broadcasts, her voice heard across a continent. But in her childhood, travel beyond Burnie to the west was still dependent on a coach and horses. On one mild sunny day, she set out with William for a trip to Stanley, fifty miles away, in an open coach drawn by four bays, where up to twenty travellers might sit on cross benches facing the team ahead as they dragged the coach to the half way stop where the horses would be changed while passengers ate tea and scones. A kilometre from the coaching house, the driver offered Enid the reins; she was sitting right behind him. "Never shall I forget it," she recalled. "The team was galloping at full stretch. My hair streamed in the wind and my body quivered with excitement… I was Boadicea! I was Diana! I was Apollo driving the chariot of the sun!" Enid Burnell, pretty daughter of a strict but fearless and ambitious mother, could be seduced by the adventure offered with William. She was ready for a challenge.

The Burnell children lived to a strict code like most children of their era. They had their chores and helped about their mother's business. But it was still a long day for Eliza, even if she was now more involved in community groups. Her health broke down in 1910 with a lung condition she suffered. She needed rest and warmth, so that winter Eliza took her two youngest children for an extended stay with her relatives in New South Wales. A friend had offered to mind the shop but was unable to at the last minute. With Nell at work as a junior teacher at the Burnie school, the only alternative was to leave the shop in Enid's hands, with just the help of a sixteen year old domestic. Enid spent several months, at just thirteen, filling in as postmistress. "I have no doubt that I was the youngest unofficial non-official postmistress ever to occupy that office," was her wry summing up. Nell would take over the shop after school and Enid harness the horse to drive to collect her father from the Van Dieman's Land Company mill where he worked. As a fifteen year old, Enid, not surprisingly, was mature beyond her years. That same year, she saw Alfred Deakin, Australia's founding father and early prime minister.

By her early forties, Enid had transformed herself. In the photo of Eliza with Bertram, taken around 1912 and published with Iris Milutinovic's profile piece in the Burnie *Advocate*, October 1981, she is a well dressed and striking woman, her dark hair coiffed fashionably above her brow, her well cut dress with ribbed shoulders and high necked frill a far cry from the worn work clothes of her early married years. This is not the wiry figure, with hair dragged back, that she presented in another family photo taken in northern New South Wales before Nell was born. In her forties, her face is fuller, her eyes are bright and wide, high cheekbones accentuate her small, well cut nose. This is a portrait of a known figure in Burnie circles; someone whose picture would appear, in time, in the Burnie Pioneer Museum, and who would be part of a recruiting committee during the First World War. Eliza was active in many local groups and would go on to become a Justice of the Peace and sit on the Children's Court Bench.

Enid always believed her mother was the most outstanding influence on her development. Walking with them to Burnie wearing her best dress, Enid could still sensuously feel her mother's presence decades later as she "shimmered like a sea beside us, shot with two shades of silvery grey" in a "high necked bodice, vest of blue silk and black velvet ribbon round the throat". There is no clue here of the woman who washed clothes for timber workers. Her teenage daughter was so proud of her: "I walked a few steps behind, to watch the play of the sunlight on the folds of her flowing skirt, and I quivered with love as I gazed at my pretty mother."

Eliza, like a free range chicken, had long since absorbed the free wheeling ideas of working men as they moved through the itinerant settlements of Tasmania's mining and forester towns. She may even have been encouraged in her determination to a better educated mind from her very early encounter and long conversations, a few years before, with Aloysius Joyce who would have been well versed in the attitudes of the labourite west coast, the area that produced John Earle, the founding father of the Tasmanian Workers Political League. In addition, her Methodist upbringing had instilled in her the belief in temperance and hard work as a way to self development – what Victorian liberalism saw as a cure for social ills. She was a natural Fabian. Any move she might make towards political involvement took her to the left of centre, but also to a branch of working class politics often in tension with the rugged drinking man's political affiliations. Enid Lyons described her mother in a 1972 ABC TV interview saying, "She read a good deal, and read a good deal about the movement in England, and the Fabians interested her very much ... she gradually came to see that at least in Australian politics, you had to have some sort of party allegiance to get anywhere."

Tasmanian women were able to vote in State elections for the first time in 1906. At the State election that year, the fledgling Labor group – known as the Workers Political League – increased its members to eight in a lower house of 35 where three were independents. The WPL became quickly recognised as a serious political force against the so long entrenched conservative members. By 1909, when Labor won twelve seats and Joe Lyons entered parliament for the first time, Eliza Burnell was part of the growing Workers Political League, where she had met and befriended Joe Lyons' sister Adeline. And one of her regular customers at the Cooee post office was King O'Malley, the radical and forceful MP for the federal seat of Darwin from 1901, one of the first to join the Labor caucus when the federal parliament assembled in Melbourne.

As Enid Lyons acknowledged in her interview in 1972, her mother was very much someone who recognised the unambiguous power of men in the political world. At her dinner table, the interesting invitees were all men and, as Enid witnessed, "They would sit around the table and have the most splendid discussions, and that's when the interest in politics began. They, of course, all supported Labor. My mother, no, she supported a man; she used to argue with them, it didn't matter what party a man belonged to, if he wasn't a good man ... she didn't subscribe to the general idea." Adeline Lyons' brother Joe was one man who interested Eliza in the political struggle. So it was, over the next few years, that this newly aware and self educated Eliza Burnell would direct the most significant chapter in her middle daughter's family story – and masterfully so.

CHAPTER 5

THE TEACHER

Enid Lyons told the *Australian Women's Weekly* in December 1947: "From 14 to 16, when I was at Teachers Training College, I spent a good deal of my study time drawing brides – and married at seventeen! I don't know what the moral is," She added that any merit her school reports contained had been due to her mother – "It was easier to work reasonably well at school than to take home news of any failure."

It is not clear that Enid Burnell had very much interest in studying to be a teacher. But her more studious sister Nell had gone on to Hobart to study at the Teachers Training College and it was assumed that Enid would too. Teaching had become a profession where students from less well off backgrounds could study at tertiary level, there being no free education at secondary level. Enid would matriculate at teachers college. Entrance to Teachers College was by a competitive examination which could be taken after completing the eighth grade. Once accepted for college, the trainee was given a modest living allowance which meant those coming into Hobart to study, from other parts of Tasmania, had just enough to support themselves while boarding away from home.

Training lasted five years, balanced between college and as assistant teachers, after which there was a three year bond to the Education Department, to be repaid should the young teacher leave the profession or Department for any reason before completing three years of teaching. As part of the Memorandum of Agreement with the government, signed by William Burnell as guarantor on 9 April 1912, Enid was bonded to the Tasmanian Education Department for seven years, until the end of December 1919. Her trainee allowance was £20 (annually) for the first two years, £24 for the third and £30 for the fourth after which she would take the regular teacher's salary.

Compulsory and free schooling, throughout Australia, had ensured that public education was a growth industry. In late 1915, as war in Europe sucked away more and more of Australia's able bodied men, Tasmanian Education Minister Joe Lyons proudly opened Tasmania's first State high school in Hobart, seeing it as a milestone, which it was. Education of Australia's next generation would continue whatever the calamities abroad or budgetary constraints at home. Governments in all states had seen the advantage of offering teacher training with living allowances and bonds as a way of adequately filling the teaching places needed to educate children far and wide. But many young teachers, fresh out of college, could find themselves posted to back-of-beyond one teacher schools where conditions were primitive. They would become lonely spokespersons for communities dependent on not much more than the strength and generosity of their schoolmaster, to provide not only basic schooling for their children but often the bare essentials needed to set up a school.

Joe Lyons himself began his career as a schoolmaster, albeit one who had come into teaching as a monitor teacher in 1895 at Stanley well before attending Hobart's Training College in 1907. Over more than a decade, the experiences he endured with teaching spurred him on to political involvement and eventually Labor politics. As a monitor teacher, on just fifteen pounds a year when he began, he was appointed to outlying and remote areas such as Irishtown near Stanley, Apsley Meadows in the Midlands, Conara near Evandale and then to the west coast mining town of Tullah in 1905 where he began his complaints to the Education Department about the appalling conditions for both teachers and children in these outreach schools. School was expected to open but he had no desks, blackboards or rulers for forty pupils. He postponed the opening of the school much to the chagrin of his masters in the department who replied that it was his fault that school had not opened – he should have made temporary use of makeshift boards and boxes until the ordered desks and blackboards arrived.

Joe Lyons was hastily moved from Tullah after a few weeks and sent to Smithton where he met up with an old mate named Horace Pithouse who later recorded in an article eventually published in *Tasmanian Ancestry* (March 2004) how it was at Smithton that Lyons first became politicised after a debate entitled "Capital versus Labour". Lyons came into his own, defending protection against free trade as well as the platform of the Australian Labor Party. Lyons and his mates formed what Pithouse called "the first Labor League on the north-west coast of Tasmania" and Joe was the fourth man to pay his sub. After this, the Education Department, as Pithouse put it, "not only forced him to resign from the Labor League but warned him against taking further part in any factional matter whatever".

This bureaucratic, distant and superior attitude was typical of the way bureaucracy dealt with harsh conditions for many in the teaching profession. Teachers were servants of the State, mostly drawn from aspirational working and lower middle class families, and they were expected to be grateful for the opportunities offered them in the way of free training and good jobs. Later, when Minister for Education, Joe Lyons would find himself in a unique position to make reforms, although he would find this easier wished than done.

Enid recollected that she had less than seven shillings a month after paying her board in her first year and just over eight shillings a month in her second year. With this she bought all her other needs – from stationery to occasional tea and cake at the "Grotto", a favourite tea rooms in a basement where arches and ornate walls and ceilings gave Enid and her girlfriends a feeling of sophisticated luxury. They would order individually and then move to sit together after their orders came. This meant extra cake. Tea and cake for one included three slices; but an order for two came with only five slices. It was the same for crumpets, toast or sandwiches. Needless to say, Eliza sent a little money, from time to time, so Enid and Nell were never destitute. The students came from similar financial backgrounds and Enid observed in her memoirs how they "all worked and played happily together in a penny-pinching confraternity".

By the time Enid began at the Training College in Hobart, her sister Nell was back there after a year as assistant teacher in Burnie. Nell began teaching at a Hobart city school for her final year. In this way the girls were able to board together, in Liverpool Street about seven blocks from the college, and Enid quickly adapted as a student away from home. It must have been exhilarating to have such independence so young, although when addressed at College as "Miss Burnell" Enid felt "devastated". Enid contributed short items to the College magazine, *The Tasmanian Trainee*, and saw them in print. Her writing style reflected her extreme youth in its sense of the dramatic and mock heroic tone, and overuse of the exclamation mark. Her "Pen Sketches" snippet for April 1913 was entitled "French – Not Latin" and is a good example: "French! Can I never escape the baleful influence? For years French has followed me ceaselessly, relentlessly dogging my steps! ... French haunts me day and night. Always beside me never away! These are the verdicts of three fair maids, and yet French is not a flirt! What is he?" French was clearly not her favourite subject.

College life, Enid recalls, was full of the sharper moments of self awareness. The superficially assured Enid, whose mother had coached her to stand before audiences fearlessly, was not as hardened to criticism as she seemed. She never forgot the lecturer who almost reduced her to tears with sarcasm telling her, "You're wrong, Miss Burnell, although you appear so confident." But air-headed she was not for in two years she had completed all subjects for her Matriculation, possible under the training college's intense program.

In Burnie, through 1914, Enid enjoyed her experience as a trainee teacher. She maintained control well, often with a psychological wisdom beyond her years. Precocious little Charlie, an exhibitionist with no boundaries at home, waged a war of wills over time. Enid called him to the front of the class, just what he wanted. But then Enid dramatically swept him up and cradled him like a baby, rocking him to and fro and telling the class how people should be gentle with babies. In spite of his fury, Enid kissed Charlie and sent him back to his desk where he buried his face in his hands. He was never a problem again.

Deftness at keeping order or maintaining discipline, Enid regarded as her "strongest asset as a teacher". She was singled out for a special project when the main school building in Burnie became overcrowded. In spite of her junior years, she was given responsibility for a subsidiary group of students, to be located in another part of Burnie. Her class there consisted of 69 pupils. Each school day, Enid and another student teacher took charge of a total of 150 children.

Young teachers at the time often faced classes with many pupils not much younger than themselves. Enid had a number of tough teenagers. One named McCarthy was older than her and the saucy disrespect of this good looking lad finally got the better of Enid. She asked him to stay back after school, a command that delighted him. His mockery got the better of her; after reprimanding him for winking at her, Enid "weakly waved a hand in dismissal".

During her assistant teaching year, William Burnell spent time out of work; maybe it was his excessive drinking or a lack of jobs around Burnie. By the time of her engagement in October, he was working at Scottsdale. With unemployment in her own family, Enid had a deep and personally felt appreciation, from then on, of its devastating effects. During 1914, in the Burnell household, there was no chance of even small luxuries. Enid's two pounds a month salary was handed over to supplement the family budget.

Generally there was little indulgence of any kind under Eliza's roof. Having encouraged her daughter in public confidence, Eliza seems to have been intolerant of any sort of display. Eliza made cutting remarks after Enid first appeared with the Burnie Methodist choir: "You thought you looked nice and never for a moment did you forget it," Eliza told her afterwards. "You thought you were being admired. You were not. You were being laughed at. And I was thoroughly ashamed of you." Conceit on Enid's part that she had "graduated" and was "mature" at sixteen was quickly flattened by Eliza's down-to-earth reminders that housework still had to be done and that the Matriculation and its higher curricula, from works of literature to complex mathematics, had little to offer in the way of "housewifely arts". Enid had charge of the weekly cleaning and upkeep of the family living room. This included ironing, with flat-irons heated on an open fire, three large damask table cloths. Seeing a little of Eliza's point, Enid reflected wryly that "reciting Tennyson's 'Dream of Fair Women' did little to help me".

But Enid was one to make good out of low moments. In a letter to Joe, she described a concert she and four other female assistant teachers had performed during a lunch time. Each item was a funny story. "I can tell you," she recalled, "that between the five of us there were some amusing gems unearthed and by the time the bell rang we were all of us quite exhausted with laughter. If you ever hear a particular amusing anecdote, please pass it on." She confessed to Joe, "I think I love a good laugh beyond anything." Eliza's ability to improvise served her well. One day her class was spent outdoors when examinations took the room. She read stories and recited, having the students do the same. "We varied the program a little," she told Joe, "by singing and marching. ... The children enjoyed themselves and I enjoyed myself ... Mrs Lee and I are on the very best of terms."

The headmaster, Robert Lee, and his wife liked Enid. They would keep in touch with Enid over many years. Enid did well at Burnie; she underestimated her abilities by saying only her discipline made her a successful teacher. She was entertaining and made information accessible – like her speeches did much later. In 1935, when headmaster of the Moonah School in Hobart, Robert Lee wrote to Enid asking if she might address a teachers conference, Enid wrote back, referring to herself as a "very green assistant". Robert Lee replied, "Not so green I can assure you. I often quote your name when discussing the type of teachers coming from the College today."

Like her mother, Enid was a gregarious and public spirited member of Burnie's local community. She gave recitals at church gatherings, fund raising concerts and the like, and played the organ on Sundays at church. The Burnell parlour remained a centre for entertainment with Enid now pianist as guests came by; on one occasion George Martin, a Labor MP for Franklin and Joe's friend, told Eliza he was surprised at her accomplishment and didn't realise she had time to study music, which of course she hadn't. Enid was good at passing herself off. She was Madame Sophie in the Burnie amateur dramatic society's performance of *The Country Girl*. It opened the day she and Joe became engaged and she wrote of hearing his "laugh floating up behind the scenes" . She put her name down for the Burnie opera the following year wondering if she would be Mrs Joe Lyons by then. Instead she would appear as "Queen of the Public Service" in September 1915 in Hobart, with a very young Errol Flynn as her pageboy, the son of one of her maids of honour in the pageant.

Years later, as the recently widowed former prime minister's wife, Enid would receive a letter from a woman she had taught with at Burnie. Alice Moore, the woman's married name, had written a few words of encouragement to Enid, after Joe's sudden death. Time had not lessened the feelings of friendship: "We were junior teachers together at Burnie, along with the other juniors, Queenie Hall, Rene

Atkinson and Tom Lee … I wonder if you realise just how deeply the ordinary, everyday folk, like ourselves, have felt for you during the last three months."

The lower middle class teaching profession was very much Enid's social circle at this point, with its government sponsored ladder to social acceptability. Another of her good friends was Ivy Haywood of Stowport whom she had known since childhood. Ivy married Leonard Russell in December 1914 and Enid was their bridesmaid. Leonard, also a teacher, became headmaster at the Elliott school. Sixty years later, they would celebrate the Russells' sixtieth wedding anniversary together. Meanwhile Nell had become engaged to Norm Allison, also a Burnie teacher. Soon after Norm would join the AIF to leave for active duty in the War in Europe, and be killed in action. Nell would marry Hubert Glover in December 1922, also a teacher. Hubert would later work for Joe Lyons on the mainland and make a career in the federal public service.

Indeed, it was partly as a result of Enid's years at Hobart Teachers College that led to the most significant step she would take in her life. As Enid ended her first year of assistant teacher, wider fields were opening to her. Letters had been arriving at Cooee and addressed to Miss Enid Burnell from no lesser person than a Minister of the State Government. By the end of October, Enid would be privately engaged to one very special former teacher who had made the jump into State politics, namely Joe Lyons, no longer protesting over the conditions foisted upon lowly school masters and who was now the "chief", in charge of it all as Minister of Education, now engaged to one of his Department's assistant teachers. With just three years of her teaching commitment completed, and about to marry, Enid would have to extricate herself from the Department.

Even before the engagement, their letters reveal that Joe considered using his position to have Enid transferred to Hobart, for her second assistant teacher year, to be nearer to him. Events of their own making, however, would overtake them. By October 1914, Joe was insisting Enid not worry if she left her teaching bond early, as he would "count myself a lucky man to be allowed to pay instead of having to wait", no small matter since she still had five years of her agreement left. From his own experience, Joe knew the exactitude of departmental procedure over lost trainees.

After almost fifteen years in the Education Department, Joe Lyons still had 21 months left before his bond expired when he resigned from the Department to take his seat in the Tasmanian parliament in 1909. Because of his penurious family circumstances, he had not been able to attend College for some years. Instead he had worked his way to a full state school salary with experience in what the department classified as "half-time" schools, working up from a monitor teacher over time. So, in 1909 and after fifteen years with the Department, he still owed the government six pounds, payable in monthly instalments, to finish off the bond begun when he entered College. It was a lot of money even for a newly elected politician. Lucky Enid, however, would have Joe to pay the cost of her leaving early.

The proposal had not been as unexpected as accounts from Enid sometimes suggest. Eliza Burnell had visited her daughters on occasion in Hobart, something not surprising for a mother with teenage girls so far away from home. During 1912, Eliza had come to Hobart (wrongly recorded in Enid's memoir as 1913) just before Enid's sixteenth birthday. Letters between Enid and Joe make it clear this was the correct date. Enid began visiting parliament when she was barely fifteen.

Eliza's political involvement meant she would make a visit to State Parliament while in Hobart. And she invited the girls to go with her. Typical of a teenager ignorant of the possibilities of new experiences, Enid relates how she declined to go the first night. But Nell's account of the occasion next day stirred her, and she joined her mother and sister on the next night's visit. She wore a dark grey velvet frock trimmed with silver grey braid and a large grey hat lined under the brim in blue to match her eyes. A confident girl and more mature than her years, she was dressed to catch the attention of admirers. Nell's account of the previous night's visit had made it obvious that Parliament was full of men, some even eligible bachelors. Enid later recalled her mother's entrance to the foyer where they assembled: "Members on both sides of the House knew my mother from her long years of political work and came to greet her." The women were the centre of attention.

After this, there were a number of evenings when Nell and Enid dropped in on Parliament to "see our show" as Joe called it. Lyons and his friend George Martin escorted the women back to their lodgings on the first visit and assured Eliza that if the girls came again to see Parliament they would always see them home safely. Thereafter, as Enid put it, "Nellie and I went along not so much to hear the debates, I think, as to be escorted home." She added, "Both men were considerably older than either of us so, in the fashion of the day, we never used their Christian names, although to them we were Nellie and Enid".

Eliza's attempts to chaperone her girls appropriately were not in question. But, unwittingly or with design, she had presented her daughters formally to eligible bachelors of considerable standing in the Tasmanian community. In a letter to Joe after their engagement, before it had been announced publicly, Enid assured Joe that he should not be jealous of George Martin's recent visit to the Burnell home. After all, she had always thought it was Nellie whom George had preferred, although Nell by then was engaged to a teacher. The walks home from parliament had certainly had their chemistry. Whether Eliza hoped it might happen to one of her daughters, or not, soon after the evening walks home from parliament began in 1912, Joe Lyons had become besotted with Enid Burnell, then a fifteen year old student – and he more than twice her age.

Joe Lyons was very well known to Eliza and William. Eliza's visit to the Tasmanian parliament with her daughters had been not so much for the girls' edification as for Eliza's own pleasure in keeping up with acquaintances in public life from whose company she drew stimulation. Lyons acknowledged his familiarity with the Burnells when writing to William Burnell in 1914, saying "there is no need to say anything of myself as you have known me for so long". Eliza's line cast, Enid had hooked the most eligible bachelor MP, and with just one throw. Enid's teacher training had delivered her far more than a classroom of smiling faces.

Newly engaged to Tasmania's Treasurer and Minister for Education Joe Lyons, Enid Burnell (far left) was bridesmaid at the wedding of her friend Ivy Haywood to Leonard Russell in December 1914.

A young Joe Lyons campaigns in the Tasmanian State seat of Wilmot (1912) for the fledgling Labor Party.

CHAPTER 6

BRIDE AND GROOM

Enid recalled the day of her engagement as one of embarrassment.
It was an era of extreme formalities. This added to secrecy.
Apparently, only when Enid used Joe's first name did her siblings
and mother know instantly the couple had become intimate, a term
at the time which meant nothing more than that the pair were openly
known to be in love, with a courtship accepted. But this was not a
normal engagement. In Enid's words, thirty-five year old Joe "had
already lived more than half his life before I knew him." That she
had continued to refer to Joe as Mr Lyons, even in their letters, says
something about the unusual environment surrounding this love
affair.

The weekend Enid starred in "Country Girl", Joe stayed with Enid's
family at Cooee. Nell had just become engaged to Norm Allison; the
family was in high spirits. During Sunday (1 October 1914) after the
Saturday evening's opening performance, Joe and Enid walked alone
on Cooee beach, where Joe finally proposed and declared how she
had stolen his heart. There is no doubt he was fully aware of the
scandal that might ensue. There was his position as a State Minister,
Treasurer and even the Minister for Education. And Enid so young,
still.

Enid, of course had accepted instantly, knowing full well that their
letters and conversations over months had ached for their chance to
be together. She was overjoyed to have a "man" as she would call

him. The lovers' walk on the Cooee sand has become something of a small legend in the timeline of their continuing romance. No longer the distance of formalities, the dance of pretence that they might run into each other, or share a walk with others, or meet at parliament, the teasing humour that they were just "good friends", or the need to find ways of being informal in supposedly formal letters. No hints needed from here on.

Returning to the Burnell house, however, their cover had already been blown. A huddled family greeted them. They didn't need to be told the couple was engaged – it was enough for Enid to confirm she had called him "Joe". This done, Enid became the butt of their collective humour as they made her say it again. Enid claims she was so embarrassed she could only blurt out "Josephine". In the weeks that followed, her young brother Bert would cheekily enquire if Enid had sat on Joe's knee and request a demonstration from Enid of their moments alone. When daily letters did not arrive on time in Hobart from Enid, Joe would express his disappointment and invariably Annie was blamed for missing the post, since she had taken on the role of assistant post mistress for Eliza. His fiancée so young, Joe often allowed Eliza's dictates to prevail whether it be how many times Enid might write to him in one week or what the timeline might be for their wedding plans. The engagement was a family affair.

Innocence and risk are qualities that haunt the Lyons partnership from the outset. In 1912 and 1913, Joe's letters to Enid exhibit a mixture of responsible man at his desk – "Earle [Labor leader] did not bring up that matter in Caucus so I presume he has dropped it. Just as well." – coupled with the quips and teasing of a lovesick adolescent – "I've been showing your photo to everyone and they all approve". Reading them, all written in immaculate copperplate handwriting, is at times a startling experience.

Joe is seemingly formal, on 11 December 1912, with, "If you want to have a look at our 'show' [parliament] you had better not wait until

Friday as it's just possible we may finish early on that day." Yet this note, on House of Assembly writing paper and from a distinguished Member, also contains the barely disguised hope of a schoolboy that Miss Burnell, aged fifteen, will not wait till Friday to come for a visit to Parliament as he longs to see her. And if she waits he may miss another opportunity. He writes again on 18 December 1912, thanking her for a copy of the College magazine she has sent him. He mentions they may be travelling back north on the same train. This is the hope of a shy boy who has no chance or right to say what he really feels.

The letters continue like this through the next year. In January 1913, Joe responded to Enid's tongue-in-cheek offer to be a Labor candidate in the snap election just called with, "I'm afraid your age is against you – with your plenitude of years you should be standing for the Council! We need *young* candidates for our young Party ... I shall turn you down because if you were successful in securing a seat the rest of us would not get a word in edgewise!" He added a "PS" joking that he would endorse her as a candidate if she would run with him. No wonder Enid confessed much later to drawing bridal frocks throughout her College days!

It was Enid Lyons' wish, when she donated Joe's letters to the National Library, shortly before she died, that they would reveal to historians and others a different side to Joe from that apparent in his all too well recorded public life over three decades. These letters are undoubtedly the most intimate collection of personal exchanges of any Australian political couple.

Joe Lyons, a confident political activist from the outset, won the seat of Wilmot after a fairly public stoush with the Education Department over teaching conditions. But in his relationship with Enid, however much smitten, he was no Don Juan. Their letters to each other reveal how they anxiously tried to gauge each others' feelings over some time, unable to declare their real thoughts. On 28 October 1914, Joe wrote:

That last visit to the House ... Each of us wanting the other and playing a game of cross purposes. If only I had known your thoughts that night I would have been crazy with delight. Oh, how I longed to go home with you ... I can see you now standing there by the table and I can feel again the mad impulse to take you in my arms and kiss you because you looked so tempting and because I loved you then as much as I do now ... And all the time I was hiding my feelings in case I should be laughed at.

To which Enid replied a couple of days after: "Will I ever forget it? I distinctly remember that on the way home, I saw a falling star and in my excitement I caught your arm to draw your attention to it. Afterwards I felt extremely silly and wondered whether or not you noticed it. Did you?"

Joe's reserve was partly because of Enid's age; he was her mother's friend. How could he make known his feelings for such a young girl without some sort of a scandal? He would have had more scope as a lounging lad in some respects. Added to that, there was his Irish background, and the ancient tendency for some Irish sons to stay close to their mothers and marry late. Joe seems to have fallen into this category.

The Lyons family

One of eight children, Joe Lyons had been born in the fishing village of Stanley, the port for Circular Head in far west northern Tasmania. His parents, both of Irish stock, had prospered for many years. Joe's grandfather Michael Lyons migrated to Tasmania to work as a labourer for the Van Dieman's Land Company. Under Edward Curr, a pastoralist and controversial figure from Victoria, the Company, or syndicate, owned most of the land in the north west of the state and operated out of a grand colonial house a few kilometres out of

Stanley, built high on land overlooking Bass Strait. Today, gradually renovated, it is one of the many tourist sights at Stanley. In time, grandfather Michael Lyons became a tenant farmer and then moved on to buy the Emily Hotel in Stanley village which he renamed the Freemason's Hotel. Later it became the Union Hotel and is still there, set among the other quaint Georgian cottages and shops that line Stanley's main street, winding down to the jetty. Joe's father was Michael Lyons junior, the second child of five and born in 1845.

In 1870, Michael Lyons married Ellen Carroll who had migrated from Ireland in 1857, aged eleven, with her mother Catherine, her older sisters Etty and Mary and a half-brother John, whom Enid Lyons described in her memoir as "born of the wrong side of the blanket", although as Kate White has shown in *A Political Love Story* he remains something of a mystery. Their father John Carroll had died in New York State in a work accident and they had been sponsored to Tasmania by Dennis Carroll, an uncle, who lived at Forrest, near Stanley.

Michael Lyons junior at first helped manage his father's produce store and later established himself in business in Ulverstone where Joe spent happy years as a young boy, exploring the river and mucking about. Joe was the fourth child in the family and born in 1979; his older brothers were Jack, Arden and Elwin and after Joe were three sisters – Adeline, Mary and Gertrude – and a younger brother Thomas (Tom) who would be the uncle all Joe and Enid's children remembered as the brother Joe was fondest of, the one they knew well.

Life was good for the boy Joe Lyons – and then came disaster. Michael Lyons had taken to betting on horses after dreaming the winner in the 1884 Melbourne Cup. In 1887 it was very different. At great expense, he travelled to Melbourne to attend the 1 November Cup and waged five hundred pounds on a horse called Tranter at 20 to 1. It lost and Michael Lyons returned to Ulverstone a broken man. The family was ruined. Michael Lyons took years to recover and never worked again. Joe, aged nine, was forced to find employment. Beginning as a printer's devil in the afternoons and evenings after school, Joe earned six shillings a week. By twelve he was cutting scrub.

Eventually Joe's Carroll aunts saved him. They still lived in Stanley, making a living from sewing and dressmaking. These two unmarried ladies took pity on their unfortunate nephew whom they believed to be bright, bringing him to live in their four roomed cottage at the foot of the "Nut", the core of an extinct volcano, a 100 metres high square of a hill jutting out from the coastline and into the sea like a giant block of earth. Joe went back to school where he stayed and excelled and began his monitor teaching. Through all the troubles in the family, it was his mother Ellen Joe worried about. She had been his guide as a child when he had listened to her stories of Ireland and the injustice there. Joe's political leanings could be traced back to his mother's influence. Joe Lyons had a soft heart; his letters to Enid reveal this intensely.

Joe Lyons MP

How proud Ellen Carroll must have been when her son Joe won a seat in Parliament as a Labor Member for Wilmot in 1909. In the very Anglo Protestant state of Tasmania, Irish Catholics were a very small minority. In the 1890s, the Irish born made up just 3.9 per cent of the Tasmanian population compared with 7.31 per cent on the mainland. When Joe Lyons won his seat, the fledgling Tasmanian Labor Party was still better known as the Workers Political League (WPL) and very much divided between union organised action and those who, like Joe, meandered into Labor politics by simply taking a stand on issues. Surprisingly, it was only in 1907 that Joe had become interested in active politics after he realised more and more, from his various outlying teaching postings – Apslawn and Apsley Meadows, Smithton, Pioneer – how unfairly some teachers in the Department were treated, and how feudal the system was where local landlords, like Aloysius Joyce senior in Branxholm decades before, were often in charge of teachers' accommodation and exerted their own pressures for teachers to conform to the status quo.

At various localities, Joe Lyons had complained to the Education Department and spoken out publicly in frustration, but it was only in Hobart that Joe enlisted, so to speak. He attended a discussion group organised by the Denison branch of the WPL while studying at Teachers College. Posted to Launceston the next year, he continued to attend WPL groups and was elected to the WPL committee of the No 2 branch there. He helped set up a WPL branch at Perth, south of Launceston. In June 1908, he attended the conference of the newly formed State School Teachers Union in Hobart, where he was used as an example of the inequities among teaching ranks of conditions and pay – those with the worst conditions received the lowest pay.

Joe continued to speak on WPL platforms, criticising teaching conditions and the Department and eventually was forced to admit that, as a public servant, he had been supporting the Labor opposition against the government in public speeches. The case caused a debate in parliament. As a result, Joe Lyons gained a small reputation within Labor ranks. Then the Royal Commission Report, in March 1909, seemed to support Joe Lyons' complaints against the Department of Education. It recommended a number of reforms, including an increase in the salaries of teachers in small country schools. By then, Joe Lyons had resigned from the Department intending to be a Labor candidate at the April 1909 State election. Yet, it was not until June 1909 that Joe Lyons attended his first state Labor Party conference, when he was already a Labor MP. That is hard to imagine nearly a century later.

Lyons won a Labor seat in parliament while still hardly known inside the state WPL. Tasmania's multi-member electorates and proportional system of voting called the Hare-Clarke system, introduced across the state in 1909, has long encouraged personality politics alongside party politics. Each Tasmanian state electorate returns a group of successful candidates and, in earlier times when the parties of candidates were not listed on voting tickets, it was possible for a popular candidate to edge out another from the same party who was not so popular. From 1907 to 1941 candidates' names were listed ungrouped in alphabetical order on the ballot paper.

Joe Lyons had the common touch. This was evident throughout his political career. Enid wrote of him being a "dropper-in" or someone who perennially thought of calling on people if he was passing. They even did it at Deloraine the morning after they were married when they called on Joe's old friends the Scotts. Enid found it disconcerting but went along with the practice all their married life. Not surprisingly, riding his bicycle over weeks across the undulating electorate of Wilmot, around Deloraine and the outskirts of south Launceston, Joe Lyons became known to thousands and liked by many. In 1984, the seat of Wilmot was renamed Lyons in honour of Joe Lyons' representation of the area for thirty years, the largest electorate in Tasmania stretching from the west coast to the mouth of the Tamar River in the north and across the island to the east coast. At the 1909 election, Lyons scored just under the quota needed and with just a third of the surplus from the top Labor candidate Jensen he won the second Labor seat for Wilmot. In his next election, he topped the poll.

Labor politics had brought the Burnell and Lyons families into contact. Eliza Burnell seems to have joined her local WPL branch around 1908 where she became a friend of Joe's eldest sister Adeline who became a frequent visitor to the Burnell home. In a letter to Enid after their engagement, Joe would remark that his sisters had known Enid "as a child and liked you". The families may not have been close but they were certainly not strangers to each other. After their engagement Joe wrote of his sister, "When I told May [Mary] in one of my letters she seemed quite pleased about it." Eliza Burnell herself had her political debut in 1910, making a vote of thanks to federal Labor MP King O'Malley at an election meeting. Four months before Joe won his seat in parliament he had visited the Burnells with his sister and heard Enid recite. Eliza Burnell had introduced her daughters to parliament in Hobart and some of its younger Labor MPs, including Joe, in the winter of 1912.

By March 1914, the seats in the Tasmanian parliament were evenly balanced. Then, a disgruntled independent, Joshua Whitsitt, whom Enid would write fondly of in *Among The Carrion Crows*, voted with Labor on a motion of no-confidence on April Fool's Day and brought down the Solomon Government. Labor came to power suddenly. Joe Lyons became Treasurer, Minister of Education, Minister of Railways and Deputy Premier within days.

On 8 April, Joe wrote to Enid, then teaching in Burnie. In his letter, his tongue-in-cheek comments and teasing barely hide his pride at being able to pass on the good news. "My dear young subordinate [he is now her ultimate boss] … you will need to treat me with the greatest respect or meet with summary dismissal so be careful how you act." On 6 May, he wrote asking if she would like tickets to the opening of Parliament: the letter opened with jocular familiarity – "I know it is unusual for His Majesty to so condescend as to address one of his menials so familiarly, but I'll risk the loss of dignity for once", adding re the tickets, "If you desire it you may have it". Enid, however, could not make the opening.

For a time it seemed the delicacy of his special position was lost to Joe. Labor was in its infancy in a parliament where there was no Hansard and the total number of MPs in the House of Assembly numbered just 30. The debating chamber had all the appearances of a gentlemen's club meeting room. The whole "show", as Joe called parliament, was extremely parochial and somewhat quaint by today's standards. In this setting, and with inexperience of office, young

Minister Lyons allowed a relationship to unfold that by modern standards would have been scandalous.

Joe wrote to Enid over some months suggesting he might be able to use his influence to have her posted to Hobart the following year. Today the mere suggestion of possible misuse of political position, especially in a written record, would be political suicide. On 21 August, just over a month before they became engaged, Joe wrote to Enid in his usual familiar but formal style. It needs to be remembered that this is the Minister for Education writing to a trainee teacher of seventeen, within his department – and that the letter is on official paper marked "Treasury Hobart":

> Dear Enid,
>
> First of all I want to remind you that your manner is not marked by the respect which is due to your chief, and I strongly object to having my words hurled back at me by way of quotation. I hope you realise the severity of the rebuke but I suppose it is all a waste of time.
>
> To be serious and deal with your desire to come to Hobart, let me say that I am not too pleased with the Director lately for certain reasons and I may find it a bit more difficult to get him to agree to your coming down, but I'll try my hardest....
>
> ... I guess you'd better suddenly put on the necessary 2 or 3 years to your age, by magic for preference, and take pity on the loneliness of your minister!

The letters continued in this vein almost until the engagement. But then the responsibilities of office gradually impressed themselves on the rookie minister. By 15 September, even as he tried to assure her he would think of something, it is clear he knew he couldn't front the director of his department with such a request: "I'll have a word with the Director. To tell you the truth I'm a bit diffident about it lately. I'm afraid McCoy will accuse me of asking for the transfer for my own benefit. It would be dreadful to be accused of that wouldn't it?" And then Joe makes a joke of it all: "I think you will have to be transferred to Hobart if you will undertake to look after me and keep me on the right track. I promise that the task will not be a hard one if you are the guide."

Engagement

Kate White, in *A Political Love Story*, pinpoints Joe's readiness to declare his love for Enid as coming after his mother died in Devonport in July 1913. White explains: "He was experiencing a much deeper, numbing loneliness since the death of his mother, his closest friend … With her death, the family was without its centre … Enid Burnell came to fill that great inner loneliness." From September 1914, Joe's letters increasingly become anxious that Enid play the role of backstop, adviser, friend to count on. But he was also very physically in need of her.

Even when engaged, their long separations due to Joe's parliamentary and administrative work in Hobart became equally burdensome. Just a month after their weekend at Cooee, Enid was so missing Joe she wrote at the end of her letter on 30 October 1914: "Two hundred miles is a long way when you are at one end of the distance and your 'wife' at the other! The 'poor little wife' wants you very badly tonight and would love so much to be felt in your arms." Around the same time Joe wrote: "I felt just a bit elated last night because of the feeble efforts of the opposition to criticise me and any success I achieve I always feel that I want you to share. That was one reason but I am afraid the chief one was that I wanted to feel you in my arms again and be really happy." By December, he was writing, "I know that my embraces are fierce and sometimes you must feel that I overdo it, but I seem to be mad with love when you are in my arms and I am scarcely responsible for my actions."

There was to be many a hurdle for the lovers even after they had told their families they would marry. First Joe had to seek William's permission to marry his daughter. Enid assured Joe it would be fine: ""He [William] told me when he was at home that he believed in allowing people to please themselves. Where I look for resistance though is in the matter of early marriage. He doesn't think girls should marry young and neither did I until – well – er – very recently." William gave his consent much as Enid had foreseen.

It was Eliza, always the manager, who came up with a most unusual query. In a letter to Joe, written on 5 October 1914, she enquired about a recent medical operation he had undergone in Launceston. The letter is interesting for a number of reasons. Her tone to Joe is friendly, partly formal but very much of adult to adult. Eliza's discussion of Enid, however, is very much mother and child, confiding in Joe as if to a father figure around Enid. She reveals Enid's rather young and excited reference to Joe ("Mum! I thank God every night that a *Man* loves me and I love him.") and from this goes on to explain the context of Enid's comment as coming from Eliza's having spoken of a man who had praised Joe for his efforts at the Pioneer school. One gets the impression Eliza is more interested in flattering the Treasurer than letting him know his fiancée is happy. Eliza knows Enid's use of the word "man" is as she herself means it – important and influential. The whole reference exaggerates Enid's youth, although Eliza does say Enid "has a maturity of outlook and ideas".

The other "delicate" matter Eliza moves on to discuss is surprising. She asks, supposedly for Enid's sake ("the maternal instinct is strong in her and she looks forward to some day sharing the joy of a child with someone"), if the medical operation Joe has recently undergone might in any way affect his ability to have children. Eliza was certainly fearless, if not a little overbearing. While she wanted all that was best for her "girleens", as she called them, she could not help trying to pull the strings. Should Joe have said yes, he would never be able to have children, would she have stopped the marriage? Fortunately Joe could answer "no".

Joe very soon was writing that the word of their unofficial engagement was out. On 2 October 1914: "At Devonport, Walter Miller informed me that the story was being circulated that you and I were married, that in fact the priest had been seen going out to Cooee for the purpose." On 6 October: "I think my fellow boarders [his Hobart boarding house] are beginning to realise my case is a serious one." The rumour mill was growing. Enid recalled, "Even among those who knew the true position, there was a great deal of hostile comment. Few condemned me, of course, but Joe and my mother were subjected to the unkindest sort of criticism. 'Cradle-snatcher' was the hackneyed and obvious taunt reserved for Joe, but my mother was accused of sacrificing her young daughter to satisfy her worldly ambition." Some rumours were caustic, even bigoted with their differing religions being used against them – Joe refers to this in November, writing: "Isn't it contemptible for those people to send you such things as occurred in the 'Watchman'? They may be religious but they are anything but Christian." They had chosen a rocky path by becoming engaged across religious boundaries. Enid would recollect in an ABC interview in 1978 how the sectarianism of the time was so entrenched, and her friends so disapproving of her decision to marry a Catholic, that she had none of the usual pre-wedding parties before her wedding day.

The idea of waiting until Enid might be a year or two older before she married was soon fraying at the edges. Joe grew more and more desperate to have Enid with him and, having become engaged, perhaps they might as well think more seriously about marrying as soon as they could. Joe began to use every persuasion he knew – especially as he realised for Enid to marry before turning eighteen relied on her parents' consent. The Labor government lived most precariously with the Independent Whitsitt always prevaricating and, as Joe wrote to Enid in November, "the sooner we know what side he is on the better because I decline to put up with what has been my lot lately … if he attempts to shuffle then we'll go to the Governor and ask for a dissolution." On 9 October, Joe had written: "I would wait longer but as I told you I want you to marry the 'Treasurer' if possible." Again, on 26 October, he assures her he is happy to wait another year for them to be married but adds, "if I were absolutely sure of remaining in my present position until the end of next year". Yet within months, the Burnells had agreed Enid could marry before she turned eighteen, sometime after Easter 1915.

In December 1914, Enid was bridesmaid in Stowport for her friend Ivy Haywood when Ivy married Leonard Russell. Together at last on Boxing Day, Joe gave Enid a brooch of pearls set with small olive semi precious stones. Her engagement ring of five small diamonds set in gold, briefly lost on the sand at Cooee and found by a young boy to whom they gave a reward, sparkled on her left hand. Enid then returned for a short holiday at Joe's boarding house in Hobart, the Ventura, where she was introduced to his landlady Mrs Manning who was dying to meet her. They spent days wandering the city, enjoying long hours together by the river, in picnics, completely absorbed in each other, so that when Enid went back to Burnie Joe was even more depressed. In spite of his busy schedule, his tennis with friends and the odd race meeting, he could not but think of Enid. On 27 January 1915 he wrote:

> You say that you want me more than ever now, well I have the same feeling, so strongly sometimes I wonder if it is 'wise' for me to go to you so often because it unsettles us both and makes us wish for the barriers to be removed and that is not good for us. … I feel sure that I cannot be as much to you as you are to me. You see there were plenty of opportunities for you in life but I had gone back to a state bordering upon despondency and disgust with everything that had reference to the relations of men and women, and you have altered everything by holding out the hope of happiness for me.

Enid had ended her contract with the Department, with Joe paying out her bond. She would not need that transfer to Hobart after all. For a short time, she seems to have helped out as an unofficial monitor teacher in Elliott, staying with her friends Ivy and Leonard Russell. By 16 February 1915, Joe was writing to say he would be going to Devonport to look at a block of land and discussing their wedding outfits. But there was still one more hurdle – the question of religion.

Conversion

Shortly after they became engaged, Enid had written to Joe (9 October 1914) with thoughts that belied her youthfulness. She confessed that she had been thinking what their marriage would mean to each of them. And she had been reading about the Catholic sacrament of marriage: "From what I have read, I gather that your marriage to me will entail great religious sacrifices (if I may call them so) on your part – far more so than to me. Naturally my Church people will resent my action but, as far as I know, I will be breaking no law of my Church in becoming your wife. But you will, won't you?" Within a week of their engagement, their difference of religion had become an issue.

Mixed marriages a century ago were not unusual in Australia. Catholic and Protestant might bicker and divide the community, but where love was concerned religion often played second fiddle. But it could still be a problem where Christians took their religion seriously, as a lot did at the time. Religious bigotry and sectarianism languished alongside many a mixed marriage. This was a nation largely divided between Protestant Anglo and Irish descended Catholics. The divisions of the old countries could just as easily tear families apart as be healed by a mixed union. Aloysius Joyce would cut his children off if they married a non-Catholic. Eliza's Methodist family was for a time bitterly divided by Enid's choice of a Catholic for her husband.

Joe wrote to Enid (26 October 1914) after their unofficial engagement: "Miss Fahey was a bit concerned because she heard you were not an RC [Roman Catholic] and when I told her you were a 'Methodist' she gasped!" After some discussion, with Eliza very much involved, Enid concluded that it was important to a Catholic (Joe) to be married in a Catholic church but not so a Methodist (Enid) to be married in a Methodist church. So a Catholic wedding ceremony was agreed to.

But it did not rest there. With Eliza her guide, Enid came to believe that it was far better for a husband and wife to share the same religion for their peace of mind, harmony and lifelong unity. This was as much a measure of Eliza's sharpness of mind and practical tolerance as anything. Moreover, she was anxious to have her daughter as happily married to Joe as possible. She, herself, had married a man whose interest in religion was indifference at best while she had become a regular churchgoer. And the Burnell union had been a disappointment to Eliza over years. So Enid chose to take instructions in the Catholic religion with a view to conversion. As far as Joe was concerned, though, it was entirely up to her.

In March 1915, Enid and Eliza travelled to Stanley to stay with Joe's close friend Fr Thomas O'Donnell, in the presbytery at Stanley, a quaint timber house with attic bedrooms next to the church in a street that sloped down to a half moon cove west of the Nut. In this idyllic setting, Enid would be guided in the fundamentals of the Catholic religion, with a library at her disposal to read up on its creed and belief structures. Joe wrote on 5 March 1915, just after purchasing the orchard (nine acres for £375) for Enid in Devonport, that his heart was aching: "Do you know that when I think of these things and your image rises up before my mental vision my pen refuses to act and I have to sit back and just dream of you. I love you with every fibre of my being.... When I begin to think of you the desire to be with you gets more and more intense and finally it assumes the position of real pain... sometimes it takes all my self control to keep me here."

Enid Lyons gives a full account of her time in the Stanley presbytery in *So We Take Comfort*, and of the pressures she faced from her own "side" to the idea that a Methodist might convert to Catholicism, the religion of the dreaded Papists, coming as it did in the public glare of her marriage to the Deputy Premier and Treasurer. Her local Minister was shocked that such a staunch member of his congregation might go to the Catholics. Even on her wedding day, Eliza received a bitter letter from her mother Louisa Taggett condemning Enid's step in marrying a Catholic. But matched with this is Enid's account of her visits with her mother to Joe's old aunts Etty and Mary, on their arrival in Stanley, a description alive with the atmosphere of their homely charm, Irish brogue and warm acceptance of her, including their suggestion they all "take a glass of wine" which the teetotal Eliza had prepared Enid for. In spite of their differences, they managed to find common ground and come away touched by their new friendship.

Enid began badly at the presbytery, however, having an argument over religious and state schools with O'Donnell on the first day. The housekeeper Mrs Conway was horrified that a young sprat of a girl might speak out so confidently to a parish priest. Then O'Donnell was called away to his dying sister in Ballarat and Enid was left to read and think with Eliza, at the presbytery. She went forward and backward. After a week Joe was writing that it was a bad idea and she should come home.

But Enid persevered — much of her understanding coming out of Eliza's reading, as she would later recall. One day, Enid was sitting by the fire sewing while Eliza researched from the priest's large library when her mother suddenly handed her a volume of the *Catholic Encyclopaedia* and pointed to a section headed "Authority". Enid started to read and became absorbed. She would write in her memoirs: "I had been accustomed since childhood to follow closely reasoned argument; and as I read, I pondered. Finally there came upon me so overwhelming a conviction of the truth of the Catholic claims that had my wedding plans been cancelled, I still should have felt compelled to seek admission to the Church." Enid had accepted the Catholic line of authority from Peter as the one true church, and also the argument that subsequent breakaway Christian churches were not the true Christian church. Old Aloysius Joyce would have been proud of her.

While Enid was still in Stanley, near the end of March, Joe had to travel to Melbourne for a meeting that included Labor Prime Minister Andrew Fisher. Returning to Tasmania, Joe was by now so desperate to see Enid, he had his driver detour to Stanley when he came off the ferry. "[we} went up your way," he wrote to Enid afterwards, on 23 March, "in the hope that I'd meet you. I got to the gate but was afraid if I rang that Tom O'Donnell might appear. Then I returned sad at heart. I got along the top of the hill and sat on the fence gazing toward the presbytery but no Enid appeared and I went down to the driver again. The driver, as soon as he saw you said, 'Shall I pull up?' You can imagine what I said." After their fleeting rendezvous, Joe spent the night at Cooee and then headed back to Hobart.

Enid became a Catholic, baptised by Fr O'Donnell at Stanley, shortly after Joe's brief visit. And then she received her first Communion. Joe wrote of his joy: "Oh Enid, was any man ever blessed as I am without deserving it, or was any man happier than I am today… the thoughts that came to me as I read, the kindness of O'Donnell to my little queen, and your anticipation of the happy ceremony to come, each and all wrung from me the tears I have tried to keep back." In many ways, as the years progressed, Enid became a stricter adherent than Joe. Enid's sister Nell confided to her daughter, decades on, that after Enid's many pregnancies it was Joe who wanted to use some form of contraception to try to ease Enid's heavy burden of childbearing. But it was Enid who would not agree because to do so was against the Catholic religion.

Wedding Day

Enid and Joe were married at St Brigid's, Wynyard on Wednesday 28 April 1915. The Dardanelles campaign had just begun but war was far from anyone's thoughts that wedding day – except perhaps Nell thinking of her fiancé Norm who had enlisted. Fr O'Donnell was the celebrant in spite of a territorial dispute between the clergy that had almost upset the wedding plans. Burnie's parish priest since 1898, Fr Pat Hayes, was eager to preside over the wedding of Tasmania's second most important politician. He argued that Miss Burnell must be married in her parish church, and by himself no less. Joe went all the way to the archbishop over the matter and won.

The relatively new red brick Catholic church at Wynyard saw a great number of important guests at Enid and Joe's wedding, among them Joshua Whitsitt, William McCoy, Director of Education and James Belton, Minister for Lands. Enid was beautiful in a dress of white embroidered voile with a long satin sash. Her train carried monograms, in pale blue, of the bride and groom. Her veil was embroidered with lovers knots and shamrocks. Around her head, a wreath of pale blue flowers, matching her eyes, caught her veil in place. Nell was her bridesmaid in white silk striped voile over pale pink with a wide pink belt and tassel; Tom Lyons was the groomsman.

They celebrated their wedding breakfast at the nearby Federal Hotel and left for their honeymoon by car, spending their first night in Deloraine and afterwards going on to Sydney for a Premiers Conference, with a stop over in Melbourne on the way. Enid left the reception dressed to disguise her tender years in navy blue serge, a black hat and the black fox furs Joe had given her as a wedding present. It would be a while before they would need to keep in touch by letter.

Seventeen year old Enid Burnell on her wedding day, 29 April 1915, about to marry Joe Lyons, aged 35.

Chapter 7

A Political Spouse

When Enid Burnell became Mrs Joe Lyons, she could not have known to what extent her life from then on would have both a public and a private sphere. Reading her letters to Joe as they approached their marriage – and his to her – there is not a lot to indicate the political and public canvas that backgrounded all their actions. Among their numerous letters during their engagement, there is just Joe's reference to the embarkation of troops, affecting Nell's fiancé Norm Allison who was among them, to indicate the international turmoil that was in play.

In October 1914, walking from his office in the Treasury to the parliament across the street, Joe spent days marvelling at what must have seemed like an invasion of the Hobart docks nearby. "[The harbour is positively alive with ships," wrote Joe on 20 October. "They are a great sight as most of the transports are the big European liners. One warship is a Jap. The city is alive with all sorts of sailors and soldiers and each day they march about 4000 N Zealanders up to the Domain for drill … Nell's boy is down the harbour somewhere."

As the *Geelong* sailed around Sandy Bay point that day, Norm Allison was among 1000 Tasmanians leaving for the war. Many, like Norm Allison, watched the outline of Hobart's suburbs, on the slopes of Mt Wellington, for the last time. The enlisted men's departure was not mentioned in the press; relatives living beyond Hobart would have not known it was happening.

Britain had joined the European war against Germany in August 1914 and Australia was immediately, and eagerly, part of that conflict as a member of the British Empire. At the September 1914 federal elections, for which Enid was still too young to vote, Joseph Cook's Liberal government lost to Labor, installing the mannerly Scot, Andrew Fisher, for his third term as prime minister. Within a year, Fisher's deputy Billy Hughes would succeed him and go on to split federal Labor over conscription. Hughes would head up a new coalition of conservatives, much like Joe Lyons two decades later.

In Tasmania, Labor had failed to gain the seat it needed for a clear majority in the House of Assembly in the state's November 1914 Bass by-election. Joe's disappointment showed in a letter to Enid as he told her how impossible it was to govern while depending on the mercurial independent Whitsitt. Joe was ready to advise Labor should "go to the Governor and ask for a dissolution". He even mused about making a run for a federal seat, such was his frustration. He could have a go federally and if unsuccessful still stand again for his state seat. Joe Lyons may have stumbled into politics out of anger with the Education Department but he quickly became a keen political player. Joe Lyons would remain Treasurer and Minister for Education in the Earle Government until Labor lost the State election of March 1916.

Until their marriage, Joe and Enid were so caught up in their romance, much of this vaster world around them became somewhat peripheral. Joe would download every so often to Enid about the constraints of office – "there is nothing in being a minister even from a monetary standpoint", at one point claiming he'd prefer to be a private member and nearer her, writing, "I am very little better off than when I took office because of the constant calls on all of us." Watching the wives and girlfriends wave the troops away from the Hobart docks in October 1914, Joe's emotions had been deep – but he admitted they were a reaction to his separation from Enid rather than any empathy for Nell or more sobering thoughts about war: "As I stood on the wharf and saw the girls waving farewells I felt for them all more than I had thought possible and it is all because of my little girl and all that she means to me."

These private reveries would change with their marriage. The political stage took precedence from then on. The war on the home front very soon engulfed Labor, debates over conscription and recruitment dividing families, individuals and politicians across the nation. The laid back excitement of the war's early months faded fast as casualty figures rolled in. Recruitment fell far short of the numbers needed in the field and conscription became a catch cry. Enid's family was split over conscription; her sister Nell would lose a fiance at the front; her mother Eliza on a recruiting committee was in favour of conscription; and the older Burnells were from the "mother country" with allegiances to empire. While Joe campaigned against conscription, his friend Father Tom O'Donnell became an ardent supporter of conscription and the war effort. Labor leader Earle split with Labor's anti-conscription stand and, in January 1917, resigned from the party to join the Nationalists, led by pro conscriptionist Billy Hughes. Earle topped the Tasmanian Senate poll a few months later.

Of the conscription campaign, Enid would write, "Those who did not experience it cannot imagine the bitterness of feeling it evoked. Long standing friendships were broken and families divided ... but true to the lessons of our childhood, we did not allow our differing views whether on politics or religion to divide us [family]." Even her bigoted grandmother, Louisa Taggett, whom Enid described as a puritan, anti-Irish and a "conscriptionist with all the strength of her strong mind and emotions", was brought around. She arrived at Cooee for a visit on the day of the first conscription referendum in October 1916. In no time at all, she fell for Joe's gracious charm and pronounced, "I like him." So, remarkably, the issue of conscription was put to one side in the Burnell home.

Honeymoon

All this was in the future as Enid and Joe set off for their honeymoon on 28 April 1915, arranged to coincide with Joe's trip to Sydney for a Premiers conference. No doubt Joe saw an opportunity to get away, and for no expense at a time when he was not all that well off. Writing to Enid just before their wedding, "I am anxious in the first few weeks especially to keep down expenses to the lowest possible level in order that I may make a big effort to pay the full value of the orchard and the extra acre of land before the elections." If Labor lost, as he feared, his salary would drop significantly.

Joe and Enid Lyons began their married life in the public glare of society and meetings between the nation's leaders. It is hard to imagine what personal toll this might have taken. In her biography, Enid Lyons gives honeymoons short shrift; hers might have been too overwhelming in some respects as a beginning to married life. Still, it was exceptional; their days away had moments rich in detail and significance, often lightened by humour. Enid, the student teacher from Burnie, would be duchessed like a princess and dine with the highest in the land, on one occasion with a group that included three politicians, Fisher, Hughes and Lyons, all (in time) prime ministers and notable for their years in office.

In Melbourne, the city where the federal parliament sat until 1927, she failed to recognise her name when Margaret Fisher called to ask "Mrs Lyons" to dinner at the Fishers' Albert Park home. In Sydney, non Labor Victorian premier Sir Alexander Peacock announced the Lyons' presence with a jocular but cumbersome gaff, "There he is. He's only been married three days and she's only seventeen!" Enid looked back and marvelled at how tolerant their hosts had been, confronted by that parochial and somewhat naïve newly married Lyons couple from Tasmania. What gossip might have been ferried back to the respective other couples' bedrooms at their hotels each day? Those old hands at the political game and their seasoned wives.

For Enid, it must have been a strain to sit for hours with people of her parents' generation, discussing matters she barely understood. And with her manners and sense of decorum moulded by Eliza's rather puritanical and prudish sense of ladylike behaviour in their very conservative world of far flung and colonial northern Tasmania, the sight of the New South Wales Labor Premier's wife Ada Holman (the Sydney hostess) wearing make-up, painting her lips bright red on the train to the Blue Mountains and smoking in public, as well as handing around to the other wives her own specially made cigarettes with her signature in gold, was mind boggling for Enid. "She was to me a being from another world," recalled the much older and by then worldly wise Dame Enid in her memoirs.

For all her lack of years and familiarity with society, Enid seems to have left a good impression. "Our stay in Sydney," Enid wrote, "had been for both of us a magic casement opening onto a world of wealth and elegance and sophistication to which we were total strangers. Occasionally I had been shocked by the sumptuousness of my surroundings." She had dined at a *thé dansant* and felt she was in ancient Babylon when told the dance floor was mounted on springs. The New South Wales government was Labor and made up of men from working backgrounds, and yet their Labor hosts could move with ease among the rich of Sydney, entertaining State visitors elegantly and with style. Enid returned to Tasmania with new benchmarks in her estimation of what to expect from political life with Joe.

Nesting

The sight of homely Hobart was a welcome one as Enid steadied into married life. She hadn't yet seen much of the world, notwithstanding their honeymoon trip to Melbourne and Sydney with highlight excursions to the Blue Mountains and a visit to the BHP steelworks in Newcastle. Her life in Burnie had been set around family and friends.

Hobart was far from familiar faces and darling Joe had gone straight back to work with a new bounce in his stride. Occasionally she socialized with his parliamentary colleagues, such as Jim Ogden and James Belton and their respective families. There were a few of her former student colleagues though most were off around Tasmania in new postings. After that, it was up to her to make a new start.

They spent as much time together as possible, Joe taking Enid on his political journeys whenever he could. Then there was "homemaking". Enid had joked to Joe in letters of "practising" ironing while making clear home duties were not her liking. In time, however, she became quite expert. Her sewing practice would be her most successful preparation. All her life Enid could decorate and refurbish her surrounds with pleasure. Success in the kitchen took longer. The happy snaps of her at Home Hill rolling out pastry while the wife of Prime Minister Joe Lyons were an unimagined scene in her first married digs in Hobart.

Their small furnished flat in Liverpool Street was not far from the parliament and her lodgings when a student with Nell. How distant that seemed now. Going from girl to woman in 1915 was an overnight transition. Blackened saucepans and a smoking kitchen often left her in tears and reaching for a tin of salmon. Her landlady passed on advice and Eliza was never further away than a letter in the daily post, but it took longer than the dear girl had imagined. Joe was inclined to teasing, writing to her as she visited Cooee that her mother should buy some "fowls" and show her how to cook them. And then she found she was pregnant, a few months before her eighteenth birthday.

What followed would leave its imprint on Enid the rest of her life. She suffered bleeding after twelve weeks, so she travelled to Cooee where her mother could watch her and give her extra care. But Joe missed her in Hobart and, after a month and feeling better, Enid returned home. Within days she had miscarried. Kate White records in *A Political Love Story* how Enid Lyons did not speak publicly about her miscarriage until three years before her death in 1981, when she was interviewed for an ABC series entitled "Women in Question".

In the interview she told of a local nurse, whom later she realised was also an abortionist, attending her after the miscarriage because her doctor was out of town. As eighteen year old Enid, in shock and pain, faced the upset of losing her baby, she watched the nurse pick up the foetus, announce it was a boy and throw it into the fire heating her bedroom. In her memoirs, written half a century later, Enid still could not write that when she fell "ill" in 1915 she had in fact had a miscarriage, much less discuss the upset of what followed. Not till she was 80 would Enid reveal what had actually happened to her. So skilled did the political spouse become in the art of subterfuge – and all for the sake of presenting an image of being superhuman and capable of serving the public without distraction.

Enid returned to public campaigns soon after her miscarriage, in one to help the Red Cross as Queen of the Public Service. Joe and Enid's first wedding anniversary, on 28 April 1916, was the day chosen for the first commemoration of Anzac Day. That year, Hobart was inundated with fundraising events – concerts, shows, fairs, charity fetes. In August 1914, Joe Lyons had agreed to the setting up of the State School patriotic fund to supplement the mayor's fund and the Red Cross Society. Thereafter, schools and their students worked feverishly to raise funds or contribute in kind to the war effort. Australia Day itself began in 1915 to raise money for the Red Cross. By 1916, Australians were starting to feel overtaxed from their efforts. The inquiry into the worldwide Relief of Belgium fund found that, of the £1.5 million given, Australia and New Zealand had donated £1 million.

By the end of 1915, with an election looming for March 1916 and Labor's prospects not appearing very good, Joe Lyons decided Enid should move in with his father Michael, brother Tom and sisters Mary and Gertrude in Devonport. Joe and Enid would eventually build a house on the orchard Joe had bought for Enid. Joe had also promised his mother before she died that he would look after the family, and he continued to believe they were his responsibility, even when his siblings were full grown adults. With this mindset, Joe arranged for his new young wife, of barely eighteen years, to take charge of the Lyons household. Enid described her situation in Devonport with characteristic humour:

> My poor optimistic, innocent husband ... on the one hand asking two women, one thirteen and the other fifteen years older than I, to step aside for an eighteen year old girl; and on the other expecting his wife, whose experience in housekeeping extended over a period of exactly nine months, to assume responsibility of managing an established household of six people, two of whom had long been its joint mistress. The marvel was that the arrangement lasted as long as it did.

Labor lost the March 1916 election. A backbencher again, Joe spent some months taking an interest in his apple orchard and the new house they were building on the land. They had chosen house plans that had won a newspaper competition for small house design, a weatherboard construction of seven rooms on bluestone foundations. It would cost them £425. The stone for the foundations was quarried on site and their builder left the frame to season for four months. As they waited, Enid often felt her house would never be finished. It was September before they could move in. By then, Joe had relieved Enid of the role of domestic head of mission to the Lyons family, but she was also heavily pregnant, with a birth due in November.

Labor and war

Labor still held 14 seats in the House of Assembly, but the war took its toll on the party. Labor, however, could not satisfy average workers that if it were to take government it would make any impact on rapidly rising prices. Food and groceries prices in Tasmania had risen more than 16 per cent in the twelve months to July 1915. Radical labour now argued that the class war at home was more important than the Empire's war abroad. There was concern at the cost to the state of drink and drunkenness and bigotry against citizens of German background had reached xenophobic levels. As Minister of Education, Joe was accused of allowing "Germans" to advance in the teaching profession. Lyons replied that there were no "German" teachers or inspectors in his department, only four Tasmanian born teachers of German parentage.

But the message was out. Any who did not fall into line with accepted standards of loyalist and patriotic fervour were somehow traitors. Tasmanian Labor's opposition to conscription, the party seen to have strong support from Tasmanian Catholics, attracted widespread sectarian outbursts. Hobart's conservative *Mercury* had begun openly suggesting that the Catholic Irish were disloyal and that the Pope was somehow in league with Germany's Kaiser. After the sinking of the British liner *Lusitania* in May 1915, the town of Bismarck, west of Hobart, had changed its name to Collinsville.

Enid was still mostly absorbed in her new personal setting: "I think it could be said that I was more interested in politicians than politics, certainly in one politician." She had accompanied Joe on much of his campaigning for the March election where she became aware that his voice was high pitched and nasal. She advised him how to correct this from her own years of elocution lessons. But she also recognised how polished he was as a speaker, having what she called "the gift of exposition" or persuasion. She pitied the other candidates' wives for their partners' weaker performances. A few years later, Joe would advise Enid not to be too conversational in delivering a public address. From the outset, theirs was a true political match.

Enid's memoirs recall scant particulars of the bitterness of campaigning in the 1916 election and its deep divisions. Her account of their time on the road is devoted mostly to anecdotes about a new Labor candidate who was a poor public speaker, entertaining herself at meeting after meeting with his familiar routine. Enid was now a political spouse, travelling to meetings and functions with Joe, where her role was to greet and meet Labor supporters and officials along with people she would never see again, sitting up front in draughty halls listening to familiar speeches, over and over. Amusing herself watching Joe's inept colleague was her earliest strategy in staying interested and appearing to be keenly involved.

As a backbencher, Joe was home a lot more. Even so, Enid's weeks were long as she took her doctor's advice to spend most of her days in bed until her pregnancy was well advanced. She forced herself to master the sewing machine, covered an old couch and armchair, and even made a box couch for her bedroom. In October, a month before her baby was due, Enid moved back to Cooee while Joe took to the political road to argue against conscription.

Labor Prime Minister Billy Hughes had returned from London in July, determined on Australia sending a vast increase in troops. If Australia could raise 32,000 volunteers by the end of September and half that number in each month following, there would be no conscription. But this did not happen. As recruiters like Eliza Burnell tried to enlist more men, thousands were falling in the battle of the Somme. A referendum or plebiscite to gain public support for conscription was announced for 28 October 1916. The question to be asked was, "Are you in favour of the government having, in this grave emergency, the same compulsory powers over citizens in regard to requiring their military service, for the term of this war, outside the Commonwealth, as it now has in regard to military service within the Commonwealth?" Hughes was confident the "Yes" case would win.

The fight over conscription in Tasmania, as in Australia generally, was not only bitter but also sectarian, even violent. A bomb exploded at one Beaconsfield conscription meeting, injuring a policeman and a caretaker. At Deloraine, Joe Lyons was all but thrown into the river as he tried to cross a bridge, and later was hit with a rotten egg. Enid wrote of exchanges between Joe and Fr Tom O'Donnell that became so extreme they remained unable to speak to each other for years.

Nationally, the referendum would end in defeat with 1,087,557 in favour and 1,160,033 against, but in Tasmania a large majority voted in favour – 49,493 to 37,833 – recalling Billy Hughes' claim that Tasmania was the "anti-Socialist's Arcadia". An angry and disappointed Tasmanian Labor caucus met in Hobart on 1 November. Labor leader John Earle, who had supported conscription, was not present. His role in the campaign was seen as the reason for the strong "Yes" vote from mining areas on the west coast. Caucus targeted Earle a Labor "rat", passed a no-confidence motion in both him and Charles Howroyd for supporting the "Yes" vote and Earle resigned. Lyons was elected State Labor leader the next day.

Growing pains

Against this backdrop, Joe and Enid became proud and delighted parents. Enid gave birth to Gerald Desmond, whom they would always call Desmond, on the morning of Friday 13 November 1916. Through the weeks of conscription fever, Enid had missed Joe and endured all the misery of a difficult pregnancy nearing its end. Her feet and legs had swollen so much she could not put on her slippers. Her hands swelled so badly she had to give up sewing and waste away the hours in bed. She worried the baby might come early, writing to Joe, "If there were no danger of the baby's not living, I would welcome his arrival any day I have become very weary of my burden."

The separations were difficult for both of them. Enid wrote to Joe, a few weeks before the birth: "Today I was trying to imagine that I was holding him, and I thrilled at the mere thought. My word, what hours of loneliness he'll save me when you're away and I'm able to see you in him and hear your voice in his little gurgle!" This craving for an infant lasted all Enid's adulthood: "All my life, even in childhood, I have felt myself potentially a mother, and never for one moment have I dreamed of a life without babies."

They had agreed to try not to make partings overly painful, but Enid pined nonetheless: "These promises not to hold you in the mornings are very difficult of fulfilment, I can tell you. My arms seem to ache when you leave them and I realise that you are going right away. I was only half asleep when you left but I couldn't sleep again." And she worried Joe would not make the birth: "I am determined to go through 'like a man'. I hope to goodness nothing happens to prevent your being with me at the time, because I'd feel heaps braver with you near me."

But Joe was there by the Thursday Enid's waters broke, trying to ease her pains holding her hand and by her side in the early hours of the long labour through the night. It was to be what Enid would record as "a day of agony ending with a slow emergence from unconsciousness to know my child was born". She was left unable to turn in bed without help for days and had to strain with every effort just to whisper in Joe's ear that they had a "little boy". It would be four decades before Enid would learn, after an X-ray, that her pelvis had been slightly fractured during Desmond's birth. She would give birth to another eleven children in this condition. None of that spoilt her joy at Gerald Desmond's arrival – nor Joe having to leave for Hobart the next day, writing to her from the train, "You don't know how I loved the two of you as you lay there together – my wife and son!"

Critics of the Lyons' partnership have, over decades, seized on a picture of Enid as the stronger of the two, the one who pulled the strings behind an otherwise weak and gentle Joe. This was not so. Joe had entered politics and seen rapid success well before he declared his love for Enid. What's more, Enid's letters to Joe and her recollections of the years before she became the prime minister's wife reveal a homely, if very intelligent and perceptive, younger woman. Until the Lyons couple took to the national stage, with the exception of Enid's efforts as a candidate in the 1925 state election, Enid's preoccupations as the political spouse were overwhelmingly domestic, unless asked by Joe to make a speech or stand beside him during an important campaign. Although he encouraged her at every step to take time out from the daily domestic routine, this was mainly to spend moments of leisure with him in the evenings after the children were asleep or during campaigning when they had a chance to travel together. They rarely entertained beyond their family or even went out socially. She delighted in her memoirs to recall, albeit tongue in cheek, that Joe saw her as "the cleverest little wife in the world", "the best little wife and mother", (in time) "the best little cook [or dressmaker] in the world" or the "best little upholsterer". His devotion to Enid, whom he called "girl", was very much that of the doting older man to his much younger and sweet bride. He preferred Enid to dress in styles that aged her – a way of keeping her sweetness all for himself.

Enid might offer Joe tips on voice projection and in time help with the electoral paper work, but for political wiliness, or endurance, it was Joe who was the practised one. It was Joe who positioned himself carefully but not too radically at the head of the anti-conscriptionists in Labor and found himself elected Party leader. It was Joe who spent eleven hours travelling from Devonport to Hobart to take his seat on a Monday evening in the House of Assembly, or nine hours from Deloraine when the family moved there soon after Desmond's birth to cut down the travelling time. In an interview for the Australian National Library in 1972, Enid stressed that on her marriage she was a mere girl and had little interest in politics. Joe became her political awakening and it was only with Joe's encouragement that she took to it at all: "He got me out on the public platform; I used to go along to the Labor conference and I'd battle hard ... and he on the other [side] so that we weren't a sort of echo of one another."

At five months pregnant with their second child, Enid accompanied Joe to the May 1918 State Labor conference in Hobart where she successfully had a motion amended that committed Tasmanian Labor to putting to Federal conference a policy "that no action be taken in any future wars without the approval of electors as expressed by means of a referendum – unless Australia be directly attacked." This positioned Joe and Enid among the isolationists increasingly to be found with Labor. At the conference, she also worked with Labor's Dwyer Gray to sponsor a proposal to enforce compulsory training but not compulsory enlistment. From a Labor perspective, this was a neat middle way position for the times – very much the Joe Lyons approach.

It was also Enid, the girl Eliza had rebuked for being too precocious in the limelight, who had to be pushed onto the stage at the Deloraine Town Hall on the night of the Armistice but who made her political husband "burst with pride" by being able to lead the singing of "Pack up your troubles in your old kit-bag" and "Keep the home fires burning". And it was Enid who, after her marriage, had made Joe's friends her friends which left her to recall that, "For most of my married life I had little contact with my contemporaries."

Joe Lyons set the pace and Enid followed, picking up tricks of the political trade as they went – and finding she had a talent for repartee and presentation. In her memoirs she wrote, "I married a man who liked change for its own sake and who had chosen a career of which the very essence is uncertainty. Throughout our married life we lived from election to election, always aware of the fickleness of public opinion." Their rapidly expanding family meant Joe was under pressure to earn well. With Tasmanian Labor in the doldrums in the immediate post war years, Joe began studying law with a mind to leave politics, but when new political opportunities came Enid never once stood in Joe's way.

Enid followed the political debate, and knew and accepted the constraints politics imposed on their domestic affairs. Their living arrangements were complicated by the fact that Joe represented a northern seat and the train between north and south Tasmania wound about the pastoral estates of the midlands making the distance and time between north and south far greater. Unlike Eliza, Enid adored her husband which gave her added vitality. As well, she had the support of her mother as the babies came, a mother who would be there if she needed to travel with Joe, and a mother who was still morally and physically uniquely stoical.

The green years

The war had barely faded in Europe and the US when the notorious pandemic known as the Spanish influenza would ravage some six per cent of the population there. Australia did not see it until 1919, and experienced a lesser fatality rate, but even then it would take some three per cent of the population, and this after losing 1.2 per cent of its able men in the war and enduring the highest percentage for any Empire country of war casualties of enlisted men. In August 1918, Enid came down with influenza, a month off giving birth to her second child. She thought it was the Spanish flu pandemic but this is unlikely; the pandemic arrived in Australia only months later. Enid recovered and then travelled to Cooee to have her new baby.

Tragically, Enid may have taken her flu bacteria into the Burnell home. Just two days after the weak little girl they called Sheila was born, Enid's much loved brother Bert came down with influenza. The weeks passed, Enid struggling to nurse baby Sheila while little Desmond needed caring for as well. Eliza had the help of Nurse Harper, midwife at Sheila's birth, but the ailing Bert eventually developed meningitis and needed additional nursing.

While Enid saved Sheila with a remedy of soaked arrowroot biscuits

97

and condensed milk, Eliza and the nurses struggled with Bert. He died after two months from what Enid described as exhaustion, his body unable to take the strain. The loss broke William with grief; Eliza resorted to losing herself in going about the neighbourhood helping others. The girls remained in shock. Bert had been their adored baby brother since his birth and his death was the only fatality in Burnie at the time from a flu virus.

As Sheila began to grow, Enid and Joe decided to move back to Devonport. They had not gained a lot in their move to Deloraine. The pretty hamlet may have been two hours closer to Hobart but Devonport was closer to their extended families and there were problems with the tenants at Home Hill. So Enid, who had become an expert packer of household goods ("I could pack china and fragile glass, boots, blankets and a clothes wringer all in one case."), once again settled the family into the home they had built, but in which they had barely begun to live. Only then did Enid realise Home Hill was no place for a politician with a young family. It was so far from town, constituents could not readily call on their local member, and they had no car which made shopping difficult, as well as no phone, no sewerage and no mains water. Added to all this, Joe was away for most of each week, as he would be throughout their married life.

By 1919, Enid was pregnant again and finding her legs so painful she could barely walk and made worse by two bad teeth which she soon lost. Dental decay was a curse of an otherwise healthy population at the time – of the 2020 men who enlisted in Tasmania during the first two weeks of the war in 1914, only 700 passed their medicals. The most common reason for rejection was tooth decay. Meanwhile, Joe had decided to try for the federal seat of Darwin. Busy with campaigning, he missed the birth of little Enid just a fortnight before the federal election on 13 December. When the votes came in, he had lost badly. He would have to continue as a state MP. Debates at state and federal conferences showed Labor deeply divided between moderates who wanted to win government and radicals spurred on by the One Big Union movement with ideas for the socialisation and nationalisation of industries, ideas that echoed socialists in Europe where the 1917 Russian Revolution was still taking its toll.

In this atmosphere, and with three young Lyons in the den and another on the way, Joe and Enid sold Home Hill in 1920. It broke Enid's heart to watch their possessions go under the hammer, even the horse they had bought from her parents. After the sale, they moved to live for a while with the Burnells, who had relocated to West Burnie having sold up the Cooee shop to a family by the name of Burrows. This gave Eliza a chance to take a badly needed holiday to the mainland. It was during their stay with the Burnells that Joe and Enid's fourth child, Kathleen, was born in December 1920.

When Joe and Enid returned to Devonport, they bought a small brick bungalow near the centre of town, a practical choice and a wise one, as Enid soon realised. The purchase left them with money over from the sale of the orchard and Home Hill. Even so, Joe's salary at £400 a year, twice the average, was still stretched with the costs of electoral and political demands. On 7 February 1922, Enid gave birth to another daughter whom they named Moira. In their Devonport home in Fenton Street, Enid employed a girl, named Thirmuthus, as a home help. In time, another girl would fetch Desmond and Sheila from school in the afternoons. Vera Ferguson would write to Dame Enid Lyons in 1968, after reading Enid's memoirs, and recall those days:

> I am the girl who took Desmond and Sheila to the Convent school in Devonport. I was Mrs Linton's grand daughter and we lived next door to the Bond Hall, just over the road from your home. Enid was only a little tot and you had a rocking horse on the side verandah which we all played on…
> I remember Desmond cutting his foot on our way home one day from school and how he cried and I carried him home

to you on my back and you gave me 1/- for lollies which I thought was great. Also the milk and biscuits you gave us when we arrived home at your place.

Enid Lyons was never without some help. Apart from her mother, who could be relied on in any crisis, Enid had her sisters, Joe's sisters and later, in Hobart, Joe's brother Tom and and his wife Mavis. The Lyons home was rarely without a house girl or someone to do the laundry. Kathleen Lyons remembered "there was always someone" and so many over the years she couldn't recall any of their names. They came and went; local girls paid small amounts of cash to clean and mind children when needed, and as Enid was called out.

With her many pregnancies, Enid certainly paid a physical price. A lot of her illnesses were undoubtedly the result of nervous exhaustion and Joe worried he had married her when she was far too young. Eliza warned her to try to make her sixth pregnancy the last, to which Enid laughed "but they're all the last". There was no other way. She adored Joe, was even by some accounts a very sexually charged young woman, and yet took no precautions whatsoever against conception. To Enid, a devout Catholic of her day, any form of contraception would have been sinful. If she had to manage with a large family where Joe's ambitions were concerned, what Joe wanted was all that mattered.

CHAPTER 8

HOBART

The great social divisions of the war years, 1914 to 1918, would run their course into the politics of 1920s Australia. Out of this, sectarianism would raise fresh converts, leaving a new generation of Protestant Australians with jingoistic suspicions of "papists", that significant Catholic minority who felt alienated and targeted by an Anglo Protestant ascendancy. Groups like the Catholic Federation seeking state aid for Catholic schools only encouraged this distrust. The Lyons partnership and its political success, however, defied the bigotry. Joe and Enid Lyons were very much identified as Catholics – especially with their large and continually growing family. Yet, they were to rise smoothly up the political ranks. Their rise says much about Australian society and its deeply pragmatic heart.

Labor's loss of Billy Hughes, and MPs who followed him, drained the Labor party of many non Catholic parliamentarians, the Empire loyalists in Labor ranks. This left Labor increasingly thought to be run by disloyal Irish Catholics. Bolshevism and radical left wing agitation after the war years further complicated Labor's image with movements like the One Big Union push, with aims to replace parliament with a Supreme National Council, and the ultra radical Industrial Workers of the World faction with talk of revolution and collectivism, alongside a call at party conferences for the socialisation of industries.

These were lean years for Labor at elections – state and federal – with Joe Lyons, ever the pragmatist, among those who came close to despair at the divisions holding Labor away from government. In *Eighty Years' Labor*, historian Richard Davis wrote of Lyons' "ambiguous lethargy" at this time. Labor's ninth federal conference in Brisbane passed the notorious "red" resolution binding parliamentary members to the "socialisation of industry, production, distribution and exchange". In spite of being hastily diluted by the Blackburn amendment, its impact tagged Labor as the party of Marxist extremes.

The heady days of Joe's mid thirties, his engagement and marriage while Treasurer and Deputy in the Tasmanian government, had become distant all too quickly. For all his love of Enid and his children, Joe had seen his early success and ambitions fall into nothing as the war divisions ruined Labor and its electoral hopes. Now he was 40, and Opposition leader of a party continually at odds with itself over policy. The increasingly radical proposals at conferences left him doubting Tasmanian Labor would ever recover its mainstream image enough to win government. At the 1922 election, so divided was the Labor team that in three of the five electorates, Denison, Darwin and Bass, separate campaigns were organised. It was vexing times. If he'd had better prospects outside politics, Joe might have given it away, if only to give his family a more settled future.

At home, Enid was regularly pregnant and with every birth came a new mouth to feed and provide for. And yet, Enid would write of their happiness after the 1922 election which Labor again lost, at home with the children tucked into bed soon after six, and Joe grilling their chops while she put her feet up. One of their saving features was that neither fussed over domestic tidiness and both could relax inside a home of gently organised chaos where Enid concentrated on Joe and the children.

None of this could satisfy Joe for very long. Soon after their marriage Enid recognised she had married a man who was driven by his need to go after political opportunities and the feeling he enjoyed when taking charge. But if Labor's prospects did not pick up, Joe needed more secure and profitable employment. At the June 1922 state election, with five small children in their Devonport home, Enid found herself more and more part of Joe's campaigning. With an infant in her care, she was handling most of the paperwork like any experienced electoral assistant. As wife of the Opposition leader, she also appeared increasingly beside Joe or in place of him on election platforms, often relying on her mother and other family to do the baby sitting. Without that invaluable extended family back up, Enid could never have taken such a public role in Joe's ambitions.

Her first speaking engagement came in 1922. One of the rotating Labor team for different venues suddenly fell ill and Enid had to stand in. It was a "hair-raising experience", speaking to an audience as Joe made his way there from another meeting 12 kilometres away, over bad roads in an unreliable car. He arrived to hear the end of her speech and complimented her on it – offering advice on how to do better next time. Enid's calm ability to take her place on an electoral platform thereafter was helped by Joe himself. Unlike many men of his generation, Joe never felt threatened by his wife's competence in public. He valued women as voters and thus as campaigners. He coached Enid, telling her to be frank, but to side step trick questions and to "crack back if you can". And if she didn't have an answer, he advised her to admit it. "Remember," Joe told her, "the man on the platform always has the last word – even if he's a woman!"

In general, Enid went onto platforms to speak to the women in the audience, an effective way of bringing more of them out in the days before compulsory voting. Until 1928 in Tasmania, the task at state elections was not only to win votes but also to get electors to go to the polls. Enid presented the female perspective most effectively and her references to home and hearth would remain her skill in public debate throughout her public life.

At a meeting in 1922, in a farming district, Enid complimented the local farmers in the all-male audience for their well-equipped farms.

Then she "wondered" if an average kitchen on such farms "still needs a sink and if mother still boils the washing over an open fire in a kerosene tin". In speaking up for the wives, who in many cases were the last to see anything of the farm investment, Enid had spoken up for the underdog. She made her point so vividly that, in giving the vote of thanks, the chairman expressed his surprise at hearing a "lady politician" and added that he was glad that his wife wasn't present.

For Enid, political campaigning added on to domestic life was never easy. But she managed what for most would have been impossible and all of it for her darling Joe. There were moments when she may have thought he took her for granted. Then she would simply let him know her breaking point and he would make up the difference. Asked to speak at a meeting in a federal election campaign, around this time, she found herself preparing a speech with a baby on her knee and the little ones squabbling around her. She was reduced to tears until Joe came home. He took charge of the children, wiped away her tears, after which she went out to make a fine speech, talking of "politics in terms of pots and pans and children's shoes", as she described it. Joe gave her new energy.

Labor having lost yet another state election in 1922, Joe made enquiries about how he could do his articles for a legal career. This meant the family would have to move, yet again, and this time to Hobart, where Kevin, their second son and sixth child, would be born in February 1923. Without a glance back, Joe and Enid sold their small Devonport home and headed south in what Enid recalls as the spring of 1922. A few months later, just days before Christmas, Enid's older sister Nellie married Hubert Glover, the principal of Burnie High School. Burnie's *Advocate* noted that the bride wore "an extremely beautiful gown of ivory charmeuse, trimmed with silk lace and hand made embroidery in silver and crystal beads" designed by Madame Wiltshire of The Beehive in Burnie. The wedding cake was decorated, the report continued, "after the American fashion" in asparagus ferns and pansies. It was a happy family affair with a ceremony at St Barnabas' Church and refreshments and celebrations at the Burnells' new home in The Avenue. Eliza and William by then were significant figures in Burnie society.

For a year, life for Joe and Enid took on a less publicly driven momentum. Joe began to seriously consider leaving politics for the law. In Hobart, they lived in the suburb of New Town, once a colonial village about six kilometres north of the city and docks on the Derwent. New Town combined both well to do and worker along its winding and undulating streets. At first, the Lyons family may have rented a house on the main road, where the trams ran and which Kathleen well remembers. Enid writes of the family one morning all watching a spiny anteater making its way between the tram tracks towards the city. But the house from where they saw the anteater was not the house they eventually bought. Around this time, newly married Tom and Mavis Lyons also lived on the main road at New Town – at first in rooms at 45 New Town Road. Mavis, like Enid, was a convert to Catholicism. The two women had an instant bonding while Tom, warm, generous and unassuming, had a special closeness to his big brother Joe. Mavis had been an only child, and yearned for children of her own. For some years, however, she found it difficult to carry a baby full term, suffering a couple of miscarriages.

With time on her hands and a delight in Enid and Joe's six little children, it wasn't long before Mavis was happy to help as fill-in mother, especially when Enid had functions to attend. From this began a strong friendship between the sisters-in-law that lasted all their lives. The support Mavis gave to Enid over the next sixteen years was invaluable to Enid's public role while the mother of a large young family. At one time, in Hobart, Tom and Mavis were to mind all six children while Joe and Enid visited Eliza's mother Louisa in the Tweed River district. On this holiday, Enid caught up with her cousins in a large extended family gathering at her Aunt Matilda's house at Billinudgel.

Joe and Enid did not buy a property in New Town until 1923, the house Enid describes in her memoirs. In June, they bought a small brick home at what is now 67 Pedder Street (then No 59) on a large block of land, well away from the tram tracks of the main road. The now white concrete rendered house is still there, adjacent to the Sacred Heart church and school in New Town and on the corner of Montague Street. The title deeds list Enid Lyons as the sole owner of the house between June 1923 and August 1927. Today, the house has been renovated and enlarged. When the Lyons bought it, the one storey dwelling was very much as Enid described it – "three stone steps led down from the unprotected back door which opened directly from the kitchenette, and into it swept the bitter winds driving upward from the South Pole. The room itself was little larger than a closet, too small even to accommodate a table."

With something of an historical irony, a few doors up Montague Street, Agnes Joyce's daughter Kathleen, who might have been Enid's first cousin, and her husband Hugh owned property. And as New Town still had large blocks of undeveloped land, in time Kathleen and Hugh's daughter would keep her horse on a paddock not far from their house. A neighbour grew rows of vegetables, given to the convent for needy families. Around this time Kathleen would wheel her babies along the New Town streets and be mistaken for Enid Lyons.

All up, the Lyons house in Pedder Street was a tiny home for a family of two adults and six, later seven, children. But with its large block of land and the school and church so close, the family was well placed for its needs. Enid joined the church choir and they managed their Sunday obligations happily, with Joe at the eight o'clock Mass while Enid dressed the children, after which she attended the ten o'clock Mass and sang with the choir.

Choir practice often took place at the Lyons' home with locals like Jack O'Callaghan and his brother Graham, the talented Freeman family – Kath, Nell, Dora, Bernard, Ted and their mother Henrietta who could fill the church with the organ sounds of "Mozart's 12th" – Rita Fox, a gifted young pianist, Charles Clay, the Ultrichts and Ted Keady. Years later, Jack O'Callaghan wrote to Enid describing their choir practices and recalling "Nell Freeman holding one of the babies in the midst of Agnus Dei whilst you had to attend to something on the stove that had bubbled over unexpectedly – preparing one of the many late meals for Mr Lyons when he was hard working Premier of the State". Jack also remembered Enid's vignette at the Concert Party where she did her old Irish mother number complete with shawl.

Enid remembered their family life at Pedder Street, New Town as domestic tranquillity, with Joe often home during the week so that he and Enid had hours together after the children were in bed. He sometimes read to her or helped cook the meals. Joe was studying as an articled clerk for the law at night and working as the Opposition leader by day. Labor expected to be out of government for some time. And then, as often happens in politics, all this changed. Government, quite abruptly, fell into Labor's lap.

The post war years had been rife with conservative rhetoric and a mainstream belief in the good judgement of the conservative side of politics. Populist Prime Minister Billy Hughes would be replaced by the smooth upper crust Anglophile Stanley Bruce. But in Tasmania, Labor and the Nationalists each had twelve seats in the Tasmanian parliament and the Nationalists governed only with Country Party support, at a time of deep economic malaise, partly due to the state's stagnant population and lack of growth. There was instability in the conservative leadership through 1922 and 1923 and, in October, the premier Sir Walter Lee lost the support of two Nationalists leaving the conservative government unable to command the numbers it needed to retain government.

Joe Lyons, meanwhile, was a rising star. His growing moderation, after a flirtation with socialist objectives at Labor conferences, had caught the attention of his parliamentary colleagues; his popularity in Wilmot in spite of Labor's downturn also made him noteworthy, and he could make a good case against Premier Lee's large deficit on the Hydro scheme.

Within hours of the vote of no confidence in the Lee government, Tasmanian Administrator Sir Herbert Nicholl, standing in for State Governor Sir William Allardyce who was in Newfoundland, phoned Joe Lyons. Having no phone of their own, Joe took the call at a neighbour' house. Would he be able to form a government, Nicholl asked. To accept would mean a significant change of tack for Joe and Enid. It was a risk; Labor could lose at the next election and Joe would be back to square one. Enid was just 26, their six children aged between almost seven and infancy. As wife of the premier, she also would be expected to take on a public role. On the other hand, they had lived the whirlwind from the time of their marriage and Enid knew it was what Joe wanted. If she was to choose, he would have it.

Joe Lyons became Premier of Tasmania on 25 October 1923. Richard Davis, in *Eighty Years' Labor*, says "Lyons' accession to power in 1923 was a victory for his personality rather than the party machine which was in a parlous state". Economics and the desire for good government had triumphed over latent hostility to Labor or Catholics. Premier Joe Lyons would lead a minority government of just ten Labor members in the House of Assembly until after the 1925 state election.

Tasmania was in financial crisis, the state debt having increased by 65 per cent since 1914 alongside a population increase of 6.5 per cent. Half of the government's revenue was earmarked for interest payments. Yet Lyons would become Australia's Prime Minister in the Great Depression, less than a decade later, largely on the back of his years as premier. He took advice where it was best sought, working to conciliate differences in parliament He sought (and received) substantial federal government financial assistance alongside contributions to Tasmania's finances from such sources as the Tattersalls lottery. Joe Lyons was not only something of a financial squirrel, he was also a good public beggar. Philip Hart wrote in "J A Lyons A Political Biography" (1967 Ph D thesis, ANU/unpublished), "His years as premier were the happiest and most successful of his political career."

With Joe Lyons' acceptance of the premiership, Enid was thrust onto the political stage in ways she had never yet experienced. The wife of the premier she was the state's first lady. This meant having her own public life to some extent. A lot of the time she was able to fall back on fundamentals. Eliza had bred in her good manners and a sense of community involvement; her years with Joe had helped her develop an instinct for the "do and don't" of endless political engagements.

Taking stock, Enid set about her duties much in the style she had developed for a decade. Her abilities were obvious – an uncomplicated understanding of ordinary people's lives and her natural warmth when meeting strangers. But these were times of dogmatic compliance with codes of behaviour in public, from whether or not to be introduced or to introduce yourself down to the correct way to hold a knife and fork, where to place a napkin or what to do with a coat. Enid admitted in her memoirs to nearly refusing her first formal luncheon invitation because of not knowing what to do with her hat and gloves – to remove or not to remove after arriving at the venue.

As for issues like her wardrobe, it was with a sense of humour that Enid described her ease at choosing what to wear to her first social engagement; she had one shop bought outfit for "going out" and the rest were "home-made cotton house frocks". Joe's increase in salary, soon allowed her more regular home help and some shop bought clothes. And off she went to a schedule of addressing meetings, opening fairs, fetes and flower shows, attending balls and parades and appearing at Hobart's grand neo-Gothic Government House which still dominates Hobart's landscape on the slopes of the Derwent in Queens Domain. Decades later she would speak of how Joe would send her alone to Government House functions, preferring to stay out of the pomp and ceremony himself. In the 1920s, the governor's mansion was the pinnacle of the state's social scene with its direct link to the then far more relevant sovereign, and an integral part of the British empire.

Today any first couple would be given access to transport, staff and extra allowances for their public duties. There was none of this for Enid as a premier's wife. In spite of her large family and her need to be at functions every week, she did not have the use of a government car. Severe budgetary constraints had done away with all ministerial cars. Joe was not ready to indulge his own wife against the budget cuts. So Enid travelled to her engagements around Hobart using what public transport might be available – or, as she described it, on "infrequent tram services". Although young enough to find the energy, it was not easy. She would arrive at venues blown about in a Hobart wind, or puffed and hot after having to run for a tram, or exasperated from a trying wait for connections.

Tasmania's Labor administration, with Joe Lyons at its helm, demonstrated that Labor was fit to govern. The Lyons administration was different. Even as a minority government, Lyons appointed an advisory council of businessman to investigate ways to improve the state's financial situation. His committee to examine Tasmania's special needs, headed by a former premier and treasurer, Sir Elliot Lewis, and including Sir Alfred Ashbolt and government statistician Lyndhurst (L F) Giblin, found Tasmania deserving of more particular consideration for Commonwealth grants.

Enid Lyons wrote later of how Joe "conferred with pastoralists, industrialists, trade unionists, farmers and businessmen" which, she added, not only revived a new confidence in government but took away the "prevalent belief that Labor would govern only in the interest of its own supporters".

On becoming first lady, however, there was a protest at Labor's Denison branches when, as wife of the premier, Enid became an ex-officio vice-president of the Victoria League, an organisation promoting women's involvement in community affairs, but also with a strong loyalty to the Empire. By 1924, Enid had been a member of the Victoria League for ten years. Eliza had been a member and Enid had won a League writing competition, entered when at College. This gave her a life membership. Her Labor critics saw this as "fraternising with the enemy". In a move that illustrated a new confidence in her role, Enid wrote to the Denison ALP with what she called not a little "heat nor sarcasm", justifying her acceptance of the ex-officio position with the Victoria League and concluding that she would not be consulting with members of Denison ALP branches over her choice of friends or associates.

It was joyous times for the Lyons family when, on 8 October 1924, Enid gave birth to their seventh child, born at Hillside Private Hospital with Nurse Hawson as midwife, a little boy they named Garnet. Even with regular home help in the figure of the reliable Ada, Joe and Enid had been living life at a breath taking pace. Moira and Kevin had been born exactly a year apart and Garnet had arrived twenty months later. No doubt, in her long years of childbearing, Enid added to her fertility at times by not breastfeeding her children. Kathleen recalled that there was "some difficulty" that stopped Enid being able to breast feed. And this also meant Enid was more able to leave a baby with a minder and accompany Joe when needed.

With Garnet's birth, the state celebrated. Baby Garnet Lyons was the first child born to a Tasmanian premier in office. Joe's Cabinet colleagues presented him with a miniature silver cradle mounted on a blackwood base and inscribed with the poet Meredith's lines:

"Keep the young generation in Hael/And bequeath them no tumbled houses." After this, the Lyons couple continued their routine, the older children moving over to accommodate another little body in their limited space at Pedder Street and Enid taking up her public duties as before.

Tragedy, however, was not far away. In her memoirs, the messiness of the next year shows in the jumbled way Enid Lyons attempted to recall the family's experiences in 1925 – when Garnet would die, aged ten months, after a most bitter winter that brought the whole family down with measles, chicken pox and whooping cough as the Lyons government fought to win a desperately needed Labor majority in the House. Amidst and between all that, Enid would stand for Denison at the state election in June. A close study of the turmoil for the Lyons family during 1925, says much about the character and stamina of both Enid and Joe, and why they remain Australia's outstanding political couple.

CHAPTER 9

THE HEART OF THE MATTER

January 1925 opened happily enough at 67 [59] Pedder Street, New Town. Seven little Lyons children were growing healthily as the offspring of Tasmania's premier and his pretty young wife. In Burnie, their grandmother Eliza Burnell had been made a Justice of the Peace. Joe Lyons might have looked at his son Desmond, then aged eight, and wondered at his own eight year old misery of being forced out to work after his father lost everything on a horse in a Melbourne Cup. How marvellous that a family's circumstances should so improve in just a few decades.

Newspapers carried stories of the Australian cricket side's convincing wins over England as Australia hosted and won the 30th Ashes Test series. Racy silent movie screen star Gloria Swanson shocked her fans in a headline grabbing divorce with stories of adultery with thirteen men, including Rudolph Valentino. It was confident times, albeit lived between margins of risk and vulnerability. Australia's population had reached six million, although the population of Tasmania continued to decline adding to its economic woes.

Enid was at peace with the world that January. Her infant son Garnet, then three months old, was growing fast. She had Ada in the house till bedtime, her backstop for a busy mother of seven under nine. Kevin and Moira both celebrated their birthdays on 7 February – Kevin turning two and Moira three. Except for constrictions of space, the regular changing of napkins and toilet training gave the

Lyons household the appearance of a modern day-care nursery. Noise and chaos would have been a familiar part of the Lyons scene. Enid happily admitted to leaving the dusting and tidying undone in place of the children's needs and Joe. The Lyons children would prove bright young minds – Desmond something of a prodigy, Sheila distinguishing herself at St Mary's and Kathleen fit to study medicine by the end of her schooling. But all this was in the future in the summer of 1925.

For Joe, the year began less harmoniously. Nation wide seamen's strikes had disrupted the ferry service to Tasmania with passengers stranded. On 17 January, volunteers had been found to crew the *Nairana* and other vessels vital to Tasmanian transport. Joe's health broke down soon after. With an election year ahead of them, Joe and Enid decided on a trip to the mainland. Leaving their seven children with Mavis and Tom Lyons, they left Launceston aboard the *Nairana* on Wednesday 25 March.

Joe and Enid spent their holiday with Louisa Taggett and Enid's cousins at Billinudgel. Enid had given up her Methodist roots but delighted her grandmother when she was the only family member who could play Louisa's favourite "old-time Moody and Sankey hymns" – the music of US evangelical partners David Sankey and Dwight Moody from the 1800s, verses and choruses to attract crowds with heartening phrases like "Safe in the arms of God's infinite love", or "Into the summer of endless delight" and the redemption themes of "the bright crown and eternal reward" in "the beautiful mansions above".

It had been a seamless move from Methodism to Catholicism for Enid, her faith set around soulful church music. As an elderly woman, she would play Methodist hymns in the Devonport Catholic church with the Catholic congregation singing along. The sentimentality and colour of those hymns often resurfaced in her arguments on podiums and writings. In the National Library there is a fragment, among her sheet music for the songs and hymns she often played; a single page of notepaper embossed with the Australian Coat-of-Arms and "Prime Minister's Lodge, Canberra F.C.T". Across one side of this blank page of official writing paper, Enid has written a note to remind herself, "Hymn to the Little Flower – EML"; the Little Flower being St Thérèse of Lisieux.

Joe and Enid returned to Tasmania on the steamer *Oonah*, arriving in Burnie on Friday 11 April, with Joe declaring he was ready for work. Within a couple of weeks, however, Enid was confined to bed with tonsillitis and cancelled her appointments. The State election ahead was vital for Joe Lyons' minority Labor government. Joe Lyons and his Labor colleagues wanted a majority Labor government to bring about reforms the Party believed were needed; a Labor premier must be capable as a Labor man not just as a good manager.

The Tasmanian election campaign started in May with the election set down for Wednesday 3 June; and it involved the extended Lyons family. Joe and Enid as well as Eliza Burnell all stood as Labor candidates. The Tasmanian Parliament had passed Labor Mick O'Keefe's Bill enabling women to stand for State parliament and Joe had asked Enid to stand. Labor needed women candidates and, while Enid could not possibly win, her candidacy would draw women's votes to Labor and away from the forceful Edith Waterworth, an independent who was standing for Denison and attracting press attention. Voting was still voluntary and Labor knew it must have women candidates to broaden its vote. In Burnie, Eliza Burnell stood as one of Labor's candidates for Darwin.

From newspaper reports, there is no indication of the struggle it all was for the Lyons family. Joe and Enid were reported attending meetings almost daily as if they had nothing else on their weekly agenda. In fact, they had a house of sick children. The 1925 winter in Hobart was particularly bracing with deep snow on Mount Wellington, heavy rain and days of chilling southerly winds. This was before infant inoculation. The Lyons children, three of whom were at school, came down with various contagious illnesses, starting with measles, which they passed on in mild form to their parents, moving on to chicken pox, whooping cough and then mumps. Joe was at one point that winter forced to withstand the embarrassment of a colleague saying that he had come down with a "childish complaint". As campaigning began, Joe and Enid employed a nurse to help Ada.

The candidate

Involvement in the 1925 campaign, both as a candidate and premier's wife, stretched Enid to her limits; she had meetings day and night, and regularly through the week. At one point, she even travelled north with Joe to rally the vote in Darwin and Wilmot. Joe, meanwhile, was barely home. Enid caught up with sleep for a few hours in the mornings after she settled the children with Ada and the nurse. It was an extraordinary burden to survive. For all that, amid the disruption of her children's sickness, going out to campaign was an escape for Enid. Indeed, all her life, her political involvement so often was. She revelled in the chance to take on a public role. In her memoirs, she wrote of coming home during the campaign at around 10pm to her seven little ill Lyons children. She would then send Ada to bed and the nurse home and sit by the fire in her dressing gown for an hour or so "too stimulated from the meeting to sleep".

On podiums, with her ability to chide opponents and debate the weaker points of the other side's case, Enid was a natural local candidate. She had a talent for drawing people into her arguments emotionally, of being able to touch an audience of strangers with metaphors of ordinary life, all the while posing, just a little, as the underdog, denying that she was standing "as a woman" while at the same time exploiting her lower female status. Her strategy was quite brilliant. In the end, with the complicated Hare Clarke formula for proportionally allocating preferences, Enid could declare she had only lost by 60 votes.

The reports of what Enid and her mother Eliza chose to speak of suggest that Labor's female candidates were designated areas of politics that fitted their domestic experience. In her first speech, Eliza Burnell argued that she would not "apologise" for standing as a female candidate. She emphasised her interest in community matters and also her concern over "matters relating to the home". In a later speech at Strahan she admitted to leaving all "financial matters to other candidates [men] who knew the issues better". in a developed metaphor, she compared parliament to the home with separate tasks for mother and father – the "mother" function of parliament was provision of social benefits for the needy, as well as prohibition. Eliza's platform was very much a personal one, and built around social action.

Enid opened her campaign at the Hobart Town Hall on the night of Monday 11 April. A high attendance was a feature of all meetings where Enid spoke. Word had gone out that Enid was an entertaining speaker. Her love of the stage, and the high it gave her, would be a lifetime romance. Audiences who came to hear Enid as something of a curiosity discovered she knew how to perform.

Women as parliamentary candidates was unnerving to many – women included. A woman candidate had to find a line of attack appealing to voters and convincing enough to have them listen to what a woman at the podium might be saying. Most of the electorate saw a woman working in a man's profession as depriving some man of a job. As Enid and Eliza stood at meeting after meeting addressing audiences, the parliaments across Australia had seen only one woman elected to parliament – Edith Cowan in the State parliament of Western Australia who had been elected in 1921 only to lose her seat in 1924.

Enid Lyons began with a straight bat. At her campaign opening, she attacked Labor's Nationalist opposition for its financial mismanagement of the state when in government. She honed in on the reduction in liabilities for the Tasmania with the Lyons government. Then she moved to a field she knew from experience – Labor's pledge to have state funded secondary education for all. The Lyons Government had restored teachers' salaries after the Nationalists had reduced them ("the teacher is worthy of his hire"), and re-established dental clinics ("doing wonderfully valuable work for the health of children") which the Nationalists had abolished. She urged upon her audience the dignity of labour making reference to the "central figure in all history" who had worked at a carpenter's bench [Jesus]. She was for Australian made goods being at the top of local shopping lists (loud applause), government control of milk distribution to guarantee supply, a health levy on all salary earners for the upkeep of hospitals, and forcing the Town Planning Act to clean up Hobart's slums. Enid was an exemplary Fabian. At meeting after meeting, it won her very loud applause.

Life with a seasoned politician like Joe had taught Enid well. In campaign appearances, she variously lobbed back the jibes and attacks as fast as they came. She "thanked" the pro-conservative *Mercury* for opining that voters should "forget altogether the good work done by the Labor Party and return a Nationalist Government" (laughter and applause). On 26 May at West Hobart, she berated her opponent John Soundy for his confusion about the state's finances saying he had fallen into "the very error against which she had uttered a warning". She then defended a family interest, arguing for a Commonwealth sawmill to ensure that Tasmania's remaining blackwood was not bought up by mainland firms and taken from local craftsmen.

Enid fended off criticism that as the wife of the Premier, already getting a good "screw" [wage], as an MP she would be taking the job off a man. She singled out an MP with a private income who was also being paid as a parliamentarian, saying "nobody questioned *his* right to an MP's £300 a year". She extended her "sympathy" to a female correspondent who referred to the Premier "permitting" his wife to stand for parliament, declaring she simply had a husband who accepted that women in the community, including his wife, had equal civic rights with himself and other men. For this she received loud applause.

To the man who thought women standing for parliament were encroaching on "men's domain" Enid queried just what was men's domain? Men and women were cooks and milliners and men handed silk stockings to women over shop counters (laughter). She added that men were also shingling women's hair and giving them bobs (loud laughter). "The class of men who said that women should not encroach on man's domain," she argued, "was the class which did not object to women cutting up firewood". By then the audience was eating from her hand. Her best line that she was not so much a woman candidate as a candidate among the men. Modern feminists might cringe, but it was one of her most popular arguments.

Labor won the 1925 Tasmanian election and handed Joe Lyons the majority government he longed for. Labor could finally make headway as a responsible government. Within two years, the retiring President of the Hobart Chamber of Commerce admitted that business had changed its attitude to Labor saying, "Tasmania never had a man more ready and more capable to work for his country's good, irrespective of party or of party politics". Enid had lost, in spite of her first preference votes being more than double the number cast for Edith Waterworth. But her efforts had helped her Labor colleagues take four of the six seats in Denison.

Eliza came in second last in the Darwin poll but her votes helped the Labor victory. And it was with much ironic pride that Eliza had stood with other Labor candidates to address a meeting at Smithton during the campaign, where Eliza had congratulated the people of Smithton on the interest they were taking in the election judging by the very large attendance at her meeting. It was a far cry from the simple wife she had been, living on the outskirts of the town, when her daughter, now the Premier's wife, was born. Enid acknowledged her mother's achievement in her memoirs: "The mere fact that during her life she had achieved a parliamentary nomination was a matter of intense gratification to her. She had done political work at a time when, for a woman, it was regarded as scarcely respectable, least of all work for the Labor Party."

While never really contemplating winning, Enid did find the loss a blow – especially as she had come so close to taking a seat. She had felt the stimulation and adrenalin rush of public acclaim, only to come back to earth with the daily round of domesticity. Enid had developed a taste for more. While principally Joe's accompanist, she nevertheless loved and belonged on the stage. In later life, Enid was nicknamed the family's Sarah Bernhardt, after the French actress.

In sickness and in health

With no warning, however, Enid's greatest test of all was to come in the following twelve months. Her own account of that year is vivid but lacking in precise chronology. In the eighteen months that followed Enid's defeat at the polls, she would suffer the death of her baby, a miscarriage soon after and the shock of Joe's serious car accident which kept him out of politics for four months. And by the end of that year she would be three months pregnant with her eighth child.

Shortly after the 1925 election, Enid came down with mumps and was confined to the house for two months. She wrote later that her appearance resembled one of Charles Burnell's Berkshires at the family farm in Somerset. In August she resumed her public schedule. On Monday 3 August, she had a long standing engagement to attend the annual meeting of the Child Welfare Association. Baby Garnet was showing signs of a cold and Enid had his cot brought into the sitting room for Ada to keep a close watch on his breathing and temperature. When Enid returned home, Garnet was feverish; by night time his temperature was rising rapidly. They called the doctor who, after an examination, informed Enid that Garnet had pneumonia in both lungs but that it was not dangerous as the child was in good health otherwise. But Garnet continued to deteriorate and developed meningitis. On Wednesday 5 August, little Garnet died.

Enid makes no reference in her memoirs to wider events at the time of Garnet's death. Mount Wellington was covered with snow. And it was a huge week for Hobart as four US Navy cruisers had docked at Queens Pier early on the morning of the day Garnet died. Preparation for the important visitors had been overwhelming with media coverage intense. In the reports of the festive welcome of Tasmanian dignitaries to the Admiral of the US fleet, Joe Lyons is listed absent – explained by "illness in the family". So it was that, while the crowds on the wharves, made up of local and out-of-town Tasmanians, waved and cheered and made eyes at foreign sailors, Joe and Enid watched their baby boy die.

The sound of the Trinity Church bells peeling in the distance and the muffled volleys of the salutes to the US Navy visitors would have all sung out a tragic death knoll for the Lyons family as the couple made arrangements for a small white coffin and a family funeral. Garnet was buried at the beautiful Cornelian Bay cemetery on Friday 7 August – a funeral attended by the cream of Hobart and Tasmanian public life. Those who were there from the family included Eliza Burnell, but not William, Desmond but not his siblings and Tom Lyons without Mavis who was probably minding the other Lyons children. An array of beautiful wreaths, from all manner of people and institutions, accompanied the coffin, from the Matron of St Virgils College, Hobart and the Tasmanian Journalists Association, to US Rear Admiral T P Magrudere who left Hobart with the US ships that day.

It was a terrible wrench for Enid. In her memoirs she writes of living for days in "an unreal world … the people passing in the street outside my window like puppets moving unnaturally on a stage". Yet her public schedule continued, a schedule not recorded by either Enid or Kate White. Within five days of Garnet's death and burial,

Enid joined Joe on a tour of northern and western Tasmania leaving Hobart on Wednesday 12 August. Joe made a parting statement on his hopes for the shale industry and Hydro Electric business in Tasmania's future. The Lyons couple travelled north and west for ten days. Perhaps Joe thought the trip would enable Enid some time to avoid the house where Garnet had died. But it was also an important trip for Joe, especially in making an impact on business as a Labor premier. For anyone reading the media at the time, life hardly missed a beat in the Lyons' public life after baby Garnet's death.

Enid, though, did not recover easily. Her grief hung on for months. In the midst of her suffering she received an anonymous letter. Its effect was dramatic enough to have her recall it bitterly decades later. Enid believed the letter to be from a woman, its author seething about money put aside for the Lyons couple to travel abroad. The trip, which never happened, was to attract overseas business to Tasmania. The letter accused Enid of killing her baby from neglect. Enid was not unfamiliar with anonymous letters, even from the time of her engagement. But given the strong feeling against women in public life and Enid's turmoil of emotions after the death of her baby, it is also possible the letter touched a raw nerve, and that Enid subconsciously did blame herself, albeit unjustifiably, for what happened to Garnet. Her lines about this episode in her memoir are extremely emotional, even after four decades.

Their baby's death hit both Lyons parents. Two months later, on what would have been Garnet's first birthday, Joe was reported being too ill with the flu to make his appearance at the Launceston Show and a number of northern meetings. It was Joe, Enid wrote, who decided the family should leave the Pedder Street house. They relocated to "a suitable house, warm, comfortable, spacious". Joe also bought Enid an electric stove, a model imported by the fledgling Hydro-electric department. By mid 1926 they were settled at 115 Main Road, New Town, a few blocks from the Pedder Street house. The Main Road dwelling was a Federation brick bungalow, wide and square and close to shops and transport. A change of house, especially to a larger one, may also have come with Joe and Enid wondering, after Garnet's death, if their house at Pedder Street had been far too crowded for a family of seven children and live-in home help. Looking back, they may have realised how their cramped living conditions had not helped with the sickness their children suffered that year.

But there was never any question of the Lyons family not being involved in politics. It was not only Joe's best chance of earning enough for his large family, more importantly it consumed his ambitions — and Enid's beside him. They were in their element as a political team. The family tagged along behind; hurdles when they came were surmounted, even a baby's death.

Enid and Joe lived by a faith in divine providence; they followed the guide of their church and believed that whatever crosses they might be asked to bear, they would manage. And since their church offered no advice on birth control, apart from abstinence, Joe and Enid's family continued to grow. On the positive side, Enid was still very young to be the mother of seven children, and in spite of the many physical ailments she endured she was more than able to keep going. Sickness and pain were the order of the times — from toothache to sciatic nerve pains, most individuals pioneered on. Around this time, Enid was told a foetus had died in her uterus. She carried it for three months before the doctor would agree to a curette which left her with toxemia.

However, 1926 did prove more stressful than normal. On 15 July, Joe accompanied by the Speaker of the House, Mick O'Keefe and the Manager of the Hydro Electric Department, Harry Curtis, travelled north in a Hydro Electric Department car which was an open roadster. Nineteen kilometres out from Launceston, the driver Mr Fulton, who was a clerk in the Department, hit the back of a goods train as it snaked its way across the narrow highway at the Perth junction.. The crossing was unlit and on a bend in the road.

Along this part of the main highway, train tracks frequently cross the road at similar intersections. Railway gates had been successively removed from Tasmanian crossings over years. And it was dark, the accident happening at about 7 pm. Joe Lyons, who was in the back with Mick O'Keefe, said afterwards that he had a feeling the car might hit the end of the train but as the driver had a better view he did not sing out. None of the men seemed to know just what had caused the accident. In an era without seat belts, all of them had been thrown from the car which was badly smashed – the photo of the wreckage in the *Weekly Courier* suggested the men in the front were lucky to be alive. But it was Joe Lyons and Mick O'Keefe who sustained the worst injuries. To the grief of many in the Tasmanian parliament, Mick O'Keefe would die from his injuries on 2 October.

Enid received the call that gave her the bad news very soon after the accident happened. It was from the stationmaster at Western Junction who had known Joe for years. He sounded unalarmed ("a bit of an accident … no one is seriously hurt") and told Enid she could have a talk to Joe by phone at the hospital. Two ambulances would collect the men from Launceston station and take them to St Margaret's Hospital. It was a little time before Enid realised that men who were unhurt did not go to hospital. She rang St Margaret's and was told Joe had complicated fractures to his right leg and was in danger of losing it. They asked her to come at once. For three days Joe would be in danger from gas gangrene.

Enid was always at her best in a crisis. Although the children were in bed, she had to find a babysitter and get to Launceston as fast as possible. Fortunately the Lyons families had telephones, although by then it was almost 10 pm. Tom and Mavis took charge of the children. Mavis' mother who was staying came over to live-in at the Lyons house. The head of the Premier's Department, Edward Parkes, organised a car immediately and came himself to accompany Enid on the long journey north. The top speed for cars in 1926 was a relatively slow fifty kilometres per hour and Launceston some two hundred kilometres away, reached on a winding unsealed road in an unheated and open car. The journey took four hours which was "good time" and Enid was frozen with the cold on arrival. Then, after reaching the hospital at three in the morning, the wife of the Premier was told by the nurse on duty Joe must not be disturbed.

A very apologetic doctor met Enid soon after daylight. He had left orders that no one should see his patient as he had never imagined Mrs Lyons could have made the journey so quickly. He hadn't counted on what Enid's devotion to Joe could accomplish. But he did have faith that she would make a difference to Joe's recovery. In a rare move for the era, Dr Ramsay told Enid she could stay with Joe at the hospital.

Over three days, Joe hovered close to death from poisoning since the marrow of his bone had come in contact with the dirt of the road. In the press, however, Joe was described as resting up and taking visitors. The Burnie *Advocate* cheerfully reported him saying, "Goodness knows when I'll get out of this. I have been battling for a long time to try and do something for the State and here I am." In the the the car, while he had light, Joe had been preparing proposals to be submitted to the opening of parliament for a reduction of taxation. Now the table by his bedside was covered with messages of sympathy from all over the country. The State Governor, Sir James O'Grady had made a number of visits.

Newspapers of the day made no mention of Joe's wife or family who were suffering most throughout the ordeal. Enid wrote of having to handle the media and many phone calls in the months Joe recovered. None of her statements appeared in print. In fact, soon after the week of the accident, progress reports on the premier stopped. Within a few days, *The Mercury* was far more absorbed with news of a Royal visit by the Duke and Duchess of York in April the following year. Joe Lyons next appeared in the news after his return to Parliament on 16 November. This was not an age for news about political personalities.

It was a different story for Enid and the children. She was by Joe's bed for the first three days as he passed the most critical stage. If he could make it through the next fortnight, the serious danger would be averted. After the first three days, Enid returned to Hobart, made arrangements for nine-year-old Desmond to board at St Virgil's, for Sheila and the youngest two, Moira and Kevin, to stay with Eliza in Burnie, and for young Enid and Kathleen to accompany her to Launceston where they would stay in a private hotel near St Margaret's. The landlady, a Mrs Berkery, looked after the girls, aged five and six, while Enid was with Joe. Enid had returned to Hobart by train, packed bags and returned to Launceston on the next train north.

Every day for nine weeks, Enid sat with Joe. Then she took him home in a hospital bed set up in a closed railway goods truck – probably not much different from the one he had hit in the accident. Enid sat in a chair by his bed, talking with Joe, as they moved south. An ambulance met them in Hobart to take them to New Town. Thereafter, Joe had to learn to walk again. He did this with the help of a retired British Army officer whom they engaged for regular physiotherapy. From that time on, Joe Lyons would walk with a limp, and the help of a walking stick.

The Lyons Government had continued with James (Allan) Guy, the Chief Secretary and a long time mate of Joe, as Acting Premier. In her memoirs, Enid jumps these months, her chronology suggesting her eighth child Brendan's birth was imminent as Joe returned to parliament. But this would have had to be something of a miracle considering the accident and that Enid was recovering from a miscarriage at the time it happened. In fact, Brendan would be born in June 1927, seven months after Joe resumed his public duties.

The Lyons Government was a success in spite of increasing union demands for a more socialist agenda and a conservative and obdurate Legislative Council which had the power to amend Assembly legislation. But the strains of having to constantly conciliate would take its toll on Joe's Labor principles, even to the point of his moving from republican to constitutional monarchist. As Enid wrote in her memoirs, his "early dreams of socialism were tempered now by awareness of the danger to individual freedom that lay within it". With this came Joe Lyons' confidence in his management skills, his belief in financial caution and a modern understanding of the power of the media. Philip Hart, in his biographical thesis, argues that Lyons "by taking leading pressmen into his confidence ... gained favourable coverage for Labor". Joe's careful cultivation of the press would no doubt have been a factor behind Enid's work on press releases and phone calls while he convalesced. On his return to parliament, Lyons thanked the press for the sensitive way they had treated him during his recovery.

Lyons' most important achievements as Tasmania's Premier undoubtedly included his ability to bring the Commonwealth government onside, resulting in better financial arrangements for the State. Lyons established good relations with Nationalist Prime Minister Stanley Bruce and his government. Lyons was wily enough to realise that his success at the polls in 1925 had come with what is now known as the "swinging voter" – a group of electors who wanted good government but who did not subscribe to the more radical proposals of the union arm of Labor. The unions saw it differently and ignored Lyons' practical wisdom. Lyons caused friction in 1926, when he refused to initiate the 44-hour week saying that this was not in his election policy speech. Joe Lyons and some of his ministers supported the Bruce-Page Government's referendum proposal that there be increased powers for the Commonwealth government over labour disputes. When the 1926 referendum was lost, Lyons faced increasing opposition from the unions.

Along with numerous dignitaries, Joe and Enid welcomed the visit of the Duke and Duchess of York at Easter 1927. Enid was seven months pregnant and missed the State Dinner on Saturday 16 April but joined the Duchess a few days later, happily admiring dolls house furniture presented to the Royal couple for their daughters Elizabeth and Margaret. By June 1927, Joe Lyons could declare the State was in surplus to the tune of £100,000.

In this buoyant climate of success, Enid gave birth to Brendan on 27 June 1927; as she would describe it decades later, "a wonderful welcome in our house". Enid was happiest with a new baby in the house. Babies made the family whole. "For two years now," she wrote, "ever since little Garnet's death, we had no baby and my heart had never ceased to cry its need."

But Enid was also impulsive, led on by the easy help of others and a husband who petted her in ways that released her from being trapped in an endless round of domesticity. This was leading, without her realising, to a psychological crisis. By the time she had recovered from Brendan's birth, perhaps even before, there were days when Enid felt she had lost her energy and confidence in managing the whole of her schedule. She was close to a nervous breakdown. One meeting at a university around this time illustrates how she was skating perilously near to collapse. On the dais, this confident and daring woman began to see herself diminished by the academic gowns of those she sat with. She managed to wing it, speaking ironically of the learned figures sitting either side of her and musing on what it might feel like to sit between an expert on the mind and an expert in the law. It amused her audience but she returned home quite spent, near complete collapse.

Ironically, just as Enid sensed her downward spiral, events would overtake the Lyons Government itself. That decline would take just a year and yet it would usher in an even bigger chapter in the Lyons saga.

CHAPTER 10

A SEA CHANGE

The Lyons Government did not survive the 1928 State election, held on 30 May. Its defeat surprised the pundits. Labor had righted much of the economic woes of the state in just a few years and Lyons was still popular as a leader. But, looking back, it was around mid 1927 when the uneasy balance in Labor's ranks began to go wobbly. And it was around this time that Enid felt she could no longer manage as Premier's wife in Hobart and began making arrangements to return with the children to Devonport. Then came the Albert Olgilvie scandal and relations between Joe and his former Attorney General, who was allied with the more radical union elements of the Party, broke down irretrievably. Along with all this was Joe's slow recovery, still ongoing after his accident and which lessened his energies at a time of increasing frustration.

Enid records that she was still just thirty when she returned to Devonport, too exhausted to play the role of Premier's wife day after day in Hobart. "Invitations can be refused, of course," she wrote, "but to refuse is often as emotionally trying as to accept and keep the engagement." She had reached an emotional crisis in her public role. And Joe was still exhausted and on edge after his accident. The couple was overdue for a change of pace.

Enid and Joe had agreed that a move back to the electorate was best for all of them. He would board with Tom and Mavis and rejoin the family on weekends. In fact, as it turned out, Tom and Mavis simply moved into 115 Main Road, New Town and Joe took the spare room. It suited Tom and Mavis who had started their own family with the happy and successful arrival of their first child, a daughter they named Carmel. Mavis hoped to have more children and a larger home was exactly what they needed.

However, in the Lyons way, moving back to Devonport was not without the unexpected. In a remarkable twist, Enid was able to take her children back to live at Home Hill, the house she had romanced in her stories to them for so long. By some quirk of fate, while Joe and she were making enquiries for a new home in Devonport, Joe learnt that the owners of Home Hill wanted to shift to Hobart. In a matter of weeks they had negotiated a direct swap of the two properties. On the 11 August 1927, the Jensens, owners of Home Hill, were granted ownership of what is now 67 Pedder Street (then numbered 59) in return for the Lyons family taking over Home Hill with its more than eight acres of land and the house the Lyons had built as newly weds. Enid's heart sung with the joy of it as if she had won a fortune. The transaction once again listed Enid as the sole owner of the house Joe had given her.

It was in August that the scandal involving Albert Olgilvie began to break and this may have delayed the family's move some weeks. There had been growing tension between Joe Lyons and Albert Ogilvie over years. Ogilvie's high personal vote in the 1925 election encouraged him to challenge Lyons' deputy and friend, Allan Guy, for the deputy position. He did not succeed, as Lyons worked the numbers and bettered him at political rivalry. Then, after a Nationalist MP accused Ogilvie of improper use of his responsibility for the Public Trust Office, the Lyons Government was forced to a Royal Commission to enquire into the allegations. The charges involved loans on mortgage from the Public Trust Office to clients of Ogilvie and his partner T A Okines who gave evidence and then committed suicide, further adding to the scandal. The outcome was better for Ogilvie than it might have been, but he was found guilty of inefficiency and lack of supervision, sins of omission rather than overt corruption. Even so, Lyons asked him to step down from Cabinet which he did on 12 October, resigning as Attorney General, Minister for Education and Minister for Forestry. Albert Ogilvie would retain his high personal vote in the 1928 election, even as Labor lost, and go on eventually to be Premier. But the rift between Lyons and Ogilvie would openly divide Tasmanian Labor just six months out from a State election, and with it take much of Joe Lyons' energy and drive.

The Lyons family made their return journey to Home Hill in a new Morris Oxford car given to Joe by a group of Hobart businessmen who believed that, with his lame leg, as Premier he needed relief from using public transport. However, Joe was not a good driver and his lame leg made him even more of a risk at the wheel. It was Joe's decision, then, that the family should take the car to Devonport and that Enid should drive them there. She had no driver's licence but soon got one. It is a measure of the unsophisticated times and the relative small amount of motoring on the roads that Enid was able to get her licence in a matter of days after Joe decided she should drive north. In her retirement and even old age, Enid would still be driving the highway between Hobart and Devonport, by then in her tank-like Humber, barely able to see over the steering wheel.

They set off on a Sunday after Mass. Enid writes that just "half the family" made the car journey, presumably some of the children were taken north by train with a relative; Eliza perhaps or Mavis. Even so, complete with infant, toddlers and the rest, it was a squeeze with packed cases, household goods and travelling gear. But they were full steam ahead, no doubt baby Brendan in front on Joe's knee in a basket of some kind, cruising along at 50 kilometres an hour and Enid gaining confidence in her driving ability. Then a back tyre blew and Joe reached for the hand brake, stopping the car broadside onto the traffic. A passing driver helped change the tyre and they were back on the road. It is possible they spent the night in Launceston with friends as the following day both Joe and Enid addressed a meeting at Westbury which, driving at twenty to thirty miles an hour, is just under an hour's drive west of Launceston. Here Joe urged local businesses to connect up to his government's publicly acquired Hydro-Electric power. Having made it a public enterprise, the government now needed as many Tasmanians to use hydro-electricity as possible. While Joe made a tilt for businesses, Enid appealed to the housewives telling them of how housework might be halved by the use in the home of electric appliances.

The day they arrived in Devonport was what Enid described as "all that a day in spring should be". Today, Home Hill looks out to the northern coast across rows of houses long since built in many subdivisions over decades but Enid recalled that in 1927 the "valley in front and the long line of the hill beyond, clear cut against the blue rim of the sea, were green with the new season's grasses". They returned to a house modernised as they had not previously known, with electricity, telephone and town supplied water. And Enid now had a car.

But the family had grown in number and, as the children ran excitedly about the rooms, Enid and Joe could see they would need extensions. In the dividing up of bedrooms, one had to be used for the live-in home help and a six foot by ten foot breakfast annex was all they could afford at the time. Over the years the house was regularly added to and extended. Tom Lyons' daughter Carmel remembers her father saying that they never knew where the back door was going to be, it was different every Christmas. Enid described how it grew, writing, "Even the kitchen and its annex would be changed to become a dining-room and later still a sitting-room lined with books, the heart of the house and of all its rooms the principal treasure-house of family memories." In 1927, the four girls shared one not very large bedroom – still known by the family as "the girls' room". The long beautiful side room they later added, with its full length, north facing widow, and the room where Enid lived most of her last years, at one time accommodated five beds set out in a row.

Enid's account of their return to Devonport in 1927, even after decades, is full of emotion.

> Here and there a group of trees or a rooftop stood up sharply against the horizon, and east and west blue hills carried the eye into the vast distance," wrote Enid in 1964. "I was back in the country of my childhood. It was scenes like this my mother had taught me to love. There had been a wonderful moment on the road where the forest ended abruptly and we came into open country within sight of the sea. Even today, as I approach a spot on a homecoming journey, memory never fails to recall the scene and the sensations of that morning long ago. The mounting excitement of the children, our own feelings as we approached the goal of our hopes, and then, suddenly, the sight of the lovely rolling farmlands warm in the spring sunshine, and the distant shimmering sea.

She must have desperately needed the change. It was as if life in the big city had smothered her, in spite of her full and public life which would have been the envy of many ordinary Tasmanians. And she was so very homesick for the north of the state, where even today one can sense a different ambience. While, in later years, Enid would enjoy the odd occasion when she entertained friends on a visit to Home Hill, Janice, Enid's youngest daughter speaking in 2007, remembered her mother as someone who needed her home as her private space. She didn't really like too many visitors, said Janice. Once home, Enid wanted nothing more than her family around her, and to shut out the world she found so very appealing at other times. Throughout her life, Enid moved with great surges of energy separated by severe collapses from nervous exhaustion. In 1927, Enid had not collapsed but she was ready to shut out the public world.

In spite of relatively good economic management, the Lyons government lost the State election of 30 May 1928. In hindsight, various reasons were offered: the Olgilvie affair had damaged Labor and Ogilvie supporters had divided the party; an industrial candidate had disrupted the Labor vote in Denison; Lyons had a high regard for the opposition leader John McPhee and had been far too kind to him in the campaign; this was the first State election with compulsory voting and it seemed to have disadvantaged Labor; unemployment was on the rise. All probably had some effect on the result. But, also, Tasmanian governments had for some time governed with very narrow majorities because of the Hare Clarke system of voting. It only took a couple of seats to fall and the opposition became the government.

This was the year Joe Lyons stepped back somewhat from the endless round of public duties, slowed by his still recovering leg, and refocused on family life with Enid. The growing children he had realised, more and more, missed his fatherly presence. And when, in the early days of their return to Home Hill, Kathleen had slipped off the mudguard of the Morris Oxford as the children had happily clung to the car making its way down the drive, he had only narrowly avoided running over her. Kathleen, left badly injured with deep abrasions and gravel in her face, arms and legs, had a nose break and a crushed antrum. If Joe felt any guilt about his absence as a parent, it was now. For months, he was in deep remorse, desperate to make amends to Kathleen, and Enid who spent hours each day dressing the girl's terrible wounds.

After the 1928 poll, Lyons spoke of looking forward to having a rest; and he praised Enid saying the public would never realise the extent to which he had been helped by her in public matters: "Her brilliant intellect, combined with the natural sagacity of her sex, have helped me to elucidate many of the problems with which the state has been confronted. Many decisions which have come from me have come only after consultation with her." It was a passionate statement, and one that would leave a legacy to haunt Enid far into the future, the idea that she was the power behind a rather weak political spouse. Nothing could have been further from the truth. Joe Lyons was the politically ambitious one always in the Lyons partnership. But Enid gave him added energy, and it is significant that before the election loss in May 1928, she had already withdrawn into her private world at Home Hill.

Enid wrote of the year that followed the 1928 election loss as a "golden" one; both she and Joe "knew deep contentment, loving the tranquil pattern of our lives". When it was put to Joe that he should contest a federal seat that November, he turned it down for family reasons. Labor candidates did extremely poorly as it turned out so he made a wise decision politically as well. Enid, meanwhile, revelled in their being just like an average Australian family, "father at work all day, children at school, mother at home with the babies". Joe opened a small business agency in town and Enid was glad of the irregular profits as they came in, as he no longer drew a premier's salary. At home, she delighted in preparing meals that were novel, appetising and frugal – "a dish for Fridays, meatless and nutritious, a pudding without butter or eggs". Tom and Mavis' daughter Lynette never forgot what a wonderful cook Auntie Enid was. Over the years, on days at the beach, Mavis would stay with the children and Enid would come in the afternoon with pasties, pies, scones and cakes for the hungry mob of children they shared between them.

Enid wrote nostalgically of that time, of building a garden wall with the children, of sitting at night reading aloud with Joe, of the steaming wet shoes and socks lined up at the back door while the little ones had hot cocoa and scones by a blazing fire after their kilometre and a half walk home from school. Idyllic? Certainly. Recalled with rose coloured glasses? No doubt, especially with the air brushing of years. But it all left Joe and Enid far stronger in facing the future. Barry

Lyons was born, eleven days after Enid's thirty-first birthday in July 1928. They would eventually discover Barry was an achondroplastic, or dwarf, and spend years seeking any sort of cure that might be available. But Barry would tackle life with no less vigour than any of his Lyons' siblings, in 2007 riding his motorised buggy from his townhouse in Devonport, across a freeway, up the drive to Home Hill, and into its main rooms for a meeting.

Joe Lyons, October 1929, now Postmaster General in the Scullin Government – Enid holds baby Rosemary and Joe holds Barry with (l-r) Enid, Kathleen, Desmond and Sheila standing behind (l-r) Kevin, Brendan and Moira sitting in front.

It was on her return to Devonport and Home Hill that Enid began in earnest the garden she would treasure all her life, not just the orchard and the small grove of pine trees that no longer survive, but the colours and perfumes in spring of borders she would describe as "big splashes of rich crimson and pink sweet Williams, and some tall spikes of Russell lupins in apricot and rose and pink ... with the lupins, masses and masses of them on a high bank. ... ambrosia (giant forget-me-nots) and then Canterbury bells, corn-flowers and campanalo and love-in-the-mist with drifts of mauve-blue cat mint ... delphiniums in a burst of glory, all the shades from blue to purple." In Enid's view, "to watch small growing things, to cultivate the good earth, to tire the body with healthy, honest toil, is, I believe, to come very close to God".

Amid this fecundity, Joe and Enid had their tenth child, in September 1929, a pretty little girl they named Rosemary. It was while Enid relaxed with Joe awaiting Rosemary's birth in Burnie at the Burnell home (Eliza at Home Hill with the Lyons children) that the Prime Minister faced a showdown in the federal parliament, by then in the fledgling chambers of Canberra. The uproar brought down the Bruce Nationalist government. Joe Lyons public figure, as Enid described him, was suddenly back in form. He came in excitedly with the morning newspaper and they discussed for hours what he might do with new possibilities opening for him. Would he resign his State seat yet again and try for Wilmot federally? His instincts told him Labor would walk it in. The country was overwhelmingly against the industrial relations bill Stanley Bruce had introduced; with it Bruce was showing all the high handedness of his devil-may-care manners. Enid now faced her hardest decision yet, for Joe had told her it was her call.

The 1920s was an era of union militancy, in particular the maritime unions. The Bruce-Page conservative government had been good for Lyons when he was Tasmanian premier, with Bruce recognising the

Commonwealth funding arrangements of per capita grants to States had disadvantaged less populated areas of Australia over decades. Bruce had stood up to the powerfully more numerous Victoria and New South Wales premiers and passed legislation that ushered in the start of new Commonwealth funding arrangements that would be fairer to States like Tasmania. But it was to be Bruce's mercurial handling of industrial relations that would hand Joe Lyons a new career.

Having stood strongly against industrial action and done his best to talk business into being reasonable about some union demands, Bruce was still unable to quell the agitation on the wharves. By 1929, unemployment was at eleven per cent and rising and the economic downturn was starting to bite. Under Jim Scullin, the new federal leader, Labor tried to censure the government over immigration alleging it was adding to unemployment. The coal industry was in a woeful state and miners' pay had been reduced for longer hours.

With a system of industrial arbitration complicated by the overlap of state and federal jurisdictions, wages determinations were often delayed and incurred the annoyance of unions whose only weapon was industrial action. Bruce had also brought in "volunteers" when industries were crippled by strikes. Then, as tension on the wharves continued, the Bruce Government introduced the Maritime Industries Bill by which the Commonwealth would vacate all fields of industrial relations except shipping and waterside industries, which it would take over under the Trade and Commerce power conferred by the Constitution. The legislation caused division in an already divided party. In the second reading of the Bill, former Nationalist leader Billy Hughes, by then expelled from the party, introduced an amendment that would hold the legislation until it had been put to the people. Hughes' amendment was passed and within two days the Bruce Government was forced to a federal election.

Enid was silently agonising over how she should react to Joe's proposition that he should stand for a federal seat when a telegram arrived from Jim Scullin, asking if Joe would stand as a federal candidate in Wilmot. It was a concerted campaign on Scullin's part – he had sniffed the wind was going Labor's way and had contacted other Labor members in state electorates. David Riordan would resign his state Queensland seat as well as Joe's close friend Allan Guy in Tasmania to contest the federal election.

Enid's account of how Joe and she made their decision is conflicted. Should he resign his State seat, Joe could no longer return to State politics if he lost; the rules had changed. She was also dreading his winning which would mean more and more absences from the family, attending parliament in Canberra, then a night's ferry journey away followed by another night on a slow train. Two days each way. It made Hobart seem very near: "As time went on we would see less and less of him. How could I say Yes? How could I let him go? But how could I say No?" And yet she knew Joe was challenged. And so confident she would decide for him, that he would tell her of his keenness to have a go. The worst, she knew, would be for her to stop him and know he might blame her for standing in his way. Enid agreed that Joe should stand.

Joe made it back to Burnie, outside the Wilmot electorate, for Rosemary's birth but only for an hour. Otherwise, for the weeks of the campaign for the election on 12 October, Enid kept in touch with Joe by letter as he travelled from town to town. She admits to being depressed and miserable, but when she saw him briefly a second time she was too proud of him to wallow in self pity. As always, when with Joe, Enid gained strength in his presence. But their all too brief couple of years of domestic tranquility were over. They weren't to know it then, but these two years at Home Hill would be their last as an ordinary family. The rest of their married life would revolve about the vagaries of political highs and lows.

Joe won the federal seat of Wilmot, a seat that had never before been won for Labor. Llewelyn Atkinson, the Nationalist Lyons defeated, had held it since 1906 and retained it easily in 1928. Allan Guy also won in Bass. The election was a landslide for Labor and even Bruce lost his seat. Enid had barely returned to Devonport with baby Rosemary when the results were known. Joe had his prize; and he was soon heading for Canberra where the caucus would select Labor's ministry. While Enid writes of the hard game of politics that awaited new boys such as Joe and Allan Guy on the mainland, in truth Joe was heading off reasonably confident of a ministry. He had a good track record as premier in a party of rookies taking office after being in opposition for twelve years. The family waved him off from the wharf at Devonport. On his return days later he had bought them all presents. And news that they would be moving to Melbourne as the family of the new Postmaster-General.

CHAPTER 11

THE BREAK

It was Stanley Bruce, master of the tactless if accurate comment, who prophesied that the rout the Nationalists had received at the 1929 election was "one of the most fortunate things that could possibly have happened to us", a view which he expressed to Senator George Pearce in May 1930.

Bruce was a long-term thinker and very much secure in his conspicuous wealth and influence, both in Australia and Britain. It was Bruce who drove about in his Rolls Royce as the unemployment queues lengthened. His comments on the 1929 election referred of course to the parlous state of the nation his government had bequeathed to his successor Scullin, both economically and industrially. Frank Anstey, Labor's Minister for Health in the newly elected ministry, put it another way when he described the situation Labor inherited as like "sitting on the eggs of a serpent". By April 1930, the Scullin Government was resorting to increasing tariffs as a buffer for home industries. This incurred the wrath of both exporters who complained, rightly, that this would bring retaliatory higher duties overseas for their goods and maritime unions who complained that the new tariffs had increased unemployment on the docks as imports dropped.

The signs of growing economic and industrial catastrophe were indisputable as the Lyons family of eleven, complete with belongings, crossed Bass Strait on what would become a sweltering January day in 1930. The miners' lockout in northern New South Wales, source of the black coal needed to power coastal steamers, was well underway. The ferry crossing the Strait was forced to a snail's pace, burning only "soft" or brown coal.

At night, without the steam needed, the ferry rolled and jerked in the cross sea and most of the children were sick. Joe and Enid had little sleep. As day came, they moved slowly towards the Victorian coast, docking seven hours late at 6pm after enduring a day of over 40° C as they neared Melbourne. A fellow passenger told Enid Lyons years later how many of the passengers had watched what he called the "Lyons circus" on the boat, but that he remembered how well the children behaved. As mother of such a large family, Enid had instilled discipline in her youngsters. Peter Lyons believes his mother's skill at controlling her children came from "her strength of personality which was such that we never bucked her".

In scenes that would be recognisable to many undergoing a shift of house with children, the family's woes continued after disembarking. In spite of offloading their belongings onto a van ahead of other cargo, there would be a long wait at the house they were moving into, at 309 Dandenong Road, East St Kilda, situated on a long arterial road in a neighbourhood of tidy Edwardian houses. The driver entered Dandenong Road a number of suburbs east of the house, driving away from it at first and having to find his way back. When the van finally arrived, shortly after 10 pm, the driver found family members spread out on the lawn, exhausted or asleep, and a surly Joe waiting at the gate. By midnight, calm was restored and life in Melbourne the next day seemed a good move. But it was a big city, by Devonport standards, and the children and Enid had a lot of transitions to make. New schools for the older girls (Presentation Convent, Windsor) and Kevin off to the Christian Brothers at St Kilda. Desmond would return to St Virgils in Hobart as a boarder a week or so later.

The heat that summer was intense. It preyed on the family, so used to the mild climate of Tasmania. When baby Rosemary became sick from heat exhaustion, Enid took her back to Burnie for treatment at the hospital there. The Bournes, Mavis Lyons' parents, had shifted into Home Hill as caretakers, so Enid spent time with her mother while Rosemary recuperated. One of Enid's friends moved into the Lyons home in Melbourne, to care for the children left behind.

Enid certainly never let family stop her travelling when and where she felt she must. What effect this may have had on her children is hard to quantify. Some of them spent years being moved from school to school and boarding from a young age, or being left with minders or relatives at any moment. Kathleen Lyons grew up never feeling comfortable about going to her mother when she was upset. Mother was efficient, a good cook and a good manager. And after each baby there was a great deal of fuss because Enid did get an intense joy from giving birth and cradling an infant. But her numerous and growing brood of children were individually something else. Enid's primary focus was on Joe, that man who had become her inspiration, the one who generated the excitement in her life; Kathleen recalled that the various paid help did nearly everything day-to-day around the children.

It could be said that Enid Lyons was the prototype of a modern high powered mother, ready to delegate her home duties and child minding responsibilities when needed. Joe's choice of career had set her in this mould at a very young age. She took Joe's lead and he was a person who let nothing stop him making a change. By the time Enid took baby Rosemary home to Burnie that summer, it seemed as if Enid herself could no longer stay in one place for very long. After all, babies have long survived Melbourne heat waves. Whatever the real reason for Enid's trip to Burnie, by the autumn she was back in Melbourne and Joe was spending less time than ever with his family who hardly saw him.

The Wall Street stock market had crashed, formally ushering in the 1930s Depression, just days after Scullin became Prime Minister.

Barely months in office, the government was limping from crisis to crisis, with unemployment rising steeply. Among trade unionists, unemployment would reach more than 18 per cent by mid year. And then, on 4 July, the Campbell Royal Commission set up to examine Treasurer Ted Theodore's role in the sale of the Mangana Mine to the Queensland government when he was premier, handed down a finding against Theodore. On 8 July, as Sarah Scullin and Esther Theodore watched their respective husbands from the gallery, Scullin announced Theodore's resignation as Treasurer. Theodore was a larger than life figure, with strong support in caucus; Scullin relied on him hugely. In *J H Scullin – A Political Biography*, John Robertson writes, "Never before had a federal government sustained such a humiliating injury."

There was speculation that either Joe Lyons or Jim Fenton would take the Treasury portfolio, but Scullin announced he would add it to his own responsibilities. The work on the Budget had been done and Theodore was confident he would clear his name with a judicial inquiry in a couple of months. But the Queensland government took a civil action against Theodore and the case dragged on. Then Scullin announced that he would be attending the Imperial Conference in London which would sit from 1 October until 14 November; James Fenton would be acting Prime Minister in his absence and Joe Lyons acting Treasurer. The Prime Minister would be away from 25 August until 6 January 1931, coming back east by train from Perth.

Enid absorbed the news in Melbourne. It clarified one important decision she needed to make. Joe was in Canberra most of the time. Not even his Postmaster General's office in Melbourne saw him all that often, as Cabinet and caucus meetings took up more and more time. They had looked for a house in Canberra, then a very small settlement of 5000 spread out over some kilometres where large important buildings dotted the landscape, separated from one another by open pastures, much of it with grazing sheep. Government housing had been built for single men or young, smaller families who might have had to move there. No Canberra house existed large enough to accommodate them all. And Joe worried about the children and Enid in a city where they had no extended family. Enid and Joe now agreed it would be best for her to move back to Home Hill.

It was a hard decision as there was no telephone link at the time between Tasmania and the mainland – that would not happen until 1936 – and the distance between them would be vast. But, overall, it was a more satisfactory arrangement for the family's needs. Once more, Enid made plans to take the "Lyons circus" on the ferry across Bass Strait. After just nine months in Melbourne, they were going home. However, the move was timely. Over the next year, the stability of extended family support would be vital for the children. Their parents were about to be tossed onto the national stage in a whirlwind of political uproar and acclaim.

Historian Philip Hart describes how Joe Lyons had found mainland Labor and its "bitter factionalism and doctrinal controversies of caucus" hard to tolerate. He got on well with his colleagues but disagreed with many caucus decisions. In the first months as Postmaster General, with the exception of issues affecting Tasmania, he stuck to departmental matters in his speeches to parliament. But, as acting Treasurer, he now had to take personal responsibility for hard decisions at a time of deep economic malaise. And a belligerent caucus stood in his way. Looked at from the viewpoint of either the Liberal Coalition or Labor seven decades later, it's hard to credit that politicians such as John Curtin could have been so ignorant about international credit ratings as they were at this time, and of the danger in ignoring financial realities.

On the radical side of Labor thinking, New South Wales Labor leader Jack Lang, who had been premier from 1925 to October 1927, led Labor once again to victory in the State election on 25 October 1930. Lang was a populist Labor figure who believed in repudiating loans in a time of economic crisis. His victory would give added weight to extremists in federal caucus, in crisis over monetary policy. Lang's extremist behaviour over monetary matters would split Labor and eventually provoke a constitutional crisis in New South Wales, in May 1932, leaving State governor Sir Philip Game no option but to dismiss him as premier.

In August 1930, Sir Otto Niemeyer of the Bank of England had arrived, invited by Sir Robert Gibson, Chairman of the Commonwealth Bank, to advise Australian governments on financial policy during the global economic crisis, or Depression. Government spending and wages must be reduced. A special premiers' conference, held in Melbourne that August, decided on economic measures to handle the crisis.

Between 1921 and 1931, the Commonwealth and State governments had borrowed some £624 million, described in *The House of Were* as a "reckless course of public finance". The Melbourne premiers' meeting devised the Premiers' Plan or Melbourne Agreement, reaching consensus that, among other measures such as increased taxation and conversion of loans to bonds at lesser interest, governments across Australia would cut "adjustable expenditure" by 20 per cent to reduce the price of imports and encourage trade. There was an outcry from the unions. In caucus, heated confrontation over Lyons' slightly more moderate proposals for balancing the budget by reducing government spending, public service wages and possibly pensions, led to Ted Theodore offering a program involving additional government spending. Caucus chose Theodore's plan and, in October, forced Lyons to seek extensive credit from the Commonwealth Bank for public works. Monetary hard head Robert Gibson, a dour Scot, refused the request.

Lyons was not an economist but his success as Tasmania's premier and treasurer at a time of budgetary difficulties from 1923 gave him an edge in financial matters with his Labor colleagues. He was in many ways at sea over what exactly was the cause of the international financial collapse but, as Philip Hart has pointed out, "was more willing than most other Labor members to heed the advice of economists and businessmen". Here Lyons counted on the intellectual back up of men he valued and trusted such as Lynhurst Giblin, formerly Tasmania's statistician, and Professor Douglas Copland who had advised Tasmanian governments.

Around this time, Lyons would also come into contact with a young Robert Menzies, a rising Nationalist in the Victorian parliament and a strong supporter of orthodoxy in economic management. He was also a close associate of Staniforth Ricketson, a stockbroker with J B Were and Sons, who had known Joe Lyons in northern Tasmania when reporting for the *North Western Advocate and Emu Bay Times* from 1910-11. Ricketson later had brief contact with Joe Lyons when Joe was premier of Tasmania, no doubt while pursuing contacts for business at a time of increased government borrowing and opportunities for companies like JB Were.

Scullin's absence for five months in London, as John Molony describes it in Michelle Grattan's *Australian Prime Ministers*, was "the most telling mistake of his short prime ministership". His one notable achievement in London was to stare down the King and get agreement that he could appoint Australia's first Australian born Governor General – Sir Isaac Isaacs. Scullin's telegrams from London protesting at various decisions of his party colleagues, including the appointment of E A McTiernan (causing a by-election in Sydney which would be won by the Nationalists) and H V Evatt to the High Court, appear to have been largely ignored. On finance, Lyons and Fenton had the numbers in Cabinet, but were outvoted by the parliamentary party in caucus.

As Enid eagerly awaited each day's newspapers, she remained in Devonport with not even phone contact with Joe for long weeks. Few of their letters from this time have survived. Joe badly missed Enid's company and support throughout the government turmoil of these months. Warren Denning, a member of the Canberra Press Gallery at the time, recollected the mayhem and uproar among Labor members in his *Caucus Crisis: The Rise and Fall of The Scullin Government* writing, "So terrific became the tumult at times that all Parliament House was aware of it, although there were double and padded doors separating the party room from the lobbies." Joe wrote to Enid in October, "I suppose I'm in for a strenuous day or two … We expect a wire from Scullin tomorrow as to what he supports. If he is with us the majority in Cabinet is set, if he isn't I'm getting out … I've been terribly blue lately and I wish I could lay my head in your lap." The cable from Scullin had arrived that night supporting Lyons, but within days the struggle with the left in caucus began again. Joe was close to breaking point. Characteristically, as he had done so many years before in standing up to the Tasmanian Education Department, he was ready to walk if he could not effect change.

The turmoil among the Labor factions reached a climax in November. Backbencher John Curtin, who would be Labor leader in just five years, with Frank Anstey put a proposal to caucus that was accepted. They proposed that the government postpone, for twelve months, redemption of £28 million of Commonwealth bonds. Lyons was shocked – he would never countenance such a financially unsound move. He would leave a government that adopted Lang style repudiation. After another bitter caucus meeting, Lyons and Fenton said they would consider their positions. If Australia did not obey conventional financial obligations, it would be a pariah in international circles. Lyons also believed that reckless credit expansion would cause a financial collapse, much like that of Germany in 1922. He cabled Scullin in London for an umpire's decision, making it quite clear what he wanted to do, and left Canberra for Devonport, and Enid, while he waited on Scullin's reply.

Enid related how Joe had left the party room angry and white faced. And how he had, very soon after, left Parliament House to catch a train to Melbourne leaving many thinking he had resigned. His colleague Defence Minister Albert Green and a group of reporters followed him to the Canberra station and saw him off, still believing he had left the government. At Spencer Street station in Melbourne, the next morning, Lyons was mobbed by reporters as he got in a cab to the docks where he would catch the ferry to Tasmania. On board, he confirmed to reporters that he was awaiting his leader's reply from London and would resign if Scullin supported the Curtin resolution for repudiation of the loan.

In Burnie at 7.30 am, Enid met Joe when the ferry docked. She had driven there in the family car. "As he came down the gangway," Enid wrote, "the signs of strain showed plainly in his face and in his gait. He was infinitely weary, and he only had a few hours before once again he must be on the boat." But Joe's weariness lifted shortly after disembarking, when he received word from the mainland that Scullin had approved his action and denounced the Curtin-Anstey proposal. There would be no repudiation. Scullin went on to make a public statement saying, "The sufferings of the people are now acute. They would become more acute and more widespread if confidence is shaken in the government's honesty. ... The government will honour its obligations"

Joe and Enid spent one happy day together, talking for hours about their future, their options and the children. Leo Broinowski, political editor of the *Hobart Mercury*, and a reporter called on them. Broinowski would break confidences of the visit discussions in *The Sun* some months afterwards: "We were in the pleasant living room of the house at Devonport, Mrs Lyons holding a large tea-pot, children in the offing, and one of us said, 'Well Mrs Lyons, Joe has taken a big risk not only for himself but for you and the youngsters.' And she waved the large tea-pot – I feared she might throw it – and said (I wish I could reproduce her attitude and tone): 'If he had done anything else I should have been ashamed of him.'"

It was no simple gamble; Joe Lyons, with Enid in the background, was a formidable force. His stand against the populists in caucus would attract the attention of business leaders who sought courageous political leadership in economic hard times. But having staked his reputation on no repudiation of government debt, acting Treasurer Lyons now had to deliver. Back in Canberra, a day later, he and Fenton avoided caucus.

. Joe and Enid had entered a significant crossroads in their Labor affiliations. As Enid admitted, over some years Joe's earlier radical views had moderated. He had gone from being a republican to supporting the monarchy and they had cancelled their subscription to the AWU's journal *The Australian Worker* when Enid had thought it too full of recriminations and "class hatred" for the children to absorb. With a precociously clever child like Desmond in the house, they perhaps had good reason.

In Tasmania, Joe Lyons had been able to run a pragmatic line with his Labor colleagues and survive because of the vulnerability of that small state. Its economic difficulties forced Labor radicals into a back seat, again and again, at election time. Labor in Tasmania was a pale imitation of its mainland counterparts when it came to ideology. In 1930, the turmoil Labor encountered was largely the result of a significant section of the party strongly locked into socialist theories while having no idea how vulnerable Australia was to economic collapse which would explode those theories in a moment. In 1931, Warren Denning, a Labor sympathiser, believed that if only the party had better managed its members, had not suffered the loss of Ted Theodore at a crucial moment, had been able to accommodate the positions of Anstey and Curtin on the loans, or had a majority in the Senate, then it would have governed well and not lost office so quickly. In all of this, there is no recognition that financial markets cannot be handled by mere command. Curtin and Anstey, left to their beliefs, would have brought on a disaster.

Joe Lyons may not have been an economic whiz kid but he knew that much.

The best published accounts of Joe Lyons' move from Labor to non Labor is found in Allan Martin's *Robert Menzies – A Life* and in Anne Henderson's *Joseph Lyons – The People's Prime Minister*. Both capture the significance of the loan conversion campaign, as Martin puts it, "a seemingly quixotic enterprise at a time of such deep depression", and in what followed for both Labor and the conservatives.

Joe Lyons had vowed Australia would not default on the debt repayment of £28 million, due in late December. He was strongly supported by Enid who gave him the stamina to go on, regardless of the gamble he was taking. The loan conversion was to be a breathtaking achievement. "In his much publicised struggle with caucus," writes Martin, "Lyons had won the favour of financiers, businessmen and prominent conservative politicians." And, to raise the money, or float, for the conversion, Lyons needed help from such financial players. He had one very important contact in Staniforth Ricketson who was a close friend of Robert Menzies, already making his mark and leading the Young Nationalists Organisation. Menzies supported financial orthodoxy in many a heated debate. Ricketson and Menzies would strategise the conversion campaign – with the persuasive and likeable Joe Lyons speaking at rallies and moving from city to city asking Australians to invest in their nation. They were joined by three others – Charles Norris, CEO of the National Mutual Life Association and a friend of Ricketson, Sir John Higgins, a retired Chair of the British and Australian Wool Realisation Association, and Ambrose Pratt who was a prominent but retired journalist with business connections and also a good friend of Menzies.

These men, "the Group", formed what Pratt would later describe as a "special bodyguard" for Lyons in the campaign. They would be joined by Kingsley Henderson, a leading Melbourne architect and friend of Pratt and Ricketson, in mid 1931 when the United

Australia Party was evolving and become known as the "Group of Six". Whether he admitted it or not, by December 1930, Lyons was moving among an opposing camp; nominally he was still Labor but increasingly his followers and associates were the men of capital with silver plated Nationalist credentials. It wasn't a thought out plan, but emotionally and intellectually Lyons no longer considered himself governed by Labor's so-called bottom-up workingman's principles. He was more and more fixed on the belief that, like any household, an economy which was not solvent and thus which could not function in the interests of its citizens was the greatest risk in the long run for ordinary Australians and their living standards.

The loan conversion was brilliantly run, and much like any modern day successful fund raising campaign. The spin of its message aimed to raise average Australian feelings to support the campaign as a patriotic move, to save Australia from disgrace and financial ruin. Across Australia, business was aroused to the call. Ricketson's *JB Were and Sons Weekly Share Market Letter* urged clients to over-subscribe the loan.

Advertisements went into daily newspapers; one from the Group in *The Argus* was called "Message to All Who Wish Australia well". In Melbourne, the Young Nationalists held open air meetings insisting it was a "non-political" campaign. There were crowded midday meetings in the Town Hall, and at one Joe Lyons spoke alongside a Nationalist named William Watt giving the non partisan message of the campaign full exposure. Businessmen bought bonds for their employees, paid back with deductions from future pay packets, banks and finance companies offered advances on risky terms while other individuals re-invested their savings. Friday 12 December, the day the loan closed, was popularly named "All For Australia Day" and Lyons called on everyone to do their "Christmas shopping" on that day. The campaign, of a few short weeks, became a giant national appeal. In the end the loan conversion was oversubscribed by £2 million.

It was a joyful 1930 yuletide at Home Hill. Exhausted, Joe was back with the family. Enid was proud of him "beyond words, and of his courage, of his honesty of mind". There had been some protest, but the overwhelming result had raised Joe's image to saviour of his country. He believed he now deserved to be offered the Treasurer's job but Enid was doubtful of any such move. Around this time she lunched with Joe and Sir Keith Murdoch in Melbourne, where Murdoch spoke confidently of Joe assuming the role of Labor Treasurer. Enid had disagreed, opining that Joe was too unpopular with the radical wing of the party and that Scullin not only had a high regard for Theodore's abilities but also thought his reappointment as Treasurer would hold the party together.

Enid was as right about who would be Treasurer as Scullin was wrong about Theodore's influence with the radicals. In late January, Scullin reinstated Theodore, even though he had still not been cleared of the charges forcing his earlier resignation. This set in train a series of events which would see Labor in disarray well before the end of 1931.

According to Enid, Joe was not particularly fussed by whether Scullin would make him Treasurer or not on his return to Australia. But Joe's disquiet with Labor continued. Joe and Enid crossed Bass Strait on the *Loongana* on Saturday night, 10 January. Joe met with his Prime Minister the following Monday to report on his portfolio while the PM had been away. Scullin relieved Joe of the Treasury portfolio. A day later, it was announced that Joe would be returning to Tasmania for a week's holiday with his family. It was the January summer holidays and no doubt a good time for a spell with the children. Still, it led to speculation that Joe was not happy with Scullin's decision to relieve him of Treasury. At a dinner in Devonport a week before, Tasmanian Labor had showered Joe with congratulations on his successful loan conversion campaign. At home he was a hero, he thought, if not with his mainland colleagues.

Late on Monday 26 January, caucus voted Theodore back into Cabinet; he was then reinstated as Treasurer. The same day, a report got through from the Mawson expedition to the Antarctic of how they had encountered intense fog and snow and a day long gloomy darkness; within a month, Dame Nellie Melba would die from ongoing complications after a face lift done in Europe in 1929. Both were harbingers of the risks of experiment in seemingly modern times. Joe's idea of just where he stood politically was cloudy. He was a member of the Labor Cabinet and yet in December 1930, at the height of the loan conversion, he asked caucus to vote on Nationalist leader John Latham's proposal for a non partisan government of all parties to handle the financial crisis. It was a proposal from the enemy and caucus strongly voted it down. Such a move by Joe indicated how non-partisan he had become. To Labor colleagues, he had forgotten his roots. Understandable, but also a half-way move to another loyalty for Lyons.

Events moved swiftly. After the caucus vote to reinstate Theodore, Joe returned to Devonport saying he would not make a decision on his future until he had been home. Yet again, it was Enid who would be his guide. Without her resolve and strong support at Joe's back, he may not have gone through with his resolve to leave Labor and cross to the other side. Instead he may simply have left politics altogether. Having such a large family to support also forced him on, although this had mixed effects. While he knew he must earn sufficient income to support his family, more importantly he felt it also his duty to secure his children's and the nation's future by doing whatever he could to stop financial mismanagement. By the end of January, Lyons had resigned from Cabinet, arguing that to make Theodore treasurer, while still under investigation and siding with much of the radical agenda in caucus, was a "grave political error". Lyons had cabled Fenton in Merricks, Victoria, of his intentions. From February 1931 until the election later that year, Joe Lyons moved as if he had become a man caught by destiny, and pulled by circumstances.

Australia was in a state of political flux. Government was floundering in the economic storm, while ordinary and not so ordinary Australian investors, business operatives and their families were dismayed at the information they were hearing. As will happen in democratic communities in times of stress, the populace was ready to take its own measures.

By the beginning of 1931, a grass roots movement of concerned citizens was well underway in the southern states, backed by advertising and funded by business. The Citizens' League of South Australia had 30,000 members by the end of 1930 and 130,000 within another six months. The All For Australia League in New South Wales and a Citizens League in Victoria followed. These loosely aligned groups were non partisan but steady in their resolve for responsible action to handle the financial crisis. With Labor reverting to inflationary measures under Theodore, the Citizens Leagues were ripe for a leader like Joe Lyons In Melbourne, Ricketson helped set up the Victorian Citizens League in February 1931, after a "Monster Mass Meeting" in the Town Hall. The group had 80,000 members by May when it held its first State convention. This overlap of business funding with a mass organisation of politically active citizens outside government was remarkable.

Theodore's proposals for a moderate increase in government spending disturbed Joe; he was fixed in a belief that any expansion would signal dire inflation. In Melbourne in February to hand over his portfolio, Joe met with "the Group" in the JB Were offices. They asked him to leave Labor and bring over any disaffected Labor members to form a coalition government with the Nationalists. Joe said he needed to consult Enid and returned to Devonport with no agreement. He was ready to split with Labor, but this would be throwing away twenty years of his life.

Enid had never been as locked into Labor Party politics as Joe had. Explaining this much later, she described herself as being "by nature a nonconformist" and too like her mother "to sink my independence of thought in a mass of common acceptance". But it wasn't easy for Joe. Enid wrote: "To those who have never belonged to the Australian Labor Party, an understanding of the mind of a man in public office who contemplates leaving it is impossible." Labor's tribal nature governed then as now. At the 25 February Tasmanian State conference, Joe would suffer a bitter Ogilvie led vote against him for not obeying caucus.

James Fenton resigned following a party meeting on 2 March when caucus had agreed to Theodore's £18 million fiduciary note issue, an inflationary measure. Lyons prevaricated but realised he did not have the numbers to vote down Scullin's policy and so finally joined Fenton, walking away from Labor on 13 March, after rousing words in parliament. Ambrose Pratt had prepared a speech for Joe but it arrived too late to be used.

It would be an all night sitting, James Fenton speaking at 4 am. Joe delivered a speech from his soul. He attacked Theodore and his proposals, so pointedly it was clear a personal animosity had grown between the two men. He accused the Treasurer of attempting to undermine him while Joe was acting treasurer and added that he no longer had any faith in the Scullin leadership. With rising emotion he said he was prepared to resign his seat of Wilmot that day and challenged Scullin and Theodore to stand for it, a seat he had held by only 1200 votes in 1929. In heart grabbing words, Joe spoke of the many thousands across the nation suffering while politicians and public servants drew their salaries: "I speak as one who has kiddies of his own. I would not like to see them suffer as are thousands of other kiddies in Australia today, while we are talking about these visionary schemes." The speech was pure Lyons – a style Enid herself had mastered. As the bells rang for a vote on Theodore's note issue, Joe and his followers crossed to the other side of the House to vote with John Latham's Nationalists and the Country Party.

At this point, Lyons was merely coalitioning with the Nationalists at the head of an independent group. The breakaway Laborites were James Fenton, Allan Guy, John Price, Joel Gabb and David McGrath. Meanwhile, the Lang Laborites were sucking MPs from Scullin at the other extreme. But Lyons was by now too large a public figure to leave on the sidelines. Henry Gullett, a conservative colleague, would later describe the emotion of that day: "That dramatic and overwhelming speech had instant and far-reaching consequences … Until Mr Lyons electrified the House that morning there was honest doubt that he was qualified for national leadership. But the speech settled all doubts."

Joe immediately made his way to meet Enid at Spencer Street Station in Melbourne. As she approached the train, she recognised the wife of a Labor minister who had always been friendly. The woman saw Enid and turned away with what Enid described as a "haughty movement of the head". Only then did the full impact of Joe's decision become clear. In Labor circles, regardless of his achievements as a Labor member and leader, Joe had joined Billy Hughes in the gallery of "Labor rats". It was a hurt that Enid would not bear easily. Yet this was not how it seemed in the popular press that day. Such recriminations would be buried in the acclaim sweeping the nation. Joe stepped from the train not only to Enid's proud and loving welcome, but also into a large cheering crowd. The Lyons phenomenon had begun.

Enid and Joe Lyons as the nation's first couple.

158

CHAPTER 12

ALL FOR AUSTRALIA

Dockside in Melbourne, the *Nairana*'s captain had held his steamer for Joe Lyons on the Monday evening following his defection from Labor. But only Enid came aboard. Joe had suddenly taken the express to Sydney, alighting in Goulburn and going on to Canberra where he met Nationalist leader John Latham at the station. The two men left the platform deep in conversation. After discussions with the opposition, Joe and Allan Guy returned to Tasmania the following Wednesday.

The political plates were slipping again. Realignments were needed to satisfy the voters. A group of Melbourne businessmen had heard the cry. But it would take weeks for all players to recognise what could be done. Enid was one of those who saw it early.

What followed in the next seven weeks, from mid March to early May, was as breathtaking as it was bold. Australia would not see its like again, certainly not in the first century of federation. In moves as secret as they were successful, a handful of political and business operatives transformed the conservative side of politics and, with it, the course of Australia's history. In the 1980s, Liberal John Elliott would try to snatch the Liberal leadership from beyond parliament; he failed. Queensland premier Joh Bjelke Petersen thought he could win control of the Liberal National Coalition in a popular bid for Canberra; he failed also. But in 1931 key figures in the Nationalist machine working with Staniforth Ricketson's "Group", which included

Robert Menzies and was in touch with Keith Murdoch, successfully reinvented the Nationalist Party as the United Australia Party, with former Labor premier and federal cabinet minister Joe Lyons as its leader. In doing so, they tapped into some of the strongest veins running in the body politic.

Popular and honest Joe Lyons aroused a deep and emotional following. He talked of prudent financial management from humble experience, as the self made man from a worker's background. He had a home spun wit at the podium which engaged ordinary voters and he was a deft hand at electioneering.

All of this Enid herself had absorbed, a powerful ally by Joe's side. He was never far from the everyday lives of those he addressed. At one crowded meeting, he urged a mother with a crying baby not to leave saying he was used to that at home. And although he'd been many years in the political trenches, he brought with him a young and pretty wife, by then the mother of nine children, who had once stood for parliament herself and nearly won a seat. A phenomenon in itself. And she was an accomplished public speaker who could draw out the emotions of a crowd, from twenty to thousands, within minutes, touching mothers, even fathers.

There was more. While Australia had elected its first Catholic prime minister in Jim Scullin, he was Labor where the Catholic vote until then had largely rested. No surprises here. But for the conservative and Anglophile side of politics, in particular the men of gentlemen's clubs in Melbourne, to anoint as their leader Catholic Joe Lyons, late of the Labor Party, this was indeed a revolution in Australian politics. It would prove a brilliant election winning move. At the 1931 election, Catholics had a choice between Labor's Catholic Jim Scullin and the UAP's ex-Labor Catholic Joe Lyons.

Melbourne's Catholic Archbishop Daniel Mannix did not give his vote to Joe Lyons, arguing that he would not be voting for "sectarians" (code for conservatives) but, as historian Michael

Hogan concluded in *The Sectarian Strand*, at the 1931 federal election which took Joe and Enid Lyons to The Lodge: "Not surprisingly, the total ALP vote fell to an almost catastrophic 27 per cent, compared with the 49 per cent of the first preference vote which had elected Scullin in 1929."

While Labor would win back much of its middle class Catholic voters in the 1940s, Catholic Joe Lyons' leadership of the UAP stole an election winning advantage for the conservatives through most of the 1930s. From then on, the Catholic vote was up for grabs at every election. Lyons did not need to parade his Catholicism; one only had to see the size of his family and hear his wife, albeit a convert, to know where the Lyons family stood.

Enid does not dwell in her recollections on Joe's gradual acceptance of his new role as leader of a conservative force. By March, she was ready to jump but for some time Joe was not sure what he was ready to accept. For a time, he thought he might form his own party from more disaffected Labor MPs abandoning Scullin and Theodore. It didn't happen. When the new opposition party developed by the Group took shape, Enid tells of how Joe was at first staggered by the task before him as its leader, believing the highly educated John Latham more worthy of the role than he. It took the press and the crowds to convince him he was the one. "It's not for you," Enid told Joe. "Australia wants you." From Enid's description, never had one so unassuming taken the role of leading Australia.

Yet, there was another factor in Joe's reticence. He was turning his back on all Labor, an allegiance from the time of his political awakening in the first decade of Federation, and a strongly held one. This was not something Enid shared. Her affiliations to any organisation, with the exception of her church, were quite fluid. She would often say in later years that her social and political beliefs never altered whichever party she belonged to. She was always something of a Fabian, and able to argue the cause of the less well off or stand for her moral view regardless of her position on who was best to form government.

But Joe was very different. As a breakaway, he was one of a small band in parliament planning to abandon Labor irrevocably, just when mainstream Labor had become dangerously divided by its more extreme elements gathering around the eccentric and ambitious NSW premier Jack Lang. It was going to take time for his breakaway colleagues to accept that they would be happy being absorbed into a non-Labor party. Joel (Moses) Gabb would not follow Joe into the United Australia Party, although he had proclaimed Joe the hero of the hour, the man who would save Australia, when Lyons broke with Theodore. Enid describes how Joe, who so loathed the rancour and bitterness of caucus, in taking up the job of leader of the UAP would be required to sit opposite Labor's parliamentary benches each day facing "a concentration of contempt and hatred … vitriolic abuse and political slander as have seldom disfigured politics in Australia".

Labor was in turmoil. The election in March 1931 of Lang's candidate Eddie Ward in the East Sydney by-election unleashed the Langites in a bitter struggle with Scullin and Theodore in federal parliament. Ward was not welcome in caucus and the party was now split, leaving two Labor parties in New South Wales and on the Canberra parliamentary benches. By the end of March, Lang was refusing to pay NSW loans, due to the Westminster Bank, and expecting the federal government to pick up the tab. Around this time, Lyons issued a "Seven Point" policy platform, in fact written by the Nationalist executive but issued without their support so as not to alienate Joe's Labor colleagues whom he believed were not ready to be seen as part of the conservative opposition. By then, Lyons was also planning a tour of the nation, to take his message on financial management to the people. He often spoke of a new political party, but at this stage he had not thrown in his lot with Latham, merely had given his assurance he would support the Nationalists on the floor of the House.

Staniforth Ricketson, who more than any other acted as go-between in Lyons' defection, wrote to Lyons' biographer Philip Hart in March 1965 recollecting the vital meeting in the J B Were offices in Melbourne with Lyons and the "Group" – the meeting which convinced Joe he should move to a new conservative alliance. Ricketson had escorted Lyons and Bass MP Allan Guy from the Commercial Travellers Club up lanes connecting the Club and his office. In his letter Ricketson recalled, "Over the next twelve months, I had a close association with the Honourable J A Lyons, one of our then staff (Captain H T Lanyon – ex Duntroon graduate) being seconded to be a private secretary to Mr Lyons for most of that time."

This correspondence with Hart reveals that Ricketson believed Joe Lyons was "activated by the best and purest of motives" in his move to the conservatives, adding "any idea of self aggrandisement was completely absent from his mind". Ricketson took umbrage at Hart's contention that "some people – particularly in Tasmania – had referred to what they described as his treachery" adding, "I have never heard such a thought … and I think the people who hold that view can have very little appreciation of the situation which was here in Australia at the time when Lyons withdrew from the Labor Party". In a letter to Enid Lyons, Ricketson wrote of Hart having a "bee in his bonnet" that the Group had been acting under influence from the Nationalists or the press. "Nothing was further from the truth," he assured Dame Enid adding, "The idea [leading a new party] originated from those five men, and whereas I was the only one privileged to have a friendship with Joe, it was natural that I was used as a liaison with Joe to bring about a meeting with the Group."

Keith Murdoch was another hovering around the Group. Ricketson believed Murdoch "saw the opportunity to continue in the role of his erstwhile leader – Lord Northcliffe – and the role of kingmaker". At his Toorak mansion Heathfield, acquired from Clive Baillieu with its twenty-seven rooms and a dining room to seat twenty-four when

The Lodge in Canberra at the time only seated ten, Murdoch retained an influence. Staniforth Ricketson recalled Lyons dining there while he was pondering his next move after leaving Labor. Henry Gullett, a close friend of the Murdochs and a conservative MP, had joined them.

An undated letter to Joe Lyons from Murdoch around this time confirms the part played by Gullett and Menzies in the new conservative grouping that would soon unfold. On 16 April, Country Party leader Earle Page received a letter from Nationalist leader John Latham inviting the CP to join the proposed new single Opposition party. Until the Country Party declined that invitation, preferring to retain its autonomy, plans for a single opposition party took the Country Party into account. It appears that Lyons may have even suggested offering the inducement of Deputy Leader to Page. Murdoch, writing from Heathfield to Lyons in these weeks, advised that he had talked with Menzies "as promised" – with Gullett present. Murdoch reported to Lyons that Menzies "would accept Paterson [CP Deputy Leader] as No 2 but Page – No!" Murdoch surmised this may have been because of Menzies' own ambitions although he added, "I cannot get his final position – I doubt if he has one. ... but I will not believe that his views are due to personal ambition until such is proved."

During Lyons' April 1931 tour of the south eastern states, organised by the network of citizens groups mushrooming in capital cities and large regional towns, Joe Lyons was dependent on careful chaperoning by members of the Group who introduced him to significant business leaders and political strategists in Melbourne and Sydney. These same business leaders would later publicly back Lyons as the new conservative leader, giving him a boost with those who found it hard to accept a Labor man leading their party.

On the April tour, Joe and Enid would speak at huge League gatherings, from Adelaide to Sydney, conducted with the tenor of revivalist meetings. Joe had told Enid she was part of the touring team as much as any of them. Enid recalled, "To Joe it was unthinkable that it should be otherwise. He had tremendous faith in my powers of persuasion as a public speaker." Joe knew Enid's value in bringing over the female vote. Throughout his political career, he recognised the importance of women. He had used Enid before with great success and he knew she revelled in appearing on a platform, indeed was quite a performer. Using Enid's words he told her, "I need you, and Australia needs you too!"

This trip across southern Australia would be the start of the Lyons personality cult at the federal level. By year's end, Joe and Enid Lyons would have coasted into The Lodge on a mini tsunami of popular appeal born out of their combined talents at the podium, the unworkable divisions in Labor ranks which made it unfit to govern strongly at a time of national and international financial disaster, alongside a groundswell of organised citizen activity that would close over sectarian divides in a populist clamour demanding a government that could restore economic well being and save the ordinary Australian from both penury and inflation.

At times, Lyons came across as a non-party man, something of a non politician in his straddling of the two sides. A man who wanted national unity above all. His catch cry in the election campaign that November would be "Tune in with Britain" – taking up the fervour of middle Australia for a government devoid of party difference and national in its aspirations. Britons had just elected Labour Party defector Ramsay MacDonald as Prime Minister leading a group MPs from the major parties who had come together at a time of national economic crisis.

Bitter divisions had opened in the Australian community following the stock market crash. Growing lines of unemployed (thousands a week) inspired erratic, and to some very dangerous, theories of how to solve economic problems. Jack Lang in Sydney operated at one extreme, while armed militias were secretly grouping at the other, albeit with no armed action ever taking place. In such a climate of dysfunction and fear, advertisements in the press inspired by anti-socialist and patriotic emotion called for a "United Australia". They called for a new leadership, perhaps a new politics, to hold back Labor's inflationary urges and incompetent economic management. The nation was seen to need a "saviour". Joe Lyons would become just that, balancing his Labor appeal with prudent economic ideals and leaving conservative colleagues like John Latham to rally diehard conservatives to a unique new grouping.

After Joe and Enid arrived off the Bass Strait steamer on 8 April, Melbourne's *Argus* heralded the new personality cult with a report that although Mrs Lyons no longer had political aspirations of her own, she still took "a keen interest in politics". Never had the nation seen a political spouse like her.

Allan Guy and Jim Fenton accompanied Joe and Enid to Adelaide where, within an hour of arriving at the central station on 9 April, Joe would open a conference described by Keith Murdoch's evening *News* as "a huge crowd, representative of all classes of the community". Joe assured the crowd that "the country that had cradled the Anzacs never could lack confidence for long". An accompanying article was headed "Meet Mr and Mrs Lyons" and, in a style not common for the time, offered a personality piece introducing a remarkable couple:

> Meet Mr and Mrs Lyons – and half Mrs Lyons.
>
> "Only half of me is in Adelaide – the rest of me is with my babies at Devonport," she confided on arrival in Adelaide this morning. She did not worry that "Joe" was beginning the greatest campaign of his career, but she did worry that he had a headache.
>
> That is Mrs Lyons.

Cameras clicked and she was away. A long arm shot out. "Come back here my girl; you are the main one in this!"

That was Mr Lyons.

A modern political spin doctor could not have organised it better. The article gushed over Joe – emphasising his common touch. The nation could trust Joe Lyons and his amazing and most admirable wife.

In Adelaide, that same day, Enid and Joe addressed a women's rally at the Exhibition Hall, filled to overflowing in spite of its 6,500 capacity, then left by car to drive through the Adelaide Hills and address meetings at Algate, Ambleside, Mount Barker and finally Murray Bridge before boarding the train to Melbourne. They entered a compartment full of flowers, the start of many welcomes at stations and crowded halls, crowds of not only well organised League members but, as the mood grew, many ordinary Australians out to see this newsworthy couple. At the Melbourne Town Hall a few days later the crowd flowed out into Central Hall in Collins Street where people listened with the help of newly invented amplifiers. Similar meetings followed in Victoria's Ballarat, Numurkah, Cobram, Wycheproof and Nunawill. The slogan was "All for Australia".

Enid had become a whizz at what she called a political "game of bridge", where Joe was her partner – "I played to his lead and never, so far as I am aware, did I trump his ace!" Her ability to move an audience was extraordinary. Robert Menzies once said she could make him weep about the state of a railway track. In Ballarat, on 13 April, Enid used her housewife analogies which resonated often in her addresses over decades, such as the analogy of the housewives who, in difficult economic times, had to be content with a "shinbone" rather than "a succulent joint of meat":

"Who is the best financier in Australia?" Mrs Lyons asked. "Is it Mr Scullin? I think not. Is it Mr Theodore? Scarcely.

(laughter) Or is it Mr Lyons? Decidedly not. (renewed laughter) It is the mother of a family. If a woman raises a family on a small wage – a wage that many a young man spends entirely on himself – she is engaged in high finance! (applause) The essence of the science of finance is to pay your way, and we women understand that, and I look to the women to be experts in the crisis confronting us today."

She made teasing references to Joe's small defects, "You've heard how good my husband is with the millions! I wish he was as good with the single pounds!" In Ballarat she confided in the audience, relating Joe's personal reasons for leaving Labor: "He worried for weeks and months ... Then one day he said to me, 'Look my girl, we have no money, and I suppose we never will have any; but we have our children ... They are going to live in Australia when you and I are no longer here and, by heaven, I am not going to allow anyone to ruin Australia if I can lift a finger to prevent it.'"

It was all a well spun message – but also deeply felt by the Lyons couple. They had found a moment in history when their own lives and personalities reflected back to ordinary Australians the hopes and aspirations of millions. But while Joe had the political breadth never to feel himself in Enid's shadow, there were some who felt her appeal might draw attention from Joe as leader. It was Robert Menzies, with his wife Pattie far more traditional in her role, who suggested that when the Lyons couple made it to Sydney Enid should only "pronounce the benediction" or closing few words rather than give a speech. In her memoirs, Enid is considerate of Menzies' judgement in this, but manages a characteristic Enid comeback writing how she pronounced the benediction to the large Sydney audience, but added a few patriotic lines for good measure, only to have a voice in the audience with an Irish accent shout, "You are Queen of Australia!" after which, she recalled, the crowd "went wild".

In this atmosphere, Nationalist leader John Latham, agreed to step down for Joe Lyons. Enid would write to Latham, in May 1951, telling him of her admiration for what he had done: "You held Joe's admiration and regard in a way unique in his life. When the time came that you stood aside for him to take your place as leader, he suffered real anguish of mind and I think would not have consented to such a course had I also not joined those who put it to him that circumstances had already decided the issue if he was not prepared to refuse a duty and a responsibility which he found so greatly against his desire."

By 7 May, the United Australia Party had been formally declared, bringing together most of Joe Lyons' breakaway Labor MPs and the Nationalists. John Latham had agreed to step down as party leader in favour of Joe Lyons and take the Deputy Leader position for the sake of unity. He swallowed his bitterness at the time and would be remembered well for it. He would be a minister in the Lyons Government and also Chief Justice of the High Court.

The Lyons couple was on a roll – and it would last for most of the coming decade – what Mary Pridmore, one of their grand daughters, much later would refer to as a "heady broth". Through it, Enid would grow mightily in public stature; out of it she would emerge as a personality in her own right, the girl from Burnie and mother of twelve who, alongside entering the hearts of a nation, would dine with the king and queen as a guest of honour, befriend Neville and Anne Chamberlain and gain the affection of Franklin and Eleanor Roosevelt.

All of April 1931, Enid had been batting above her average. On the eve of the Lyons' eastern states tour, Enid found she was again pregnant. Her feelings of nausea had raised her suspicions. But the doctor had encouraged her to go on tour, nonetheless. As usual, nervous energy and excitement helped Enid muster buried stamina in the face of physical discomfort.

As the coalition of Nationalist and Labor breakaway forces evolved into a new party, Joe informed Enid that it was again time for them to make Melbourne their base. The older children, and those "babies" she fretted for while on tour, would once again have to leave Home Hill while their parents bowed to the political agenda.

Enid packed up the house, left Desmond, Sheila, Enid, Kathleen, Moira and Kevin at boarding schools in Tasmania and relocated to a flat in Melbourne with Brendan, Barry and Rosemary. Within a short while they had moved to a furnished house at 150 Barkers Road, Kew, across the road from Xavier College. Peter, their eleventh child, was born in Melbourne that September. A month after his birth, the Burnie *Advocate* reported that Joe and Enid had taken Peter across Bass Strait for the first time in an old fashioned dress-basket. After they came aboard, Joe told *Nairana's* captain John McIntyre that they were taking the little chap to "the home of his ancestors" and Enid called over her shoulder as they went below to their cabin that "it is wrong to handle babies much, you know. Carrying them in a basket is much better". Enid had picked up this priceless piece of advice from New Zealand's Dr Frederick Truby King. His writings had dictated radical methods over decades. This may also explain Enid's ease at handing her babies over to others whenever public life called.

As the year wore on, federal parliament grappled with divided Labor ranks and four separate parties haggling in the House. At one point, there was even a suggestion of forming a national government to get through the crisis. In late August, British Labour's Ramsay MacDonald and a number of senior Labour colleagues had split with their party to form a National Government with conservative opponents. The UAP would use this precedent in their election advertising during the election campaign.

Whatever misgivings he might have at times felt over his Labor roots, the United Australia Party was now Joe's reality; there was no going back. To the end of his life he remained convinced he had made the only move his conscience allowed him. Lyons did hate having to face those he had deserted, whatever his principles. While able to wear decades of political intrigue and backbiting, Joe Lyons never relished it like some at the top. The stress of it in the late 1930s would eventually kill him. From 1931, Labor would start its campaign against Lyons and seven decades on there would still be those who on hearing Lyons' name would simply sneer – "Labor rat". Mary O'Byrne (nee Sullivan), a close friend of Rosemary Lyons when a boarder in the 1940s at Sacre Coeur, Melbourne, recalled that her father, who had businesses in Deloraine before moving to Launceston, had been one of Joe Lyons' most generous financial supporters when he was Labor Member for Wilmot. Sullivan cut Joe off after his defection to the UAP. And so the Labor dirt mill began. In Canberra, rumours began to circulate – from Joe being hopeless in parliament to the idea he was merely a puppet of big business and would soon be pushed aside if the party took office.

Wanting Enid closer to him in Melbourne was no doubt partly because of Joe's isolation from his long time colleagues, even if he was the hero of the day to millions of unknown citizens. At one rally in Sydney they had addressed a crowd of 12,000 adoring fans. The move might also have been to get Enid away from Tasmania where there was so much ill feeling from old friends towards the member for Wilmot. Enid was too caught up with family matters to do much to help Joe day by day, but she did register her feelings against his detractors in her writings much later.

On Wednesday 25 November, in a vote of no-confidence, Lang Labor voted with the conservative opposition parties and brought down the Scullin administration. The next day, prices rose on the stock market. On 26 November, Scullin announced that a federal election for both houses of parliament would be held on 19 December – the third federal election in three years with a campaign of just over three weeks, the shortest ever. Labor strategists believed a short campaign would prevented Jack Lang from resigning as NSW premier and contesting a safe seat. Former prime minister Stanley Bruce, who had re-nominated for his old seat of Flinders was in London doing business. The UAP would take government in such a landslide that Bruce would win Flinders, *in absentia* and by 31,000 votes, and Lyons would have an overall majority and be able to govern without the Country Party.

Enid was still recovering from Peter's birth when the election was called and admitted to being more interested in preparing to take her younger children to Tasmania to join their older brothers and sisters for the Christmas holidays than take part in the campaign. But when Jim Fenton asked her to speak at his opening meeting she felt unable to refuse. He had been a true ally of Joe throughout the defection and even before that with the tensions in caucus over the loan conversion in Scullin's absence the year before. And Enid believed Jim Fenton had not been given the credit due him for the part he had played in the formation of the UAP.

Fenton held the seat of Maribyrnong, a heavily industrial area of Melbourne and a Labor heartland. Jim Fenton would have been worried he could lose such a seat by standing as a UAP candidate. Enid must have realised she would be walking into a hostile crowd the night she addressed that opening meeting – her courage in this should not be underestimated. She was certainly her mother's daughter when it came to fearlessness.

Enid recalled: "As our party walked on to the stage, such a din of hooting, cat-calls, shouted insults, football whistles and counting out broke forth that throughout the entire evening, except for the space of three drama-laden minutes, no single voice could make itself intelligible beyond a radius of a few feet." In the din, she heard cries of "traitor" and "rat". Fenton battled against it for thirty minutes – with no microphone or amplifier. It was the same for a local committee man who followed him. Then Fenton came across to Enid and, apologising, asked would she try – "they might listen to a lady" was his reasoning. She lasted five minutes against a jeering crowd: "Get back to your kids"; "Get back to Tasmania".

Eventually the meeting broke up in extraordinary circumstances which no one could have predicted. A local man, of Jewish background, named Sergeant Issy Smith VC, had appeared on a seat next to Enid. He was appalled by the crowd but thought he could manage them, many of whom he knew. Yet it was no different when Smith took the stage until a man in the audience raised his hand and stood long enough to have the audience quieten and listen. The man asked Sergeant Issy Smith VC, in a voice that rang out, "Who killed Christ?" Enid recalled that a shock of silence took over until Sergeant Smith found his comeback: "Well if you're a fair specimen of a Christian, thank god I'm a Jew." The meeting broke up immediately.

Looking back, Enid Lyons could see that the Fenton campaign meeting captured much of the ugliness of a year. Tribal loyalties in many had blurred their good sense. Beyond it, the majority of ordinary Australians wanted closure. Enid played only a small part in the 1931 election campaign. Joe toured the eastern states endlessly while Enid stayed for the first fortnight in Melbourne before taking the five youngest children back to Tasmania with Joe on 7 December as he travelled south to campaign for a couple of days in Bass and Wilmot. They kept the lease on their Melbourne house in Barkers Road until 1932.

Joe and Enid were photographed for the Burnie *Advocate* leaving the *Nairana* in Burnie, and a lead article proclaimed the visit of "A leader and his helpmate". They had become, yet again, northern Tasmania's darling couple. Joe had joked that his cabin was "Number 13". A photo in the Burnie *Advocate* on 16 December, had Enid speaking at an election meeting in Melbourne. This suggests she had done some mainland campaigning and was not nearly as cut off from events as she herself suggests in *So We Take Comfort*. Nor was she as lonely and far from Joe as Kate White pictures her in *A Political Love*

Story. Enid was a consummate traveller; the idea that she waited by the kitchen sink or sitting room window, week after week, for Joe to return was never a reality. They did endure many separations, but mostly as a result of Enid's frequent illnesses and times when she was hospitalised in Tasmania or Melbourne. For all that, Enid was no drover's wife.

The 1931 election was the first where Australians heard campaign broadcasts on radio, a medium Joe and Enid Lyons used brilliantly in the years that followed. Lyons made his final message to Australia in the election from the studio of 2UW in Sydney on Thursday 17 December. He was already using any means of transport he could muster to make appearances as often and wherever he could. At one stage, on Sydney Harbour a couple of days before polling day, Lyons used a speed boat, according to newspaper reports, to dash from the Cremorne wharf to arrive at the Man-o'-War steps below Government House in just two minutes saying on arrival that he preferred the exhilarating experience in the boat to his flight from Adelaide, which had been rough, the Tuesday before.

The campaign took its toll. By the final week, Joe was losing his voice and as throngs of people greeted him at railway stations and the like he was forced to preserve his voice for more formal meetings. By 16 December, he was quite exhausted with some reports that he might have to cancel some engagements. He refused.

In 1931, Joe Lyons and the UAP fought the first modern election campaign in Australia. It was impossible to get as far as Western Australia or Queensland in such a short campaign, but Joe Lyons made scores of meetings to all other states and was available almost twenty-four hours, in person or on the airwaves and in print. He could meet a deadline between states with, on rare occasions, the use of aircraft. When public transport failed, he had used other private vehicles. Early in the campaign, he ended a speech at an Albury venue and was on stage in Wodonga within half an hour. Here, when asked if he was Labor or Nationalist, he shot back with, "My hope is that I will be returned to power to set in operation a policy which will put the jobless back into jobs and so prove me a better Labor man than anyone in the Ministry which so far from putting men into jobs has actually forced them out of jobs." (loud applause)

For three weeks, his family barely saw him. Enid listened to the radio and read the daily papers, monitoring the acclaim Joe was receiving from his public meetings. While she remained in Melbourne, they could talk by phone. She wrote later that the 1931 campaign took her husband "to the edge of utter exhaustion".

The votes came in. It was a triumph. Even Jim Fenton had won the hard bitten Labor stronghold of Maribyrnong. Enid welcomed Joe home to Devonport – once again, while not actually living inside the electorate of Wilmot, he had held it easily. As Christmas approached family and friends were around them, unbelievably joyous. Joe had to dash back to the mainland for meetings to put in place the myriad of matters for government. Meanwhile, press, photographers and well wishers besieged them. Joe would not arrive home for Christmas until the morning of 25 December, exhausted by the campaign but high on the adrenalin of his win. On Boxing Day, he was off visiting the Latrobe Carnival and on 28 December he opened the Latrobe aerodrome before leaving on 29 December from Launceston, on the *Nairana*, for more meetings over his ministry and government.

Enid and the older children returned to Melbourne on the *Loongana* on Saturday night, 2 January, to spend time in the rented house at Barkers Road. Enid had seen a chance for a brief holiday before they had to give up the house and the children return to boarding school. Interviewed for the *Advocate*, she spoke of The Lodge as too small for the entire family to live there. And there was no way she would allow "ten noisy young people" to disrupt Joe's need for some peace away from his political duties. The younger children would join their parents at The Lodge, while the older children would continue to board during school terms. Tasmania and Home Hill were there for holidays. On 8 January, Home Hill was only narrowly saved from a bush fire that set alight some of the pine trees on its western boundary.

Meanwhile, in Canberra, it was reported that The Lodge was being made ready to be a home again, freshened up for whoever among the Lyons family would reside there. The Tasmanian ash panels on the walls of its large welcoming vestibule gave off a new sheen as staff and workmen hummed about the building. Weeds were being chipped away from the grounds and coats of paint applied where necessary. Renovations were also being made to the verandah over the entrance to the six bedroomed Lodge; it would be closed in to make a large nursery for the Lyons children. Pattie Menzies would return the verandah to its original condition when the Menzies family took over The Lodge in 1939.

Joe Lyons was sworn in as Prime Minister of Australia on 6 January 1932. He immediately wrote to Enid words that are now legendary:

> My first act as Prime Minister is to write to you, because whatever honours and distinctions come are ours not mine. Girl, we have seen some changes and we've lived full lives in our years of married life and it is grand to know that our love for each other is still our most cherished and valued possession. It has grown sweeter and more beautiful with the years and with God's help it will still go on increasing as the years come and go …
>
> "It has been a great day for me but I would be happier on the hill with you and all the children … Give my love to them all and kiss the little ones especially for me. Tell them how I love them. I'm longing for the time when you will be here with me.

CHAPTER 13

FIRST LADY

Canberra welcomed its new first lady to the official residence on 11 February 1932. A photo in the *Daily Telegraph* showed Joe and Enid and their four youngest children arriving by car at the front of The Lodge and being greeted by the wife of Joe's private secretary Martyn Threlfall. Joe in a hat is carrying Barry, as he so often did in photos, Brendan is standing in front of Joe with his hands on Rosemary's shoulders and Enid is carrying baby Peter. The rest of the family is at boarding school. A week later, on Wednesday 17 February, the first parliamentary sitting of the Lyons Government was opened by Governor General Isaac Isaacs.

In 1932, Canberra was a scattered small settlement in the midst of nowhere in particular with a population of just over 9000. Surrounded by rural estates, it was not uncommon for stock being driven to the abattoirs at nearby Queanbeyan to stray into Canberra's civic centre. Barry, Brendan and Peter Lyons, and their cousins Carmel and Lynette Lyons, recall the white two storey, slate roofed Georgian style home known as The Lodge as not unlike a large country house looking out over sloping lawns and paddocks beyond. As they played in the grounds, they would watch out for occasional buses of tourists driving up to view the prime minister's "Lodge". According to Sheila Lyons, there were more sheep than people in Canberra when her parents lived there.

Chosen as a compromise location between the major capital

cities of Sydney and Melbourne, federal MPs had only sat in the federal houses of parliament (now what is known as "old Parliament House") since May 1927. A highway from Goulburn to Canberra had finally been completed in 1931, giving jobs to many of the nation's unemployed and making road travel an alternative to train journeys into the nation's capital. The Depression years slowed Canberra's massive building works program so while the Lyons family brought life back to The Lodge, they took up residence at a time of stagnation for the national capital. Robert Menzies, commenting on the Canberra he found on entering federal politics in 1934, spoke of it as a "place of exile".

For some years, since Stanley and Ethel Bruce, The Lodge or official residence had been closed. Jim Scullin had saved on costs by taking a room at the Kurrajong Hotel and his wife had remained in Melbourne. So it was with a sense of excitement that Canberra residents welcomed the lively and noteworthy Mrs Lyons. Enid Lyons was a curiosity piece – the mother of ten and just thirty-five, but a woman who could hold an audience from two to thousands in thrall. And while very heavily built ("I weighed more than my husband!" she once recalled of that time) and could seem overly dowdy in photos ("my hair too long, my hats too matronly"), she was also vivacious in other presentations, with extraordinary blue eyes that lit up her clear skin and merry round face, which turned her housewife image to one of beauty. People of every class responded warmly to her personality wherever she appeared.

Within days of arriving in Canberra, Enid Lyons addressed a gathering in the Albert Hall of 250 women from the Housewives Association and other women's groups. After speeches of welcome and piano solos from Peggy Shepherd, songs by a Mrs Edwards and recitation by a Mrs Laud, Enid said spoke of how pleased she was to meet the people of Canberra through the medium of the Housewives Association and added she hoped during her stay the women of the city would regard her as their friend. She dismissed a newspaper report describing her as strong minded and hoped that in fact she would be someone easy to get on with.

All her life, Enid Lyons played to the middle class crowd's appetite for the gentle, if bright, homely woman, appearing to suppress her ambitions and ego. The crowds loved it and Enid basked in the glow. It gave her strength. Seventy years later, Janice Lyons would observe that her mother never really liked people in her private world where she preferred to escape from the outside. What she really loved was the "adulation" of her public appearances. Enid Lyons was indeed Australia's first modern political woman, however homespun her speeches.

Taking charge

The Thelfalls, Martyn (a former journalist) and his wife, had moved into The Lodge to ease Enid's arrival there. In the first weeks, Enid had been overwhelmed by the task ahead and confessed later how it was the hardest undertaking she had ever faced. This was "making mountains out of molehills", according to Joe. Instead of worrying about how to cope with employing people in an official capacity, as he saw it she should jump at the chance to have paid staff taking charge. Enid had managed for years with home help but recalled,

> Every full time household help I had employed in my own home had lived as a member of the family, and had been selected not so much for her efficiency as for her personal attributes ... I quailed at the thought of my deficiencies as a mistress, none of which, as I very well knew, would escape detection by the shrewd eyes of those who would serve me. I was not even sure where a housemaid's duties ended and a parlourmaid's began, and the professional cooks I encountered in novels terrified me!

Perhaps Enid had read too many novels. As the public demands grew, she would steel herself with the facts of the life she wanted with Joe: "I had accepted long before that, for me, there was no escape from the life of compromise I lived. As long as he carried the burden of his office I must give the major share of my time and energy to the man I loved and had married, saving for the children away from home the weeks when they were on holiday, remembering that he loved them as I did, and saw them even less." From the outset, there was no chance Enid would pass up moving to The Lodge like Sarah Scullin or, in the future, Elsie Curtin or Elizabeth Chifley. But, as her official and private life panned out, the longest stint Enid Lyons ever spent at The Lodge at one time was five weeks – and this only once.

By 1932, the ten Lyons children ranged in age from fifteen to five months; as well Enid was expected to be available for public appearances, often without Joe accompanying her. As a recognised public speaker in her own right, she travelled about the nation to functions and would recall that her average over the time as first lady was three speeches a week, "sometimes several in one day, and once in a headlong tour of 300 miles, ten in twelve hours". It was not surprising that Robert Menzies once wrote in his diary that Joe and Enid were "inclined to extract the last drop of juice from the orange".

It was a very relieved Enid who arrived in Canberra to find all domestic arrangements had been taken care of by the Threlfalls. She wrote to a friend in Tasmania that same week saying, "We have only been here two days but everything in and about the house is so lovely that I have almost forgotten to be homesick." Enid was initiated as "a household accountant" under the "expert guidance" of Martyn Threlfall whose efficiency left Enid fulsome in her praise. She found the hired staff all that was required for their needs; the "kind, capable" Hilda becoming her mainstay until Hilda's marriage some years later. And then there was Elsie Bush whom Enid wrote of so warmly in her memoirs. She had also enlisted the services of Sister Blanche Clare, a well known nursing sister and midwife from Burnie who had attended at the births of Barry and Rosemary and delivered Peter Lyons in Melbourne in 1931. Sister Clare lived at The Lodge in the early months of the Lyons family's residence there and took charge of the younger children as Enid settled into her job as prime minister's wife. Enid would return to Burnie in 1933 so Sister Clare could deliver her twelfth child, Janice. For baby Janice, the Lyons also engaged a Sister Carmody to take care of the Lodge nursery – Carmody's methods were strictly set around the popular Truby King baby care methods of the time. Some would later refer to Janice Lyons as the "Truby King" baby.

First couple

It had been a whirlwind two months getting to The Lodge. Joe was caught up in the inevitable wrangles over ministerial portfolios and admitted much later that as a new boy in the conservative side of politics, he did not really know his colleagues' personalities till much later. John Latham and the UAP's non parliamentary leaders made most of the decisions about portfolios in 1932. No doubt Joe's geniality as leader – and his Labor Party origins – gave rise to the continuing rumours that Lyons would not last as UAP Prime Minister and would soon be replaced by Stanley Bruce who had by then returned to Australia.

Joe and Enid made a triumphant tour of northern Tasmania in late January. At Stanley, on Saturday 24 January, Joe visited sister Mary and aunt, Mary Carroll, in the cottage in Wharf Road where he had lived as a young boy. Then he and Enid had been guests at a public reception at the Stanley Town Hall where the entire population of Stanley had waited for them for over an hour. Asked to add a few words to her husband's address, Enid admitted it was the first time she had ever found it hard to speak. The emotion of the moment had taken over. In her few words she said there had been "some hard knocks during the last few months" but that it was great to know that the people of that small island, even if they did not agree, "would at least understand". They had gone on to rousing receptions in Burnie and Ulverstone and a huge reception at the Devonport Town Hall. Joe had continued on to Launceston, more celebrations and a return to the mainland.

The step up to the role of nation's first couple was a tremendous moment of pride for the Lyons and Burnell families. For Eliza and William, it was their crowning social glory. By 1932, Eliza and William were living at 12 High Street, Burnie, and William was a mill manager with the Van Diemen's Land company. The loans on the Cooee block, subdivided over years, had been fully paid off to Mr Tracey by 1920. Annie Burnell had married Jack Gilmour and remained in Burnie; Nellie and her husband Hubert Glover had moved to Sydney. Hubert, who had worked as a secretary to Joe in 1931, had become private secretary to the new Assistant Minister for Customs and Member for Bass, Allan Guy.

In Hobart, Tom and Mavis Lyons continued to be Desmond and Sheila's mainstay while they boarded at St Virgil's and St Mary's, the schools adjacent to the cathedral in Harrington Street. In 1933, Desmond became the youngest student ever to enter the University of Tasmania's Law school. During Enid and Joe's long months overseas, in 1935 and 1937, Mavis would take her daughters, Carmel and Lynette, to The Lodge in Canberra and live there while looking after the younger Lyons children. She would recall much later how she had known and mixed with the wives of four prime ministers, something she treasured as a special experience. Joe and Enid may have lived precariously at times, but the excitement of their stature was not lost on the extended family.

As Enid prepared to join Joe in Canberra at The Lodge, letters went out on her behalf from Martyn Threlfall, replying to requests she attend functions, accept gifts, respond to appeals and so on. In the PM's office at this time, secretarial staff were seconded from the Department. Hazel Craig, for years secretary to Robert Menzies but also with Joe Lyons, recalls being part of the brigade of typists who went over to the PM's office to type correspondence. "There would be piles of mail waiting," recalled Craig, "They [Private Secretary] would send across to the Prime Minister's Department to have somebody to come over and take the letters that they dictated, then we did them, took them back and they signed them and sent them off. You didn't see the letters again after they were typed, and you didn't know what happened." Enid's correspondence was handled in this fashion. To Mrs Britonarte James JP of the Victorian Women's Citizens Movement, Threlfall wrote on 4 February 1932: "I am now directed to say that owing to her absence in Tasmania Mrs Lyons was not able to accede to your suggestion that she attend the meeting of your movement on Tuesday, February the 2nd." And so the correspondence files were filled, with some requests being accepted and many refused ever so politely.

A public life is lived successfully around a diary maintained by secretaries. Acceptance of an invitation, a request or favour is carefully considered against a busy schedule, political expediency and private obligations. In Enid's case, her family obligations were significant but she juggled her load with an expertise developed over years, and home help. She often found herself ill from the effort. In late 1932, Enid was rushed to hospital and all her appointments cancelled. Joe's telegram on 12 September to Mavis and Tom in Honora Avenue, New Town, informed them that Enid was in St Vincent's Private Hospital in Sydney and that she would be there at least a week. He was hoping no operation was needed. In another wire that day, Joe thanked Governor General Sir Isaac Isaacs and Lady Isaacs for their telegram to Enid and was able to report by then that Enid was much better.

Enid had been forced to decline an invitation to attend the Australian Women's National League's opening session in Melbourne. The organisation was a powerful support group for the UAP, its leader May (Elizabeth) Couchman one of the towering figures of conservative politics. Mrs Couchman wrote to Enid of the delegates' "great regret at the illness which prevented us from seeing you". May Couchman was one of many influential women Enid would become close to in her years of political life. The AWNL was delighted when Enid was able to open its conference in Melbourne in November, just weeks later, where she spoke out on the "art of living" and encouraged women to stand for parliament.

In all their public actions, Joe and Enid never lost sight of the acute economic hardship so many were suffering. Janice Lyons recalls that, during the Depression years, the older Lyons children each received a cake of soap as a Christmas present on one occasion, and were told to understand that many children had less that year. Their parents were donating the money saved on their presents to charity. Where Enid or Joe was not in a position to help, or oblige a request, they had to reflect consideration or empathy in the replies they sent. Even some relatives and acquaintances made representations to them for help in finding employment.

Sarah Lyons wrote for over a year begging Joe to help his nephew Stanley find a position; at first it was the Navy but he seems to have failed the physical tests; she then thought Joe might find the lad something in the Post Office. A friend of Enid in Hobart, Tess Moore, wrote asking if Joe could put in a word for her husband Allan who was doing a few days work with the Shell Oil Company. She was desperate to stop living with the in-laws and he needed a permanent position if they were to afford their own accommodation. But even the word of a prime minister didn't always make a difference. Joe tried through a number of letters to help Albert Taylor (married to his niece Jean) find work. He wrote to the Premier of Victoria,

Stanley Argyle, in regard to work with the State Rivers and Water Supply Commission and also tried the Curator of Parks and Gardens in Melbourne. Joe was still trying in mid 1934 to help Albert.

Enid received many letters from unknown individuals telling of personal hardships and begging her to help. Her public speeches using simple anecdotes and housewife analogies, made women especially feel they could write to Joe Lyons' wife for assistance. This need for ordinary Australians to contact Enid Lyons would be a feature of her public life for many years. During the war years, after she became the Member for Darwin, she once responded to a request for titles of books she was reading with: "Lately I seem to have been reading nothing but letters since it would appear that half the women in Australia write to me, and about a quarter of the men, whenever there is any problem worrying them."

The letters came in all manner of handwriting and composition. Alexandria Crofts chose to itemise a budget on a meager allowance – rent, insurance, light and gas, food and "no fire of course" – concluding, "I don't suppose I can live much longer." And there were the opportunists. One letter, on 18 February 1932 from a Mrs Reynolds of Nowra in New South Wales, urged Enid to consider acquiring one of her Pomeranian puppies, describing them vividly as "pure-bred prizetakers". In reply, Martyn Threlfall wrote, "Mrs Lyons would like to know what is the cost of a puppy?" There is no record that the Lyons children ever received one as a gift.

The role of the wife of an Australian prime minister in 1932 was quite undefined. According to Diane Langmore in *Prime Ministers' Wives*, it remained ill defined many decades on. The first lady was expected to play something of the role of a successful businessman's wife, to entertain, to support, to keep the home fires burning so to speak and to be as inconspicuous as possible when not needed. Enid and Joe had never had such a relationship.

For all their appearances of the traditional man and wife – the concentration on children, the older man leading the young spouse, however accomplished, and the single breadwinner – Joe and Enid Lyons enjoyed something of a late twentieth century partnership where the husband allowed his wife her independence and where, considering his professional responsibilities, he also spent a reasonable amount of time helping rear his children. True, Enid's independence was squarely based on her husband's success but, within a very full on domestic whirl, Joe was always anxious that Enid have her time out, and even to have her own space in the limelight.

Family life in the fast lane

The full Lyons family as such was never "in The Lodge" while Joe Lyons was Prime Minister – it was in fact split between Devonport and Canberra, boarding schools at Deloraine, Hobart, Yass and Goulburn and wherever Joe and Enid travelled. Photos released to the newspapers of the Lyons brood arranged as in tiers in front of The Lodge – all thirteen of them – or walking across the lawn in a long line of varying shapes and sizes were rare moments when the family came together on special occasions in Canberra.

In an interview in Adelaide in early April 1933, Enid explained that she was heading back to Canberra but only for a few days as she would be going to Devonport "to spend Easter with our elder children". On this occasion, as on many others, Joe would be with half the children in Canberra and Enid with the others back in Tasmania. The burden of coordinating a family rendezvous in Melbourne, or Home Hill, would often be left to prime ministerial staff like Jack Swanson and driver Ray Tracey and happen with the precision of a military operation. Sheila who spent her last three years boarding at St Mary's in Hobart often played surrogate mother in Enid's absence after 1935 when she joined the family at The Lodge.

Around this time, Enid, Kathleen and Moira moved from school in Deloraine to board at the convent in Yass and occasionally spent their weekends at The Lodge where they played tennis and helped with the younger ones. Kevin, who had been at St Virgil's, moved to board at Goulburn, also within easy distance of Canberra. Nellie's daughter Marian Paul believes the responsibilities the older Lyons children often carried in looking after the younger ones, left them with resentments large and small at times. In later life, Desmond and Sheila often visited their Aunt Nell in Sydney to whom they seemed closer in some ways than their mother. As youngsters, Nell had often minded them in Burnie with Eliza. At Aunt Nell's in Sydney, they would off-load their frustrations; sometimes, with parents so caught up with younger children and busy public lives, the older ones could feel they took second place or at least were expected to cope

Enid and Joe with their eleven children on the lawn outside The Lodge in 1937.

without much parental involvement. Sheila remained a backstop for Enid throughout her mother's life, at her beck and call even as Sheila reared eleven children of her own. Desmond, who briefly worked as a parliamentary secretary for his mother, did not attend Enid's funeral.

It was very common for parents of large families to expect older siblings to take charge of the younger ones. In the case of the Lyons family, Sheila and Enid seem to have been called on quite a bit. Sheila often had charge of the younger ones on trips back to Devonport. The small group of siblings, travelling home to Devonport with Sheila in charge, would leave from Canberra in the evening by train in a sleeping compartment at around 7-8pm. At Goulburn they connected with the train from Sydney and would be in Albury by 7-8am. They would transfer to the *Spirit of Progress* and arrive in Melbourne around noon or just after. Here, they'd rest before leaving South Wharf around 5-6pm on the ferry to Tasmania with the first stop Burnie and then Devonport, coming into port around 8-9am. One mid winter trip was delayed by seven hours. Sheila just had to cope. There was no talk of her going to university as Desmond had done in 1933 and she did not take up any paid work until after her father had died when she went to work for ANA. Young Enid, likewise, could be relied on to step in. During Joe and Enid's trip to London and the coronation in 1937, they took Sheila as a help for her mother, while young Enid, at seventeen, was left to play carer for the younger Lyons contingent at The Lodge, helped by the faithful Elsie Bush.

The Lyons family did become a feature of Canberra life when they were there. Just as the Menzies family would later on. Bob Menzies' daughter Heather can remember how the family at "The Lodge" mixed in with their neighbours, some of whom would drive through the Lodge grounds as a short cut. When it rained, they all picked mushrooms from the paddock which is now the Italian Embassy, and neighbours would give their share to the Lodge kitchens to supplement food needed for formal dinners. The Lyons family lived as a normal family on the weekends, The Lodge becoming any ordinary family home. Heather Menzies recalls that it was far more like a family home at that time, where the Lyons children would all just fit, with a squeeze, around the dining room table.

Joe and Enid, with children in tow, attended Mass on Sunday at St Christopher's Catholic Church in Manuka, the same building where the small ones attended school on weekdays. They would then dismiss the Lodge staff after lunch, and Joe and Enid would wash up in the evenings so that on Monday mornings the staff had no Sunday clearing to do. The Lyons couple could mix with elites all over the world but remained fairly ordinary on their own. At Mass, Joe refused the armchairs Father Patrick Haydon, the parish priest, put out for them saying that before the altar there was no room for distinction. Some bishops would not have agreed. At times they took off in the car with driver Ray Tracey for picnics or a few hours at a country spot out of town or the golf course. A report in the Burnie *Advocate* on 26 July 1932 captured something of their rare moments of leisure:

> A visitor to Canberra relates that he was interested in a party of seven on a local golf links ... Investigations proved the group to be the Prime Minister and Mrs Lyons out for a round with four of the little Lyons following up with a few clubs of their own.

Joe and Enid Lyons were the first political couple to exploit the modern media for their political ends and to deliberately create a personality cult around their images. In this, Joe Lyons was a politician beyond his time. In the 1930s, they created a virtual reality of the Lyons family in The Lodge.

Public image

In 1932, photography in newspapers was in its infancy – broadsheets still had the classifieds, beginning with births and deaths, on their front pages. The top news stories and political reportage was pages in and sensational writing was discouraged. In the broadsheets, a heading across two or three columns signified a news breaking story and would be placed around page 10. Joe and Enid did not discourage photos of their children in print. They allowed them to mix with reporters as they invaded the family home for interviews.

In January 1932, in Melbourne, Enid recalled being with the older children when a reporter called at their home in Barkers Road. "There they had their first experience of a newspaper interview," she wrote. The article described them as "neat little figures in navy blue tunics and white blouses" indicating that Enid had especially dressed them in their uniforms for the occasion even though it was school holidays. Neatness and order, and the "rosy apple cheeks" the journalist noted, all added to the cosy picture of domestic harmony around this extraordinary family.

During the 1934 election campaign, in spite of widespread fear of flying at the time, Joe Lyons clocked up 7,000 kilometres in a few weeks. On one flight from Tasmania to Laverton air base in Victoria, Sheila Lyons accompanied her father on the legendary "Faith in Australia" plane piloted by Charles Ulm. The plane was tossed about by fierce winds and rain as it raced to outpace a storm. In the middle of the turmoil, the plane had found a brief calm near Devonport where it managed to drop ten thousand leaflets over the electorate – they read "Have faith in Australia – pull together and pull Australia through".

The pictures of Joe and Enid at The Lodge with their entire brood of children were ground breaking. Canberra was in mothballs with the depression, government funding for building works had dried up. The Lyons children were the first children to occupy The Lodge and suddenly there was a real family at the helm of the nation, and pictured for all to see and follow in their progress, playing tennis, going to university, being born and even little Barry struggling with his condition and for which his parents would continue to seek medical advice and pay for expensive treatment.

The Lyons family was forever moving about in small bands; a group here, another there. Added to this, during the course of their time as prime ministerial couple, Enid spent much of early spring in hospital, a collapse in 1932, a birth in 1933, a curette in 1934, exhaustion and illness after her trip abroad in 1935 and a hysterectomy in 1936. This did not stop the photographs. After a long stint in St Benedict's Hospital in Melbourne in 1934, Enid and Joe were pictured in the gardens of the hospital, Enid seated and warmly rugged with Brendan on one side, a walking stick resting on her lap – probably her husband's – and Joe with Barry on one knee at the other. The perfect media opportunity a day before the polls. "Mrs Lyons is recovering from her illness, but it will be some time before she is able to leave hospital," the caption read. Enid looks young, relaxed and extremely pretty, beaming over Brendan's shoulder, surrounded by loved ones and with Joe by her side.

It took no spin doctors to craft Joe and Enid into salt-of-the-earth family folk. Like the distraction of a royal wedding in London, this first family caught the imagination. Joe and Enid Lyons and their children in The Lodge were a comforting and unifying symbol for the many seeking security in these years. And with this came Joe and Enid's use of radio to communicate their story, with a weekly broadcast on policy from Joe and, on occasion, Enid too. Then there was her voice, heard by millions, deftly modulated yet unpretentious but with the dramatic quality of the stage – clear, well educated and very much a product of Eliza's enforced elocution lessons. Enid Lyons became a mother to the nation, one in need of a mother's touch in the 1930s. After yet another function, where she was fulsomely praised and could not attend, Joe wrote to her, "Ug, [the pet name they had for each other] you don't know what a place you have in the hearts of the people of Australia, nor how interestedly and sympathetically the women are looking toward you just now."

Politics and personalities

The big clash between the Labor Party and banks was gone. The UAP government under Joe Lyons, however, was cautious and inclined to exactitude in its financial management. Argument continued over how much money might be released, or borrowed from the banks, for relief works. There were no unemployment benefits in 1932; it was work for the dole if a man could get it and called sustenance work. In the view of many, there was too little of it. In C B Shedvin's *Australia and the Great Depression*, he estimates that around £50 million was needed to provide full time work for just half the unemployed at award wages and only £5.8 million was actually spent from the loan fund. But economising, however hard, seemed the only way to solvency for the Lyons Government.

Critics of Lyons' approach to spending included the new UAP premier of NSW, Bertram Stevens, who succeeded Jack Lang after Lang was sacked from office by state governor Sir Philip Game on 13 May 1932. Enid Lyons would write that if Joe had never accomplished anything else in the federal parliament, he "would always remember with the greatest pride that he had the honour and the pleasure of introducing the legislation that brought about the downfall of John Thomas Lang".

Stevens was taking over a state cowed by debt and stagnation and wanted to see increased spending for recovery. He believed Lyons thought all he had to do was lower costs and wait for something to turn up. Stevens wanted investment in the domestic market to stimulate recovery. After the 1932 Premiers Conference, Lyons wrote to Stanley Bruce, "We have got rid of Lang but unfortunately we now have Stevens to contend with. At least one could go out and attack Lang in the open. In the case of Stevens, one is continuously sabotaged from behind." Relief money for public works did, however, trickle out into the community; restricted to males it caused a controversy with women's groups who argued that single mothers and older women were being left to starve. Water supply, sewerage, road construction and rural development became priorities. And with the setting up by Lyons of the Commonwealth Grants Commission in 1933, money eventually flowed more readily to the states for public programs.

With Joe Lyons' win at the polls, he brought a field of new talent to the government benches, and a lot of egos. Some thought he was a stop gap leader and would not last long as Prime Minister. John Latham was in the wings. Archdale Parkhill, who had never been happy with the formation of the UAP, believed he could take the leadership from Joe. Stanley Bruce was mentioned continually by *The Sydney Morning Herald* as the Prime Minister should Joe stumble.

In August 1932, however, Bruce was sent to the Imperial Conference in Ottawa and from there to a new posting as Resident Minister in London. He had been Assistant Treasurer which hardly ranked as sufficient for a man of his stature. With Bruce in London, the loyal Richard Casey took over the Assistant Treasury post which brought him close to Lyons who was also Treasurer. In October 1933, Bruce resigned from parliament to become Australian High Commissioner in London. After the announcement of Bruce's appointment to London had been made, Joe wrote to Enid, "The *SMH* continues to campaign ostensibly for Bruce but in effect against me ... It must have been a blow to them today to publish Bruce's resignation when yesterday they demanded his return."

John Latham went to the High Court as Chief Justice in 1935 and Robert Menzies won his seat of Kooyong. He was immediately appointed Attorney General. Joe Lyons had encouraged Menzies to stand for a federal seat, telling Enid this was "in the expectation that he would succeed me". At no stage before Joe died, however, did the

UAP party leadership regard Menzies as "ready". Bruce would still be considered for the prime ministerial position in 1939, as Joe and Enid wearily sought retirement.

These machinations were never far from Enid's understanding of the job she had taken on. Her role was to listen to Joe download, or read his outpourings of how lonely he was without her by his side. "Last night we sat till about 2 o'clock and I'm pretty sleepy, and I wish I had someone nice to sleep with! What about coming over?" he wrote on one of the many nights he missed her in the midst of his political burdens. In Canberra, she could only hope for his continued success, trusting to Joe's astute and long practised skills in managing colleagues and contacts, while being ready to evacuate her comfortable temporary quarters there should her husband be rolled by his colleagues or an election.

Shortly after taking office, there were months of bitterness around Premier Jack Lang's defiance of his financial obligations and, in particular, after the dramatic scenes at the opening of the Sydney Harbour Bridge in March when the New Guard's Jack de Groot slashed the ribbon before the Premier could do the honours. Enid recalled how she and Joe were warned not to go into the streets alone, a warning she ignored only to discover later that she was carefully tailed by security officers whenever she did. They received threatening letters, although eventually Enid chose to ignore them as merely outlets for "minds over-pressed". On their trip to Queensland in mid 1933 at a stormy meeting of tobacco growers, a gesticulating and angry man in the crowd aimed a revolver at Joe. He was quickly disarmed and Joe stopped the incident being reported.

But it was advice given to her by Stanley Bruce, as ever frank and cutting, that provoked her most. Bruce, she claimed, had told her early on that Joe would need her as never before. As he put it, "For this job a man really needs three things, or some of them anyhow; a hide like a rhinoceros, an overpowering ambition, and a mighty good conceit of himself. And your poor husband has none of them." Enid quickly understood that, as a political wife, "the wounds her husband receives are hers to heal" and that she "must keep alive whatever small conceit of himself he had".

As for Joe's lack of ambition, Enid knew he had something far more enduring; in her words this was "an intense desire to pull Australia out of the depression". In August 1932, Joe wrote to Enid, "I can't help recalling that one day just after I had crossed over [parliament] and I was greeted with cat-calls and an organised attempt to prevent me from speaking, I said then that they would not stop me from playing a part that would help Australia to get through her troubles. Well, we've travelled a long way already, haven't we?"

On with the show

On 25 October 1933, Enid gave birth to her last child, a daughter they named Janice Mary. In the fortnight she lay in bed in Burnie awaiting the birth, Joe wrote anxiously and kept her updated on Brendan, Barry and Rosemary who were in Canberra. Enid had taken Peter to Tasmania, and fourteen year old Enid as a help. Janice's birth was an historic occasion; the first child to be born to a Prime Minister in office. The "Group of Six" proudly presented Enid with a special gift of a silver porridge bowl to mark the occasion. Joe, however, could only manage a few hours with her after the birth, flying in and leaving within hours. He wrote a little later from the Menzies Hotel in Melbourne:

> Goodnight my sweetheart – sweet dreams and a pleasant awakening, and remember that the chap that came to Cooee because he loved you, loves you more than ever tonight and wishes he could take you in his arms and kiss you and squeeze you and just tell you how he thrills at the very thought of you.

Janice's birth left Enid very unwell. Travelling between the mainland and Tasmania became an increasing burden in the year that followed, as much as the long road journeys in and out of Canberra. The invitations came and went and attendances at important occasions could not be avoided. Enid hung on grimly, finally going into hospital in August 1934 as Joe prepared for the federal election in September. She did not take part in the campaign for the 1934 election on 15 September, Joe's birthday.

Left with the five youngest, Joe managed in The Lodge with Hilda, Elsie and Sister Carmody who took care of Janice. He wrote every other day or as he paused in his travels, keeping Enid up-to-date with developments. He was concerned about Brendan's cough. Nurse thought it was whooping cough, and even that an epidemic might be threatening. Eventually he sent the children to Devonport and received a letter from Enid telling him how displeased she was that he had done so. Gentle Joe was contrite, blaming the doctor who had advised it.

This was a modern marriage of sorts indeed. A prime minister like Joe Lyons was certainly a role reversal in a first family – a prime minister who, when in Canberra, came home to listen to his children's accounts of their day, who shed tears in a doorway as little Barry stood by the grand piano singing a hymn with a touching reverence, who reflected on how pretty little Rosemary was and how loving Brendan could be saying goodbye on the way to school, who bought material for school uniforms and organised the dressmaker, who checked the household accounts and noted how the small items his many children needed all added up, who wrote notes to school teachers, or took a sick son into his own bed at The Lodge to keep an eye on him overnight. He once wrote to Enid after buying clothes for the children in Myer, Melbourne, "You see I'm quite a good mother."

By late October 1934, Enid was well enough to attend the visit of the Duke of Gloucester to Canberra. Her photo with Joe and the Duke on the steps of The Lodge would be chosen for the cover of *The Canberra Times'* "annual" that year. Enid looks is elegant in a stylish wide brimmed hat and full length floral dress. There is no indication she has recently been so unwell. Celebrations throughout the Duke's visit were extensive in every state. During the Duke's visit to Canberra, Enid oversaw a "Royal Dinner Menu" so elaborate it was published in the Melbourne *Herald*, no doubt to assure readers that local taste in fine dining was adequate for the Royal guest. The dinner was described as a "work of art … decorated with a large reproduction of a magnificent painting by Elioth Gruner of the Murrumbidgee Ranges near Canberra".

Early in her time at The Lodge, Enid became aware that political differences were rarely personal. Asked what she was going to do regarding her association with the wives of men who had helped bring down the Bruce-Page Government, namely Dame Mary Hughes and Lady Groom, wife of Sir Lyttleton Groom, former Speaker of the House, Enid replied that she would receive "anyone who is kind enough to call on me". In time both ladies became her good friends. To these she would soon add Penny Gullett, wife of Sir Henry Gullett, Lady Zara Gowrie, wife of the Governor General from 1936 and Richard Casey's wife Maie, whose rather pompous brother Rupert Ryan Enid found to be "courteous and delightful". These and many others in political circles kept close to Enid through years of political ups and downs.

Within a very short time of taking over The Lodge, Enid went with the Canberra flow, picking up clues rapidly and playing hostess. "Dear Mrs Grosvenor," she scribbled on 5 November 1934 back in Canberra after her illness, "I am enclosing two lists containing the names of people to whom I should be very glad if you would kindly send formal invitations for tea at The Lodge on the afternoons specified." The invites to tea went out to wives of MPs in Canberra and other dignitaries. Sheila recalled her mother would sometimes give a party in the Prime Minister's office. In spite of the Depression and the fact that she preferred Devonport to The Lodge, over seven years Enid went a long way to promoting Canberra as the nation's first city.

Back row standing: Kevin, Enid (jnr.), Dame Enid, Sheila, Desmond. Middle row sitting: Kathleen, Joe, Moira. Front row sitting: Barry, Rosemary, Brendan, Janice and Peter (late 1938).

CHAPTER 14

NOT JUST A PRETTY FACE

While Tasmanians of a particular generation had come to know Enid Lyons as their premier's wife and one of very few women to stand for parliament, it was only as prime minister's wife that Enid came into prominent national recognition. Her headline grabbing moments at podiums in South Australia in May 1931 may have been swiftly abbreviated on the advice of Robert Menzies, but Joe Lyons could make his own rules on how to present his government and he knew Enid was an asset. Enid would be heard and seen on podiums across the nation, not simply as a first lady supporting causes or speaking to party gatherings, but as a leading figure addressing major issues of the day or simply rallying support.

In this, Enid Lyons still stands tall and unique among all prime ministerial spouses since federation. Diane Langmore in *Prime Ministers' Wives* has pointed out how Margaret Whitlam and Zara Holt were colourful, but their contributions in public were not always helpful to their partners. Zara Holt was stylish but Langmore writes, "Some, mindful of her exuberance and impetuosity, her garrulousness and 'bungles', referred to her condescendingly as 'zany' or 'daffy'." Likewise, after being praised for her outspokenness in the role of prime ministerial wife, Margaret Whitlam gave few speeches but entered the public arena through her columns in *Woman's Day* and her sound bite comments to reporters. This culminated in controversy – and uproar when she said, as inflation and unemployment rose,

"All this hoo-ha about inflation in this country can be said to be encouraged by the press." Then there was Pattie Menzies, who made countless speeches to small gatherings across the nation but never on policy or as a spokesperson for government. Tamara Fraser, Annita Keating and Hazel Hawke contributed to sponsored causes and gave an occasional personal interview. For the rest, most were tireless in support of their husbands, but hardly heard.

Pattie Menzies believed there would be unhappiness if husband and wife were both "political at the prime ministerial level". But the Lyons marriage had a very liberal interpretation of spousal roles for the time. Speaking to Mel Pratt for her Australian National Library interview in 1972, Enid Lyons explained, "If we were out on a little country tour somewhere, and of course I wouldn't be on the formal program, Joe would just lean across to someone as the proceedings went on and say, 'Ask my wife to speak; you'll enjoy it.'" As Joe read the reports of his wife's success or sat listening to her sway a crowd he swelled with pride.

Waiting for the birth of their twelfth child, in October 1933, Joe wrote, "Jennings [UAP colleague] came home with me and you would blush to hear his praise of you and his description of the way you thrilled the people at Randwick. He says it is your wonderful personality that appeals to them all. Is it any wonder I am proud of you Ug?" Further on he responds to self doubts she has expressed, "Ug, you need not worry about the general attitude. You will go even higher than ever in public esteem. I'm real proud of it and of my part in it!" Before their first overseas trip he wrote, "I am thrilled to death with the reports of your speech – you're a marvel! What with the packing, travelling, children, dress worries and all the rest there isn't anyone in the world who could do as you did. It was just wonderful and it's just impossible for me to describe my pride and admiration for you. I'm almost reconciled to the London trip when I think of the way you'll put it over the natives there."

In spite of his immense popularity and being one of the longest serving among Australian prime ministers, Joe Lyons would never completely head off fringe chatter that he was the tool of more powerful operatives among the conservative forces and not really in charge of his government. This was nothing short of speculation by rivals and political enemies or wild contention, but it dogged his legacy and led Enid to defend him forcefully in her later writings. His death before he could write his memoirs and comment on his place in history would further complicate his record. And, with the formation of the Liberal Party in 1944 and the success of Robert Menzies as the first Liberal Prime Minister in late 1949, Joe Lyons would fall between the two party traditions and fail to gain his rightful recognition in the history of the major parties; each would seek to ignore him.

In all this, it would be Enid who would both save and impinge on her husband's legacy. Impinge, because she would outlive Joe by some forty-two years and become a national figure in her own right, in politics and in the media. For reasons of necessity and interest, she would write and broadcast over years and develop a huge fan club. Dame Enid, as she would be known, became such a strong personality at a time of sophisticated film and sound media from 1943 until her death in September 1981, the idea grew among the many who had never experienced Lyons as prime minister that she was the talent of the couple, with Joe her weak puppet. Nothing could be further from the truth. As Brendan Lyons put it in an interview in 1999, "Mum was tremendous, but if you analysed their achievements in government, Dad was a mile ahead."

Ironically, Enid's fame, name and perspicacity would save Joe Lyons' historical legacy while also threatening to overshadow it. Enid Lyons' public personality was such that she would always be of interest to historians and, in exploring Enid and her unique contribution as a prime minister's wife, something of the character of her husband shines through.

Joe Lyons' time as prime minister was overshadowed by depression and slow economic recovery; and his manner in government was always to administer well and save the histrionics for others. This does not make for colourful material in the archives. Former prime ministers Harold Holt and Gough Whitlam, whose brief periods in office were far less distinguished, have captured the interest of writers much more. Not only because of the issues from their time in office (war and social change) but also because of the controversial ways that they lost office – one to drown in strange circumstances and one to be dismissed by the Governor General.

Secession in the west

Enid Lyons referred to it as "speeching", that schedule laid out for her of public appearances after taking up life at The Lodge. A woman had written to her "be a good, sensible little woman and stay at home. Don't go around speeching and making yourself ridiculous." Enid, as it turned out, did a lot of speeching.

In March 1933, Enid found herself preparing for a long train journey with Joe over days to Western Australia on what she called "a mission that had a touch of the Lincolnesque", Joe's mission to preserve the Federation. Western Australia could not secede from the Commonwealth under the Constitution, but ever since that state had been the last to accept federation in 1900, Western Australia had retained an underbelly of protest against being cheated by the eastern states.

As Western Australians geared up for a state election and a plebiscite on whether to secede, set down for 8 April 1933, the secessionist Dominion League had split WA voters on the issue of withdrawing from the Commonwealth. Both conservative Nationalists (who held government) and Labor opposition were anxious the debate over secession not ruin their chances at the polls. As the WA campaign had progressed, Joe Lyons felt troubled over the controversy. He believed he should speak to Western Australians personally. To add to his forces, he took Enid and UAP Victorian Senator Tom Brennan with him to address rallies in Perth.

Facing hostile crowds was nothing new for Joe Lyons, or Enid. But Western Australia then was akin to another country for someone from the east. Their initial reception was cordial. During their welcome in Perth's Town Hall on 28 March, Enid expressed her surprise to Labor member and Perth local John Curtin. "Everyone seems delighted to see us," she commented. But Curtin warned her of subtleties in the Western Australian character replying, "Ah, here we affect a manly, breezy insincerity, but don't let it mislead you. Wait for tonight!"

At a packed gathering in Fremantle Town Hall, there was uproar. Headlines next day reported the meeting had to be abandoned shortly after the Prime Minister spoke, such was the heckling and interjections. Outrage at being lectured to by easterners like Lyons and Brennan further fueled the meeting. An appeal from the Mayor for calm and for speakers to be heard was ignored. Abusive remarks rained down on Joe from the gallery as he spoke, but he ploughed on, pausing occasionally to let the hubbub subside. When Senator Kingsmill rose to speak after Joe, the noise was such that the Mayor asked the band to play "Rule Britannia" which silenced the audience. When the hecklers started again before anyone could resume speaking the Mayor silenced them once more with the National Anthem, "God Save the King". At least the Mother Country could qualm these Empire loyalists a while.

In the midst of this volatile atmosphere, it was Enid who seems to have had the best hearing. Asked to speak before her husband, perhaps as a warm up act, Enid stood before the hostile crowd. She tried an appeal for rationality, arguing that "whatever has been suffered [in the Depression] in Western Australia, in Tasmania or in South Australia is nothing compared to what has been suffered in Melbourne and

Sydney during the past two years … In Western Australia one person in sixteen is receiving government relief … the proportion in New South Wales is one in six." When heckling began, she resorted to national symbols, as reported in the *West Australian*:

> "We have kept the Union Jack in the top corner of the Australian flag and on the vivid red background [as it used to be] there are six stars."
>
> A voice (derisively): "How lovely." (laughter)
>
> "I appeal to you," resumed Mrs Lyons, "not to have one star removed. Keep them intact." (applause)

UAP Senator George Pearce was a particular target as Joe Lyons appeared before a crowd at Perth Town Hall a little later. The crowd chanted for Senator George Pearce whom they wanted to hassle, now ready to pillory a Western Australian traitor. Enid describes the rowdy meeting in her memoirs: "The end came with a shower of pennies from the nearer galleries. One of them hit me on the ankle. The chairman immediately closed the meeting."

At a women's meeting, next day in the same venue, the anger at Joe had abated somewhat, perhaps shame at reports of such bad manners dished out to their federal leader had shaken the locals. Joe Lyons was now given a hearing for his brief introductory words and then he had to leave for another function. Senator Tom Brennan spoke after Joe, defending free trade between states. This was too much – the crowd began to boo and jeer. They called for Mrs Lyons.

Enid rose to speak, choosing her customary humour to settle her listeners. "I'm not too sure about this 'We want Mrs Lyons,' she began. "It sounds alright, but I was at the theatre last night. I heard them chanting 'We want George,' and I knew why they wanted George." By now, she had her audience laughing. But interjections were not long in coming and soon the chairman, Bessie Rischbeith, was calling for a policeman. Enid stopped her, insisting she would talk her way out.

"Fair go," she said loudly across the audience from the microphone, towards the rapid fire of questions, "One at a time." Taking the first question, she was conciliatory in response. A master stroke. "Just the point I was coming to," she replied. "But I'd like to finish the one I was on. Okay?" The meeting became attentive.

There was a dialogue – Enid listening, women querying, Enid responding. Enid was quick to drop what finer points she might have made; the notes she had brought with her were of little benefit, so emotional and parochial the crowd. What use a speech she had brought with her by nineteenth century American nationalist Daniel Webster, arguing against secession from the Union? Words from Webster she had noted included: "If I have my senses, my last prayer shall be, Heaven save my country and the Constitution." It would seem Enid's papers became so irrelevant, she left them behind. They were posted back to her some time later by a journalist from the West Australian *Mirror* who found them. It was Enid who saved the day on more than one occasion during this visit, either as a result her sex, wit, unassuming demeanor in the face of rowdy audiences or a combination of all three. Joe sent young Enid, at boarding school in Deloraine, a telegram on 29 March that read, "Mother had best reception of tour at a big meeting of women in Fremantle yesterday."

Secessionists in WA were furious about competition from mainland firms in products such as jam and crockery. Western Australian goods were not holding their share of the market. Enid challenged the locals, however, to consider just what the problem was – were they eating Western Australian jam or using Western Australian china? Not nearly enough it would seem. And higher tariffs on goods from other states or overseas simply pushed up the price of all jam and china. The struggling family would find it even harder to purchase the basics. This was the universal problem of protection, a problem Australians as much as Western Australians would grapple with for many decades to come.

Using basic arguments, like the school teacher she had been so long before, Enid's commonplace illustrations and humour restrained her opponents, and caused them to think, perhaps even to fall back in their recognition of the complexities. It made sense where more elaborate arguments could be howled down. But it would not change the outcome of the plebiscite. Reading Enid Lyons' account of the meeting one might have thought it should have made a difference. Enid described how this particular meeting ended with almost every woman coming up to shake her hand, writing, "almost without exception they announced they would vote against secession". But, as Enid went on to admit, almost with a sense of paradox, "in spite of our efforts, the referendum was carried". For all that, Western Australia did not secede.

On message

At the time of her visit to Perth in 1933, Enid probably knew she was in the first stages of pregnancy. This did not stop her continuing her program and joining Joe on a trip to Queensland in June. They would travel by train as far north as Cairns attending what Enid recalled, "as many as seven different receptions in a day (complete of course with speeches)". Arriving in Brisbane, Enid was feted as a woman who "can successfully combine public life with the bringing up of a family". She was described in the *Brisbane Courier* as taking interviews in her room in the Gresham Hotel "surrounded by flowers" of welcome. In her public comments she continued her push for women of all backgrounds to be part of civil society: "I like the mother on the hearth but that does not preclude her taking part in other things. It is the duty of every woman to take an intelligent interest in outside affairs." She added that while she believed women with young children should remain with youngsters while they were little, "everything that can possibly be done to help the mothers who have to turn out to work to keep the home together should be done".

She also had a dig at "child study and analysis" adding that "every child is a law unto itself, and a mother's adaptability is the measure of her success".

The Lyons era of government in Australia fell between two international crises – the Great Depression and the Second World War. Joe Lyons' governments would be returned at three consecutive polls in what Clem Lloyd, in *Liberalism and the Australian Federation*, has described as a feat of "outstanding quality". Lloyd points out that no prime minister in the first century of federation won "three consecutive elections with such imposing authority". It was no surprise that the leadership of the party remained with Lyons in spite of a vipers' nest of conflicting egos in Cabinet wanting to topple him and take the prize. Joe Lyons's mastery of personalities kept him in The Lodge – but in the end it would kill him.

By 1934, unemployment figures were dropping and in May 1933 the full bench of the Arbitration Court devised a scale to increase the basic wage in line with increases in the cost of living. This did not fully restore the ten per cent basic wage reduction of 1931 but was a step that signaled continuing recovery. In October that same year, the Lyons Government felt confident enough, albeit not without a struggle in the party room, to raise parliamentary salaries. By 1935, as Joe and Enid prepared to leave Australia, the talk was of new trade agreements Lyons might secure while abroad, in particular a lessening of the duty on Dominion (ie Australian) meat exported into the UK. Australian producers and the government were worried that a renewal of the UK-Argentine agreement on imported chilled beef might bring restrictions on Australian beef products. The delegation's visit to North America on their return continued talks on trade.

While it is often acknowledged that Prime Minister John Curtin in the 1940s brought Australia closer to the United States through allied defence in the Pacific, it is forgotten that important groundwork was initiated in Washington by Joe Lyons' visit there in 1935. In all of this,

Enid played her role of informal diplomat, heralded on her return to Australia in 1935 as "the ambassador who laughed her way into British hearts". In the United States she was described as a "human dynamo" and in Canada "all mother" but also "a clever politician in her own right" who has "lectured all over several continents". No Australian had quite taken on the world in this way; a woman combining so many diverse attributes in her image, so homely and intellectual at the same time and so able "to put it over the natives".

Enid was good at what we now call "spin", something she had long before learnt from Joe. Asked in Toronto by a journalist for *The Star* how she managed with so many young children to stand for parliament, she gilded the lily quite a bit, portraying herself as a "super" dynamo. Forgetting her daily housekeeper at the time, the reliable Ada, and the nurse they had employed for the campaign, she replied: "I had no help in the house and had to do my own housework, but I'd make up my speeches as I worked, and then at night when it was time to go out campaigning, I'd get a friend to come in and stay with the children." Wherever she went, Enid was a sensation – the mother of so many who spoke so confidently in public was a phenomenon indeed. But Enid also kept to well honed themes and avoided lengthy written out speeches. Her thespian sense of timing on stage and repartee in front of a fractious audience were other skills she had picked up as she watched Joe on the campaign trail over years.

Enid earned a name among UAP leaders for her quick wit and ability to phrase the sharp one liner. Writing to her in October 1933, Joe remarked on her reputation among colleagues: "A very great compliment was paid to you at the final Cabinet on the budget. We wanted a good phrase to stress the beginning of better things indicated by the concessions and everyone had a shot, including Thelfall but we seemed stuck ... Pearce said: 'Is Mrs Lyons here in Canberra – she'll do it.' What do you think of that?"

Joe and Enid had chosen the middle way which meant expecting fire from either extreme. They were Catholics through and through. Joe would often stop by Pellegrini's, Catholic bookshop in Melbourne, where Molly Carroll worked. On one visit to the shop he bought Enid the "music of the *Boree Log*" adding that Molly "brought Pellegrini to meet me and he proceeded to discuss his tax troubles". In Melbourne, Joe would drop into St Francis Church in Lonsdale Street, a haven for busy Catholics. He often mentioned his church visits to Enid in letters: "Last night I went to St Francis' and this morning to Communion at the little church round the corner... the racing people were there from all states."

Catholics they might be, and faithful to their religion in no small measure, but this did not prevent the Labor leaning Catholic press often taking a swipe. Enid felt it deeply – especially as a convert. Joe regularly assured her not to worry about press reports. He was contemptuous. In October 1933 he wrote: "I wish you could see the Catholic Press. Two leading articles dealing with racketeers and an absolutely lying par ... It is disgusting. Mr Lyons was the "sorriest figure" of all waiting to speak; no reference to Mr Scullin who didn't speak at all but quietly voted ... thank God they are not the Catholic church."

As a political partner, Enid easily attracted public notice but never wavered from the message. She described this as not trumping Joe's hand. In one Feminist Club address she spoke of women's power in these terms:

> I have heard that women make the best bridge players – Australian women particularly. If the bridge playing brains of our women would concentrate on solving our difficulties, better conditions would prevail in our country. Great wealth, great poverty and great idleness are the three problems of this country. There are those who talk of equality of sacrifice. Some make forced and others voluntary sacrifice – let us be among the latter.

Enid Lyons received debutantes, opened flower shows and fetes, addressed annual meetings, charity fund raisers and the like but also put the government line where needed, albeit in phrases which added simple philosophy to the prosaic economic arguments of policy. At the conference of the National Council of Women of Australia in Melbourne, in November 1932, Enid spoke of the "art of living": "We have come to make living a business, rather than an art. Everyone must live by some philosophy and I am sure that the greatest philosophy ever propounded to the world was that given two thousand years ago in Palestine. The art of living is not the art of getting but the art of love." She then added that the restoration of prosperity was not merely a matter for governments and monetary policy but rather a matter of spirit.

Taking the high ground and speaking as a political player also meant Enid had to roll with the punches afterwards and take the criticism of cynics. After her "Art of living" speech, *The Daily Telegraph* responded: "Men who have to spend 40 per cent of their time working for the tax gatherer have not much chance of cultivating the art of living ... No doubt the restoration of prosperity is, as Mrs Lyons put it, not just a matter of governments. But they have a deal to do with it." Like any seasoned politician, Enid just kept on going.

On the eve of the Lyons' departure for seven months abroad in February 1935, there were various send offs. Certainly Enid's attire caught newspaper attention – in Melbourne at Greenknowe in Toorak, the residence of Sir Robert and Lady Knox, she was described as wearing "a gown of deep lobelia-blue tissue matelasse woven with a silvery thread to repeat the shimmering note of her silver slippers". But, as for no other prime minister's wife, what Enid said at many of these gatherings was also noted. *The Argus,* on 19 February 1935, reported that Mrs Lyons had described women as "the shock-absorbers of the world" and had added:

We can always make privileges for ourselves and some come to regard them as our rights, but the claim to equal citizenship cannot be regarded in the light of claiming a privilege as a right. It is the natural heritage of every citizen of every community in the world where justice is done.

Here, as in other speeches, she gave "two great reasons" why women as a whole were not equally alongside men in the "work of the world". The first was that "they were opposed by the majority of men" and the second that "they were opposed by the majority of women". Women, such as she was addressing, were the key to change. "If people like you go on working as you are doing, full of energy, full of human kindliness, understanding and humility – and the last three are perhaps the most important – the day will come when we will know that all these things are our right." Julia Rapke, president of the VMCM, closed the meeting speaking of the affection and esteem felt for Enid by the women of Australia.

On her return from overseas in 1935, Enid expressed her hopes that world peace might be sustained. Interviewed after disembarking in Sydney, Enid expressed her unease at seeing "a detachment of mounted cavalry swinging through the streets of Rome, all of them young boys". She told her listeners that it made her think, "Why must people take up arms?" Her mind turned to the battlefields of France she had just visited and the thousands of young Australians killed there in the First World War. She recalled Joe saying that "every statesman and politician should be made to go to those battlefields where our boys lie with the sons of the rest of the mothers of the world". By the time of her second trip to London in 1937, not all of Joe's colleagues felt her pleas for peace were all that realistic.

In 1938, as war threatened, Enid continued to believe peace might prevail. In September, *The Age* reported Enid as speaking of Australia as facing a very grave crisis saying, "Empire policy is informed with the object alone of preserving the peace of the world, if that could be maintained with honour. It is only within this century that the idea of striving for peace for the sake of peace, not for the promoting of political ends, or purposes of development of Empire, had come into being."

Enid, an ardent pacifist, strongly supported Neville Chamberlain and the Munich Agreement. A growing group among UAP members believed this was a naïve approach; Henry Gullett had fallen out with Joe and resigned from Cabinet and Sir Keith Murdoch believed Enid was the major influence over Joe in his continued belief that Hitler could be reasoned with. Writing to his friend Clive Baillieu in London early in 1939, Murdoch described Enid Lyons disparagingly as "an ardent pacifist, even a belligerent pacifist". Joe, who had found a soul mate in Neville Chamberlain during the 1937 visit to London, did not need urging from Enid, however, in his support of Chamberlain's heroic belief in negotiation as a way to peace with Germany.

Her personal commitments, to family and faith and somewhat Fabian principles held from childhood with Eliza her guide, took Enid into areas of public policy she felt strongly about. Keeping clear of too much theory or the idea that a grand plan could solve all ills, she often relied on her personal experience in making judgements. In the late 1920s, Enid had become enamoured with the Truby King baby care methods, only to find herself in 1938 at odds with Mary Truby King, Frederick Truby King's daughter and successor, when personal experience challenged the theory. The Truby King method emphasised increased education for mothers in hygiene, nutrition, regularity of children's functions and, in an early treatise, eugenics and patriotism. The method was credited with improving child mortality. However, a slavish belief in non familial methods could also leave traditional mothering out of the equation.

A speech Enid had given was reported to advocate a return to more natural mothering, and for mothers not to slavishly adopt instructions before using their instincts. She also called for more home births.

Separately, she had told the editor of *The Australian Women's Weekly* in an interview that she believed Mary Truby King's weekly column on mothercraft relied so much on the advice of nurses and experts that young women were being put off having babies at a time when the nation needed an increase in births. In a long letter to Enid, on 1 March 1938, Mary Truby King sought Enid's views directly, thinking Enid may have been misreported. Enid replied extremely courteously on 3 March, and admitted to feeling "ill" at having to criticise aspects of the mothercraft profession ("so many of my friends who are child welfare nurses and voluntary workers"). But she nonetheless reaffirmed her views:

> ... although theoretically it is safer to have a baby in hospital, actual figures seem to show that such is not the case ... it is safer to have one's baby in one's own home that is only clean than in a hospital that is sterilised but which nevertheless houses many patients ... What I advocate is this: a reversal of putting more and more maternity cases into hospital ... organise our resources to allow this function take a more truly natural function. A midwifery service in conjunction with medical and clinical practice and, of course, some hospitals should provide what is necessary.

Enid's grandson, Peter Lyons, who spent a good deal of time with her in Devonport in her last years, says that she was always able to see both sides of any argument. She could empathise. But when a decision had to be made on principle, she made it. In time she conceded that no appeasement was possible with Hitler or Mussolini. As the years went by and her allegiances to political parties were less important, the younger Peter Lyons believes that a lot of her Fabian instincts resurfaced. He says she might have voted for Gough Whitlam in 1972. And her green credentials came to the fore when she strongly opposed damming Tasmania's Franklin River.

Until she entered parliament herself, Enid Lyons spoke out on political issues in mostly general terms. Her role was not to argue the finer points of tariff reform or budget priorities. She kept to her script, sending out strong messages that women must become more involved in public life, that family life underpinned a moral society, that citizens and government should support an environment that would lift the birth rate, that young women be encouraged to be mothers, that women with children who needed to work should be assisted, that women had a natural right to equality, that Australia was the best country in the world and that she was in every sense Australian and proud of it. Her philosophy was straight and simple, and somewhat timeless. In a letter to a Mr Chisholm of Kooyong in Melbourne, in 1948, Enid Lyons outlined something of the framework that kept her "on message":

> Our generation is obsessed with the idea of security. Tell youth to forget all about it. Tell them that to live only for security is scarcely to live at all. But a life lived without fixed principles of conduct is a life wasted. Tell them to have faith in God, self-discipline and a sure standard of moral integrity; then let them dare to do the things they dream about.

None of which would have stopped Hitler or Mussolini, or solved the problems of budget spending or constraint, but as a message to many ordinary Australians it hit a nerve and offered a sense of direction which made Enid Lyons a voice to be reckoned with for decades.

CHAPTER 15

PUTTING IT OVER THE NATIVES

A photo page in the Melbourne *Argus* for 20 February 1935 recorded the moment – streamers from three decks and more than 1600 waving passengers as the Orient Line's *Otranto* of 20,000 tons eased its way out of port bound for Europe, Robert and Pattie Menzies were just two of many esteemed passengers embarking. Menzies had arranged his own tickets to join the Commonwealth delegation, after much planning was now finally off to London. Joe and Enid Lyons meanwhile took the train to Adelaide and Perth, making use of the journey to attend functions, before embarking at Fremantle on 25 February.

Saying goodbye to her young children in Canberra was heart wrenching for Enid. The idea of not seeing them for six months, or even being able to talk to them except on a rare and brief phone call, at long distance, was something she dreaded. Wealthy families like the Caseys or Murdochs were bred for it, even carried it as a sign of a superior class to have children growing up with long separations from parents. Within a week Enid was writing in her diary that she wished she had not joined Joe abroad such was her homesickness for "a pair of little arms around my neck".

Nothing brought an end to Australia's tyranny of distance like the Boeing 747. Before modern air travel, making a trip to the other side of the world, as Australians had to do in order to make contact with their origins or leading world powers, was a major and expensive undertaking. The Australian delegation in 1935, led by Joe Lyons and making the trip to coincide with celebrations marking King George V's Silver Jubilee year, was planned over months. Included in the group was Sir Henry Gullett, a minister without portfolio directing negotiations for Trade Treaties, and Harold Thorby, a Country Party minister who at the end of the trip would be appointed to assist the Minister for Commerce. There were also senior representatives from the Tariff Board and Department of Commerce and prime ministerial staff. In London, Stanley Bruce had become Australia's High Commissioner in October 1933. He had a reputation there, as one senior British government official revealed to Bruce's biographer Cecil Edwards, for being "bluntly polite, or politely blunt" and in some ways "a hawk among the chickens". He would guide the delegation in making contacts and appointments.

Trade was Lyons' first priority, but events in Europe had long since taken on sinister omens. Adolf Hitler was strongly entrenched in Germany, his storm troopers out in force among the civilian population from the first. The day the *Otranto* left Melbourne, newspapers carried gory reports that Germany had beheaded two aristocratic Prussian women, charged with stealing War Office plans for the invasion of Poland – the style of execution was unprecedented in Germany. In March 1933, Albert Einstein arrived in Britain from New York saying, "I cannot go back to Germany where freedom of opinion has been abolished." There were already stories of atrocities against Jews in Australian newspapers.

By May 1933, the Nazis had begun their book burning and photos had appeared of Prince August Wilhelm, fourth son of the ex-Kaiser, giving the Nazi salute before speaking at a Nazi rally in Berlin. By the time Enid and Joe arrived in Europe, German rearmament was well advanced, its air forces reconstituted and conscription reintroduced. Clearly Hitler had no interest in abiding by the Versailles Treaty of 1919. On 20 March, Joe and Enid stopped briefly in Rome, and were given an escort of planes as they approached from the coast. As a Secretary of the Italian Government met them, delighting Enid with orchids "from Mussolini", Il Duce was already making plans to invade Abyssinia, a member of the League of Nations. At a diplomatic level, heads of government and their emissaries continued to hope that negotiation could prevent the shadow of war. By the time the Joe and Enid returned to London in 1937, a clear division would have opened up between those who still believed negotiation was possible (Neville Chamberlain's appeasement) and others like Winston Churchill who saw war as the only option to stop Herr Hitler's aggressive takeover of Europe.

Life at sea

The weeks on board the *Otranto* left Enid convinced that long sea voyages were not her forte. She had crossed Bass Strait many times over two decades and was certainly not prone to sea sickness. What troubled Enid was the constant need to be social, and the lack of time and space for escape from the crowd. "Deck games distress me," she wrote, "I am the delight of bores." While Robert Menzies had a similar inclination to ration his time at general socialising, he did do better on deck as Enid noted a few days into the Indian Ocean – "Mr Menzies is a favourite for the ball tennis tournament". By contrast Enid had to swallow her pride in games – "Finished my part in quoits match, thank heavens! Was sorry for my partner though who was only a child."

Some historians have concluded it was Enid Lyons with the confidence Joe lacked in political life – this was never true. Enid could perform when needed but it was Joe who loved continual company on the road, the endless "dropper in" as Enid called him, and making his case before a group however big or small. And while Enid always appeared at ease before a microphone, she told Natalie Scott in her "Woman in Question" interview for ABC TV in 1976 of how before any major public event where she would have to appear, her bones would be "turning to water" as she took the stage. Then, after a few words, she would relax into the performance and enjoy it.

So while Joe might be selected to chair a "sports committee" or accept an "award" from "Neptune Rex" Enid did her best to be cheerful, "dressing for dinner with a towel in my hand to mop my steaming neck and brow, stoically distributing prizes [in third class] while the ship plunged in a thirty-knot gale." She played "appalling" accompaniments – "Concert on board last night. F J McKenna [Joe's private secretary Frank] sang and I accompanied by ear. Was very nervous. Also conducted community singing of 'Auld Lang Syne' and moved vote of thanks to performers". There were costume balls on occasion that were more fun – "ball last night a great success with some very good costumes."

For all her nervous exhaustion, Enid was not without friends and people she could relax with. Accompanying Joe were journalist and UAP supporter Irvine Douglas with his wife, and Jack Swanson whose parents had looked after young Barry during his weeks of hospital treatment in Melbourne. There was also Joe's Private secretary Marjorie Grosvenor, Marge as Enid called her.

Enid became good friends with Penny Gullett during these weeks at sea. The Gulletts were close friends of the Murdochs and Elisabeth Murdoch later recalled Penny Gullett as being quite unique and, "very amusing … if she spoke about anybody, she spoke in their voice, an absolute mimic". Penny Gullett remained a solid friend to Enid over years, in London jollying and supporting her in moments of apprehension and depression through the many weeks in foreign surroundings – "My dear Mistress Lyons. Just a slight note to say how pleased & proud we were of you both yesterday. You did nobly by us all & 'dear old Aussie' & no prime minister & his lady did us greater credit. Have a good rest today & get to it again tonight. Yours affectionately, Penelope Gullett."

One newcomer who would form a bond with Enid was Lady Swaythling, a noted London society hostess and world traveller who had joined the ship in Adelaide after being in Australia during Melbourne's centenary year celebrations. Lady Swaythling had been the guest of four state governors as she toured the country. Interviewed before her visit, she claimed to be quite anti-social at sea preferring to read and catch up with sewing – "I won't join in the sports. And I refuse to play bridge." But she fascinated Enid with her conversation on board ("Lady Swaythling full of details at lunch. Amazing woman") and equally Enid appears to have interested Lady Swaythling who went on to host functions for Enid in London and keep in touch by writing to her in Australia for years. They had interests in common; Lady Swaythling's extensive involvements and advocacy of women in public life attracted Enid.

Among the entrapments at sea by 1935 was the relative ease with which official parties could continue to conduct business. There was no let up from the job. Press aboard were now in radio contact with the world. On 5 March, *The Canberra Times* reported that the Australian delegation aboard the *Otranto* had been able to learn of the overwhelming victory for the UAP and the Argyle Government in the Victorian elections held on 2 March – "A constant stream of Victorians visited the wireless office all day … Ministers are still consulting officials daily … The wireless has proved a boon." With this sort of contact possible with Australia and London, much of the preparatory work for the London program was done on board. By the end of the sea voyage, the Lyons party had sent 8000 code words by wireless to London and received 10,000 code words in reply. The wireless operators had worked sixteen hours a day.

As compensation, Joe and Enid had their own company to enjoy over weeks; and were never long separated over six months. A photo of Joe and Enid, solitary figures leaning near each other on deck, gazing out to sea in a quiet moment, captures the sort of escape Enid craved. She would write that highlights of her first ocean voyage were "small glimpses of other and exciting worlds, and sharing it all with Joe."

Enid's daily summaries of life abroad were nothing like the 400 pages of handwritten record Bob Menzies would produce. Hers are truncated, typed later by a staff member and appear to have been the very much abbreviated because of her weariness at the end of a day. Enid's and occasionally Joe's comments were posted back to the Lyons children by way of correspondence about what they were doing.

Her tone is characteristically chatty and irreverent, sometimes with small asides (near Aden, she saw two exotic "hoopo" birds on deck "black and grey with little crest of feathers. I did not see King Solomon, however!") that suggest her sense of the ridiculous. Jottings after society functions often showed a tendency to lop tall poppies in private. There are other moments when Australia seems not too bad at all; passing an island in the Red Sea she wrote, "2 miles by 1½ miles. Looks very desolate, Nullabor Plain need not blush." Later, in Cairo, "Pyramids did not move me at all – a great pity." In London, "Attended High Mass at Westminster Cathedral – not impressed with the building, prefer St Patrick's Melbourne." As they did their media round in London one occasion left her deflated – "Went to make a talkie in morning, Joe to talk, myself as decoration." Her asides to the children reminded them to check their history books, "Great ceremony at Westminster Hall (Read your history children!)."

Britain

The official party disembarked at Naples and continued on to London by rail and the Channel ferry. The sight of the White Cliffs of Dover produced notably different reactions in the two Australians keeping diaries. Menzies felt as if he'd reached a personal "Mecca", like "those who go 'home' to a land they have never seen", while Enid scribbled of her lack of emotion, writing, "Saw Dover Castle and cliffs but got no thrill. What's wrong with me?" The slowly healing boil on her face and the poultice applied in Paris wouldn't have helped.

Stanley Bruce and wife Ethel met the party at Dover on 21 March and escorted Joe and Enid to London's Savoy Hotel where they were given a suite overlooking the Thames, Cleopatra's Needle below them and the outline of the parliament of Westminster along the river to their right. Enid, still exhausted and disorientated from the travelling, breakfasted next day in her sitting room amid dozens of mimosa, tulips and daffodils that decorated the side tables. Far too many, thought Enid, everywhere too much opulence. The hotel was already flying the red insignia acknowledging Australia's delegation as the first Dominion party to arrive in London for the Silver Jubilee celebrations.

Late in the morning on their first day, Joe and Enid made a call to Canberra. London's *Daily Telegraph*, reported that "excited children ran to the instrument [phone] and crowded around the eldest"; the call went through around midnight Canberra time. After it, Enid admitted to feeling lonely but the business of her schedule was soon taking over. That first day, she met a representative of the Guild of St Joan, a Catholic women's feminist group ("Catholic women banded together in the cause of women's rights. Fought through the Suffrage campaign. God bless them!") and accepted an invitation to speak for the organisation on 30 May, had a visit from Ethel Bruce with plans for shopping the following day and an appointment with a dressmaker, lunched with Jack and Joe ("marvellous but ridiculous charge"), went for a shampoo and set, took a number of callers and did press interviews. She had dinner with Joe in the Grill ("Didn't enjoy it at all") and then wrote for two hours before retiring.

Reading Enid's diary gives no indication of the media curiosity the Lyons couple quickly became for the British press, as far north

221

as Scotland and in Ireland. For a Dominion prime minister and his wife, they attracted considerable interest. Details of Joe's life as school teacher in remote bush towns appeared, accounts of their very large number of children, their marriage, Enid's public attainments.

The Daily Express for 23 March focused on Mrs Lyons' amazing schedule as wife, mother and public figure under a headline "The Mother an entire Continent adores". *The Manchester Guardian* of 8 June wanted to know what Mrs Lyons thought about the Jubilee decorations and her impressions of the English countryside. Enid responded with words about Salisbury Cathedral, describing it as perfectly beautiful and added, "It is not cluttered up. If I heard that anyone wants to add so much as a tablet to it, I shall write and ask the King to have his head cut off." The reporter added, "She has not been to Westminster Abbey. One trembles to think what she will say when she goes." They found her funny, genuine and always a bit of a surprise.

On 15 May, Enid was captured in a large photo on the front page of the *Daily Express*, along with the Countess of Jersey and Lady Plunket, just three chosen ones to be pictured from among the ladies who had been "guests of the King and Queen" the night before. The report alongside opened with, "The most envied women in the British Empire last night were those who danced the evening away dressed in their finest raiment, adorned with their most precious jewels, at the first of the Jubilee balls at Buckingham Palace."

Enid and Joe Lyons came across to UK journalists exactly as the British liked their Dominion visitors to be; both of them loved what they saw of the British Isles and they were affable and well spoken. Both were nice Anglophiles with plenty of stories to keep journalists filling their columns. Shortly after arriving in London, the *Yorkshire Observer* summed up one interview with, "there are very few pleasanter personalities with whom to converse than Mr 'Joe' Lyons".

Enid's emerging success as a writer also caught the imagination. Sir Keith Murdoch had asked her to contribute weekly articles during her travels for his publications in Australia. In addition, on Monday 25 March, her article (for which she was paid twenty guineas) appeared in the *Daily Mail* over half a page, and under a three column wide photo of the Lyons couple and their five youngest children, headed, "A Prime Minister's Wife on The Joys of a Large Family". Best of all for the newspaper, it brought a number of letters in response. Robert Menzies, early in their travels, perhaps because he doubted her capacity to sustain a weekly column, had suggested, recalled Enid, that "his secretary, Mr Stirling, can help me with articles by 'devilling' for me."

After an introductory meeting with Prime Minister Ramsay MacDonald and some of his ministers on 25 March, Joe attended further meetings and lunches and gave speeches – to a British sponsored lunch at the Dorchester, to the annual banquet of the Honourable Company of Master Mariners, to the Grosvenor House Joint Empire Societies banquet, to a group of finance journalists at Australia House, and on it went. Enid joined him for many of the official receptions and banquets but also did her own round of appointments, giving occasional speeches herself. She launched a ship at Tyneside and met Australians they knew in London like Bessie Rischbeith from WA and Professor Theodore Flynn, father of actor Errol Flynn, whom they had known from their days in Hobart when they were first married and young Errol had been Enid's page boy in a pageant.

Some locals were not always gracious; at lunch with Lady Cadman Enid met some quite insouciant women, including her hostess, and one who brashly patronised "colonials". One story that became a Lyons family legend was the encounter Joe had with anti-Catholic Lord Craigavon of Northern Ireland at a London banquet. Craigavon asked Joe if Australia had many Catholics, to which Joe replied.

"about one in five". "Watch 'em," shot back Craigavon, "They breed like bloody rabbits." But the only significant bigotry, Joe and Enid encountered in the UK, in spite of their unfashionably large family and being so very Catholic, came in Edinburgh where Joe received the Freedom of the City. A demonstration, as he arrived, of hooting and shouts of "no Popery" continued inside and interjectors had to be removed. The whole event was a shameful embarrassment to its organisers. Enid missed it, having been confined to bed from nervous collapse and Joe stood in for her at another meeting. It was the familiar pattern, as in Australia. Enid would go hard until she collapsed and needed medical attention. Soon after, she would be back to her appointments.

Enid visited many organisations connected to women or babies during her time in the UK, her speciality. She was taken to a Jewish Maternity hospital, attended the annual meeting of the National Baby Week Council, spoke to the Executive of the National Council of Women and the Overseas League. Enid and Joe dined at No 10 Downing Street with the Prime Minister where one of the guests was writer Sir James Barrie; they presented wedding gifts to Prince George and his fiancee Marina. On 8 May Enid wrote,

> Dog tired but Lady Swathyling's to dinner. Wore my beautiful white frock. A nice party. Very bright people. Cahill, Queensland pianist, played for us. Met Lady Hilton Young (Lady [Capt.] Scott) And also Lord and Lady Bective (formerly widow of Sir Rupert Clark). Very nice people. Want us to go to their house in the country. Went on with Lady Swathyling to stupid party in a garden. Stayed about twenty minutes – 19½ minutes too long.

Seeing Joe in the regalia of the Privy Council after he was sworn in on 29 March made Enid swell with pride, as well as the many fine speeches he made, even though she wrote that he had begun nervously in this vast new metropolis. Before long, after a slow beginning, the delegation felt negotiations over meat were making headway.

Enid created so much curiosity that Lady Astor just had to have them for dinner. Astor's old beau, Geoffrey Dawson who was editor of *The Times*, had been taken by Enid after he asked if she had indeed a large family and Enid had replied, "Babies to burn." Enid found it hard to find a time when they could dine at Cliveden but Lady Astor managed to squeeze herself in to the Lyons' full schedule. Joe and Enid also sat in on the House of Commons debates and Enid found the Chancellor of the Exchequer, Neville Chamberlain, to be "much brighter" than she expected. The Chamberlains and the Lyons would become good friends.

On weekends the Lyons toured the countryside, taking extra time over the Easter break in April at what *The Sydney Morning Herald* described as "ancestor hunting" for Mrs Lyons in Cornwall. She managed to locate the ruins of the school where her great grandfather Taggett had taught. They made a brief visit to the south of Ireland in late April, where Enid described how Joe had brought political enemies together. Certainly, as the *Manchester Guardian* reported, the banquet in Joe's honour at Dublin Castle was the first time, since the 1921 Treaty, that representatives of all Irish political parties had sat around the one table, another report adding: "It would indeed be strange to sit opposite the man who had signed one's death warrant, to be a guest where one formerly had been a prisoner." Enid returned to London alone while Joe went to Belfast. She was trying to stop the rounds of eating – the curse of a public life where entertaining is compulsory.

One weekend in mid April they spent at Chequers with the young MacDonalds, Ramsay MacDonald away at an urgent meeting with Mussolini. Enid enjoyed the company of the younger people and took her first long walk in England. She had by then warmed to Ishbel

MacDonald. The MacDonalds were not to know it then, but their time as first family would end on 7 June when Ramsay MacDonald would be forced to resign, replaced by Stanley Baldwin.

Certainly one of the highlights of Enid's stay in London was the Lyons' night at Windsor Castle. Indicative of the sentiment typical of most Australians at the time, Joe Lyons' words on being received by the King at St James Palace, with other Dominion leaders, on 8 May are telling:

> Australia lies far distant from the shores of Britain, but our loyalty to the Throne and the person of your Majesty is not lessened by the thousands of miles of land and sea which separate us from you; rather it has been strengthened by them, deepened by the knowledge that across half the globe there dwells a monarch who understands and sympathises with those of his subjects in the homeland.

These words Joe spoke without notes, unlike words read by other Dominion leaders. It was barely a month since the Lyons had stayed at Windsor Castle with the King and Queen and the visit had touched the Lyons couple.

They arrived just before six in the evening with Enid feeling "numb" with nerves. Dinner was for eight. Their rooms consisted of a sitting room, two bedrooms and two bathrooms. Here they were met by the chief lady-in-waiting, Lady Desborough. There was fortifying tea for Enid and whiskey for Joe and a small book of instructions in etiquette for guidance. Ladies should wear white gloves whenever they left their rooms. Lady Desborough showed them some of the Castle before dinner, set down for 8.30 pm. Enid wore ivory silk marocain over pink, embroidered with rhinestones, and looked resplendent in Penny Gullett's three strands of Persian Gulf pearls and large black opal and diamond brooch. There were no gauche moments; dinner was a magical experience and Enid floated. The King and Queen were natural and polished hosts, as monarchs invariably are, conversation moved easily through topics from London to Enid's columns to the Lyons family and Australia. The next morning, Enid was given a tour of the Castle library.

As they took their leave, Enid recognised one of the Grenadier Guards standing near the King, a man who had visited Australia a year before when the Guards had toured Australia. This recognition took the King's interest – "Just imagine that," the King had commented to the Guard later. According to Enid, the King always remarked when they met, over the following weeks, on the fine speech Joe had given when the Dominion Prime Ministers had offered their jubilee congratulations on 8 May.

The visit to London, alive with Silver Jubilee decorations and celebrations, was choked with experience for Enid. There was even a "Great Jubilee Cake Knife", inscribed for the occasion, to cut the many Jubilee Cakes. On 6 May, Enid rode in a carriage with Joe through London streets for the Jubilee procession; voices in the crowd called "cooee", "good old Joe" and "Aussie". "Probably the most wonderful day of my life," she wrote in her diary. At the State dinner on the 9 May she talked with the Queen, Princess Mary, the Duchess of York and the Queen of Norway. "My frock was gorgeous," she wrote in the diary. She was also hearing whispers of important gossip circulating upper society. She had asked a lady at the court why the heir to the throne, the Prince of Wales, remained unmarried. The reply came that he was in love with a woman who was totally unsuitable. Joe later confirmed this was the talk of London clubs. Enid had stumbled on a constitutional crisis in the making which would in time involve her own husband in a significant way.

North America

After London, Joe and Enid moved on to Scotland before leaving for Belgium on 17 June to attend a trade fair. They went from there to First World War battlefields and visited Australian War Graves in northern

France which reinforced both Joe and Enid's strong opposition to conscription and war and would prey on their minds at the time of the Munich Agreement in late 1938. They went via Geneva and the Alps to Venice and Rome, taking in the sights, broadening their knowledge of countries important to Australia, so isolated from the majority of the world's population. In Rome they had an audience with Pope Pius XI, the Pope who had struck a deal with Mussolini to give Vatican City sovereignty but also the Pope who would write significant encyclicals condemning Nazism, anti-semitism and communism and find himself in the tragic position of having to weigh up how his teachings might cause further persecution of Catholics in Germany. To meet the Pope, escorted by the British Minister at the Vatican Sir Charles Wingfield, Joe wore formal evening dress and white bow tie while Enid was nunlike in a full length black dress and black mantilla covering her head.

At the coast they left for the United States on the Italian liner *Rex* which, at 51,000 tons, was a far larger and more luxurious ship than the *Otranto* with fine banquet rooms and a nine piece orchestra, all of which signified the vastly more populous and wealthy world they were among in the northern hemisphere. This was one sea voyage Enid did enjoy, writing: "With only ninety first class passengers in accommodation designed for a thousand, and with the cachet of being guests of the management, we received every service the ship's complement could devise." The *Rex* held the Blue Riband, an award for being the fastest transatlantic steam ship for 1933-35. The Lyons were moving in style.

In New York, the Foreign News Service reported the arrival of Joe Lyons with an ironic description of his heroic mission:

> Racing towards the US this week on the Italian liner *Rex* was honest, naïve, likeable, tousle-haired Joseph Aloysius Lyons, premier of the Commonwealth of Australia, soon to swap grins in the White House with Franklin Delano Roosevelt and

indulge in economic horsetrading … Today the exuberant
young Commonwealth, much sobered down and striving
mightily to pay her debts, is Britain's third largest customer
and the US's second best for motor vehicles. Australians are
also avid consumers of US typewriters. They expect premier
Lyons to rub these facts into Washington's New Dealers and
convince President Roosevelt that he should lower the US
tariff to favour Australia's wool, wine and wood.

One can hear the chuckles from behind the pages of US
newspapers. Cordial the US hosts would be to these visitors from the
distant, barely populated Pacific continent called Australia, but tariff
reduction was not an easy matter in Washington. One visit wouldn't
draft a tariff reduction bill, much less pass one. But it would be a
good try. For Australians, it would be a small initial step on a very
long journey with the United States for which Joe Lyons has been
given little credit.

On the matter of the United States' growing importance to
Australia and the Pacific, Joe Lyons was years ahead of his UAP
colleagues who were very much focused on London. Philip Hart
demonstrates in his unpublished thesis "Joe Lyons; a Political
Biography" that Lyons had from 1935 been keen to bring about a
Pacific Pact of non-aggression after witnessing the weakness of the
League of Nations over Mussolini. He took this idea to Washington
and Franklin D Roosevelt along with his hopes for a better trade
balance for Australia.

Britain had little interest in Lyons' Pacific Pact idea and when
Roosevelt offered to exchange ambassadors with Australia in 1935,
Lyons could not accept as he knew Cabinet would never agree
to the expense. Roosevelt then offered to accord any Australian
Commissioner to Washington the recognition of Ambassador. Joe
took the proposal back to Canberra only to have it killed by Senator
George Pearce. In fact most Australian parliamentarians at that time

were opposed to closer relations with the United States; Britain was all Australia needed. Lyons' later proposal of a goodwill mission to the US and Canada for 1936 was also rejected on the grounds of its being too expensive and of little benefit. The best Lyons could achieve in bettering Australia's relations with Washington in his term

of office was to have an Australian counselor attached to the British Embassy in Washington.

So it was a far sighted Lyons couple who came to the White House in 1935 where they were received warmly. The trip had been planned to take up invitations for Joe Lyons to address functions on Australia's unique economic recovery for which he was seen as being largely responsible.

Joe and Franklin D Roosevelt found the Pacific to be their common talking point and they yarned on into the small hours over the chances of any European conflict reaching the Pacific and how the US would respond if it did. For all this, neither could have contemplated the bombing of Pearl Harbor by the Japanese, in less than a decade. Eleanor Roosevelt was nothing Enid had imagined; her hostess was a "tall, quiet woman, serene and dignified, with an air of self-containment rather than the self-sufficiency I had dreaded."

Interest in the Lyons couple in the US came undoubtedly from Joe Lyons' reputation as a successful financial manager. Esther O'Neill, of Fall River Massachusetts, wrote to Enid in June 1939 after Joe's death with the following assessment of their US visit in 1935:

> In this country, his was not an empty name. I remember attending a gathering shortly after your visit to this country, and one of the men who was president of the local National Bank told me I had no idea of the standing of Joe Lyons in the banking world. He was a power in the world of finance ... A few days after the news of his death was received, Mrs Louis McHenry Howe called and asked me to extend her sympathy to you, as she remembered the delightful time she spent with you at the White House. She had told us of the morning spent on the patio at breakfast, and how much you and he were thought of by President Roosevelt and his wife ... I am telling of these incidents so that you may know the impression he made on those whom he contacted while in this country.

The final leg of the journey took Joe and Enid to Toronto and Ottawa before they embarked on the *Niagara* from Victoria in British Columbia to return to Sydney. Both were terribly homesick and ready to collapse from their life in the public fish bowl. But just three days out of port the *Niagara* collided with the *King Egbert*, a freighter. All passengers were ordered to the decks and made to don life belts but the vessels were eventually able to return to port. After the excitement, the Lyons booked tickets on a steamer to Seattle and then train to San Francisco where they joined the *Mariposa* and set sail for Sydney on Tuesday 23 July. On board was child star Shirley Temple, heading for Hawaii. Newspaper photos captured Joe and Shirley together, happily enjoying their cruise, the big names of the trip. Enid meanwhile collapsed onto a bed in her cabin and took advantage of the long time ahead at sea. There would be few quoits games this voyage for Mrs Lyons.

Back in Canberra, the younger Lyons children and their cousins Carmel and Lynette Lyons, were being looked after by Mavis Lyons and Nurse Carmody. Carmel remembers fondly their time with the cousins in The Lodge, attending St Christopher's in Manuka, and doing their piano practice on the grand piano in the sitting room off the vestibule. She recalls Rosemary getting diphtheria after playing in the cold, wet grounds and how the others tried to catch it by throwing her a teddy bear she could infect. Homeless men would come to the kitchen door for food and one day an Aboriginal man wandering in had Carmel run for her life. All the girls slept in the glassed in verandah in front of the house. Mavis Lyons, with her daughters, would help with the child minding again in 1937, when Joe and Enid went to the coronation of George VI. While they were away in 1935, Tom Lyons built his family a new house in Hobart. The children arrived home and told him it seemed very small, they had grown so used to The Lodge.

The *Mariposa* docked in Sydney on Monday 12 August. Moira

and young Enid met their parents at the ship. There were press interviews and welcomes from officials. At lunchtime Enid appeared at the Hordern Bros tearooms to address a packed function for the Women's Club of the UAP. There were excited questions as to what the King and Queen were like, was the Duchess of Kent so beautiful, the Duchess of York so sweet? The royals could not have found a more enthusiastic spokesperson in Enid. She would take positive messages from her trip to many other gatherings over the following days. But in Sydney that day, Enid apologised for her quick departure saying she had to leave for Canberra to see her baby, "They tell me she has grown into quite a woman now, and I haven't heard her yet." And off she moved, laden with a great number of boxes, and baskets of flowers that had been presented to her.

It was a sleepy and excited group of children who waited up to greet Joe and Enid around ten that evening at The Lodge. Janice did not remember her parents and it took some hours before she

Circa 1935, Enid and Joe Lyons in Sydney on deck with daughters Enid and Kathleen (holding baby Janice) and son Peter.

was clinging to Enid again. Mavis Lyons remarked how the next day some of the children still came to her to ask permission to do things and she had to remind them that their parents were back and she was no longer in charge. The family in The Lodge spent a day together trying out the presents (model yacht and mechanical motor boat for the boys) and then it was off to Melbourne for Joe and Enid, more speeches and across Bass Strait to see the other half of the family. Enid was given feature length reports in the press of her talks for the rest of the week. She made a nation wide broadcast on ABC radio. Her descriptions of English life and the aristocracy wowed her audiences. But the stress was slowly closing her down. Before departing for Tasmania, Enid told a lunch gathering at the Windsor Hotel that she would return for a lecture in the Melbourne Town Hall on Monday 26 August; after that she would be going into hospital and then returning to Tasmania to regain her health. At the Melbourne Town Hall, before a crowd of 3000, Enid spoke for over two hours to a rapt audience. Then she left the function, with her customary bouquet of flowers, and took herself off for a complete rest.

CHAPTER 16

SAYING GOODBYE

An era was closing – not that the players fully understood what this meant. Political cycles in Australia, like weather patterns, have their regular peaks and troughs. Jim Scullin and Gough Whitlam would share economic turbulance. As prime ministers, Joe Lyons and John Curtin would share triumph followed by a tragic end; one from the scars of pulling away from serious economic travail, the other the turmoil of war. Representative government is unforgiving; a leader must perform or go.

As 1936 began, Enid returned in full to her public duties which were daunting. This was the year she took to flying to meet her various schedules, the first D.C.3s flying into Canberra especially to collect her, no doubt adding many functions to her list of appointments. That year Joe opened the Bass Strait telephone service bringing Home Hill into contact by phone to the mainland at long last.

The Lyons children at school were now all on the mainland. Desmond at university in Hobart was intellectually ahead of his peers but inclined to worry his parents at times in small ways, as maturing young adults will do. Sheila had finished secondary school and was in Canberra as a help with the young ones. Life should have been easier. But Enid, who had worn out her body physically with twelve full term pregnancies and various other ailments, was suffering. By late July she was in the new Mercy Hospital in Melbourne awaiting a hysterectomy. It was an operation, she later declared, where she felt close to death.

Although Joe was not called to her bed urgently, Enid was certainly quite ill. Surgery of this kind, at the time, could often involve serious complications.

Writing to Enid, Joe wanted to make public more details of her treatment; Australians had no idea that Enid was so afflicted. She had a pattern of using hospital as a retreat for recovery from her often nervous exhaustion – and would do this for the rest of her life. So it was not unreasonable for ordinary people to fail to understand why she was out of the limelight so long. Enid would spend weeks recovering in Devonport through September, and only resurface in October to launch HMAS *Swan* in Sydney.

In July 1999, journalist Mungo MacCallum in *The Sydney Morning Herald* likened Janette Howard to Enid Lyons as both "fiercely ambitious" driving forces behind their respective prime ministerial spouses. Such a conclusion was far wide of the mark. Whatever Janette Howard's ambitions for her husband, she saw her achievements reflected in his. For Enid Lyons, it was Joe first and always but her instincts and talents were never those of Janette Howard. She had ridden with Joe where he wanted to go, but often wished they could take a different path. Her talent for writing and speaking gave her a career path whenever she felt it possible. For what remained of the Lyons years in government, Enid stood by her man more because he was caught in an impossible tussle of political egos with little escape. Unlike John Howard, who might have retired easily before 2007, with Lyons there was no clear successor acceptable to a majority of the UAP.

After 1936, Joe's health was of real concern, rapidly deteriorating in the face of tensions in Cabinet between rivals who sought to succeed him. He was the great conciliator, keeping in touch with many groupings, spending time with them separately. He would meet Staniforth Ricketson or Kingsley Henderson from the Group, on other occasions Keith Murdoch and, separately again, non parliamentary leaders of the UAP. They were assured of his friendship and returned their support. But the UAP was a disparate grouping between loose alliances and formed at a time of need, the political party that never wrote a platform. As time ticked on, various parliamentary egos believed it was their turn at the leadership. Most ambitious of all was Robert Menzies, to be echoed by Peter Costello and Paul Keating decades later. Menzies, with good reason, believed Lyons had convinced him to enter federal politics as his chosen successor.

Joe Lyons' skill in handling colleagues' ambitions was extraordinary. But at a cost. In *The Government and The People*, Paul Hasluck wrote that Lyons was the only leader the many contesting egos in Cabinet could accept since they "did not at all accept and respect each other". Philip Hart noted, though, how the "increasing ill-health resulting from the pressures of [Lyons'] work was an important cause of his weakening leadership in the late thirties. ... In his seven years as Prime Minister, he never had a relaxed holiday, for his brief snatches of peace at Devonport were always interrupted by urgent work."

At the height of the tensions, Enid felt the moves in the shadows behind Joe were nothing short of "disloyalty". This was a sad state of mind for Enid; there were legitimate criticisms to be made. By 1938, in spite of a convincing win at the 1937 election, the Lyons government had stalled from the days of bounce and planning for economic recovery; it had few ideas in a new age of risk and insecurity around an approaching war. A recruiting campaign for military enlistments began in 1938, launched by Joe and Enid in the first hook-up ever to link all Australian radio stations. But Enid admitted later that she dreaded the hostility she felt from people who were angry that the government believed war may be inevitable. Joe and Enid had no stamina for the era ahead and it showed.

Abdication

But the unsettling of the Lyons' premiership began not so much with war as with a matter of love. King George V died 20 January 1936, which immediately installed the Prince of Wales as King Edward VIII. Edward would never be crowned. The rumours Joe and Enid had heard in London society circles in 1935 were not wrong. The new King did indeed have a most unsuitable partner in waiting, the twice married (and soon to be twice divorced) Mrs Wallis Simpson. The British and Commonwealth media had kept the affair quiet but in the foreign press the story had been long out. *Time* magazine chose Wallis Simpson for their cover and made her "Woman of the Year" for 1936, possibly in anticipation of her becoming Queen of England – an extraordinary achievement for an American divorcee in 1936.

By December, with Wallis Simpson's divorce proceedings underway, the King advised Prime Minister Baldwin he would marry Mrs Simpson. A constitutional crisis loomed; as Supreme Governor of the Church of England, which then forbade remarriage of divorced people while their ex-partners still lived, this was unthinkable for an English monarch. Baldwin must act carefully; should he advise against the marriage and the King ignore his advice, the Government would have to resign. Enter Joe Lyons and his Dominion prime ministerial colleagues.

During discussions between Baldwin and the King, there was no let up in Edward's determination to marry Wallis Simpson, although he had wavered in how he would do this – vacillating between abdication in favour of his brother and a morganatic marriage where Simpson would not be Queen and their children never heirs to the throne. Baldwin contacted the Dominion prime ministers. Cables went back and forth. The overwhelming view of the Dominion leaders, with the exception of De Valera of Ireland (part of the Commonwealth until 1938), was that a morganatic marriage would weaken the status and authority of the Crown throughout the Dominions. The King must rethink his position. It was over to Baldwin. Wallis Simpson, in retreat in the south of France and under extreme pressure, released a statement written for her that she would give up the King. But the King would not give up Mrs Simpson.

In her memoirs, Enid Lyons devotes a chapter to refuting a claim made in John Lockhart's biography of former Archbishop of Canterbury Cosmo Gordon Lang in 1949. Lockhart claimed Baldwin was finally convinced abdication was the only alternative because of "the attitude of Mr Lyons – a Roman Catholic". Using copious notes made by Joe at the time. Enid demolished the theory. She also pointed out that Joe had acted with the help of Earle Page, and Bob Menzies who had drafted the cable to Baldwin. "The only Prime Minister to dissent from the view that a neo-morganatic marriage was not acceptable," wrote Enid, "was Mr De Valera, a fervent Catholic."

The whole matter was disturbing and divided Britain and parts of the Commonwealth. In late November, the Australian press abandoned their "gentlemen's agreement" not to publish details of the affair. Even so, newspapers overwhelmingly took a conservative approach, critical of the proposed union. But not all did, and the Crown became momentarily tarnished by the hue and cry of notoriety. As the Lyons Government tried to contain the more sensational reporting in newspapers, there were outbreaks of feeling in favour of this good looking and popular King. George Fairbanks, in an article entitled "Australia and the Abdication Crisis, 1936", noted how "The King's name was cheered in theatres, cinemas and restaurants in all of the capital cities." A report in *The Sydney Morning Herald* on 8 December declared "the King is on the side of democracy ... Baldwin, who is a diehard Conservative, is certainly not speaking for the mass of the people". In pockets of opinion, the people's saviour Joe Lyons appeared no longer such an affable bloke, even though there is no doubt a majority of electors would have agreed with his advice. The matter was unsettling and Enid felt it.

Coronation voyage

With the Abdication, there was a new King and a coronation. Enid and Joe were off once again to London, now aboard the *Orontes*.

The delegation would also attend the Imperial Conference, timed to coincide with an influx of official guests in London for the Coronation on 18 May. Enid's 1937 diaries are more detailed than those of her initial voyage in 1935, though often more pedestrian. Nothing is quite as fresh. There is a new interest, however; nineteen year old Sheila had joined her parents, partly to assist Enid who had been so unwell. Enid wanted to introduce her lovely daughter to London society and wrote in her diary on 8 April how pleased she was that Stanley Bruce had arranged for her to be "summoned" to Court where she would be able to present Sheila. No doubt she and Joe hoped (echoes of Eliza here) that Sheila might return with good connections among English society and the chance of a good match romantically. It was the trip of a lifetime for Sheila whose diary reveals a happy young woman discovering the world at a very fast pace, even if after three months she was a little moody and very homesick. Jack Swanson, Eileen Lenihan and Irvine Douglas from the prime ministerial staff joined Sheila on many outings like members of a family; embassy and consulate staff escorted her to dances, shows and dinners. There are hints of an occasional would-be suitor in her diary, but she returned home very glad to be back and later married a Tasmanian.

The Lyons entourage made use of the journey to explore Italy, Switzerland and France, with extensive motoring about England in between the many official functions. Enid sent back her regular columns to the Murdoch press and was given the nod to do an Empire Day broadcast. Her reputation in Britain was such that a number of newspapers approached her for articles, offering attractive sums of money. Only her contract with Murdoch and her lack of time stopped her from accepting. She was very tempted to say yes.

The Lyons couple had a fan club – even in the United Kingdom. During a weekend at Chequers on 16 May Sheila wrote, "After Mass we were besieged by autograph hunters and we were fully twenty minutes signing prayer books and holy cards." The days of Sheila's diary in

London are a round of visits to prominent landmarks sprinkled with the names of various notables; "Lady Swaythling came to see Mum this morning and lent her a beautiful tiara."; "Lord Craigavon... took me into supper. ... met several well known people including Ishbel MacDonald, Lord Derby and the Sultan of Johore"; "sat between Duff Cooper and Ramsay MacDonald"; "Lord Glendyne lent me his box [Royal Opera]".

Britain was the centre of international power, its empire stretching across the globe. Joe and Enid being so feted at the heart of that empire was indeed "a heady broth". Enid entered Westminster Abbey for the Coronation alongside the formidable Mrs Baldwin, whom Enid once described in her diary as "looks like a public building and behaves like a steam roller". The women followed an usher dressed in tails and breeches, black silk stockings and silver buckled shoes. The ladies were dressed in white like all the other senior spouses behind them, with "sweeping trains and low cut bodices and on each head three nodding ostrich plumes and a flowing tulle veil". Enid thought they looked like a veritable "model for Britannia". The next day, 13 May, the King summoned Enid for a private investiture of her honour as a Dame Grand Cross of the Order of the British Empire. The King wanted Enid to wear the decoration he would give her to the State banquet at Buckingham Palace that evening. "This is what I have never desired and I feel in a false position... [but] The whole thing is beautiful and there is a gold collar which even the King was admiring," Enid noted in her diary. Henceforth she would be known as "Dame Enid" as a sort of pet name.

The UK government was still called National, but it was more Conservative at the top, with Prime Minister Stanley Baldwin who retired after the Coronation to be succeeded by his Conservative colleague Neville Chamberlain. Joe and Enid Lyons met the Chamberlains at a number of functions in their visits to London and in 1937 enjoyed a private lunch with them at 10 Downing Street, on

11 June, a get together that Enid recognised as a meeting of kindred spirits. Anne Chamberlain won Enid's lasting affection, "captivated by her beauty from the first moment I saw her," she wrote, "Her expression was one of complete repose, giving an impression of a still spirit within, rarely disturbed."

Neville Chamberlain, like Joe, was a very able manager of national finances but not a man for the difficult decisions that lay ahead against a predatory Hitler. He was steadfast in his belief that every possible negotiation should be tried in order to avoid a war like 1914-18. This impressed the like minded Lyons couple. But his approach would end in the disastrous Munich agreement of 30 September 1938 that dispossessed the Czechs in order to appease Hitler in the name of peace. Enid would hold fast to her belief, held by others, that Munich was a positive move, giving Britain time to rearm. In fact, it has since been argued that the British and French were better armed than the Germans and it was Hitler who needed the extra time for rearming – what he gained from Munich. At their lunch with the Chamberlains, Enid recalls how Joe's suggestion of using Mussolini, who had shown Joe great respect in Rome, as a go-between with Hitler struck a cord with Chamberlain.

Anne Chamberlain sent Enid an inscribed Coronation Spoon after their lunch and Enid sent the Chamberlains a small box made of Tasmanian blackwood decorated with a map of Tasmania. Enid wrote on Savoy Hotel writing paper as they packed to leave, "Please do not bother to acknowledge it as we shall be on the High Seas in just a few hours". Anne Chamberlain did write to thank Enid and they would keep touch long after their respective husbands died.

The 1937 trip disturbed Joe and Enid. The word feminism was taking on a far more strident tone and Enid clashed with some among the women she met. She was "glad not to be asked to sign a message of protest to Mayor of Brighton because no women were invited to a reception to Indian soldiers there". She encountered members of the upper class who felt Edward VIII had been treated unfairly, "knowing nothing, as is often the case, but suspecting a great deal, as is the way with so many 'left-wingers'", she would jot in her diary. At Chequers, "Joe nearly quarrelled with Mrs Baldwin" who insisted they keep to her regimented program.

Joe and Enid both knew a European crisis was threatening; photographic pages in British newspapers ran pictures of Hitler and Goering inspecting German troops while in Spain revolution and civil war had seen the slaughter of hundreds nuns and priests, all deeply disturbing for Catholics like Enid and Joe. As Britain celebrated its Coronation on a wet London day, ("universally hailed as the most magnificent piece of pageantry the century had seen", wrote Enid) a British destroyer hit a mine near the Communist controlled Spanish port of Almeria. At Toulon, as the Australian delegation prepared to board the *Orford* to return to Australia a month later, they saw what Sheila described as "a lot of firing" beyond the harbour, with searchlights tracing planes in the sky for some time. As if reflecting the mood in Britain, ("hatred and distrust" she called it on one occasion) Enid experienced considerable ill health in the latter part of their London visit. This did not help her feelings after exhausting functions.

Menzies and Murdoch

Back in Australia, political developments continued to underpin a growing dissatisfaction with the Commonwealth government. In March, the referendum seeking Commonwealth regulation of marketing and civil aviation had been soundly defeated. In May, the UAP lost the Gwydir by-election and the government was criticised for being tired and out of touch. But as Joe Lyons arrived back in Australia at Perth on 20 July, he predicted his government would win the election later that year. On 30 July, Joe and Enid appeared before a

UAP rally of 2500 people in Sydney where Joe spoke of "the inherent dangers of the world situation" and how the country needed "an Empire strong and undivided, not as an instrument for war, but as an instrument for peace".

The UAP went on to win the 1937 election on 23 October, only losing a handful of seats. Joe made super human crossings of the continent; Enid took no part in the campaign and tried to regain her health. That Christmas, as Australia sweltered, the family stayed in Canberra at The Lodge, because of an outbreak of polio in Tasmania. Enid, who was at Home Hill during November, would not risk the children crossing the Strait. The following year she wrote, "I made speech after speech on the subject of peace". In her 1937 diary she had described peace as "my favourite topic".

During 1938, Joe would regret the loss of Sir Archdale Parkhill who had been defeated at the 1937 election. Parkhill was ambitious, one of those who saw himself as a potential successor to Joe, but his rival was Menzies not Lyons. Menzies now gained confidence. Another rival, Charles Hawker, would be killed in a plane crash late in 1938. As Europe drifted to a confrontation with Hitler, and Sir Keith Murdoch worried about the British and Australian governments' muted reaction to Hitler and Mussolini, Lyons supported Chamberlain's appeasement of Germany, as did Robert Menzies. Elisabeth Murdoch saw part of the problem as English people's closeness to Germany – "we were related ... but Keith was very alarmed in 1936, he was very alarmed." At the end of September, Chamberlain met with Mussolini and Hitler in Munich to decide the partition of the Czech nation and returned to London brandishing a sheet of paper declaring a new deal for peace. In less than a year, Britain would have declared war on Germany.

In the lead up to Munich, Australia had sent top secret telegrams to Britain in support of Chamberlain's strategy of negotiation. In one to Chamberlain, drafted in the presence of Menzies and Page, Lyons wrote, "Your latest projected personal course excites our warmest admiration and will in our opinion completely consolidate British opinion over the whole world." But while supporting Lyons in this, Robert Menzies also believed national government needed more assertiveness against a "small Australian mentality" preventing long range national interests. Lyons was trapped hanging on and government was drifting. In October, Bob Menzies gave a speech to the Constitutional Club in Sydney calling for stronger governments throughout Australia, "to take people fully into our confidence and give them leadership along well-defined lines". Regrettably, he used both Mussolini and Hitler as evidence of strong leadership. The speech became greatly controversial and seen by some as a tilt at Lyons from a man who wanted his job.

Enid Lyons reacted very strongly to the speech as reported. At The Lodge, reading the morning papers, she cried out to Joe, in bed beside her. "It's a direct public hit at you." "Not at all," was Joe's reply. The scene is recorded vividly in her book *Among the Carrion Crows* in a chapter devoted to her interpretation of the relationship between Lyons and Menzies. Enid believed the speech was remembered not "so much for its content as for its intent". Her ironic sense of what was happening to Joe's government was clear in a letter to Anne Chamberlain at No 10 Downing Street, London, on 8 November 1938 when she wrote, "We too are in stormy political seas, the worst yet encountered by our ship. We are still afloat but, I fear, leaking rather badly!"

Kate White, in *A Political Love Story*, takes the anti-Menzies approach and agrees with Enid's reading of the speech at the time. White adds how, after his visit to Berlin that August, Menzies' advice to Lyons that Germany was no threat to Britain meant that Joe was taken aback when the Czech crisis had broken in September. He had rung Enid in Melbourne asking her to return to Canberra immediately. Joe thought war was about to break out. In her abbreviated memoir for *Woman's Day* in 1949, *My Life*, Enid writes of how she convinced

Joe at that moment that he should phone Chamberlain and suggest he talk to Mussolini who might avert the crisis as go-between with Hitler. Joe rang Chamberlain and, in Enid's words,

> Mr Chamberlain had thought of it but had dismissed it as a forlorn hope. Now hope sprang to life again like a flame in a darkened room. "Do you feel that way out there?" he asked. "Then I shall act on it immediately." Mr Chamberlain did. He telephoned Mussolini and Mussolini, by telephone to Berlin, talked to Hitler. Hitler agreed to stay his hand. The way was open to the Munich Pact.

In *Robert Menzies A Life*, Allan Martin is far more forgiving of Menzies' speech on government leadership, seeing in Enid the stereotype of a manipulating and ambitious wife behind the weak Joe, "the husband she both adored and dominated". This is an unfair judgement of Enid; any reading of Joe's letters to Enid reveals it was as much Joe who encouraged Enid as she did him. He used her often as a sounding board and comfort, but he made decisions most of the time without her near him. He had been an accomplished political leader long before they met.

But Martin does have a point in arguing that Menzies had no plan of his own to overthrow Lyons. He was more the figurehead of a group around Sir Keith Murdoch creating tension in the press at the time. Enid Lyons had been informed by *Herald* journalist Tulla Brown that Henry Gullett, who had resigned from Cabinet, was writing much of the criticism in the Murdoch press against Joe. Robert Menzies was also regularly attending Sir Keith Murdoch's private lunches in his Melbourne office. Enid could feel the campaign being orchestrated. For his part, Murdoch believed Lyons had outlived his usefulness. He had been drafted to lead the conservatives by influential businessmen, and he could be removed in the same way. Writing to his friend Clive Baillieu in January 1939 Sir Keith gave a withering assessment of Joe and Enid, clearly an opinion built up from frustration at not being able to move events:

> I don't know what we can get out of Lyons, but his wife is an ardent pacifist, even a belligerent pacifist; when he speaks she speaks; when he gives a Christian message she gives one. When he appears at the microphone she wants to appear also – and she does. Her message always, if we love our neighbours enough there will be no war. It is very pitiful.

Enid would later write, "Outside parliament there was Keith Murdoch, with a newspaper empire behind him. Strangely enough, his part in the campaign to remove Joe from the prime ministership has been scantly recognised by political writers since then." But Enid was also, like many at the time, naïve in her assessments of both Hitler and Mussolini. Something Keith Murdoch and Henry Gullett were not. In an interview in 1972, Enid Lyons revealed her lasting inability to understand the real nature of Nazi Germany in these words:

> I do know that in later times, occasionally it was mentioned that Bob Menzies had admired Mussolini, and most people in the days before the war situation arose did admire his work, it was fantastic, as a matter of fact, what that man did do in Italy, and the same can be said of Hitler; he lifted the nation up by the bootstraps practically but, of course, there's the old saying 'power corrupts'. Apparently no human being can stand absolute power, they always break, and those two left Europe in shambles, and all the work they'd done in earlier years that was commendable went by the board in that terrible holocaust.

Enid's conviction the world could negotiate peace never waned. In her memoirs, she quotes the words of writer Mary Gilmore to Joe at the time, encouraging Lyons in his quest for peace. The radical and pacifist Gilmore had become more and more enamoured with Lyons after he criticised H G Wells in January 1939 during Wells' visit to Australia. Lyons believed Wells' public contempt for Hitler and Mussolini threatened the Munich attempt to hold off confrontation. "Thank you for your sane, dignified and necessary rebuke to Mr H G Wells," Gilmore had written to Joe on 6 January 1939: "I have no love for Germany as such, but ... 'a man's a man for a' that' is my doctrine whether he is Hitler, Mussolini, or the nominee of a state church sitting unelected as ruler, as in great Britain." It was all very valiant but misguided, considering what Hitler planned for Europe. Both Mary Gilmore's and Enid's unwillingness or incapacity to comprehend the realities of Hitler's Germany in the 1930s was much like Manning Clark's blind spot for Soviet Russia when he returned from a visit there in the 1950s and wrote glowingly of what was taking place, even as the gulag and "psychiatric" centres sucked in more and more political victims.

Enid Lyons came to a more balanced analysis of the political dysfunction before Joe died in her later years. All played out over an Australian summer that saw the worst bush fires on record in eastern Australia. Joe's crumbling administration was wracked by factions and facing domestic and international chaos. Joe was bearing most of the burden as Prime Minister, and his health was failing. He had been forced to take sick leave in Devonport after the Munich crisis and they had managed to snatch a quiet Christmas there. Joe wanted to retire; they both did and yet there was no way out. The UAP non parliamentary wing insisted Joe hang on till they could work out an alternative leader.

For Menzies, there had been months of speculation in the press about Lyons' leadership without result. And Murdoch was now ready to support Menzies, although still concerned about his unpopularity with the public. Barry Lyons believes many in Cabinet feared losing their jobs under Menzies. Then there was Earle Page, leader of the Country Party – he and Menzies were hopelessly alienated, an alienation confirmed when Dr Page made a bitter and personal attack on Menzies in the House after the latter succeeded Lyons as Prime Minister. In his last months, Lyons was heavily dependent on Page's loyalty and advice as resignations from Cabinet continued to disrupt the government.

Menzies' Constitutional Club speech was the outcome of frustration, however the words might be interpreted. He resigned from Cabinet on 14 March 1939, the day Hitler invaded Czechoslovakia and as newspapers heralded the failure of Munich. It was an ominous sign of breakdown in the Lyons Cabinet. Ostensibly, Menzies was going over the delay to introducing the National Insurance Scheme, although his own government a few months later would itself shelve the legislation. Years later, Enid could accept that Menzies needed out from the stalemate. After his initial anger had passed, Joe had even expressed admiration for Menzies. Enid recalled: "His feelings of relief when Menzies left the Cabinet sprang from his belief in the man himself, in his basic integrity. In Joe's eyes, incomprehensible to many, Bob Menzies had redeemed himself by his resignation."

But if Menzies had cleared the air, the pressure would not let up on Joe. Enid had taken the younger children back to Devonport during 1938. Sheila and young Enid kept house there while their mother made frequent trips to the mainland, waiting for the day they might leave politics behind them. Even so, Joe needed an alternative income. He had a family of eleven children, only one of whom (Desmond) was at work. The youngest was not yet in school.

Wealthy UAP friends had not extended any offers to enable Joe Lyons to retire – and some felt he should not retire. Decades later business groups would "take the hat around" when Bob Menzies retired to purchase a fine home at 2 Laverback Avenue, Malvern, in Melbourne for Bob and Pattie Menzies and, in November 1920, Prime Minister Billy Hughes had been given the extraordinary sum of £24,000 of privately donated money from Britain and Australia in recognition of his services during the war and at the Versailles Peace

Conference. But there was nothing to induce Joe Lyons to step into relative obscurity when he wanted to give up office. He might have a house, but how would he feed and educate his large family? Bruce had the diplomatic post in London and Australia had few embassies at the time for an equivalent posting elsewhere. Frank Green, Clerk of the House of Representatives, had known Joe from Tasmania. In his memoir, *The Servant of The House*, Green wrote that Joe faced his last months in great distress. On one occasion:

> Lyons walked out of Cabinet and came to my room, as he explained, 'to get out of the way' … he wanted to resign and end the torture but was being urged to wait for something to take place. I gathered he had been offered an appointment by the British Government and was awaiting details of the terms and conditions before he resigned as Prime Minister.

All their married life, Joe and Enid had cut their cloth fairly closely to the available material. Letters often detailed bills that needed to be paid and calculated money available in accounts. When they had a little over, they put it towards renovations at Home Hill or a few extras for the children. Enid was renovating and extending Home Hill during 1938 in preparation for their larger needs on retirement. Joe's letters often mention amounts he is sending her for their needs. He would have been under enormous pressure trying to work out how he would support his family once gone from his PM's position. They had very small savings to depend on. Joe died leaving an estate of just £344. This did not include Home Hill which was in Enid's name. But it left little to live on. They had grown used to a comfortable lifestyle, with money enough for specialist doctors treating Barry, for boarding school fees, travel back and forth to the mainland and so on. Without his parliamentary position, there would be no extras – which all added up and helped with family budgeting. Enid was inclined to trust in providence but even she had the sense to realise their financial future was a growing concern. MPs had no superannuation in 1939.

Letters from Joe to Enid in their last year are poignant, even tragic, considering neither knew how little time they had left together. In May 1938, Joe wrote, "Looking back on my brief visit home makes me think of it as a brief glimpse of heaven. It was all very beautiful and wonderful Sweetheart! I wonder will the time ever come when we can count on a long period together." He told her in other letters how he was dreaming of her in the days at Cooee, and lying in bed thinking of how he used to "wake to see the photo of yourself as Sophie [in 'Country Girl'] on the dressing table." Less than a year before he died, he would write fondly:

Enid and Joe dressed for a formal occasion, late 1930s.

251

I was loving you very much when I was home and I'm always longing for the time when, if God spares us, we can be together in our own beautiful home forgetting all the problems of politics.

Years later, Enid would take out Joe's letters and read them longingly, as if to bring him back. Peter Lyons, Enid's grandson, says she told him of one last moment she treasured; shortly before his death, Joe and Enid watched the sun setting over Bass Strait which they had crossed so often in their political life together, a red and glorious sky spread out in front of them. And Joe had held Enid very tightly, so tightly it hurt, as if he could not let her go. But, just weeks later, before midday on Good Friday, 7 April 1939, Joe had gone.

Easter Tuesday, 1939, Joseph Lyons' coffin following a funeral procession through Sydney streets and prior to boarding the destroyer 'Vendetta' en route to Devonport.

CHAPTER 17

PAYING THE PIPER

E vents carried Enid forward even as the three days of her life after Joe's death would disappear from her memory. Only later would she piece a lot of it together from newspaper cuttings. The condolence messages were so vast a bundle she saw only a sample, like a Prime Minister at Christmas taking stock of greeting cards. The famous, the Pope, US President Roosevelt and Eleanor Roosevelt, Royals and dignitaries across the Commonwealth, as well as thousands of not-so-famous wrote and telegraphed alike. *The New York Times* called Lyons "the schoolteacher who beat the depression" and the *New York Herald-Tribune* referred to him as the Prime Minister "who saved Australia from bankruptcy". Pavement artists in London were drawing Lyons' portrait on the streets the minute news came of his illness, while the Sydney *Sun* reported that the King and Queen mourned his passing as a close personal friend.

As the undertakers removed Joe's body to the morgue that Good Friday, Enid was already under medical supervision at St Vincent's Hospital. There was a week of public grieving ahead of her. Desmond's flight from Hobart had been delayed because of bad weather but he eventually arrived to be met by Kevin at the airport. This meant the six older Lyons children were now all in Sydney to support their mother. While Enid remained at the hospital, Sheila, young Enid, Kathleen and Moira stayed with family friend and MLC Tom Murray and his wife while Desmond and Kevin took a room at the Wentworth Hotel. The funeral arrangements had begun even as Joe breathed his last moments, Richard Casey given the task of asking Enid where she would like to bury Joe, chosen by his Cabinet colleagues because of his dignity and tact, according to Enid. Without hesitation she had insisted Joe's body be taken back to Devonport where she believed he belonged. And so it would be.

On Easter Monday, the body of Australia's first prime minister to die in office was laid in state in St Mary's Cathedral from 10am till 10pm. Many arrived ahead of time and thousands filed past and paid their respects. The body lay in a glass topped casket, set on two rosewood pedestals behind the high altar and before another altar below the great northern window, draped with the Blue Ensign. Six tall candles on each side of the coffin lit up the faces of the servicemen guarding it, in turn the Navy, Army and Air Force. White silk lined the casket's lid as Joe's body, in evening dress, lay with his medals arranged beside him. A tall gold cross on a pedestal, swathed in purple silk, stood at the head of the casket. The Lyons children arrived to view their father's body without their mother, still too fragile to leave hospital. They were met by Archbishop Michael Kelly and Dr Giles, Secretary to the Apostolic Delegate. By the end of that day, the cathedral floor was carpeted with bouquets left by mourners.

On Easter Tuesday, a full requiem Mass at St Mary's Cathedral farewelled Joe Lyons in Sydney, after which a cortege carrying his coffin left on an extended procession through Sydney streets snaking its way past throngs of people to the destroyer *Vendetta* waiting in the harbour to take Joe's body to Devonport. The route went from St Mary's via College Street, Park Street, George Street, Martin Place and Macquarie Street to Circular Quay.

Nell's daughter Marion and her brother watched it all from the Commonwealth offices near Martin Place. Caught by the sudden tragedy, their mother's friend had opened her Mosman dress shop just so Nell would have a suitable black outfit to wear for the ceremonies.

Enid managed to attend the Mass, heavy in a plain dark coat and brimmed hat over which she threw a veil during the service, her face wan and puffy and seated in the front pew between Kevin and Doctor Oscar Diethelm. Long afterwards, she spoke in an interview recorded for the Australian National Library of how it all seemed a terrible drama she barely got through:

> I was helped up the [cathedral] steps by my brother-in-law and my eldest son ... and I was able just fortunately to fall on my knees in the place assigned to me beside Joe's coffin. I don't know how I got through that period, but I was taken there and I insisted on going down to the waterside, I insisted on getting out of the car. I was so weak I could scarcely support my own weight, and I stood holding onto the car while the coffin was transferred to the ship, then I was taken back to the hospital, and as I got into the foyer, once again that frightful collapse occurred, which is I'm told a sudden drop in blood pressure. I just collapsed in a heap on the floor.

The family then moved on to Melbourne for a memorial Mass in St Patrick's Cathedral the following day. While young Enid, Kathleen and Moira went ahead on the Douglas airliner *Wirana*, Enid recovered a bit in Sydney and was flown to Melbourne the following day in BHP's private plane. Helped on board by Desmond, Sheila and Kevin, Enid lay down throughout the flight on a couch with a nurse in attendance. During the journey, Enid says she began to feel weightless, as if leaving her surrounds totally; in fact she had passed out. Seeing this, the nurse gave Enid a jab of a hyperdermic needle, the pain of which jolted Enid back to life. "My next consciousness was of struggling to fill my lungs with air," Enid told Mel Pratt for the National Library, her voice full of stage dramatics as she recreated the event. Enid was not well enough to attend Melbourne's memorial Mass with Archbishop Daniel Mannix where, as the rain fell, a crowd of 5000 spilled out of the cathedral and into the grounds to listen under their umbrellas.

Enid recalled hearing the panegyric on the radio in hospital, after which she was given another injection and passed out.

They all returned to Tasmania on the same plane and the Lyons children noticed how Enid brightened a little as the island's coast came into view. For months, she had been preparing Home Hill for Joe, anticipating his retirement. Now they were coming back, however sad the circumstances. But, as she arrived at the house after a sixty mile drive from Launceston, Enid caught sight of a special easy chair she had bought Joe as an Easter gift, hoping he would spend future hours in it resting his lame leg. It was all too much and she collapsed again.

The next day, Thursday, 13 April, they buried Joe from Our Lady of Lourdes, Devonport's Catholic church. Special buses and a train had brought people in from far and wide. Joe's Cabinet colleagues were all there, and the Tasmanian Governor Sir Ernest Scott who, with Archbishop Justin Simonds, had met the destroyer and taken delivery of the coffin at 1.30pm. The procession of the cortege from the wharves stretched for half a mile and moved slowly along the Esplanade, up King Street into Rooke Street, to Best Street and along Fenton Street to Steel Street and then to the church for a 3pm service. Joe was buried in the grounds, packed with mourners, at 3.30pm on the newly consecrated circular lawn in front of the church. Returned soldiers formed a guard of honour.

A crowd of 200 in the church and 5000 in the grounds heard the service, others lined the streets. Sun shone through stained-glass windows onto pews Joe and Enid had long used with the family for Sunday Mass. Dr Simonds, standing by the open grave and flag draped coffin, spoke of the unity in death of common charity: "We have gathered around this graveside, irrespective of our political allegiances, to pay a final tribute of prayer and of respect to one of Australia's most distinguished sons." Enid would return to Melbourne shortly after the burial, and spend a month in the Mercy Hospital trying to recover from her loss.

For all the pomp and ceremony, the laudatory words of praise for Joe as the nation's great prime minister, residual bitterness remained. Robert Menzies had been fulsome in his recall of Joe's abilities and their genuine friendship as he paid tribute:

> … he provided that advocacy brilliantly in Parliament and on a thousand platforms. Yet, while I admire beyond the power of words to express his public services, my clearest and most poignant memories will always be of Joseph Lyons, the man with whom I worked during some of the greatest and most distinguished years of his life… It was my honour to know him intimately in 1931 when the greatest crisis of his political life was upon him. Thereafter, our friendship was, I am glad to remember, unbroken. Even when I felt compelled to leave his government, only a few weeks ago, his attitude was generous and understanding. We parted with expressions of mutual affection and good will. It would have been impossible to quarrel with him in a personal sense.

But the last months of Joe's life had left their scars, and whatever the sincerity of a rival's posthumous comments, they did little to heal the rift for many in the Lyons family. Nell's daughter Marion recalls Sheila carrying a belief that Menzies was the cause of her father's ill health and ultimate early death. During the National Library interview with Dame Enid in 1972, her daughter Enid Austin was also present. Asked about Dame Enid's ongoing relationship with Robert Menzies when in parliament, Enid Austin was sceptical about Menzies' appreciation of Enid's abilities. Looking back on the period after her father's death, Enid Austin recalled a box of flowers sent to Dame Enid on the first anniversary of Joe's death: "You were in bed and I came in with an enormous box of flowers from Bob Menzies, and you said, 'Well, isn't that kind of him,' and I said, 'Kind … send them back! It's his guilty conscience.' I'm still sure that is what it was."

Whatever Enid Lyons' own feelings at the leadership struggles, and she did admit later they were strong and they hurt, she was not prepared to harbour bitterness, even from the outset. She would stand her ground on what she believed had happened, but it was not personal. When Robert Menzies was elected as the new leader of the UAP that April, after a turbulent nineteen days with Earle Page as acting prime minister and the rivalries playing out, Enid sent warm words of congratulations from her hospital bed to Menzies, words she confessed later made many of her friends furious and "no doubt my children would have been had they known, but I felt that was what Joe would have done". Her telegram read: "My congratulations and best wishes on your election to the leadership of a party which has still the power and the opportunity to serve Australia greatly." Menzies sent her a telegram in reply, "Your generous telegram has given me great encouragement. Pat and I hope to call on you at the weekend. Kindest regards, R G Menzies."

The weeks in the Mercy hospital did much to help Enid recuperate. She had passed through a maelstrom it would take years to come to terms with. But in her usual way, a hospital gave her seclusion, nursing support and time to evaluate her next move. Enid, to some extent, spent her life overusing her body like a favourite machine she could never trade in. Thirty-two times in the operating theatre, she would laugh in her old age. Each time she collapsed from over exertion, she would turn to the specialists and get an overhaul. Even in her later years, her grand daughter Libby Lyons recalls that she would come to Melbourne and book herself into the Mercy Hospital for time out and some special care and attention.

In the case of Joe's death, Enid's nervous exhaustion was real enough, but it did not totally stay her hand. She oversaw many personal responses to telegrams and letters that arrived from all manner of significant people in the days after Good Friday. Such was the amount of press reporting, in August that year, Prime Minister Robert Menzies sent Enid a volume containing press references to the illness and death of Joe writing, "While the events chronicled therein relate to an occasion of great grief for yourself and family, it is appropriate that you should have a permanent record of the magnificent tributes paid by the Australian people to the memory of your late husband and to his work as Prime Minister of the Commonwealth." Staff – Jack Swanson, Eileen Lenihan and Martin Threlfall – and family continued to help Enid in her formal responses. The older Lyons girls were an important backstop, arranging the removal of the Lyons belongings from The Lodge and taking over at Home Hill where the younger children were at school. Peter Lyons has fond memories of his sister Enid who often cared for him over years. But it was certainly a catastrophe the children were caught in, Janice just five and Peter barely at school. Their father whom they adored had suddenly gone, and mother was in hospital in a world turned upside down. Janice would be sent to boarding school from the age of five.

From the outside, the public figure of Enid Lyons for many was as strong as ever. One of the burdens of public life or personality politics is keeping alight the image a fan club sees as the full persona. To an adoring public, Enid Lyons would go on much as before, while in fact she was a crumpled wreck in a hospital bed. Requests to speak continued. One communication she received was from Jessie Street, then President of the United Associations of Women. Street's telegram was sent to Enid at the Mercy Hospital and requested that she nominate as a candidate for Joe's seat of Wilmot which Street said "would delight all of Australia, especially the women". A similar request came from Mrs Spotswood of the Australian Women's National League in Hobart. Enid replied politely to both of them: "I sincerely thank you all, but many things combine to make it impossible for me to do as you suggest." Instead, Joe's old friend Allan Guy, who had lost Bass in 1934, would stand and win the seat of Wilmot.

There was a chasm opening up before Enid. Her medication could help ease the pain of Joe's loss a little, but eventually cold realities had to be faced. The family had lived comfortably for years as Joe achieved the pinnacle of political success his country had to offer. But now, suddenly, they were close to penniless. There was no Joe to comfort Enid, much less to lean on in hard times. And these were the hardest of times she had ever experienced.

But Enid was never abandoned. From the outset, Richard and Maie Casey had been personally generous. Casey, who had broken down quietly in a hospital room as Joe died, had arranged for Myer Department store in Melbourne to open that Easter week to outfit the Lyons daughters in suitable black attire for the funeral. Later he offered to pay out any mortgage on Home Hill and would thereafter (overcoming as he put it "any residual anti-papist scruples") take over the fees at Xavier College for Kevin to complete his education as a boarder; and on occasion Kevin stayed with the Caseys during holidays. Enid Lyons would never forget the generosity and kindness of Maie and Richard Casey. The Gowries, Lord Gowrie and his wife Zara at Government House Canberra, kept in touch with offers of sanctuary. After Enid's first Christmas without Joe, Zara wrote to Enid, "I do hope you got through Xmas as well as it was *possible* for you. I am so glad you were surrounded with the family to help you. ... If you ever want to come up here – your Pink Bed awaits you."

As well, the fate of the Lyons family quickly touched a nerve in many of Joe's former colleagues. While Earle Page was acting Prime Minister, Cabinet initiated legislation to provide annuities for Enid and her dependent children. There had never before been a prime ministerial widow and no precedent existed for what should be done by way of compensation. Without any parliamentary superannuation scheme, here was a family of at least seven dependent children at the apex of the nation suddenly without any means of support. Whatever the differences of political opinion, the Lyons couple had served the nation in many ways.

Enid Lyons would write years after that her instincts were against any payment being made to her from the public purse: "We had planned for the years ahead on the basis of his earning capacity. Beyond that I had always insisted that with the children growing up I had within me sufficient resource to meet whatever situation arose … As soon as I was well enough, I could provide for myself and for the children until they were self-supporting."

In late November 1938, Irvine Douglas, by then with the *Sydney Morning Herald*, had approached Enid on the *Herald*'s behalf with an offer of a weekly column: "Management would like you to submit an article – which of course would be paid for when published – and state how much you would be prepared to accept for a regular weekly feature article." A couple of weeks earlier, Enid had received a letter from George Warneke, founding editor and then Editor-in-Chief of *The Australian Women's Weekly*, with a proposal that she agree to a contract for a weekly article "for which payment will be ten pounds a week". He had added, "In making this proposal to you, our opinion is that you have a personal prestige which is now established as something apart from your husband's position." Even as George Warneke prepared to leave for the United States in 1939, after falling out with Frank Packer, he was still keen for her to sign up with the *Weekly*, writing on 14 March: If you see your way clear to go ahead with the articles in the near future, I would like to fix this up before I go."

It was clear from both Warneke's letter ("glad to learn from you the other day that you now feel in a position to consider a concrete proposal") and that of Douglas ("following our recent conversation") it was Enid who had encouraged the offers. No doubt she was already thinking of Joe's retirement and the need to find alternative income. Both proposals were subject to control at the editorial end as to what she might write from any political position – "Our paper has kept clear of politics, and we regard it as essential that we maintain this detachment" (from George Warneke). In the case of the *Sydney Morning Herald*, Enid was advised by Douglas the "*Herald* would like to be able to suggest subjects from time to time".

After Joe's death, Enid believed she could support the family with her writing. However, she was quickly told her health was too fragile to think of paid employment. Moreover, it was argued by Page and others, a parliamentary annuity was only justice for Joe's family and she could not refuse what would ensure a future for their children. Their initial proposal – in the Bill that produced such rancour in the House – proposed the payment of an annuity for life to Enid of £500 a year and another annuity to her on behalf of the children of £500 per year until the youngest child reached the age of 21.

As details of the annuities proposal came to light, Enid was hit with the bitterness of Joe's legacy in leaving Labor, as well as the disappointment of having voices in the UAP party room oppose the generosity of the amounts proposed. Many Labor MPs refused to believe Lyons had died leaving such a small estate. At one stage, a woman's group published a newsletter that claimed, falsely, that Joe had died leaving a £50,000 insurance policy. Labor's Eddie Ward was the most fulsome in attack, declaring that Joe Lyons had drawn a salary of some £20,000 as Prime Minister with a travel allowance of more £2/10/0 a day and this was more than enough for him to have provided adequately for his family. Other Labor members complained that widows of ordinary Labor MPs, after rigorous means tests, were lucky to receive £3 a week. In the community, many wrote letters arguing that Joe Lyons' widow should receive no more than the widow of an Australian serviceman.

Apart from the bitterness felt at Joe's treachery in leaving Labor, many Labor members believed his well paid life as Prime Minister gave him more opportunities than most. But the heavy costs of the large Lyons family and Joe's generosity in the community had taken it toll. Just days before his death Joe had written a cheque for £60 and given it to a struggling farmer in Leongatha, Victoria so the man could buy cattle. He's a trier, Joe had declared after investigating the man's circumstances, and "he is entitled to his chance of a real start".

As the Lyons annuities Bill was debated on Wednesday 10 May, such was the indelicacy of the discussion, Labor leader John Curtin proposed handing the whole matter over to a committee for proper examination rather than have the financial state of the Lyons family become a spectacle for public debate. Menzies, who had argued strongly for the annuities, agreed. While Labor tried to reduce the payment substantially, eventually with UAP support Enid received an annual annuity of £500 and a further annuity for the education of her younger children which would be £500 in the first year and decrease as each child reached the age of sixteen, ceasing with Janet. This was a very reasonable living wage for a widow at the time. Enid would also, for some years, receive a supplementary stipend from a trust fund set up by Joe's business backers in Melbourne to cover the Lyons children's education.

The controversy over the annuities was a bitter blow for Enid so close to Joe's death. She wrote much later of: "Filthy epithets, threats, dead rats, things even more revolting, came through the post. Its effect on my already lacerated mind can be imagined. Soon I was not allowed to open my mail ... but it was more than eighteen months before the stream finally ended." It all left its scars and decades later Enid was still arguing how she would have preferred not to have needed the annuities. The bitterness says much about the petty nature of politics as, in time, payments to Enid Lyons and Elsie Curtin under special legislation were overtaken by later general provisions for widowed parliamentary spouses and by a generous superannuation scheme. In 1969 and 1970, letters between Prime Minister John Gorton and his treasurers indicate that payments to the ageing Enid Lyons and Elsie Curtin had fallen well behind normal payments to all others left widowed by parliamentary spouses, in spite of their husbands' importance. Increases in their payments had to be made.

Before long, all the Lyons children of school age would be sent to boarding schools in Melbourne, Janice barely after beginning school.

What effect years of boarding had on various Lyons children is hard to quantify. Kathleen was alienated by it, and Janice left bitter at her convent experience recalling how the Reverend Mother at Sacre Coeur in Melbourne would keep Dame Enid in the front parlour chatting leaving a bare twenty minutes to spend on visits with her daughters. But Rosemary, musically gifted like her bosom friends the Sullivan sisters, seems to have bloomed as one of the mischief makers at Sacre Coeur. Peter Lyons joined his brothers Kevin, Brendan and Barry at Xavier College but would look back and feel that they would have all been better served at local Tasmanian schools where they would have bonded more with the locals.

Then there was the fall from prominence they all underwent, today a condition known as limelight deprivation syndrome and a recognised mental challenge for all people having to adjust to no longer being in the media spotlight. Enid herself recognised this in her "Woman in Question" ABC TV interview in 1976 and reflected on how the children had not only lost a much loved father but had gone from national recognition to "coming back to their little home" in Devonport.

As a family, they had mixed among the most prominent in the nation for years; Desmond photographed with Robert Menzies, saying farewell to his important parents in 1937, Sheila written about much like an early version of Chelsea Clinton; the older girls on deck welcoming their parents back to Australia in Sydney, parents who had given a reception for 800 in London aboard their ocean liner; at the other end the little ones a centre of attention as a novelty in The Lodge and so it had gone. After Joe's death, what notoriety that came was Enid's and from that sprinkles of momentary interest in what her children might be doing from time to time – marriages and so forth – but essentially they were on the shelf politically.

It would take some adjustment. For, while they were no longer attached to immediate political importance, they continued to carry the Lyons name. "We never had any money," a much older Janice reflected in 2007. Looking back on her days at posh Sacre Coeur she felt embarrassed to return from summer holidays, when they would have spent just one day on the beach and one outing to the local pictures, with nothing much to tell or even an exciting Christmas present to reveal. "One year I was given a school bag for my Christmas present," she mused. Gone were the long days they had spent every summer with Joe and the extended family on Lillico's beach and other parts of the northern coastline they knew so well they had a stretch of sand or beach they thought of as their own.

Eliza and William Burnell had moved on to the Home Hill property in 1937 after building a cottage at the back of the block where they would eventually live out their days. By 1939, Eliza was seventy and no longer strong enough to take charge of the Lyons brood in Enid's absences. Moreover, her increasing dementia meant her health would be a growing burden for both William and Enid and the older Lyons daughters. Enid returned to Devonport after four weeks in the Mercy Hospital and her great chasm of readjustment began.

Enid was still just forty-two. Her married life with Joe had not only been companionship of the first order, it was also a very physical union. Their letters reveal not just their faith in God and family values but also their enjoyment of an occasional blue joke and saucy gossip. As Enid lay waiting for the birth of Janice in 1933, Joe had amused her with a bit of hanky-panky among the staff writing: "Tracey [driver] doesn't seem too well these days. He has had to take time off once or twice. I think he made it a welter in Sydney the week I was in Tas. Allan Guy tells me Rattan wasn't driving the car at all – it was his lady friend and she had no licence. Allan thinks they were not going *golfing*. What a turn out for Mrs Rattan."

The loneliness Enid faced now was far more than lack of adult conversation; she hungered for the physical presence of her husband as she had done over years in their separations. Only now there would be no returns from the mainland, no meetings in a Melbourne hotel or travel together where they could share not only their love of political platforms but also their marital bed. They had been one in all things, including the entertainment of good conversation. Enid recalled some of their evenings at Home Hill with Devonport acquaintances in her National Library interview:

> We had friends with similar interests and we had delightful discussions on this, that and the other. I remember two men who were journalists, great friends of ours, and every time when we would go home to Devonport, after we had settled in, we would ring up these two men [one Jack Donohue – an editor of the Burnie *Advocate*] and we'd have a gorgeous evening, finishing up in the end about one or two o'clock in the morning, out on the front steps of our home … still laughing about our discussions…. The children would say they'd wake up sometimes. … We would have discussed practical politics, we would have discussed literature, I suppose we'd have discussed everything under the sun.

Around Christmas time in 1939, writing to Kingsley Henderson from the "Group", a close personal friend, she confessed to enduring times "when the heavens and the earth are all swallowed up in utter grief and loneliness and I feel I cannot face the years that probably lie ahead of me. I am much too young." In a letter to Neville Chamberlain on 1 June 1939 Enid had written, "I scarcely know where to begin the building of my life anew. My husband's death came with such terrible suddenness that I have been stunned. The life we had made together is so completely shattered that I falter at the prospect. For the children of course I must go on but I confess that my heart feels dead within me." And with the sort of frenzy her mother had shown for public volunteering after the death of Bertram, Enid threw herself at work admitting she was "obsessed with the idea that there was work that I must do".

Self confidence and ease on stage was something Joe had recognised in Enid early on. By the end of the 1930s, her name was marketable even without Joe. She had been saleable for years not only as the wife of the Prime Minister but also as a popular public speaker and writer who could pull in a fan club. She may not have enamoured Robert Menzies or Senator George Pearce who seem to have found her style too emotional but George's Pearce's wife Eliza, like thousands of others, found her a tremendous speaker. Radio had come into its own during the Lyons years in The Lodge, Enid and Joe making use of radio broadcasts from its earliest days. When it was suggested to Enid that she might begin regular broadcasts on a paid basis, she took the plunge.

By the time of the funeral for Tasmania's premier Albert Ogilvie, in June 1939, Enid was back to reasonable form. She attended the Ogilvie funeral in Hobart, confirmation that the rift between Lyons and Ogilvie had healed before Joe died. By June 1939, events in Europe were moving fast in the direction of a confrontation between Hitler and Britain. Hitler had signed non-aggression pacts with Denmark, Latvia and Estonia and by 23 August would have signed the Nazi-Soviet non-aggression pact, all part of Hitler keeping his northern and eastern neighbours quiet while he made plans to move on Poland and further west.

Enid's broadcasts began as a re-entry of the Lyons voice into the public arena just as the nation was looking for leadership as it faced the throes of global conflict. "Long before I was fit to do so, I began a series of broadcasts," wrote Enid in 1949, "which I carried on with increasing difficulty for several months, while I struggled with the family's future." On 22 May, A P Findlay from Findlay's in Launceston – a subsidiary of Macquarie Broadcasting Services – had written to H G Horner, the Director of the Macquarie Broadcasting Network, advising that after meeting with Dame Enid at her home in Devonport, he had been able to secure her for a weekly broadcast of fifteen to twenty minutes every Sunday evening for twelve months at the rate of £10 per broadcast. If required, she would also do a second broadcast in any week for a further £5 a broadcast. The broadcasts were to commence in August or September.

However, with the declaration of war that August and some equivocation on the part of Dame Enid ("you did not at the time feel well enough to go ahead with any project and you asked to be relieved of any previous undertaking" – H G Hordern, 19 October 1939) Palmolive, the prospective sponsor, moved to an alternative commitment and H G Horner came back to Dame Enid with another proposal. Having lost Palmolive, Macquarie Broadcasting was still prepared to offer her a series of talks over four to six weeks. These would commence in lead up to Christmas 1939. Which is what finally happened. H G Horner wrote to Dame Enid on 27 November that Macquarie "shall be very glad to know fully a week in advance where you will be on the following Sunday night, so that the necessary trunk line arrangements can be made." On 6 December, H G Horner enclosed a cheque for Enid's initial broadcast, from 2CA in Canberra on 3 December, saying: "we have received many congratulatory messages from all over Australia and your further talks are awaited by listeners with interest."

By March 1940, David Worrell of the Herald Broadcasting Stations, headed by 3DB in Melbourne, was offering Enid the chance to head up a weekly program for women four days a week – "we need the cooperation of a woman whose name, character and personality would command the immediate attention and respect of women everywhere." The letter was forwarded to her by Sir Keith Murdoch. His covering letter assured her the program could be done from her home. He added by hand, "With kindest regards and best wishes from Lady Murdoch and myself". The proposal was more than Enid could manage but it would have flattered her to be sought out by Keith hiimself.

By 1940, Enid had relocated to Melbourne, taking up a lease on a Californian bungalow in the leafy streets immediately behind Sacre Coeur at 11 Valley View Road, East Malvern. Her children of school age were by then all in Melbourne boarding schools and with the war and the possibility of disruption of the ferry service between Tasmania and the mainland, Enid wanted to be as close as possible to her children. There was even a gathering in the Devonport Town Hall in late February to farewell the Lyons family, an "au revoir" it was called. As in previous moves, Enid would not last long before she was heading back to Devonport. Her gypsy character continued, encouraged as always by her nervous condition and unpredictable heath.

In later interviews, Enid spoke of her health breaking down by late 1940, forcing her to give up her radio talks. In fact, her deal with Macquarie Broadcasting, regardless of her popular appeal which had kept her on air long after the initial six week deal, was tenuous. Sponsorship money, sought to make the contract more reliable, had become scarce with the war. While she had been paid for some talks to be published and had done extremely well out of her foray into broadcasting, by May 1940 Enid was requesting more details about her agreements with Macquarie Broadcasting as she was still on a week by week arrangement.

Horner replied to Enid on 7 May writing that he would understand if she was considering an offer from a rival network (possibly Murdoch) and made clear that sponsorship was not assured for the continuation of her talks. Enid had not handled her negotiations as deftly as she might have, relying on Murray as go-between and quibbling over the commercialisation of her talks. Yet again, by the time she had agreed to a commercial sponsor, the sponsor had moved elsewhere. On 20 June, Horner wrote to Enid that talks for an alternative sponsorship had come to nothing and the last talk of her series would be broadcast on 30 June. Enid would then lose her job.

Some of Enid's scruples over commercial production for her talks would have been her concern at being seen to be promoting products while she was also getting a public pension. However, this was hardly the point. Whether sponsored or not, she was still being paid. She seems not to have understood that a commercial business had to finance its programs. And, as Horner advised her, her talks were at the high end of production costs since they were recorded live from wherever she was to be. In July 1940, Enid was offered a chance to broadcast for the ABC in a letter from the ABC's Victorian Manager Robert McCall who wrote saying, "We think it would be useful at the present time to broadcast regular talks by leading women citizens, such as yourself, on the part that could be played by women in Australia's war effort" The payment would be considerably less than on commercial radio at £4 per talk. But it had all got the better of Enid – the uncertainties and stresses of haggling in the market place had sapped her.

None of which erased the value of Enid's prominence. When Frank Maher, Director of the National Secretariat of Catholic Action, wrote to Enid in early December, he was well aware of her indifferent health problems. Nonetheless, he was keen to keep her abreast of work being done to revamp the Catholic Women's Guild. She had become a vessel for influence and would continue to be sought out for support and advice.

The requests came from all manner of associations and auxiliaries, people known to her and not; from conservative friends like Penny Gullett wanting her to speak at a rally for a war appeal in the Melbourne Town Hall to Jessie Street who wrote from Darling Point in Sydney a few months after Joe's death asking Enid how to best go about gaining a seat in parliament: "I would so like to discuss with you the possibility of my entry into federal politics. I have never been associated with any party so I do not know how to set about things." She signed off "with love and warmest remembrances".

Sir Keith Murdoch was encouraging at this time, in letters. In August, he wrote saying he had arranged for young Enid to start at 3DB and move later to the *Herald*, a position she never took up as she married soon after. Sheila had married in October 1939 and by September 1940 was the mother of a daughter making Enid a grandmother for the first time (she would eventually be grandmother of some fifty grandchildren). Writing to Enid after the happy event, Sir Keith sent "hearty congratulations" adding "splendid news for the country! We cannot have too many of this type."

Murdoch wrote more seriously in December, albeit wishing Enid and the family a happy Christmas, but more importantly advising her that he had for some time been trying to have her proposed lecture tour of America decided. The Department of Information, in October, advised the proposal should be put to both government and opposition for funds to be made available. Enid was seriously interested. She returned to Tasmania that October to sort out what would happen in her absence, asking that the cost of the Tasmanian trip be included in the US package when it was finalised. Enid never made a US lecture tour – funding did not eventuate. However, as he had been (unsuccessfully) when pressuring Enid to take part in a huge Brisbane "Win the War" rally in September, Murdoch was persistent. In his December letter he wrote, "I cannot understand delays [US trip], but I really have had little encouragement in one important quarter [Menzies] & I can do no more than leave the matter for the new minister." He wrote on 31 January 1941, this time to "keep in touch with you", but again mentioning her proposed trip to the US. He offered any help he might give her children in finding employment, adding also, "If you are going on with your book of recollections, let me help you in any way if possible". A hint that he was interested in publishing her memoirs.

Enid had withstood the aftermath of Joe's death fairly stoically, in spite of a month in hospital. Pressing forward with paid work had seemed her only alternative if her very large family was to survive – in spite of generous public and private allowances being paid to them. In the first week of October 1940, young Enid suddenly announced she would be marrying Lieutenant Maurice Austin and that the wedding would be held on a Thursday, just three days later. Her new husband would be embarking for the Middle East a fortnight after the wedding. Enid showed no hint of nervous exhaustion as she arrived hurriedly from Devonport for the wedding in St Roch's Church, Glen Iris and was immaculate in a black frock and small black hat with a cluster of flowers at the front. The wedding, meant to be small and private, attracted press coverage and a huge crowd of onlookers at the church.

By late 1940, however, Enid was spent. Neville Chamberlain's death had shocked her in early November and she had spoken in his memory a fortnight later: "There need be no apology for Mr Chamberlain. He leaves a world in flames, but a world where to the last moment he sought to prevent the lighting of the fires. It is not true to say he played the weakling at Munich … his action at Munich saved us two years ago is true, and because of that is helping to save us now." But even as she spoke these words, the Chamberlain legacy was taken as one of failure. For many, a delay that gave Hitler an early advantage.

Soon after this, in December, Enid ceased her public involvement: "In the end I began to have a nervous horror of standing before an audience… All kinds of fears oppressed me and it became quite impossible for me to follow the discussions at various committee meetings." That December she closed off her public involvement.

Enid arrived home to find her mother quite ill. Eliza lingered a month and died on 10 January 1941. She had taken her secrets with her. A laudatory obituary in the Burnie *Advocate* recognised her contribution to public life but left her part in the Lyons story for others to measure. Enid would write in 1949 of how she felt as her mother died: "I looked at her and thought of the long years behind her, of the high courage and the firm principle. No ordinary spirit had inhabited that tiny form lying so still and straight beneath the covers." A long chapter of Enid's life had finally closed.

CHAPTER 18

JOINING THE CARRION CROWS

By the second half of 1940, it was evident Robert Menzies' election as federal leader of the United Australia Party had not delivered the party harmony many had sought prior to Joe Lyons' death. Internal squabbling continued to haunt the parliamentary ranks of the UAP. *The Sydney Morning Herald* had begun an anti-Menzies campaign reminiscent of the Murdoch press campaign against Lyons in 1938-9. Discussions took place about the formation of a new conservative party; it was generally felt the parliamentary party lacked talent.

Then, on 13 August, an RAAF bomber crashed coming into Canberra, incinerating all ten passengers and crew. Menzies lost three of his ministerial colleagues who were aboard – Geoffrey Street, James Fairbairn and Henry Gullett. The tragedy left Menzies to write, "I felt that, for me, the end of the world had come." A week after the crash Menzies called a general election for 21 September, an election the UAP almost lost and which left it clinging to government by a slender one (independent) seat majority. In spite of all this, in late January, Menzies took off for four months to Britain via Singapore, returning via the US. It was a trip his wife Pat felt was very unwise. In addition to important meetings with all major players in the war effort, where he put Australia's case especially in relation to Singapore, Menzies enjoyed the usual social round and weekends at Chequers and received an honorary degree from the Chancellor of Bristol University, Winston Churchill. For all that, Churchill exasperated

Menzies with his tendency to exclude Australia when discussing the Pacific with the US.

Soon after Menzies returned home, in spite of a warm public welcome initially, the strength of the Labor Opposition and disillusionment with the war as Australian troops fell in the Crete campaign overwhelmed him, along with disaffection with his leadership within the UAP. He had by then also lost the confidence of Keith Murdoch and press attacks were constant. In late August, Menzies resigned as UAP leader. So weak had the UAP parliamentary team become, Country Party leader Arthur Fadden was voted unopposed as the new leader of the conservative coalition. Fadden would serve as Prime Minister a mere 41 days before the UAP lost the numbers in the House when it lost the support of the two independents keeping it in government. John Curtin took over as the first Labor Prime Minister in a decade. In December 1941, Japan attacked US bases in Pearl Harbor, Hawaii; on 15 February 1942, British forces in Singapore surrendered to the Japanese. The war for Australians was now very close to home.

Through 1941 and 1942, Enid Lyons was leading a gently healing existence in Devonport, watching her first grandchildren grow, sharing Home Hill with daughter Enid and her first child, gardening and welcoming the younger children home from boarding schools in the holidays. As well as, it now appears, meeting her mother's old friend Aloysius Joyce in Eileen Joyce's office in Burnie.

Enid's breakdown after her mother's death had been a delayed reaction to losing Joe. The full meaning of his loss had taken her almost two years to recognise. As she had soldiered on, family life had undergone rapid change; the older Lyons children had become adults, some had left home and were making their own contributions to the nation's war effort. Desmond had enrolled in the RAAF three days after the declaration of war, in September 1939. Kevin soon followed, joining the AIF; before long Kathleen had joined the Women's

Auxiliary Australian Air Force (WAAAF) and Moira the Australian Women's Army Service (AWAS). In time, Sheila's husband joined the Air Force.

Enid read the daily newspapers with wry despondency as the political machinations of Canberra played out. Arthur Fadden remained Opposition leader but the Murdoch press, once again, was backing Menzies for strong conservative leadership. The Labor government continued to hang on with its bare majority in the House until, on 7 July 1943, John Curtin announced an election would be held on 21 August.

Labor would record a landslide victory in both Houses of parliament in the 1943 election, the woeful result for the UAP and CP Coalition enhancing the belief that the UAP was a defunct political party and that a more consolidated and policy driven conservative party was needed. The one victorious moment of the 1943 election for the UAP, however, was Enid Lyons' win in the seat of Darwin, now called Braddon. The electorate stretched across northern Tasmania from the western and southern fringes of Devonport, to the mining areas of the West Coast. Without Joe, but with all that she had learned from him about electioneering and with many of his good supporters, Enid had risen (literally) from her bed and got back into public life.

Enid often related with a flourish how on a day in May 1943, her daughter Enid had brought her the morning newspaper with her breakfast tray. On this day, however, Enid junior was rather excited. The newspapers carried the story that Sir George Bell, their local federal member, had announced he would not contest the next federal election because of his failing health. Handing over the paper, young Enid had insisted her mother put her name forward for preselection. No amount of protest from Dame Enid had any effect on her daughter. Mentioning her indifferent health, young Enid told her mother firmly that she had the finest recuperative powers of anyone – this was undoubtedly true given the number of times her mother had taken herself off to hospital only to return to public life soon after. Moreover, clearly the Lyons family despaired of Dame Enid's retreat into a private world. That day, in May 1943, Enid Austin told her mother firmly, "The excitement alone will carry you through! But in any case, I'd rather you shortened your life by ten years than see you mouldering away like this."

After weeks of uncertainty, Dame Enid finally made the hard decision to throw her "cap over the windmill" and put her name forward for preselection. She had, after all, always urged women to play their part in public life when possible. By the time she had decided on nominating, however, the UAP was already considering two male candidates for the seat. Even so, the application of Dame Enid Lyons meant the UAP could not reject such a nomination easily. As well, the UAP had never organised itself at the grass roots, it had never even written out its political platform.

Enid spoke in her National Library interview of how her nomination was put forward by a good friend Frank Edwards, whom she had known since he was one of Joe's colleagues in the State parliament in 1915. Edwards had himself considered standing for Darwin: "[Frank] took along my nomination to this ad hoc committee, there were no rules at the time for putting in a nomination or anything like that; it was always done on this ad hoc basis, they lacked that basic organisation of a political party." There was turmoil, as Enid put it, but eventually, with the precedent of Tasmania's Hare Clarke multi member electorates for State elections, the problem was easily resolved by having three UAP candidates stand for the seat of Darwin in the 1943 federal election. They would each attract preferences to strengthen the UAP ticket.

It turned out to be quite a canny move, whether by strategy or default. The electorate had changed significantly since the previous election – industries had prospered after the war of 1914-18 and in the years of the current war the working population had grown; even George Bell was not confident he would retain anything like the comfortable majority he had. The UAP had chosen two men they believed would attract support from different kinds of voters. One was a farmer by the name of John Wright, selected because the majority of conservative voters in the electorate were from farming districts. The other was an auctioneer and devout Anglican from Burnie by the name of John Leary and expected to attract Anglophile townies, although later Enid mused that his Irish surname deflected some of his appeal there. Coming in as a third UAP candidate, Enid was, as she had been all those years before when a Labor outsider in the State election for Denison, expected to have no chance of winning principally because she was a woman but also, as Enid herself put it, "I was a Catholic and that was a point not in favour there." Among conservatives in the far north of Tasmania, Enid was well aware of a latent sectarianism even in the 1940s.

But she won. And for the same reasons women candidates have proven successful in elections since the 1990s. Enid worked the electorate hard knowing she was at a disadvantage because of her sex, backed by a fiercely loyal team of seasoned operatives, Frank and Madge Edwards, Murray White and Hector McFie her principal backers. She never took any vote for granted, presenting herself as Joe had done in every corner of the electorate where she might win a vote, travelling in freezing conditions to the West Coast to speak with miners at Queenstown and Zeehan, former stomping ground of the Joyce brothers and from where Aloysius Joyce's niece Eileen Joyce had gone on, via Perth, to become a world famous concert pianist. For decades, Dame Enid Lyons and Eileen Joyce would be two of the very few women whose names appeared in Australia's *Who's Who*.

A photo published during the 1943 election campaign shows Enid and Hector McFie on the Queenstown railway station, heavily rugged up in hats, thick coats and gloves with a life sized snowman between them. Enid recalled her weeks campaigning, with humour and detail, in *Among the Carrion Crows* (1972). Excitement certainly carried her on. Wearing two overcoats ("looking more like an overstuffed ottoman than a prospective Member of Parliament") she addressed an indoor but unheated meeting in Queenstown – "a barrage of interjections from a leather-lunged unionist, determined once and for all to demolish all female pretensions, kept the meeting lively. We felt it could be declared a success." In Zeehan, there was a power failure and she was advised against a public meeting lit only by candles ("first the policeman and then the local doctor came to say that in their opinion to hold a meeting would be unsafe") – there was a worry that in the excitement of a candle lit hall, one of the "hatters" (ageing retired miners considered a bit mad) might "throw a missile".

For all that, Enid's campaign was most successful in more closely settled districts of the north. Murray White had a very flattering photo of Enid printed so that, "It seemed impossible to travel more than a few miles in any direction without meeting my smiling countenance on posters, on handbills, on how-to-vote cards, and in advertisements in the local paper." They used the radio whenever possible for broadcasts, "It was the period of the radio 'bed-time story', and whenever I was within range of a broadcasting station, I made a feature of five minute broadcasts at 10 pm, for which the complexities of [war] rationing provided wonderful material." On one occasion she simply read out in a monotone the regulations governing drapers, the bureaucratic entanglements becoming absurd to hear. Meanwhile Enid was in her element driving over the speed limit to meeting after meeting. In later years Peter Lyons' children, Michael and Christine, nicknamed her "Nanny Brabham" after Australia's famous racing driver. She told her grandson Peter once that whenever she felt down she would cheer herself up with a long drive in her car. In the 1943 election, every drive gave Enid another thrill.

On the night of the election, Enid went to bed uncertain of

her victory. There were seven candidates – three UAP, two ALP, a Communist and an Independent Laborite. Although Enid had gained more than 1300 first preference votes than those for her two UAP colleagues put together, the ALP candidates had most of the Communist and Independent Labor preferences. Exhausting the preference count took time. Newspapers reported that Labor had won. At one point, over the days that followed, Enid conceded defeat. But as the votes came in from soldiers on active service, her tally rebounded and after eight "counts" of preferences Enid was declared the winner with 51.49 per cent of the preferred vote. She had beaten her main ALP rival, Eric Reece (much later a premier of Tasmania) by 816 votes. Today, this would be seen as a relatively comfortable win.

After the declaration of the polls for Darwin on 14 September, Dame Enid Lyons became an overnight sensation. As had happened after Joe's death, she was besieged by letters and telegrams from notable and ordinary folk, only this time it was all joy. Friends who had known her from childhood, people she had never met, all manner of women's organisations so proud of her, Archbishops and clerics, nuns and future parliamentary colleagues alike wrote and sent telegrams singing her praises and saying congratulations.

Enid had not only given hope to UAP leaders Hughes and Menzies at a bad time for the party (Hughes had telegraphed, "Your victory compensates for many defeats." and Menzies had said the defeat was like being run over by a steam roller) but she had, more importantly, become Australia's first woman elected to the House of Representatives. In Western Australia, Labor's Dorothy Tangney had become Australia's first woman Senator. It did not go unnoticed that Eleanor Roosevelt was at the same time in Brisbane meeting with US troops – women seemed to be making history all over.

The effect on Enid was invigorating; her health was never better; friends and media noted the new bounce in her stride. On 12 October, Elisabeth Murdoch wrote to congratulate Enid, starting her letter with, "Having just seen a perfectly dazzling picture of you in Collins Street, I hasten to do what I should have done weeks ago – write and offer you my humble congratulations." She added, "Keith and I were delighted that you made the grade, knowing you a little we appreciate the fact that you are one of the few women of Australia who is likely to add stature to our national life and we expect great things of you!"

Enid had taken off running. Her instinctive love of the public arena and her old habits of moving from function to function had been restored. Within days of her win, she was broadcasting on ABC radio a talk entitled "The Role of Women in the Post-war World". By November, she had done functions in Sydney, Newcastle and Melbourne and was briefly back in Devonport before taking off for Adelaide later that month. She had clashed with the Reverend Stuart Watts at a conference in Newcastle over sex education, which Enid believed should be left to parents; she had spoken up for Australian women wanting to adopt some of the "thousands of children in Britain bereft of their parents because of this terrible war".

In Devonport, she told a reporter by phone that "my nose has been glued to my desk. Just when I think I am making a big hole in my correspondence, along comes another large batch to be answered." In Adelaide while addressing the Women's Council of the Liberal and Country League she made a strong plea for "decent housing" to enable "young Australia to grow up healthy and happy". And added, "Give people some say in the kind of houses they want. Don't just regiment them into rows of mass-produced homes." Not surprisingly, she would soon disappoint Keith Murdoch with her populist views. Elisabeth Murdoch recalled that Enid as an MP "rather fell out with Keith, she became very Labor-ish". For all that, he was still keen to publish her columns in *The Sun*.

Former Liberal politician Michael Hodgman, who became close to Enid Lyons in her later years, reflected that, "She wasn't a stuffy person. She had strong ideas on social justice. And she wasn't your conservative at all. She was a reforming Liberal from good solid Labor stock. A good combination really." This was clear from the first words Enid spoke in the federal parliament in her maiden speech on 29 September, 1943.

Enid Lyons and Dorothy Tangney had taken their seats in the Houses of Parliament with the attention of a nation glued on them. Press articles noted that Parliament House, now known as "Old Parliament House", a white art deco building of square and squat proportions, was hardly ready for its first female MPs. They were, however, advantaged in one sense by their gender. At the time, Parliament House was undergoing extensions; many MPs had no room or office of their own and worked in the Common room where general gossip and banter often took the place of serious work. As women, however, Enid Lyons and Dorothy Tangney were allotted small rooms as offices, although Enid often went to the Common room just to keep in touch.

Then there was the issue of billiard room and bar – no woman had ever been in these places. Just how would male MPs react to a female "invasion"? And Governor General Lord Gowrie had to check his terms of address when opening parliament – no longer could he say "Gentlemen of the House of Representatives" or "Gentlemen of the Senate".

None of the Lyons family joined Enid as she made her debut in Canberra, but she told a Melbourne journalist, "I will be surrounded by friends on both sides of the House." And indeed she would. The Lyons couple had always maintained good relations with many in the various parties represented in Canberra. Enid held Labor's John Curtin, whom she saw in many ways very like Joe, in high regard and Curtin was fond of Enid. Months before Curtin died, Enid begged him to give up the leadership of his government as she recognised in him the health symptoms that had killed Joe. Curtin knew what she meant but said he must go on. It was history repeating itself.

Then there was Labor's Ben Chifley who almost joined Joe in 1931 during the months of the break. Jim Scullin, surprisingly, was also a friend and would often arrive at Joe's prime ministerial office for a chat.

Enid stopped in Melbourne on her way to Canberra for shopping, to do a live broadcast and interviews, visit her children at boarding schools and address packed functions, one for the Australian Women's National League. She was photographed buying clothes – interest had grown as to what she might wear once in parliament, a matter she quickly settled by deciding on a couple of black frocks and a number of what she called white "lace and muslin jabots". On the day Parliament opened, however, she wore the Lady Astor classic of white blouse and black suit, black brimmed hat and a fur draped over her shoulders, her figure notably trimmed down after her illness in Devonport and months of electioneering.

For her swearing in, Enid had taken with her a special Bible, a King James version and the one Catholic Joe Lyons had used when being sworn in as Prime Minister by a Jewish Governor General, Sir Isaac Isaacs. A remarkable combination which said much about Australia. Somehow the Bible had been given to St Patrick's Cathedral in Melbourne and Enid had been trying for years to have it found. Then, a fortnight before the federal election, Rev Patrick Lyons (no relation), Vicar General at St Patrick's, wrote to Enid saying he had found the Bible and had sent it to her by separate mail – "I could find no trace of it until this week when it turned up … Perhaps it may be a good omen and I hope that you may be able to use it in the near future for another swearing-in ceremony." On Thursday 24 September 1943, that is just what Enid did.

Sworn in she was, but Enid faced an outcry from opponents. Reports said her election was to be challenged based on a section of the Constitution that prevents a person who is being paid any allowance or pension from Commonwealth coffers to stand for parliament. Prime Minister John Curtin told the press this did not affect Dame Enid, but the stories went on.

It was all very disconcerting; Enid, wrote of how it left her standing by her bed trembling. She, who had tried to avoid the payment originally and suffered months of hate mail as a result of the annuities being granted. With her election, she had told the press she would relinquish the government annuity. One of her first acts as an MP was to meet with Prime Minister John Curtin to have the annuity stopped, which he refused to allow. Curtin was only too well aware how temporary a political career can be, that Enid was not always in good health; he had no intention, what's more, of opening old sores, and genuinely believed a Prime Minister's widow should not be left without means. It was a matter of respect for the position.

Curtin and Enid reached an arrangement for Enid to pay back the annuity each month. Later a simpler means was found for Enid not to accept the annuity while she was an MP. Nothing transpired from the threat of a legal challenge. When John Curtin died in office, on 5 July 1945, Enid strongly opposed those of her conservative colleagues who wanted to argue against an annuity for Elsie Curtin just to "hurt" the other side. "There is only one person who will suffer," said Enid "and surely death has hurt her enough." Enid later wrote that as she watched her colleagues allow the legislation to pass, in silence, "I sat in the House barely able to restrain my tears".

Over sixty years later, Australia's House of Representatives and Senate now includes many women MPs on both sides. Even so, it is still a media highlight whenever a woman "first" comes into vision. In 2007, it was Julia Gillard as Australia's first Deputy Prime Minister. Words spoken, actions made, every move is recorded. So it was with heart stopping interest that Australians waited to hear or read the maiden speech of their first female MP in the House of Representatives, made on 29 September 1943. Although admitting later to not having eaten before her delivery and being extremely nervous ("my lips were stiff when I started but all the men were wishing me well"), Enid did not disappoint – eloquent, richly written, and delivered in Enid's long practised and well trained lilting voice it surprised then and still remains one of the classic speeches in Australian political life. She opened:

> It would be strange indeed were I not tonight deeply conscious of the fact, and not a little awed by the knowledge, that on my shoulders rests a great weight of responsibility; because this is the first occasion a woman has addressed this House. For that reason, it is an occasion which, for every woman in the Commonwealth, marks in some degree a turning point in history ... I know that Honourable Members have viewed the advent of women to the legislative halls with something approaching alarm; they have feared, I have no doubt, the somewhat too vigorous use of a new broom. I wish to reassure them. I hold very sound views on brooms, and sweeping. Although I quite realise that a new broom is a very useful adjunct to the work of the housewife, I suspect that it is very unpopular in the broom cupboard; and this particular new broom knows that she has a very great deal to learn from the occupants of – I dare not say this particular broom cupboard.

It was Enid at her best. Having sorted out the metaphors, "of the kitchen rather than those of the operating theatre, the workshop, or the farm" she moved on to quote King George V and his belief that, "The foundation of a nation's greatness is in the homes of its people" warming to her oft used theme of the family. She spoke of her love of early Australian values, of the history and historical experiences that had woven "the fabric of Australian life" – "hatred of oppression, love of 'a fair go' and a passion for justice ... qualities of initiative and daring that have marked our men in every war in which they have fought – qualities which, I hope, will never be allowed to die".

Sounding at times a social reformer but also an economic conservative, she argued for measures that would support growing families and women who wanted to be mothers. On the subject of population, she said she had pondered, "not with my feet upon the mantle-piece, but knee deep in shawls and feeding bottles". She spoke out against the basic wage only for a man, wife and three children when "the three notional children of the man who has not any, militate against the success in life of the children in other families of six and seven and eight". Child endowment should cover more then just three children. And there should be a social security safety net for all and contributed to by every citizen with an income. She agreed with the need for better maternity, nursing services and better houses but added these, "cannot in themselves revive the falling birth rate". The nation had to reverse a culture where a "woman who became the mother of a family was something of a lunatic".

For the armed forces who would soon, she felt, be returning from war, she wanted a homecoming that provided them with training and jobs, and wives, mothers and nation prepared for men coming back "young, eager, and impatient … heartily sick of everything to do with the Army and with war". She then faced her demons somewhat, voicing her thoughts on the international scene:

> Because of what has happened to me in this war I have become disillusioned. For years, I went about the world preaching the gospel of peace and friendship and co-operation. I believed with all my heart in disarmament, but I can never again advocate such a policy. I believe we must arm ourselves to meet whatever danger may threaten us, but I also believe that we must co-operate with all those forces of good that are working for peace, and with all those people who have a will to peace, so that we may do whatever lies in our power to preserve peace in our times.

As she came to the end of her speech, Enid invoked a memory of her husband without mentioning his name saying, "I bear the name of one of whom it was said in this Chamber that to him the problems of government were not problems of blue books, not problems of statistics, but problems of human values and human hearts and human feelings. That, it seems to me, is a concept of government that we might well cherish."

The press and media lauded her speech. Australians were justly proud of their first female MHR. It was not only to make use of a bold one liner that William (Billy) Morris Hughes would refer to Enid in parliament as "a bird of paradise among carrion crows".

'A bird of paradise among carrion crows' – Dame Enid becomes the first female member of an Australian Cabinet, December 1949.

CHAPTER 19

LEADING LADY OF THE HOUSE

For Dame Enid Lyons and Senator Dorothy Tangney, entering the all-male realm of Australia's parliamentary chaps in the early 1940s, was an exhilarating experience. The war had seen women enter many areas of what had for centuries been the work provinces of men. For the first two women taking seats in Australia's federal parliament, there were barriers to overcome. Early on, John Curtin had learned of the long hours both women endured travelling to and from Canberra, Enid crossing Bass Strait in wartime with dangers for shipping and then making a gruelling train journey, from Melbourne via Goulburn, in packed carriages, sitting up for sixteen hours at a time and trying to exercise her deadened limbs around sleeping soldiers in the corridors. He ignored Enid's protests that she deserved no different from any of her male colleagues and ensured thereafter that both women used air travel for all their parliamentary journeys.

Amid an atmosphere of gentlemanly good manners among her colleagues, Enid observed only one disadvantage in being a woman MP. This was the undue sympathy she felt she was given after withstanding parliamentary gags, debate guillotines and abrupt rulings from the Labor Chair such as happened in an attempt to end her speech on estimates the night Ben Chifley was to introduce the Bill to nationalise the banks.

Enid had sought early to master tactics in her parliamentary career. She discovered how often when she spoke in the House, Senators would arrive to watch – she was a curiosity piece and this disturbed her. She was an MP on merit not as a piece of fine china. In the House, sitting in the back row directly behind her leader, she watched colleagues noted for their speech making and oratory and, as time went on, determined she would take a more assertive position in debates.

On the day scheduled for the introduction of Labor's Bank Nationalisation Bill, 15 October 1947, Enid's estimates speech had been interrupted by the customary break for dinner. Under parliamentary rules, she was entitled to finish her speech (a full fifteen minutes left) when the House resumed at 8 pm. But this moment also coincided with the newly introduced evening radio broadcast of parliament, a time Labor had planned for the Prime Minister's bank legislation speech so it would be heard across the nation. As the House broke for dinner, Enid's parliamentary colleagues urged her to use her entitlement of time, thereby capturing a slab of the Prime Minister's radio slot for the opposition.

For her efforts, graphically recalled in *Among The Carrion Crows*, Enid was almost suspended from the House. Earle Page nicknamed her "the woman who wouldn't be sat down" as she persisted in challenging Chair Joe Clark's rulings. Enid was not pleased with her effort, later believing she would have shown more courage to have refused to withdraw and copped a suspension. The Chair's interruptions forced her on the defensive and her time was whittled away with back and forth over standing orders. By 8.15pm she had made few points against the government and it all left her "badly rattled". Even so, Enid had found the temerity to make a few mistakes on the way to a stoush.

Then, in the weeks that followed, with all the "unwarranted" sympathy she resented, Enid took it as a feather in her cap when the Communist Party declared her "black". Her notoriety became such that news reports described how early chivalry in parliament for the "lady Member" would hereafter cease. Enid realised her criticism of the government had been more effective in the media reports that followed her speech than in what she had said in parliament. Unwittingly, she had achieved what politicians of every hue take for granted seven decades later – the power of media and communication in making a message noticed.

All this was a long way from the Dame Enid who first entered parliament. As she took her seat, those former days when she had followed politics as a parliamentary spouse, albeit of the first order, were her only guide. She had rarely viewed parliamentary proceedings, partly because Joe preferred her not to watch him in the House and because of her busy personal schedule. So parliamentary procedures took her time to conquer when an MP herself. As the lone female in the boys' House, Enid admitted in her ABC TV "Woman in Question" interview in 1976 that her feminine tactic was to never "instruct" any of her male colleagues but only to "ask" them about matters so that they felt very important and valued her conversation. And she soon realised the parliamentary ranks of a reduced opposition team left her opportunities not available to Senator Dorothy Tangney who was somewhat remote from public notice in the Senate and a novice among a far larger group, and one in government where ministerial voices took a greater role.

Dame Enid had her advantages. Her title gave her seniority in the social-political pecking order of the day. Her name was a household one across the nation. She had her fan club, and not merely in her electorate. She was continually followed by the press, asked to do broadcasts, speak at functions, lend her name to charity campaigns. Had she been a man, there's no telling where her career might have taken her. Dame Enid Lyons had influence, something not lost on her rivals on both sides of politics. That presence, along with her experience as a mature woman at ease in the public glare, gave her a head start as a female rookie in a man's world. Apart from all that,

Dame Enid stood with pleasure before microphones and on any ready podium in ways that were instinctively vote winning. Her own team would ignore her at its peril.

Women were making their mark in 1943, although feminist arguments encouraging them to overturn the male order were not yet in vogue, and certainly not with Australia's female parliamentary representatives. Enid Lyons accepted what she found in the structures and territory her male colleagues presided over. Personalities she could accept or deflect in argument; institutional mores were not her worry. She had no gripe with men – in fact loved the society of men. Her grandson Peter noticed how often she "preferred the company of men" and how in her later life "didn't have many girlfriends". The only male attribute Enid ever bucked, as her grandson noted, was the "dominant male" persona which she sometimes saw reflected in Robert Menzies, although Peter Lyons never heard her say an unkind word about Menzies. In her writings, though, she described the "awe" in colleagues that Menzies' dominance produced, which she felt often prevented the good influence of an occasional critic.

In those early days in parliament, Enid's judgements were very much influenced by her time with Joe. Colleagues who had been loyal to him were her first port of call. In her recollections, she admitted that Menzies' chief rival at the time, an ageing and cantankerous former Prime Minister Billy Hughes, quickly won her over with his charm and sense of humour. In later years she would fondly recollect Billy Hughes, mimicking his habit of saying "ah" between phrases. His wife Dame Mary, quiet and excessively generous, had been a favourite with the Lyons family since their time in The Lodge. At the Hotel Canberra, where Enid lived when parliament was sitting, she breakfasted each morning with Earle Page and shared Billy Hughes and Dame Mary's table at the evening meal. Enid would be one of a handful of UAP members who supported Hughes after he defied his party to rejoin the Advisory War Council in April 1944.

It was years before Enid felt confident enough to make her own policy strides such as when she opposed aspects of the Stevedoring Industry Bill in 1947. When told Joe Lyons' government had introduced much of what she was opposing in the Bill, Enid replied, "but I'm against it. I don't care who introduced it". Years after she had left politics, however, Enid would admit how, in the party ballot to elect a new leader after the 1943 election, she had not voted for Robert Menzies: "I had come into parliament determined to ignore the past, but all the events of the last year of Joe's life … were still too close for me to be uninfluenced by the judgements I had then formed."

Enid continued to find a natural bond with Joe's earlier allies over her years in parliament – the eccentric and professed anti-feminist Archie Cameron, and Country Party members like Larry Anthony, father of Fraser Government Minister Doug Anthony, whose wife had died in 1941 and who was sometimes her "escort" for parliamentary dinners. Anthony's friendship with Enid was more than mere professional association. It looked to some for a while as if there might have been a romantic attachment. At Enid's funeral, Doug Anthony recalls speaking to one of the Lyons daughters and her comment that the Lyons family had at one stage wondered if Larry Anthony might have married their mother. Doug Anthony, however, felt the two were just very close friends.

Larry Anthony and Enid shared an ironic humour, a self deprecating sense of fun at the pretensions of the would-bes they so often met in politics. Writing to Enid in February 1946, as she considered not recontesting Darwin and just after a snakebite (using a razor blade to cut out the poison) and a fall from a ladder, Anthony had cheered her up with amusing ruminations as to the kind of snake ("whether it is the type that inhabits the grass that the cows eat, or the figurative kind that we know so familiarly at Canberra") and ladder ("such as carpenters fashion, and not the symbolic social one which no doubt the Mayor's wife, the bank manager's wife and the storekeeper's good lady were struggling up step by step when their Exs were royalling at Devonport") before pressuring her not to give up Darwin – "In my rough inarticulate agrarian way, I am very fond of you, and your friendship at Canberra leavens life there for me tremendously. It's good to have someone who can see the humour in the same sort of things, and my happiest thoughts associated with Canberra are the laughs we have enjoyed together. When therefore you suggest that you may have to retire from the seat, I am filled with consternation – both in your behalf and in my own." He signed off "Ever loving Larry".

This attraction was something Enid hinted at in *Among The Carrion Crows*, telling of her "broken suspender" as she rose one day in the House. She had been forced to ask Larry Anthony, whom she had known for just three days, to lean over her and talk to Allan Guy on her other side while she rolled a rubber band up her thigh, unnoticed she hoped by three pairs of eyes watching her from the public gallery: "[T]here was a light in his eye [Anthony] which gave me pause when I thought of the proposition". When Anthony realised what he was being asked to do, he had replied, "Of course, if you wish it". And Enid had noticed "that light in his eye grew brighter". Anthony organised a "press free" (although she gave interviews at every stop) trip for Enid in June 1944 to visit her daughter Kathleen in Brisbane. Kathleen had married Gilbert Gordon of the RAAF in April 1943. On the way, Enid stayed with the Anthonys, Larry and his sister, at Murwillumbah. They became lifelong friends, Anthony confiding in Enid as he considered proposing to a twenty-five year old widow, Lyndall Thornton, whom he eventually married as his second wife in April 1946. As the Minister responsible, Larry Anthony had Enid appointed to the ABC Board in 1951 after she retired from her seat due to ill health.

Enid was very fond also of Archie Fadden, and close to John McEwen ("he did more to sustain me than he ever knew" [1950]) and befriended Percy Spender who approached her the minute she arrived in Canberra as an MP to offer his assistance in her battle over the challenge to her election ("we became very good friends") and Harold Holt, one of those she believed were suffocated by Menzies' dominance. Where government policy was concerned, however, and the way policy might be argued, Enid found her own art for using the language of women's domestic experience to stir male apathy.

In March 1944, when Enid rose to make her second speech in parliament, the press held their collective breaths. She did not disappoint, and gave what *The Argus* called "light and colour", arguing that coal miners deserved the nation's sympathy for requiring them to go "into a black hole in the ground", but then suggested their attitude was one of disloyalty "to the community at large" (after a month long strike in NSW) from a mentality reflecting their dreadful workplace. By contrast, she praised Australian women for accepting so many war restrictions (unlike coal miners), an example to the rest of the community – ie men. After much laughter, she went on to labour the sacrifice of women having no stockings with wartime shortages, saying "without such hose even the most graceful ankle deteriorates into a mere joint".

Days later, Enid made a speech judged as an attempt on her part to depart from her preoccupation with women's issues. She opposed the proposed referendum for increased Commonwealth powers over post-war reconstruction (known as the "Powers Referendum"), arguing it would be better to seek state co-operation than go to a referendum. Labor lampooned her case and implied a woman could never mount a sound case in matters unrelated to women's issues. In August 1944, however, when the referendum was eventually lost, Enid's case was an undisputed one for saving taxpayers' money. The government's loss of this referendum would be Menzies' jumping off spot in a come back for his party's hopes against Labor's entrenched success in government.

Throughout her parliamentary career, Dame Enid would prove more than able to stand her ground over public policy, from industrial regulation to industrial action, from arguing the need for a United Nations Association to making a rallying cry for empire loyalty, from taxes on "gifts", government budgets and public spending to the problems of shipping for Tasmania or the price of potatoes. In early 1944, she had joined child care campaigner Lady Phyllis Cilento on a federal government inquiry into the needs of mothers and children and in August 1944 had been part of the ABC's "Nation's Forum of the Air" (with Dr Colin Clark against Dr Norman Haire and Jessie Street) to push arguments in favour of families and support for mothers. "Women who decorate popular magazine covers are those with three husbands and no children," she had proclaimed, adding governments should give practical support to encourage women to become mothers. One of her well worn themes. The finances of those she represented also took her into new fields of Commonwealth-State relations and, by the end of 1944, she was laughing at how she had become a "fat lamb" expert. After President Roosevelt's death in 1945, she spoke in the House with tears in her eyes and hands trembling, "I have met many world famous men but I regard president Roosevelt as the greatest."

Yet Enid's special weapon would remain her unabashed use of personal housewife and motherly experience to take an argument into her own territory. Time after time, debates in the house were quickly reduced to plain speaking with Enid's homely metaphors or stories from ordinary Australians. She often cut across party platforms, pulling the rug out from under Labor's credentials as the party of the underdog or working family. Invariably, the colour of her metaphors captured press attention.

"The pay envelope goes in the front door and straight out the back door," was one of her jibes in July 1947, as the parliament debated the need to reduce wartime taxes and the economic squeeze on families of post war life. She added, with the tone of one much schooled in the art, that it had been a long time practice for mothers in large families to cut down father's pants for the boys and mother's skirts for the girls, but that the quality of materials had so deteriorated trousers and skirts no longer could be reused.

In parliament, Arthur Calwell often spurred Enid to action, "a source of constant irritation to most of my colleagues," she would later write, "I crossed swords with him more often than with any other man in the House." She would make something of a name for herself in the "Manila girls" affair, defending the right a group of Australian women, employed by the US military in Manila during the war, who had broken an agreement to return to Australia after one year. In 1948, a dispute arose over their status and legal right to return "home" and Enid took up the issue in parliament. The women were eventually allowed back into Australia, but Calwell remonstrated "in no circumstances" would he "issue passports to these women, who have so flagrantly violated the immigration laws of this country" and he added "they are now back in Australia and they are back to stay".

In May 1947, Enid had taken on Arthur Calwell when he tried to embarrass the Opposition by recalling that Enid Lyons had once advised housewives they could manage a household on £3 a week. It was an attack on the Lyons Government and its depression measures and Enid labelled it "mendacity". She rounded on Calwell, accusing the Minister for Immigration and Information of "acute food snobbery".

What she had been arguing during the Depression years, Enid explained, was how the Australian housewife was then "the greatest financier in the world" in being able to make £1 do the work of three. Under Labor, she added, now housewives had to make £1 do the work of four! Press articles that followed carried headlines like "Woman Member points the shinbone" and reported how Dame Enid Lyons had invited Minister Calwell to dine with her in her

Devonport home where she would serve him a three course meal made from a shinbone – soup from the stock of the bone, beef and vegetables from the meat and apple pie with a crust using the bone's marrow fat.

These were challenging years for the conservative opposition – the majority of Enid's years in parliament. As the new leader of the UAP, in September 1943, Robert Menzies began envisaging a new conservative party, writing to Frederick Lampe of the Institute of Public Affairs how the election "wreck" gave opportunity to establish a "new party under a new name". Lampe did not agree, but Menzies and an assortment of UAP and state conservative operatives, not least of all Dame Elizabeth (May) Couchman and the Australian Women's National League, would carry out that vision and, over a number of meetings and conferences, bring together disparate conservative groupings. Within two years, they had founded the Liberal Party of Australia on a similar national framework to the ALP, with the AWNL's network of branches becoming the skeleton for a full party membership to drive it towards government. This was a first for the non Labor parties which had been, from the time of Federation, a fragmented and barely coalitioned collection of state and federal operatives, lacking a written platform or organisational formality. The Country Party, however, continued its separate existence.

For the first time in nearly half a century, the major non-Labor force had a constitution, a federal organisation and six state party organisations all under the banner of the "Liberal Party of Australia". Enid was elected to the party's policy committee. Liberal colleague Bill Hutchinson told her she'd won his vote because "you had something different from the others to offer, in outlook and so on". As she did throughout her parliamentary life, Enid worked diligently on policy tasks for the new party and credits herself with gaining acceptance of the policy to provide free medical attention to old age pensioners. Her other achievement was convincing the party room, against Menzies who thought it was excessive expenditure, to include child endowment for the first child in their promises for the 1946 election . This caused the ACTU to pressure Chifley to include a similar measure in Labor's election promises which in turn had Menzies respond that the ACTU was "learning from the Liberal Party".

Approaching the 1946 election, Enid began to wonder if the exertions she had to make keeping up with her parliamentary undertakings were more than she could physically endure. In her National Library interview she said: "It was nothing for me to go

Dame Enid Lyons MP addresses an election rally for her colleague, former Prime Minister Billy Hughes (seated behind), 1946.

home from parliament, have a meal, get into my car and drive 40 miles out into the country and 40 miles back, quite alone of course. Fortunately for me, I was not nervous in the slightest degree ... but it took a tremendous toll." In Canberra, she often found herself thinking her time there was like a holiday from the many responsibilities of the Darwin electorate and her children's needs in the weeks they were home from school.

As the election year 1946 dawned, Enid remained undecided about staying on. She was weary. Apart from the lack of a secretarial assistant in her electorate, she also had no partner to share her doubts and problems. A lot weighed on her. But she had given her word and her popularity was one of the Opposition's important weapons. She stayed on, once more taking the long rail journey to the west coast and making a foray into King Island in Bass Strait. As the campaign sapped her physically, a letter from parliamentary journalist Stewart Cockburn, a fortnight out from polling day, moved her to tears and gave her renewed energy.

In a most unusual move for a Press Gallery journalist, Cockburn had written good wishes for the election, adding "the profound hope that you will be back once more in the place which you have filled for three years with such distinction". He went on, "It is people like you who give us courage – who help us to hope and believe that Parliament and democracy are *worth* believing in, and fighting for. If only one Member of the whole Parliament can show that life and experience have not destroyed idealism, sincerity, and the spirit of struggle, then Parliament is worthwhile. More than anyone else, you, Dame Enid, have helped me resist the impulse to scepticism."

The 1946 election, held on Saturday 28 September, resulted in modest gains for the newly formed Liberal Party. Enid doubled her majority but her friend Allan Guy in Wilmot was defeated, although he would be elected to the Senate as a Liberal in 1949, and continue his chequered political career. Across the nation, the Liberals had increased the UAP's seats by just three; the Opposition benches, including the Country Party, had increased to 29 seats in the House with Labor occupying 43. It was a disappointment for Robert Menzies. Enid was, naturally, delighted with her comfortable win in Darwin.

Funds became available for electoral secretaries; Enid was overjoyed. She employed Desmond briefly but it did not work out – none of the family ever discovered why and Enid herself claimed she never knew. Desmond's youngest brother Peter, who found Desmond not easy to know, believes it was simply that for all Desmond's brilliance academically he had no political nous. Desmond once told his sister Moira that she was the least intelligent member of a very intelligent family – which he meant as a compliment.

In time, Enid employed Frances Lane, a young woman from a Devonport family who had long supported the Lyons family politically. The Lanes owned the Grand Hotel and a wonderful mansion named Malunnah, a feature of Devonport. Frances was diminutive, always immaculately groomed and would become Enid's most loyal supporter and friend. Now Enid could work from home without having to write everything out long hand for typing back in Canberra – "I'd be cooking the dinner and my secretary would be in the kitchen taking notes and I'd dictate letters and so on."

While Enid returned to parliament more confident and decidedly ready to be more assertive in her parliamentary tactics, her health remained her greatest opponent. During her second term, she continued her exhausting round of extra parliamentary appearances at all manner of meetings and functions from debutante balls and flower shows to large women's meetings such as those for Helen Keller in April 1948 where she stood with that remarkable woman at four separate gatherings in capital cities across Australia. Helen Keller wrote her thanks to Enid shortly after saying, "You are like Teacher in so many ways ... the indefinable something that makes your praise not an embarrassment so much as a sweet challenge ... only the language of the heart can express all the thanks I owe to you." Not missing an opportunity, Keller went on to ask Enid to use her influence within parliament to bring the work of organisations supporting blind and deaf people in the community to governments' attention.

A personality in her own right, Enid Lyons could not hope to satisfy all the requests to appear and speak that came her way. Those not accepted were always turned down most politely, and "with regret" or with a note that illness prevented her from being able to accept. In August 1948, Kevin Lyons won a seat in the Tasmanian parliament after he and Enid spent weeks travelling the Darwin electorate. A fortnight before election day, mother and son turned their car over on a road near Yolla when it skidded on loose gravel on a sharp turn. Neither was seriously injured but Enid spent half a day in bed as a result. Kevin took after Joe as a "dropper-in". The Sunday following the election, Enid wrote to Father Walsh, one of many priests she and Joe had met in the UK, saying, "He is very like his father and we are hoping that he will do well." And then Enid discovered she had a serious condition involving a large goitre in her neck. For some time she had been complaining about what she regarded as bad ventilation in the parliamentary chamber; in fact she had been straining to breathe around two large growths flattening her windpipe. The discovery was less than two months out from the 1949 election, set down for 10 December.

There was no choice but for Enid to take her doctor's advice. Alternative arrangements were being made for her campaign as she arrived at Melbourne's Mercy hospital for the life threatening operation, scheduled for the day after the election writs were to be issued. While Enid was in hospital, William Burnell died in the Devon Hospital at La Trobe on Saturday 12 November. He was buried the following Monday and with much acknowledgement because of his family connection to Joe and Enid. Enid herself was not able to attend. Richard Casey represented the Liberal Party, and it would amuse the family to later recall how the non believing William, well known in the district for his heavy drinking, was finally laid to rest with great respect by a Methodist pastor in the presence of senior a representative of the (soon to become) historic Menzies Government.

Enid would make just one appearance in her campaign. After four weeks in hospital, all she could do was make a recording for her electors. Yet she intended to appear at her campaign's final rally even though her doctor warned her against it. Resting in bed was quite a different matter from standing before a crowded hall after such an operation. Whatever her intentions, Enid may never have got to the rally. But, as she turned on the radio that evening, she heard her opponent, a Mr Kirkpatrick, arguing that *he* had no need of a sympathy vote – the implication being of course that Enid did.

With all the mettle of a daughter of Eliza Burnell, Enid got up from her bed and dressed herself slowly, making sure a suitable covering hid her wounded neck. She arrived at the hall, driven there by Kevin, to find her friend and colleague Harold Holt at the microphone. Holding a safe Liberal seat, he had devoted the last two days of the campaign to help Enid in her campaign. Standing at the microphone, Holt saw Enid arrive and stopped his speech, asking the audience to welcome her. She now had her entrance. And, although feeling extremely ill, she was fired by simmering anger at her opponent's words. She thanked her supporters, telling them what she had heard from her opponent. She then challenged anyone who thought she was playing for sympathy to come forward. "Let me remind the gentleman who made the broadcast that it didn't take a sympathy vote for me to give him a beating six [she meant three] years ago," she added. There was uproar in the hall. Enid left soon after, helped by her doctor. She went on to win with an increased majority. It was the last election speech she ever made.

Two major factors influenced the results of the 10 December 1949 election – Ben Chifley's Government had overseen a massive redistribution of seats, bringing numbers in the House of Representatives to 121 and the Senate to 60 and, on the night of Enid's estimates debacle, Chifley had introduced legislation to nationalise the banks, fermenting a campaign that brought down his government, something akin to the effect of John Howard's Workchoices legislation sixty years later. At the 1949 election, Robert Menzies' Liberals took government in a landslide, 74 seats in the House going to the Liberal-Country Party coalition and 47 to Labor. In the Senate, with a half Senate election only in 1949, the conservatives held a one seat majority which would increase to a four seat majority after the 28 April 1951 double dissolution election.

When Robert Menzies announced his ministry, Enid was included in the Cabinet list. It had been expected, in spite of her illness. Harold Holt had predicted it months out from election day. But on the list of Cabinet names, Enid's was the only one which did not include a portfolio. Instead, she was to be the Vice President of the Executive Council. Most regarded this as largely an honorary post – influential but having no impact on government decisions through the ministerial system. Enid spoke of what she knew of the appointment during her National Library interview, saying her belief was that Menzies did not want her in the ministry but seemed to have been pressured into giving her some sort of spot.

As Enid phrased it, "[P]apers throughout Australia, all that I saw, ... named me a certainty to be included, and various portfolios were suggested. One I remember was the portfolio of Immigration, another was Social Services [Enid was in Devonport recovering from her operation] ... then the wife of one of what I call the party hierarchy rang me and asked if I would accept the position of Vice President of the Executive Council, this toothless position." Enid sensed that the woman's husband, obviously one of Enid's supportive colleagues, was trying to get her name up for Cabinet and thought the Executive Council suggestion might be a way to persuade Menzies.

Nearly seventy years later, Barry Lyons would comment that it was his mother's Country Party colleagues who had pushed for her inclusion in the ministry.

"It doesn't take much more than common sense to be a minister, let me tell you," said Enid in her National Library interview, "Of course he [Menzies] knew that I was in pretty poor health at that time and he also knew, or thought he knew, that I was a person with a rather soft heart and he'd think my heart would overrule my head. But he may have had other reasons of his own and I'm not questioning his right to them, nor the validity of his reasons." This would be another sore point between the Lyons family and Robert Menzies. As they saw it, after all she had done, she was still only a novelty to her leader, whatever telegrams he might send congratulating her on wins in Darwin.

Yet, it was not only Menzies who had doubts about Enid. She, herself, did not project confidence, one of the prerequisites in succeeding in a male dominated pecking order. Doug Anthony believes some of the communications between Enid and Larry Anthony at the time which are among his father's papers indicate that, while Enid thought she should have a portfolio, she was also hesitant about her stamina for the job. Anthony, familiar with Enid's occasional reticence about her abilities, urged her to accept and affirmed his faith in her capability. This was what Joe had done over years with Enid, pushing her onto platforms where she performed brilliantly.

Seen from Menzies' point of view, 1949 was far off either political party considering a woman for a "real" ministerial position. These were times when all working women earned significantly less than male counterparts (Enid had taken up the issue in parliament – only to be told the question could "go on notice") – the argument went that a woman didn't have to support a family. Such distinctions, of course, did not apply to parliamentary salaries – as a member of Cabinet, Enid would earn between £2,500 and £3,000. In addition, in the eyes of the majority of the public, male was the sex equipped for leadership – and Menzies was no radical. He had a list of would-be male colleagues jockeying for a limited number of ministerial positions. What's more, with her closeness to Earle Page and Billy Hughes, Enid had never been in the Menzies' camp. For that, her fate would not be all that different from male colleagues like Richard Casey, taking up a ministerial position well below what he believed he was due. Still, as many women did over decades, Enid would be left to ponder why her achievements could not make a difference.

Nellie's husband Hubert Glover told Enid the offer of a Cabinet position without portfolio was an insult and she should turn it down, but Enid accepted, telling her family she still felt far too weak to "undertake the serious work of a portfolio" and it would give her at least a place. She added, "I'll hope to break through when my health is restored".

Enid was in Canberra for the swearing in of the ministry on 19

Dame Enid Lyons, Robert Menzies, Thomas White and Richard Casey head for Canberra to be sworn in as part of the new Menzies Cabinet, December 1949.

December. Still frail from her operation, she managed to look elegant and poised in a light grey crepe suit, high necktie and black felt and velvet hat as she stood talking to the Governor General Sir William McKell. According to Enid, in no time Robert Menzies had called her in to suggest she accept leadership of a mission to London, advising she could do with the rest; the sea voyage would restore her health. She admitted to being flattered, even delighted, but turned the suggestion down. In *Among the Carrion Crows*, Enid says this was because "five of my children were still in their difficult teens and one, at that moment, was in special need of watchful, loving supervision." In fact, with the exception of Janice, Enid's children had all left school. And Janice would not return to finish her schooling the following year as Enid was worried about the outbreak of polio that had troubled the mainland throughout 1949. Enid may have had worries about one or more of her children, but it was not because five were "in their difficult teens" as only two of them were still teenagers and one of these a fairly grown up eighteen.

Whatever the real reason Enid turned down Menzies' offer of a trip to London, she did need an extended convalescence. But she resumed her duties before parliament opened and was photographed for the front page of *The Canberra Times* laughing heartily with three of her ministerial colleagues – the caption acknowledged this was the first occasion a woman had presided over a meeting of the Executive of any British Commonwealth Government. Sixteen year old Janice accompanied her mother to Canberra for the opening of parliament in March and was reported as having been voted the "prettiest" of the younger set that year in the national capital. In April, Moira married Frank Brady and in June young Enid and her husband Maurice Austin with their four children returned from Washington where Austin had been posted after the War. Around this time, Enid found herself arguing for a woman to be appointed to the Olympic Games Organising Committee, with all her usual conviction.

305

Overall, however, 1950 was a year when Enid struggled to keep pace, for various physical reasons she would only later understand. The medication for her thyroid deficiencies remained inadequate; before long she had also discovered a virulent ulcer on her nose which developed into a serious skin cancer which would take surgery and time to heal. Cabinet's decision to send troops to the Korean War disturbed her as well and reminded her of how Janet Rankin, America's first woman in Congress, had burst into tears at Woodrow Wilson's decision to commit troops to the First World War. Menzies' intuition about Enid in Cabinet had not been wrong – the times and its workings did not suit her. Still, she was a perfect hostess at functions, standing in for the Governor General and welcoming delegations to Canberra. To the general public, her name inspired fond recognition and her doings continued to be of interest.

When Enid eventually realised her health was against any reasonable performance at her job, she went to Menzies and handed in her ministerial notice, announced at the beginning of March 1951. She had been forced to take leave from the parliament far too often since the election and had made few speeches in the House over that time. The next question was whether she would remain the Member for Darwin. Her decision was soon easily made. When Menzies opted to go to an early election set down for 28 April 1951, and a double dissolution, Enid was ready to stand down from her seat, not so much to retire as to make a new start. Aged fifty-three.

CHAPTER 20

THAT OTHER LIFE

The 1950s Down Under had begun with much reporting of optimism. As parliament opened on 8 March 1951, however, a packed gallery heard Prime Minister Robert Menzies herald a significant passing as he paid a glowing tribute to Australia's first woman to have attained not only a seat in the House but also one at the Cabinet table. Enid was moved by Menzies' praise for her, but looked ill in her seat as she fanned herself against the heat of a Canberra summer. There were farewell dinners with the Tasmanian members and the three Liberal female senators, Annabelle Rankin, Ivy Wedgewood and Agnes Robertson as well as with ministerial colleagues, the Caseys, the Hughes and Percy Spender among others.

In the weeks that followed, the Menzies Government would see its bank legislation delayed in the Senate and gain the consent of Governor General McKell, a Labor appointee, for a double dissolution. With her announcement that she would not stand again for Darwin, Enid had been besieged with requests she stay on but had turned them down. Her farewell events went on for weeks across the electorate. The election for both houses of parliament on 28 April saw Aubrey Luck easily win Darwin for the Liberals. Enid's time in federal politics was finally over.

Enid had come home to Devonport once more, this time to stay. Most of her children, long grown, were now in Tasmania. Sheila, Kathleen and Moira and their husbands were settled there,

Brendan, Barry and Peter were living at Home Hill while Kevin, now the state Member for Darwin, lived on a small property he had bought next door. Rosemary was a cadet journalist with the Herald and Weekly Times in Melbourne and had been joined by Janice who had started a business course. Their sister Enid and husband Maurice were by then living in Frankston. Desmond, going on to a career teaching mathematics in Hobart, would become the eccentric of the family, a genius who never found his niche. In 1951, Enid told Mary Coles of *Women's Weekly* that he was 34 and still not married but that "of course his father waited until he was 35, so there is still hope".

Her decision to resign had cost Enid a handsome annual salary as an MP – especially her ministerial salary. In May 1951, her personal annuity from the federal government was reinstated but the annuity for the Lyons children had long ago dwindled to zero. Loss of parliamentary earnings after an election defeat is bad enough, but Enid had chosen to face the prospect of maintaining her comfortable lifestyle not only on a minimum stipend but also without the travel allowances she had so long enjoyed. But Enid had opportunities up her sleeve. Over her years in parliament, requests for her to write for payment, and broadcast, had regularly come her way – but she had routinely turned most of them down due to time constraints and the workload she carried. One offer, however, she had not refused. In 1949, Colorgravure Publications, part of the Herald and Weekly Times Murdoch stable, had sought Enid out to write a serialised version of her life for *Women's Day*.

Enid's own account of 1949 does not record her "other life" as she concentrated in *Among the Carrion Crows* on her parliamentary experiences. But on 7 November 1949, just as Enid was recovering from her goitre operation and the Liberals were looking to make inroads into Labor's majority at the federal election on 10 December, a six-part life of Dame Enid Lyons began to entertain thousands of

readers of *Woman's Day*. The series, written before Enid had gone into
hospital, was so successful that by the end of the year *Woman's Day*
was planning to quickly publish the whole as a booklet entitled *My
Life*. Enid received 300 guineas for the serial instalments and a further
£50 for the booklet rights.

After Enid left parliament in 1951, she was a free agent. Whatever
possibilities for earning an income came her way, she would consider
them seriously. Like many a successful writer and personality, Enid
not only enjoyed her moments in the limelight but also needed the
financial compensation. Initially, however, it was her parliamentary
contacts that brought her back into public life.

Larry Anthony was now Postmaster-General in the Menzies
Government and responsible for appointments to the ABC Board.
He told Enid he would like to have her as an ABC Commissioner,

Dame Enid Lyons, having just published her parliamentary memoirs, 'Among the Carrion Crows' in 1972; and with a crowd of children after her retirement.

replacing Ivy Kent, a Labor activist and mother of eight who had been appointed in 1944. Enid, in her usual style, saw complications and wondered if her health was good enough. She got in touch with Anthony to suggest he withdraw her name. Her reticence was something Anthony understood and he replied on 28 June saying, "if your doctor is satisfied, I can think of no better appointment. I suggest therefore that you do not burn your bridges at this stage, and ask that you leave the matter entirely with me." On 13 July, Larry Anthony announced in parliament that Dame Enid Lyons would replace Ivy Kent, from Western Australia, on the ABC Board and "introduce fresh viewpoints into the Commission's deliberations". Ken Inglis in *This is The ABC* writes that when Ivy Kent heard of her replacement she "knew the worst; the place reserved for a woman would go to one who rightly described herself as the mother figure of Australian public life".

Once again, Enid publicly declared that she would not accept her government annuity while she was being paid the substantially lower ABC Commissioner's fee. The day after the announcement of Enid as the new ABC Commissioner, Senator Dorothy Tangney had asked a question in the Senate that was undoubtedly hostile to Enid's appointment. The gist of her criticism was that Western Australia had been slighted and Enid Lyons' recently publicised contract to write for a Melbourne newspaper compromised her place on the ABC Board. Then Tangney added, "As Dame Enid Lyons is in receipt of an Australian Government pension of £500 per annum and as Mrs Kent, who is also a widow, has no other income is this appointment an indication of the government's policy to give to him that hath and take from him that hath not?" Enid had written to Dorothy Tangney that same day, telling her of a "delightful" letter she had just received from Ivy Kent. Enid's letter to Tangney went on to say how surrendering her annuity, which Enid was doing, would mean real hardship for her financially. Tangney's comments outraged Enid's friend Massey Stanley who wrote soon after that he was "boiling with rage" and that even "members of parliament have continued to draw war pensions after election".

But events were moving elsewhere too, as Senator Tangney had noted. In July 1949, Enid had replied to a letter from Archer Thomas, Murdoch's man at *The Herald*, who had written, "Remember how once upon a time you were going to write a weekly column for us? Is it any more practical now than then? ... I wonder if you would let me know." Enid arranged to meet up with Thomas. The short series that became *My Life* column had followed but by mid 1951 Enid was ready to take up the *Herald* offer. On 4 July, Enid began what would be, over some three years, a twice weekly Melbourne *Sun*, column syndicated with *The Advertiser* and *The Courier Mail*.

In Dame Enid Lyons' inaugural column, she took a swipe at her ego, wondering if the editor had felt a person like herself, so familiar with politics, might find the silence of retirement too hard to bear and so had given Dame Enid Lyons a place in his newspaper to say what she liked. Enid then announced that her columns would be about: "Not party politics of course – but all the things that make up life for all of us, what we eat and drink and wear; our customs and our manners; our national failings and our virtues; and all the greatness of our heritage as Australians." She noted that having to write would test her views and "undoubtedly will bring me into conflict with all manner of people". But in words that underscored her character and political populism she also noted how she was "a sentimentalist in an age that likes to think of itself as hard-boiled; a middle-of-the-roader in an era of violent partisanship". And there was the Lyons' sense of not taking life too seriously: "My children tell me I was flattered into it." She concluded with an account of her Jubilee Day appearance at Smithton:

> [I] was given the honour – to a Scotsman, I understand,
> the ultimate honour – of being piped off the ground. As

I followed the resplendent kilted figure of my escort, with the pipes skirling and the crowds applauding, I was deeply moved. I related the story to my family with great warmth of feeling and not a little pride, and an irreverent son-in-law commented, "And I suppose everyone said, 'Here comes the old haggis.'"

Her touch was light but wise and readers could digest the humour alongside intelligent comment. Enid's belief had always been that if a speaker could entice an audience to laugh, within the first five minutes, the speech would be a winner. Certainly she did that. And her columns followed similar lines. She would write of large and small issues and move from the general to particular with her ready store of anecdotes. Her output suggested her long years of experience and eye for the human interest made it easy to find a new topic every half week. They ranged from issues in the news, an evaluation of the Kinsey Report, Russia and the atom bomb, peace, the inequality of the sexes, the deaths of royals she had known, the need for green belts and protection for trees, support for farms and "those who help themselves" to why women can't but a good mop or the delight of doing the weekly wash. She took on the "experts" with homely experience, she supported hard working "new Australians", questioned the public's interest in murder trials and jokes at in-laws and women drivers. All hand written in hard copy for typing in her Norman Bros "Norman Lawn" note books, of A5 size so that she wrote across the length of each page.

Such was her appeal, it was not long before Enid was negotiating with Herald Gravure, at their invitation, for a further column, this time with *Woman's Day and Home*. On 10 October 1951, the magazine's editor, A. McElwain, had written to Enid telling her of an idea for a new column where readers of all ages would write in their problems and "have their enquiries answered by someone of experience and high standing in the community". The consensus ("Sir Keith Murdoch included") was that she was "the obvious person to do this". The editor went on to point out that Eleanor Roosevelt had both a daily column in a number of US newspapers as well as a question and answer column in *McCalls Magazine*. Enid took to the idea. The offer included payment for a secretarial assistant. By 25 October, Enid had posted in her first set of answers to questions she had been sent. Negotiations over payments were handled by Enid Austin on behalf of her mother at the Melbourne office. At first the deal was to be £35 per week paid, half and half, between the *Sun* and *Woman's Day and Home* but Enid Austin managed to up the portion paid by *Woman's Day and Home* to £20, directly to her mother, and a further £5 to Frances Lane for two days part time work. So it was that, under the title "You Asked Me", Dame Enid Lyons became a weekly agony aunt for a year, helped occasionally to meet her deadlines by ghost writers in the *Woman's Day* office. And Frances Lane returned to Home Hill on a regular basis to type up the Dame's answers.

At Devonport, in her so-called retirement, Enid found herself sharing Home Hill with an energetic and grown family of young adults, all with strong personalities. Where she had ruled with that central presence of the respected mother of a large but very young brood in years long gone, now End was living with a group of individual and strong personalities. Peter Lyons, Enid's grandson, recalls, "When they were together, even if there were four or five of them, it was absolutely overpowering. They all had huge personalities and they would compete with each other; they would laugh and tease each other. I knew this when I was a kid. Aunt Kath was the quickest wit, and had a very loud laugh. Aunt Sheila was a bit more reserved, and very religious as she got older. Aunty Moira laughed with them. And, every now and again, the Dame would trump them, just quietly. And then you'd see her sort of almost flinch, as if she shouldn't have done it; it was just that banter they'd engaged in."

Often it all became more than Enid's nerves would stand. Janice Lyons well remembered what would become known to the family as the "night under the pines", when Rosemary was in her early twenties. Rosemary wanted a party and Enid had replied, "Why tonight girl?" But Rosie was having her party and called up the guests. Enid stomped off. "I was the only one she'd talk to," recalled Janice. "She took her rug and a pillow and went out under the pines." The young ones went on with the party, also inviting Frances Lane's mother, a good friend to Enid over years. But Enid refused to enter the house to welcome Mrs Lane who must have been puzzled at being left with no one her own age. And so the evening went on. Then suddenly Enid came to her senses and realised she was making a mistake. As Janice remembered it, "In the middle of the party, in she came, Sarah Bernhardt. And she didn't say hello to anybody. She just sat down at the piano and began playing as if nothing had happened. And everyone came around and started singing. She used to do strange things my mother. I don't know where the madness comes from in my family – on both sides." Thankfully, for Enid, Rosemary settled down soon after when, on Anzac Day 1952, she married Frank (Hookey) McGrath whose father had, like Rosie's father, been a Labor Party MP in the Tasmanian parliament.

With the announcement on 6 February 1952 that King George VI of Great Britain had died peacefully in his sleep at age 56, Enid took up her pen to record her memory of "a genuinely simple and self-effacing man". In her characteristic way, she brought the ordinary and extraordinary together, telling of her opportunities to know the King from close associates and her own private audience with him which she extended in anecdote using a story told to her by Prime Minister Stanley Baldwin; the King had once allowed his two young daughters to interrupt their meeting (something that no one ever did) just prior to the King's coronation in 1937. The two princesses had come into the room excitedly displaying their new dresses with trains.

Enid then moved into a familiar theme with, "How much this loving understanding relationship with his children will mean to the future of the Crown, only the next few years will reveal, but its influence must be great."

The older of the princesses, Elizabeth, by then the mother of two children herself, was already Queen as Enid wrote these words a few days before the King's funeral. After the mourning, excitement gripped a Commonwealth absorbing the impact of a new young Queen – pretty, fashionable and with a handsome husband as her consort. The Royal couple instantly became the media stars of a generation. Coronation Day was set down for 2 June 1953 and led to sixteen months of frenzied preparation. Then, Enid received her invitation from the Queen to be present at the Coronation. A cable to Lennox Hewitt at Australia's High Commission in London dated 2 April informed him that Dame Enid was "contemplating accepting" and asked whether the High Commission could obtain "suitable accommodation for her at reasonable cost" over some three weeks for her stay in London. The cable went on to ask if the High Commission would also advise on dress for the ceremony and the cost of having "robes of the Order" made or hired.

It would be Enid's last trip to Europe and the UK, but again one done in great style. The trip was carefully co-ordinated by the Prime Minister's Department and the High Commission in London as if it were the travel of a prime ministerial spouse. In London, Vera White, daughter of Alfred Deakin and wife of the High Commissioner Sir Thomas White, took personal responsibility for the seating of Australians in the Abbey and meetings in London. Cables back and forth between Canberra and London to Enid and Frances Lane fixed itineraries, booked flights, checked on how a set of "robes of the Order" could be made in time and the cost (£14 for the hat; £78 for robes, cordons and badge, nine guineas for embossed tin hat case) and booked hotels. At one stage, Enid's head, bust and height measurements were cabled from Australia to London, in time finding their way into the National Archives in Canberra on multiple documents.

Janice Lyons, aged nineteen, was accompanying her mother as well as Frances Lane. For the three women, it was the trip of a lifetime. Along the way, Enid would be sending back her regular columns to the *Sun*. They left Sydney on 20 May on a British Commonwealth Pacific Airlines flight that made stops at Canton Island and Honolulu before arriving in San Francisco at 7 am on 21 May. They stayed at the St Francis Hotel one night before leaving for New York the following morning at 8.30am. After a weekend in New York, staying at the Commodore Hotel, they left for London, arriving there around midday on 25 May. In London they stayed at the Mount Royal Hotel.

It was sixteen years since Enid's last visit to London. Some of the people she and Joe had befriended were now gone, among them Neville Chamberlain. Enid had written Anne Chamberlain her words of condolence with special feeling at the time. But many remained and the round of social engagements took over, although these were private occasions and very different from the relentless public appearances when Enid was a prime minister's wife. Of one official occasion where she attended a reception with the Queen in the Great Hall of Westminster as one of sixty representatives from across the Commonwealth parliaments, she would write, "I met old friends and new ones on every hand, and felt the sense of loss that comes with the memory of those who once graced such occasions and now are gone."

As usual, Enid's notoriety did not escape the attention of the media. During her stay, she was interviewed by Joan Gilbert and Leslie Mitchell for a BBC program on distinguished visitors from the Commonwealth. It was Enid's first experience of television and she was surprised how people stopped her in the street after the show and told her they had seen her. "I now find myself almost as well known in London as in Melbourne," she wrote. The number of Australians abroad also surprised her: "There are Australians everywhere we go, and sometimes in the most unexpected positions." She had been made up for TV by a girl from Griffith in NSW and the traffic manager for BCPA at Honolulu airport had been none other than a boy who had pinched apples from her orchard years before in Devonport. Michael Collins Persse, an Australian studying at Oxford and a relative of the Gowries, met Dame Enid a number of times at the Gowries' London home where he often stayed. He found her intelligent rather than intellectual, good at conversation, affable and motherly, and interested in what he was doing in the UK.

On Coronation day, Enid was up at dawn, taking a quickly snatched breakfast. She drove to the Abbey in a drizzle and found her place in the gallery of the South Transept staring down on the Sanctuary and "the rose and gold of the empty Throne-chair". Enid's account of the Coronation for the *Sun* is rich in emotion and colour, her respect for the unifying symbols of State, religion and Commonwealth pronounced. London had changed in sixteen years, the scars of the War still evident, but change and progress were everywhere – "a lessening of reserve, a greater willingness to enter into conversation with a stranger".

The crowning of the young Queen had become for Enid a symbol of all she valued in the English speaking world – even in the US she had noticed New York and San Francisco had fabulous displays celebrating the new monarch of Great Britain and its Dominions. And now, her occasional public functions took her into streets that introduced her for the first time to a cheek by jowl London. She addressed a meeting of the Women's Gas Federation and at St Pancras she seconded a vote of thanks to the Health Minister while having her first encounter with "the authentic rhyming slang of cockney London".

After a short visit to Scotland, the trip home took Enid, Janice and Frances through France, Switzerland and Italy, favourite haunts that Enid recalled so fondly with Joe. She wired back columns on Dunkirk, Paris, the shores of Lake Geneva, Milan, Venice, Florence and the historical and religious wonder of Rome. In *The Courier Mail* her first column on her return to Australia was titled, "Dame Enid says, 'Australian Food as Good as Any'". By this time she was a personality in her own right, if not a media star in her own country.

A great disappointment, during Enid's 1935 visit to London, had been missing an opportunity to meet her literary hero G K Chesterton because she had a clashing engagement. On her 1937 visit, it was too late to meet the great literary figure as he had died the year before. G K Chesterton's appeal for Catholics of Enid's generation was immense. Apart from his Wildean wit and sense of the ridiculous, along with his paradoxical logic and ability to satirise elitism in all quarters, Chesterton like his good friend Ronald Knox was a convert to Catholicism. Where Oscar Wilde had had become a Catholic on his death bed, after social degradation and imprisonment following a criminal conviction involving a homosexual relationship, Chesterton maintained respectable social mores and found his way to the Catholic church after a philosophical search for meaning. His book *Orthodoxy* in 1908 had convinced readers he was already a Catholic but it wasn't until 1922 that he was baptised, after what Joseph Pearce in *Literary Converts* calls "defending Catholic orthodoxy for twenty years". Enid's favourite book was Chesterton's autobiography; the passage in it which amused her most was his account of a séance where he commented that whoever the spirit was they had contacted, he was surely a liar.

Joe and Enid Lyons adhered strongly to their Catholic faith and social circle throughout their marriage and Enid would be a stalwart member of the faithful till her death, playing the organ (not well, according to Janice, having only learned piano) at her local parish until in her advanced years. Enid always kept in touch with a number of clergy and was a good friend of Tasmania's Archbishop (Gilly) Young, who preached her panygeric and had often dropped in to visit her at Home Hill. Many of the men she admired were priests. Yet, in Edmund Campion's *Australian Catholics – the Contribution of Catholics to the Development of Australian Society* (1987), there is not one mention of Joe or Enid Lyons, while there are a number of references to people such as Catholic advocate and agitator B A Santamaria and even Labor Prime Minister Joe Scullin. A Catholic Prime Ministerial couple, such as Joe and Enid Lyons, should surely have rated a mention. Perhaps the Lyons couple had fallen out of fashion by the 1980s or perhaps this was because neither sought to use their Catholic religion in their public lives. They were Australians first and always – their religion a matter for them, not the public. Enid was never preachy, as her grandson Peter recalled. And, for that, they had made their mark among Protestant and Anglophile conservatives, indeed a first for Australia. What's more, they were careful never to become too closely, or exclusively, allied with organsations which pressured government through religious affiliation.

Enid had enjoyed the company of political activist and anti-communist Paul McGuire and his wife Margaret in their North Adelaide home when an MP. Paul McGuire was yet another (Catholic) fan of G K Chesterton. For all that, Enid did not jump at McGuire's representations to her after December 1949 to prevail on Prime Minister Robert Menzies to "consolidate the Catholic voters who went over at the election ... [because] a strong backing of Catholic opinion is essential if a serious move against the Communists is made". In a letter to "Dear Mr McGuire", dated 8 March, Enid advised that McGuire's views would be welcome to the Minister for External Affairs, Percy Spender, ("Percy, I am sure, is alive to the dangers of the Asian situation") and that McGuire should come to Canberra and say what he felt. But, Enid added, she was "very small potatoes here". Eventually, and after courting Robert Menzies and B A Santamaria,

McGuire was content to take an ambassadorship to Ireland in 1953. Enid also never became associated with the National Civic Council of B A Santamaria.

In July 1954 and 1957, Enid's appointment as an ABC Commissioner was renewed. She would remain on the ABC Board until July 1962 and retire only because of ill health. On her appointment, Chairman Richard Boyer had written to tell her it was the best news thay had had at the ABC for a long time. This was because of the high regard she had with the public which would promote the reputation of the ABC. He had also assured her that the Board would have as many of its meetings as possible (lasting over two days each time) in Melbourne to make the travelling easier for her.

Enid's contribution to the Board was to ensure practical and positive decisions were made and harmonoius relations kept between Board members and management. Ken Inglis refers to her part in Board discussions as "sparing and persuasive". From the outset, she was an enthusiatic supporter of the ABC's John Douglass who wanted to rejuvenate the *Country Hour* and she proposed that the northern Tasmania ABC station at Launceston be used as an experiment in the use of locally based farm programs. The experiment proved so successful, regional extension officers were appointed in every state. During her time as a Commissioner, the ABC became part of the television age, something already being prepared for as she took up her appointment. As an ABC Commissioner, Enid was one of the first Tasmanians to own a TV set.

Relations with her Board colleagues were warm and Ken Inglis writes of how Enid and Richard Boyer often caused their colleague Professor John Medley to wince by "singing revivalist hymns from their Methodist childhoods". When Enid was invited to take part in American Ed Burrow's world wide radio series "This I Believe" in April 1954, Richard Boyer wrote to encourage her to say yes, alongside Australian heavies such as Menzies, Opposition leader H V Evatt,

Walter Murdoch and Ian Clunies Ross. In a "PS" Boyer scrawled, "Give 'em your fundamentals of faith in the meaning of life. Very few are able to do this, or if able, not willing. Dick". John Medley and his wife Molly also became close to Enid, and Medley sometimes wrote her verse to make her laugh. The Medleys visited her at Home Hill and when John Medley died in October 1962, Enid's obituary for him in the *TV Times* referred to his death as being "as if a light has gone out". Molly Medley wrote to Enid when she read the obituary to say "thank you dear beloved Enid. I shall value it always". Enid could also recall the Board's informal lunches in the Chairman's room and how often she had been the one to introduce an occasional "lamentable state of unsophistication" at meetings for which Medley "had only to utter one short comment – acidulous but humourous – to bring the conversation back to an acceptable level". After his appointment in 1956, Victorian Arthur Lowndes enjoyed Enid's company and wrote to her from Melbourne when she was no longer on the Board, "Here for a Comm. meeting & missing you, and the time and the inclination to say hello are conjoined".

In March 1961, Enid appeared on ABC TV in an interview with Michael Charlton for the *Horizons* program, after which Arthur Lowndes had written to her to express his admiration for how she had handled the interview. "There seemed to be a nice feeling between you and Charlton – he wanting to keep control and getting as much as possible into the session – and you accepting this so beautifully, never thrown off by a too-early interruption, and without fail you communicated what you knew was important." Michael Charlton also wrote on 16 March thanking her for her kindness at her "lovely home" adding "you are quite one of the most interesting and charming people I've met". In June 1962, the ABC's Clem Semmler advised he wanted to send Michael Charlton back to Home Hill to interview her for *Four Corners*.

Sir Keith Murdoch had died in 1952 but this did not stop the offers coming Enid's way to publish and be heard. In May 1959, *The Age*'s John Hetherington wrote wondering if she "intended turning into a book the most engaging autobiography which you wrote for 'Woman's Day'". Hetherington was interested in the story of Enid writing rather than the autobiography itself but the idea had been mentioned. When Enid retired from the ABC Board in mid 1962, to be replaced by Dorothy Edwards who had been mayor of Launceston, ABC Managing Director Charles Moses sent Enid, by air freight, a "recorder" and its attachments, purchased from Phillips for a heavily discounted price and paid for by a collection among the "girls" at the ABC. He hoped it would "be a real help in writing the book you have in mind". Enid was ready to do the hard yards on her memoirs, or what John Hetherington had referred to as "much that the circumstances of magazine publication had caused you to discard".

Heinemann Australia were interested in publishing and by mid 1964, Theo Sambell, Manager for Australia, was writing politely seeking a date when she might have a completed manuscript. He concluded, "I hope your health is maintained and that you have no further problems to face in this respect." By 2 March 1965, Sambell was delighted to be able to offer Enid a contract, "Charles Pick, our Managing Director in London, has written to say that they would very much like to publish this book." She would receive an advance against royalties on publication of £350 (sterling) and between ten and fifteen per cent royalties on the sale price. There would also be payment for serial rights and it was initially hoped that the ABC would serialise it on radio. However, after a wait of some months, this did not eventuate with ABC Acting General Manager Clem Semmler writing to Enid on 18 May 1965 to say that the ABC would decline, in spite of the book's "prose beautifully written (and that is quite honestly meant)". He added that the books chosen by the ABC to be read over the air were "stories of action, adventure and so on, or novels which are to a large extent made up of conversation and are therefore, in a sense, partly dramatised."

Her working title had been "I'll Give My Heart Away" but eventually Enid's memoirs of her life until Joe's death came out in the second half of 1965 as *So We Take Comfort* – a borrowed phrase from the lines of poet W B Yeats "So we ... /Take comfort of thy worth and truth/And pluck till time and times are done/The silver apples of the moon/The golden apples of the sun." The book was well received, serialised and many articles written and interviews done about this extraordinary woman who had resurfaced in the Australian media and revived a history somewhat forgotten. Moreover, Enid excelled in her prose and ability to dramatise a life. Eminent essayist and author Walter Murdoch wrote, "the book ... sparkles with vivacity and ... is likely to take its place as a classic of Australian literature and as a source book of Australian history." By December, Theo Sambell was in touch with London regarding a reprint and Enid had more than earned her advance. But publishers are slow to pay and by 10 June 1966 Enid was requesting some of the royalties – "as your book has sold so quickly here, and you expressed a wish that some royalties should be paid by the end of June, they [London] have agreed to authorise a transfer of Stg £500 to your account". By October 1967, Heinemann had expressed interest in a new book from Enid and were "very anxious to schedule it for publication".

The idea of continuing her memoirs was more difficult than Enid could manage, so to make good use of the publishing success of *So We Take Comfort* Enid put together a collection of her columns in what would be come *The Old Haggis* (1969). The manuscript was largely the work of editor Bridget Everett at Heinemann who helped Enid sort out a selection of her *Sun* columns with appeal to contemporary readers and to come in within a marketable length. Complete with illustrations by Western Australian Allan Langoulant, the book had wide appeal among Enid's fans and those looking for intelligent light reading. In March 1973, Enid's second instalment of her memoirs *Among the Carrion Crows* was published, with extracts in the Melbourne *Herald* adding to her earnings.

This second volume came with marked controversy and involved old scores between Enid's and Menzies' differing interpretations of UAP history in the months before Joe's death. This time Enid had decided not to pull any punches and write her version of the falling out, as it had come to be seen, between Joe and Bob over the National Insurance legislation and Menzies' resignation from Cabinet in early 1939. Ironically, the story leaked to the press a full year before publication. And unfortunately at a time when Robert Menzies was recovering in the Mercy Hospital from a stroke.

Much had changed in Australian politics since Enid had left the House of Representatives. Bob Menzies retired as Prime Minister in January 1966 after which the Liberal Party had quickly gone through two Prime Ministers; Harold Holt who drowned in December 1967 and John Gorton who had quickly lost the confidence of the Party and been replaced by William McMahon in 1971. By 1972, there was a mood for change after such a long period of Liberal Party dominance. By the time *Among the Carrion Crows* was published, in early 1973, Labor's Gough Whitlam was Prime Minister. Enid had watched the change in political mood with interest; her own political instincts had often been social democratic rather than conservative. On many issues the new Labor mood attracted her. However, she had also watched how the era of Joe Lyons had become the captive of a few historians with little appreciation of the man Joe was. The real Joe had fallen between the cracks. Enid was ready to put the record straight, as she saw it.

Historian Manning Clark's view that Joe was noble on the surface but "at a deeper level he had the cunning and skill of a people who, for hundreds of years, had been striving for survival against a more powerful foe" riled her. The words had surprised one of her grandsons who had read it at school and come to tell her that Joe "couldn't have been a very nice man". Enid was not to know that within a few decades Manning Clark's history would be seriously challenged by historians as often fanciful personal musings not related to fact. But Enid had a point about such misrepresentation and its influence on Clark's readers.

When the media came fishing about her new book, Enid took up her pen and wrote to Sir Robert Menzies. She had visited him in hospital shortly before and, in 1967, when his book *Afternoon Light* had been published had written to thank him for his words about Joe – telling Menzies of her "great enjoyment" at reading his book. Now she had some explaining to do and she came straight to the point.

Her letter was dated 8 March 1972. "Dear Bob," she began. "Ever since I saw you in hospital you have been much on my mind and that makes the writing of this letter, already delayed because of your illness, all the harder to write." Attaching a draft of the chapter she had written on Joe and Menzies, she continued, "The press has been after me today. I've tried to stave them off but I'm not hopeful of the result of my efforts." She wanted him to read her chapter ("some of my observations may surprise you") and she was confident he would not be displeased. She had changed her resolve to never write about "the period just before Joe's death", and this because of "amateur historians who write books and lecture to university students".

Then she got to the crux of her feelings, "I have watched the denigration of Joe's reputation with growing concern and resentment. Somehow the story of that time always seems to leave him an ageing incompetent hanging futilely to office, or – in one case at least – as reviling you almost with his last breath. ... You will know how difficult it has been for me to write it all. I don't think I come out of it with much glory but I have been as frank as I know – and I have tried to be just."

Menzies replied at length. He was disturbed, but rational. He was away "from my office and my personal records" but he would tackle two of the issues she raised which were "still pretty vivid in my mind". He gave in full once again his explanation for supporting the National Insurance legislation against the decision of Cabinet and hence his resignation – "in the 1937 General Election, I went within an ace of losing Kooyong. You have forgotten this." He had written his circular letters to get back in touch with his electorate, and thus the letter about pledging himself to National Insurance in 1938. As for his notorious Constitutional Club speech in 1938 – this he tackled more swiftly: "It was not a speech about my Leader at all. It was addressed to all people in responsible posts in Australia, including myself." He concluded, "The whole matter demonstrates something that I have learned in the course of a long life, and that is that two people looking at or participating in a series of events can honestly come out of the process with entirely different understandings on what has gone on."

In reply to Menzies' long letter, Enid thanked him for his generosity, saying her purpose was not to injure him but to "show Joe as the man he was and thirty years have amply demonstrated your own character". She agreed that "no two people ever see the same event in quite the same way" and asked for his consent to publish their correspondence in her book. And that is what happened.

CHAPTER 21

THE LYONS LEGACY

W ho would have imagined that a woman born in 1897, married at seventeen and the mother of twelve children would be an achiever ahead of her time. In so many areas of her life, Enid Lyons was just that. Interviewed by Ruth Brown for Tasmania's *Sunday Examiner Express* in November 1969, she had wondered if she was on the way to becoming a "Grandma Moses" – a reference to the late developing US folk artist Anna Robertson Moses – as there had been so many areas of life she had taken to. "My story has run on so many different lines. Nothing would surprise me now," she added. By then, she had 69 relatives claiming direct descent. Within a year or so she would be attending her grandchildren's weddings.

By the age of 75, Dame Enid Lyons had chalked up a notable life, and celebrated accordingly. Her views and example would be recorded for all time. With the publication of *Among The Carrion Crows*, Enid began the preparation of her sole intellectual and academic address. On 19 October 1973, Enid Lyons delivered the Silver Jubilee Sir John Morris Memorial Lecture set up to honour the founding of the Tasmanian Adult Education Board. She began lightly, "I am swimming in unfamiliar waters. ... My public speaking has been of a different kind." She had given her speech the title "The Role of The Christian Moralist in Present Day Australia". The Christian moralist she defined as one who, within the Christian ethic of concern for the welfare of others, could "perceive the issues involving the rights and duties" in human relationships and "help to a solution, by law if necessary, the difficulties that inevitably arise".

Her canvas was a wide one. "Only a relatively few in any society seek the general good rather than their own personal welfare." She tackled the sorry state of Christian values and the satirists: "The most commonly advanced objection to our censorship laws is that they make us a laughing stock abroad. And practically no-one says 'So what?'" She acknowledged that "A democratic society rests on the moral concepts of human dignity; a man has rights simply because he is a human being ... the few may not coerce the many, but... by virtue of the common right they *may* proclaim their views and press their arguments in the face of overwhelming numbers." In her view, the "few" in modern Australia were those pressing for the Christian ethic. "The danger lies not in disagreement, but in indifference; not in argument but in apathy."

Enid's support for the anti-abortion cause was well known and very public. In her lecture she used the abortion debate of 1973 when the McKenzie-Lamb Bill to de-criminalise abortion was defeated heavily in the Senate as illustration of her belief that, against the clamour for the "easy way out of every disquieting circumstance", it was the moralist who would save society. "When it was shown that grave problems of morality were involved, the basic moral values were at stake, the conscience of the community was roused and the existing controversy gave parliament pause and time to reflect again." On international relations she saw membership of the UN as carrying "moral obligations", in Australia's case repaying its debt from World War II to Papua New Guinea, "But for the geographical fact of New Guinea and the human fact of the support given by its people to our purposes and to our fighting men, the Kokoda trail might well have been a track to the Atherton Tableland, or the road from Townsville to Mackay."

She called for government to look anew at the welfare of people migrating and settling in Australia, "Culturally and racially different people thrust into communities often hostile to their entry are not likely to become contented citizens." And, to all Australians, she called for frank recognition of the Aboriginal dilemma. Joe and Enid had sat down with an Aboriginal delegation in 1938 and listened; Joe had sought from anthropologists and "every person with practical experience" ways to a "coherent policy for their advancement". Forty years later, there was still no solution. "The core of the problem has always been, and, in my belief, continues to be, ignorance of a suitable method of attacking it. Palliatives applied to specific sections do not supply the answer to the whole."

Moving to industrial and economic issues, Enid regretted the "go-slow policy" that had emerged during the sluggish days of the Depression, seeing it as having taken over the culture of work. In this she blamed both unions and industrial enterprises. The three decades to come would prove her right as a new commercial landscape of productivity bargaining evolved.

On women's rights, she was more forthright, recollecting that she had recently been referred to as "the North West Coast's very own Germaine Greer". Her grandson had come to her the day after with a box of matches; "To burn your bra Nannie," he had said. But, unlike Greer, Enid would never condone the "denial of all those instincts and desires, all those little graces that express the uniqueness of her femininity". These to Enid were "precious things" but there were features of woman that men had long failed to recognise, "qualities of mind and spirit that proclaim her his human equal: intellectual capacity, fortitude, courage, fidelity." And while she could not understand boredom in a young mother, she could understand "loneliness and the longing for mental stimulus beyond the scope of the daily routine when the small one's day is over." Husbands should be house husbands too. As for the "triumphant male", she cautioned women against accepting the centuries of chauvinistic propaganda that had "robbed women of part of their self-respect".

But the Dame was not done. Standing on the podium, in conservative Tasmania, she was ready to tackle the sexual revolution on her terms, "the most remarkable social phenomenon of the post-war period". She was sceptical of the fashionable views of Paul Ehrlich that the world was doomed with a population explosion. She could not have known then that, decades later, populations in the West would be in serious decline. But sexual pemissiveness worried her more. "By television, radio and cinema, by newspapers and periodicals, literature, art and drama we encourage sexuality in all forms. Not of course with the object of promoting population growth, but in the name – the sacred name – of freedom." In this she saw "self-deception". Pornography was her worry. "Those who assert that there is no proof that pornographic material has any influence on those who read it are often the very people who, in the exercise of their advocations, by implication at least, daily proclaim their belief in the power of the printed word: educators, whose tools of trade, so to speak, are books." These concerns would be scoffed at by many only to be resurrected within decades.

Of modern attitudes to sex, Enid reflected, "Sex is no longer a secret thing, which in some respects is good. But sex is no longer a private thing and thereby is robbed of dignity." As the twenty-first century ushered in Paris Hilton and her explosive media appearances, even modern liberals might have partly agreed with this. For Enid it was a serious moral dilemma, "The young who are encouraged to think that sex is beyond control are being cheated of self-respect, deprived of belief in their own moral strength." One of her constant arguments against abortion by 1973, was that "modern discoveries have rendered pregnancy avoidable at will" so that a woman should not need abortion if she did not want to conceive. This was a very different Enid from the wife who could not countenance, for religious reasons, any use of contraception.

Her lecture was a sound case for traditional Christian moral principles. And they were her principles. She supported anti-homosexual laws, a sexual preference she pitied. A majority of Australians would have agreed with her at the time. And her worry at a growing dysfunctional society, created by a moral vacuum, would be a theme taken up by many commentators before two decades had run their course: "There is the alarming increase in divorce, partly because young people are led to have sexual expectations of marriage that no union can possibly fulfil. There is the growing number of troubled, unhappy children from broken homes; the rapid spread of venereal disease, especially among the under-twenty group and the prevalence of psychiatric disorders. The growth rates of neuroticism and eroticism show a remarkable similarity."

In all this, Enid was for proposing not imposing. The Christian moralist, she said, "had no power to prohibit". And she concluded in this vein. "The role of the Christian moralist in Australia today is the ancient role of the look-out at the mast head … And having seen must give his warning call. … His courage must not fail." And so ended her lecture.

Listening to the lecture, in Hobart's Town Hall, was Rosemary's daughter, Enid's grand daughter Mary McGrath, then a student. She remembers her grandmother's warmth to her when she noticed her in the crowd:

> There were various dignitaries but afterwards she came directly across to me (I was toward the back of the hall) and of course she introduced me to the official party. This stood out for me. I had not pushed myself forward and it seemed then and now a typical generous act.

The world Enid found herself in, as she saw out her years at

Home Hill, did not so much confound her as stretch her principles. Except for Desmond, all her children would marry. But Janice would marry a divorcee and there would be a rift for some time until Enid came to terms with it and the couple sat with her by the log fire as part of the family again, watching Enid wheel in another barrow load of wood. Peter's marriage would end in divorce in the seventies and cause family division as Peter remarried and Sheila sided with his ex-wife in the upset. On this occasion, Enid was more understanding than she was with Janice a decade earlier. "My subsequent divorce and remarriage went against everything Mum stood for over her life," said Peter. "I know it hurt her deeply. But when it was obvious my marriage had ended, Mum, not wishing to completely ostracise me, asked me to visit her with Judy [new wife]."

In time, the vast extended Lyons brood would produce a myriad of shades and lifestyles – and some who would challenge Enid's moral code. Kevin Lyons became Speaker of the House (in Tasmania) but eventually split with the Liberals and formed the Centre Party. He held the balance of power from 1969-72 until his last vote brought the government down. Brendan Lyons won a seat in the Tasmanian parliament in 1982 but was defeated at the 1986 State election. Their beautiful sister Rosemary, a talented classical pianist (in the style of Eileen Joyce) with a poet's gifts and mother of four, suffered several psychological collapses. Enid spent her last years worrying over Rosie more than any of her other children and for some time divided her Christmases between visiting Rosie, in care at New Norfolk, and staying at Home Hill. And Barry, with a fine intelligence in spite of his physical handicaps, had paid employment throughout his adult life.

There were tragedies. On 11 October 1969, Enid's sister Nell had been driving towards the northern approach to the Sydney Harbour Bridge with her husband Hubert when they were struck by a car and Nell was killed. Just months later, in March 1970, Moira's husband was also killed in a car accident, leaving her with four young children.

The visitors came and went at Home Hill. Zara Holt arrived in late 1968 to open the Devonport Show. "Darling Enid," she wrote on her return to the mainland, "It was bliss to see you again, have dinner with you in your lovely house & meet so many members of your large and enchanting family." Writers sought access to documents; Philip Hart exchanged letters with Enid as he wrote a PhD thesis on Joe Lyons and his political life. Librarian Pauline Fanning corresponded and visited from Canberra to sort through her papers and select what would be sent to the National Library. Enid took to opening her garden for an annual fair. Professor Manning Clark wrote to offer his explanation of his published views of her husband, "… the apparent detachment was imprudent. I should have made things clearer ... Permit me to add that I admire the way you defend and uphold his memory." The invitations to attend receptions continued, from Parliament House, from Government House, Hobart and Government House, Canberra – the Queen Mother came in 1964, the Duke and Duchess of Kent in 1969, Pope Paul VI in 1970 and HRH Prince Philip, Duke of Edinburgh in 1971, along with many others. In May 1972, the International Portrait Gallery in New York wrote to request she send a photograph of herself for use in a series it was holding on "famous men and women of all nations and periods of history". She was listed by the *Dictionary of International Biography* for 1974.

Her greatest thrill came in 1979, after a "summons" to Government House, Canberra by Sir Zelman Cowen. She was collected at Canberra airport and, at Yarralumla, guided into a room where she immediately noticed Prime Minister Malcolm Fraser and wife Tammy. But her surprise was total when she recognised another woman in the room, tall and elegant. It was the new Prime Minister of Great Britain, Margaret Thatcher who was on a one day visit following the G7 summit in Tokyo.

Schools, local organisations, hospitals, women's groups and the Liberal Party continued to invite Enid to appear at their functions and give the occasional address. In November 1972, just before the federal election, she went to Canberra to speak at a Liberal Party dinner. But as the speech drew near, Enid was so badly afflicted by laryngitis Senator Margaret Guilfoyle, new in the Senate, had to read the speech for her. "I remember going over that night to deliver this paper; it was fascinating and her daughter was with her. What was lovely was that she was so beautiful. I looked at her that night and I thought, she can't utter a sound but what a beautiful woman. And she was the most honoured guest. You could see that she had this respect." The Whitlams also found Dame Enid a delight to know. She turned up at The Lodge during International Women's Year in 1975; she had been asked to speak at the Women in Politics conference. Gough Whitlam opened the car door for her as she pulled up and said, "Welcome home." And gave her a hug.

In an obituary on Dame Enid, in 1981, Margaret Whitlam wrote with understanding of the role she had played as a prime ministerial wife. And of Enid's writing and public commentary: "No matter what brand of politics persuades us, we all admire an undaunted woman and [Enid] was one of the first quality. How easy it is for me to identify with her when I read what she had to say."

Home Hill remained her castle; she continued to work in her garden and potter about with maintenance jobs on a property she regarded as one of the nation's treasures. One of its rooms still features a floor to ceiling tree that Enid painted to hide a crack in the wall. She spent hours in her garden, a great passion. Grandson Peter Lyons recalls mowing her vast lawns in the morning and lunching with her on the swing in the side garden while they talked. Soup and bread or sandwiches, but always the pot of tea and lemonade. Then they would spend the afternoon digging and clipping trees. And she would often correct young Peter for his incompetence with a saw, "Don't be like a bull at a gate boy; let the saw do the work." The years her grandson Peter spent helping his Nannie at Home Hill left very fond memories:

> There were so many little adventures inside and outside the house. We cleared French drains, injected the borer holes in the antique furniture with poison and attached the Christmas decorations in exactly the same places each year. I helped her paint and put up wallpaper and cooked with her in the kitchen where she was always keen about a new recipe. Sometimes I would climb a ladder and, following her instructions, clear the guttering on Home Hill. One Sunday afternoon, we were working around the back near the kitchen where the roof is relatively low. She was in her late seventies, but couldn't resist climbing the ladder to stand on the roof with me. It was a slow process but we made it. We heard later that Aunty Sheila had been driving near Home Hill and had nearly crashed when she saw her mother on the roof.

Never one to wait for help, Enid often put her hand to the jobs needing attention around her estate, whether electrical or chopping wood. She fixed spark plugs in her 1959, mint condition, dark grey Humber car, with red leather seats and wood panelling; the car she would often drive from the north coast to Hobart, visiting her relatives and friends. Says her grandson Peter, "It was always at the garage of her mechanic Mr Hedley Cole. I think he could have retired on what she spent on it." Grandchildren would hear her coming and run out to watch her cruise into the driveway, a tiny body behind a huge steering wheel. It made a revving sound as she put it into "Park" and her son Peter said it steered like a truck. Whenever he saw it outside his house, he would say the family was "under vice regal patronage". Once when pulled over for speeding the policeman asked for her name and she replied, "Dame Enid Lyons." His face registered something of the order of "pull the other one" until he looked at her licence.

In the mid sixties, Enid began plans to have Home Hill turned into a publicly preserved museum. In March 1967, the Chairman of the National Trust in Tasmania wrote regretting that the Trust could not afford to acquire Home Hill, and expressed his "bitter disappointment". The sale of the house and contents to the Trust was not a prospect the Lyons children welcomed; their family home and the many lovely items in it would never be theirs. Family jokes over which of them might get the beautiful mahogany dining table were suddenly irrelevant. But Enid persevered, considering her options. On 7 May 1976, the Devonport Municipal Council finally purchased Home Hill for $52,000, funded under the National Estate Program of the federal government. Enid also sold to the Council

Dame Enid meets Prime Minister Margaret Thatcher, June 1979, Government House, Canberra. (l-r) The Hon Malcolm Fraser, Anna Cohen, Dame Enid Lyons, The Hon Margaret Thatcher, Sir Zelman Cohen, Tammy Fraser.

many items belonging to the house, on the understanding they would remain with the property. The Council took over the title on 2 March 1977, with Dame Enid given a life tenancy for a weekly rent of $10. After her death, the Council leased the property to the National Trust of Australia (Tasmania). The family might express regret at their mother's decision but Home Hill, as she told her grandson, would never become just another car park for a local shopping mall. It had been her life, and Joe's, and it would not be broken up. In time, her grandchildren would value what she did.

Old friends were going, her generation disappearing from the political and public stage. Larry Anthony had died long before, in 1957. Harold Holt had gone, Artie Fadden also in 1973. Ivy Wedgewood had gone in 1975 and in June 1976 Richard Casey died. Senator Ivy Wedgewood had written to Enid soon after Menzies' retirement saying, "There are many new faces in both Houses now & it will not be long before the 'foryniners' are all out."

And then, on 15 May 1978, Sir Robert Menzies died. Enid's grandson Peter Lyons was with her that evening. Having heard the news, he had decided to go up to Home Hill. She opened the back door and he said, "Did you know the big man has died?" Enid had no idea what he meant. "When I said, 'Sir Robert Menzies,' she staggered backwards and was visibly shaken. We put on the news and the phone calls started to come in from all over Australia. Mainly newspapers, but friends and family too. She did not speak ill of him to me and it was just us there. They had once watched Menzies making a speech on the television. And Enid had said spontaneously, "Bob had such a wonderful turn of phrase: a well furnished lawyer."

Local Liberal politicians came across Dame Enid as they continued the work she had done so long before. Ray Groom who represented Braddon (formerly Darwin) in the 1970s recalls dropping in on Dame Enid in 1975, after calling to say he would be coming but not giving a time. He found her in the middle of wallpapering a room which she went on doing until she had finished a section. Then she gave him some soup and they chatted for a long time across the table. He was always impressed with her as a speaker when he saw her on a podium, but this time they spoke of the electorate she knew so well, going through the meetings he should not miss and Enid suggesting how best to get around to important contacts. "When I spoke with her," reflected Groom, "she was very pleasant and affable, but also with the tone of authority, much like a senior matron running around a hospital, in charge."

Senator Jocelyn Newman's mother "held Dame Enid on a pedestal". When Newman moved to Tasmania and lived in Launceston with her husband Kevin Newman who became the local federal Member in the famous Bass by-election of 1975, she "found Lyons all around" and got to know Brendan Lyons very

Accompanying Dame Enid's coffin, September 1981, at her State funeral in Devonport are (l-r, in front) Michael Tate, The Hon Michael Hodgman, the Hon Kevin Newman, The Hon Sir Phillip Lynch, President of the Senate Sir Harold Young, Premier Doug Lowe, The Hon Doug Anthony.

well through their Liberal Party work. In 1975, Jocelyn asked Dame Enid to open a day in Launceston held to celebrate International Women's Day. She recalls a diminutive but stout lady, close to eighty, who held her audience as they all stood about her: "She spoke for quite a while, standing, and she was old. It was men and women. And she could take you from one minute of laughing with her and the next minute to having a few tears. So I looked around, wondering how it was going in a mixed group, and the men were weeping too. ... I don't know that I ever saw her again. And then I went to her funeral."

Dame Enid Lyons died on 2 September 1981 at a nursing hospice in Ulverstone. Her funeral was a momentous occasion for Devonport and attended by leaders of the State and federal governments. Among the pallbearers were The Hon Doug Anthony representing the Prime Minister, Malcolm Fraser, the Premier Doug Lowe, Deputy Leader of the Liberal Party Sir Phillip Lynch, President of the Senate – Senator Young, The Hon Ian Sinclair and The Hon Kevin Newman. Some streets were closed for two hours. Joe and Enid's children were all there, except for Desmond who for some unexplained reason did not attend. Archbishop Guilford Young preached a lengthy (what some called self-indulgent) panegyric during which he spoke of his intimate friendship with Dame Enid Lyons, which brought a cry from Rosie of "Whoopee." No-one ever forgot it.

Enid was buried at the Mersey Vale Memorial Park lawn cemetery, next to Joe in a plot she had organised when she had moved Joe's body from the local Catholic Church grounds for reburial on 14 January 1969. "I am growing old ... and it has seemed to me appropriate that his grave should be in a place more readily accessible to those of the general public who would wish to visit it," she told Archbishop Young who organised the matters needed for the shift and presided over the ceremony. She wrote her thanks to Young for all he had done shortly after, saying, "Once again, as on other occasions since you came to Tasmania, I am remembering words once spoken to me in the confessional by another Archbishop of Hobart: 'It is a Bishop's duty to give happiness.' Whenever I have sought your help – and mostly I have sought you sorrowing – I have come away strengthened and comforted and at this time my heart is full of a very conscious gratitude towards you."

On the day of Enid's funeral, as the family moved away from the church they were ushered into Commonwealth limousines for the trip through the crowded Devonport streets along the way to the graveside. Coming out onto the Old Coast Road, Peter Lyons was sitting with his sister Rosie who had lounged back in the luxury seat watching the assembled locals. "You know, Peter," she said, "funerals aside, this is the bloody life." All Peter could think, as the Commonwealth driver split his sides, was how his mother would have laughed.

'HOME HILL'

A fter Dame Enid Lyons' death, Home Hill and its contents became a museum, open to visits from the public. The National Trust of Australia (Tasmania) took a lease of the house in September 1984, having bought the contents all as Dame Enid had left them, and began to administer the property as one of the historic homes of Tasmania. It can be found at 77 Middle Road, Devonport and on the internet.

A visitor enters this quaint and rambling home, set in parklike gardens, through a vestibule flanked by two rooms that were used as bedrooms for most of the time the house was occupied by the Lyons family. However, while Joe Lyons lived at Home Hill, the bedroom to the right of the front door had, for a time, been his study – so this room is now furnished as such, albeit not authentically as Joe Lyons' own study appeared.

For such a large family, what is striking about the house is what appears to be the minimal space available for bedrooms and one can imagine how closely the children might have been tucked in at night. However, the house was enlarged and renovated many times as the family grew. And some of the current living area was once used for bedrooms. Joe and Enid's bedroom was originally what became the dining room. The house today has a layout of sitting room flowing into lounge room flowing into dining room which reflects the continual adding on of space, but it also presents a unique open plan living idea for such a large number of occupants.

The rear of the house contains the old kitchen and store area, with a separate small servant's quarters and is illustrative of an era when a large amount of domestic work, without modern appliances, was achieved with limited resources. Barry Lyons can recall the Christmas ham, at one stage, being cooked in the old wash house copper.

One room is the long L-shaped sitting room where Dame Enid spent most of her time as she grew old. Here, also, the shape of the room has been achieved by remodelling rooms – by combining what was once a breakfast room with a boy's bedroom off it. This room eventually was known as the sunroom. And with its bluestone fireplace at one end, where Dame Enid would have sat on cold Tasmanian evenings, and its wide floor to ceiling Georgian style window at the other, it became the room many family members recall so well as Enid's hearth.

In the formal entertaining rooms, there are displays of precious Lyons family collections; Dame Enid's robes of the Order purchased just in time for the Coronation of Queen Elizabeth II in 1953; antique furniture in cedar, walnut, mahogany and rosewood; the admired mahogany dining table and its matching sideboard; silver, porcelain, Venetian glass and lustre vases.

Mementos from their historical lives are prominent too - the miniature silver cradle on its blackwood base presented to little Garnet in 1924 and the silver porridge bowl given to Janice with its error listing her as Enid and Joe's eleventh child. There are also the many beautiful gifts presented to Joe and Enid Lyons from Joe's stint as Prime Minister - from the silver Coronation spoon replica given by Neville and Anne Chamberlain to gold, silver and blackwood caskets given as Freedom of the City awards from London, Aberdeen, Edinburgh and Devonport.

Dame Enid and her darling Joe have left their spirit in one small corner of the nation they both loved. Home Hill is open every day from 2-3pm except Mondays and Tuesdays.

THE CHILDREN OF DAME ENID LYONS

Gerald Desmond	13 November 1916
Sheila Mary Norma	29 September 1918
Enid Veronica	18 November 1919
Kathleen Patricia	31 December 1920
Moira Rose	7 February 1922
Kevin Orchard	7 February 1923
Garnet Philip Burnell	8 October 1924 (died 5 August 1925)
Brendan Aloysius	27 June 1927
Barry Joseph	20 July 1928
Rosemary Josephine	25 September 1929
Peter Julian	20 September 1931
Janice Mary	25 October 1933

ACKNOWLEDGEMENTS
AND A NOTE ON SOURCES

I have been especially indebted to remaining family, friends and acquaintances of Dame Enid who have contributed a rich source of views and recollections throughout this story. In this, I am especially grateful to Lyons siblings Kathleen Gordon, Brendan Lyons, Barry Lyons and Janice Wotton, as well as their brother Peter Lyons who not only provided his insights, but also readily and generously responded to queries about the family throughout – many thanks.

Mary Pridmore, daughter of the late Rosemary Lyons, spoke with me at length, sat in on many of my interviews in Tasmania, and checked out family details as requested – her energy helped tremendously as did her recall of her grandmother and mother. Mary's godmother, Mary O'Byrne, contributed valuable recollections of Rosemary and Janice Lyons and the Tasmanian Labor Party.

From Britain, Peter Lyons' son Peter Lyons (a difficulty in this book has been the tendency of families to use the same names!), who spent a great deal of time with his grandmother as a teenager, sent me marvellous anecdotes and insights into the older Dame Enid. Libby Lyons, daughter of Kevin Lyons, was invaluable in recollecting Frances Lane, Dame Enid's secretary, as were Miss Lane's nephews Bill and Tim Lane. Thanks also to Dame Enid's nieces, Carmel and Lynette (both nee Lyons), who added information about the Lyons family in The Lodge. Marion Paul (daughter of Nellie Burnell) provided memories of some of the Lyons family in Sydney. Thanks also to Brendan Lyons' daughter Katy who gave me precious insights into her grandmother's appearance at the wheel of her ageing Humber car. Ross Glover and Charmaine Brown provided important new information relating to the first family of Harry Taggett (Enid's Lyons' grandfather).

Dame Margaret Guilfoyle, former Senator for Tasmania Jocelyn Newman, and former Member for Braddon (once Darwin) Ray Groom all contributed insightful memories of Dame Enid. Dame Elisabeth Murdoch also generously gave some of her personal recollections of Dame Enid after Joe's death. Heather Henderson (nee Menzies) gave me useful perspectives on life at The Lodge in its early years. Hazel Craig contributed wonderful background to the work of parliamentary secretaries and the Prime Minister's office in 1930s. The Hon Doug Anthony added information about his father Larry and his friendship with Dame Enid. I am also grateful to Michael Collins Persse and Sir Lennox Hewitt for recollections of Dame Enid's visit to London in 1953.

Dame Enid Lyons wrote two volumes of memoirs – *So We Take Comfort* (1965) and *Among The Carrion Crows* (1972). Her collected selection of columns, from the 1950s, for the Murdoch press was published in 1969 as *The Old Haggis*. These publications have been used for many of Dame Enid's quoted statements in this biography. In addition, I have used comments which she made in interviews for radio, television and the National Library in Canberra.

The Dame Enid Lyons Papers in the Australian National Library not only have been my source for numerous references to Enid Lyons' family, friends and associates but also for an intimate insight into her relationship with her husband Joseph Lyons. They contain a significant collection of letters, largely from Joe Lyons to his wife, which Dame Enid gave to the Library.

Papers in the National Archives relating to the circumstances surrounding the annuity paid to Dame Enid after her husband's death in 1939, her trip to London for the Coronation in 1953, and correspondence involving Keith Murdoch relating to the "Win the War" campaign in 1940 and proposed trip for Dame Enid to the US for a lecture tour were also useful.

I am particularly grateful to Kate White for access to her papers in the University of Melbourne's Baillieu Library. Also to the librarians at Special Collections, Main Library, University of Birmingham for their access to correspondence between Joe and Enid Lyons and Neville Chamberlain, held in the Chamberlain collection. My conversations with Matthew Ricketson helped clarify his grandfather's part in Joe Lyons' break with Labor in 1931.

For additional details relating to the Joyce family, I am grateful to Trish Joyce in Perth who provided documents and photos of her late husband's grandfather Aloysius Joyce. Burnie librarian Judy Cocker was especially helpful in locating information relating to the Burnell and Joyce families, as was Maureen Martin of the Glamorgan Spring Bay Historical Society who put me in contact with Judy. Brian Rollins provided documents and contacts helpful in information regarding the Burnell property at Cooee, and Betty Jones assisted in identifying the old Cooee post office. Leanne Aitken of Burnie made helpful contributions from her work on the history of northern Tasmania's public schools. Jenny Ramsden, grand daughter of Ivy and Leonard Russell, gave important details of Enid as bridesmaid at the Russells' wedding. Erica Davis provided invaluable documents relating to 67 Pedder Street, Hobart. Faye Gardam and her staff at the Devonport Maritime Museum were very helpful in providing access to documents they have on file. I am also grateful to David Jones at the Devonport City Council for providing copies of documents relating to the Council's purchase of Home Hill. And, for her time and discussion with me at Home Hill, thanks to Pam Bartlett.

Special note – The Joyce family material

This biography makes a case for Enid Lyons to have been related by birth to the family of Aloysius Joyce of Burnie. This case is not made lightly. My source wished to remain anonymous. However, I have assessed the story and the witness over a long time and find the information reliable. A record of interview will be kept, along with a statement verifying the identity of my source for the Joyce family connection.

Finally …

A big thanks to a team of hardworking folk who contributed in no small way in the transcript typing and by helping the author over occasional technical hitches – Tanya Goldberg, Alice Grundy, Tenille Halliday, Lalita Mathias and Este Regos with Raffe Gold and Viren Nathoo. And to Veronica Henderson and Christine Wallace for general comments on the text. For this new edition, thanks also to Michael Gilchrist who reworked the original manuscript, and Paige Hally and Hannah Killin at The Sydney Institute. Thanks also to Ann Teesdale at the Home Hill Museum in Devonport for her help in sourcing a number of photos. As always, also thanks to the ever resourceful Gerard, for a rich home library of the period, historical perspectives and ten hours of reading the manuscript with valued comments to consider. And to Anthony Cappello at Connor Court for this fine publication along with Nick Cater at the Menzies Research Institute for offering me a chance to revise and update this wonderful story.

BIBLIOGRAPHY

Andrews, E. M., *Isolationism and Appeasement in Australia* (ANU Press, 1970)

Baird, Julia, *Media Tarts* (Scribe Publications, 2004)

Blainey, Geoffrey, *The Peaks of Lyell* (MUP, 1967)

Bogdanor, Vernon, *The Monarchy and The Constitution* (Clarendon Press: Oxford, 1995)

Brett, Judith, *Australian Liberals and The Moral Middle Class* (CUP, 2003)

Calwell, Arthur, *Be Just and Fear Not* (Lloyd O'Neill, 1972)

Campion, Edmund, *Australian Catholics* (Viking, 1987)

Childe, V. Gordon, *How Labor Governs* (MUP, 1964)

Conlon, D. J. (ed), *G. K. Chesterton - A Half Century of Views* (OUP, 1987)

Davis, Richard, *Eighty Years Labor 1903-1933* (Sassafras Books, University of Tasmania, 1983)

Day, David, *Curtin - A Life* (HarperCollins, 1999)

Day, David, *Chifley* (HarperCollins, 2001)

Denning, Warren, *Caucus Crisis - The Rise and Fall of The Scullin Government* (Hale & Iremonger, 1982)

Edwards, Cecil, *Bruce of Melbourne* (Heinemann : London, 1965)

Fadden, Artie, *They Call Me Artie; The Memoirs of Sir Artie Fadden* (Jacaranda Press, 1969)

Fairbanks, George, "Australia and the Abdication Crisis, 1936", *Australian Outlook*, Vol 20 Dec 1966

Fitzhardinge, L. F., *The Little Digger 1914-1952* (Angus & Robertson, 1979)

Fitzherbert, Margaret, *Liberal Women - Federation to 1949* (The Federation Press, 2004)

Grattan, Michelle, *Australian Prime Ministers* (New Holland, 2000)

Green, Frank, *The Servant of The House*, (Heinemann, 1969)

Hancock, Ian, *National and Permanent? The Federal Organisation of The Liberal Party of Australia, 1944-1965* (MUP, 2000)

Hart, Philip R. , 'J A Lyons: A Political Biography', PhD Thiesis, ANU

_____ 'J A Lyons: Tasmanian Labour Leader', *Labour History*, No 9, November 1965

Hasluck, Paul, *The Government and The People 1939-1941* (Australian War Memorial, 1952)

Hazlehurst, Cameron, *Menzies Observed* (George Allen & Unwin, 1979)

Henderson, Anne, *Joseph Lyons – The People's Prime Minister* (NewSouth Publishing, 2011)

Hogan, Michael, *The Sectarian Strand* (Penguin, 1987)

Hudson, W I, *Casey* (OUP, 1986)

Hughes, Colin, *Mr Prime Minister : Australian Prime Ministers 1901-1972* (OUP, 1976)

Hughes, Colin & Graham, B. D., *Australian Government and Politics: 1890-1964* (ANU Press, 1968)

Hughes, Colin & Graham, B. D., *Voting for The Australian House of Representatives 1901-1964* (ANU Press, 1974)

Inglis, Ken, *This is The ABC* (Black Inc, 2006)

Jenkins, Cathy, 'A Mother in Cabinet: Dame Enid Lyons and the press', *Australian Journalism Review* Vol 25 (1), 2003

Kiernan, Colm, *Calwell: A personal and Political Biography* (Nelson, 1978)

Lake, Marilyn, *A Divided Society: Tasmania During World War I* (MUP, 1975)

Langmore, Diane, *Prime Ministers' Wives* (McPhee Gribble, 1992)

La Nauze, J. A., *Alfred Deakin: A Biography Vol 2* (MUP, 1965)

Luscombe T. R., *Builders and Crusaders* (Lansdowne Press, 1967)

Lyons, Enid, *So We Take Comfort* (Heinemann: London, 1965)

_____ *Among The Carrion Crows* (Rigby, 1972)

_____ Enid, *The Old Haggis* (Heinemann, 1969)

McCalman, Janet, *Journeyings - The Biography of a Middle-Class Generation 1920-1990* (MUP, 1993)

Martin, Allan W, *Robert Menzies; A Life - Volume 1 1894-1943* (MUP, 1993)

_____ *Robert Menzies; A Life - Volume 2 1944-1979* (MUP, 1999)

Menzies, Robert, *The Measure of The Years* (Coronet Books, 1972)

_____ *Afternoon Light* (Cassel Australia, 1967)

Monks, John, *Elisabeth Murdoch - Two Lives* (Sun, 1994)

Murray, Robert, *The Confident Years - Australia in The Twenties* (Allen Lane, 1978)

Negus, George, *George Negus Tonight*, ABC TV, 22 September 2003

Nethercote J. R., *Liberalism and the Australian Federation* (The Federation Press, 2001)

Page, Sir Earle, *Truant Surgeon* (Angus & Robertson, 1963)

Pearce, Joseph, *Literary Converts* (HarperCollins, 2000)

Perkins, Kevin, *Menzies, Last of The Queen's Men* (Rigby Limited, 1968)

Pratt, Mel, Interview with Dame Enid Lyons for the Australian National Library collection (1972)

Reid, Arthur, *Those Were the Days*

Richardson, Nick, "Sir Keith Murdoch's Relationship with Prime Minister Joseph Lyons" - Margaret George Award Paper 2006, National Archives of Australia online

Robertson, John, *J. H. Scullin - A Political Biography* (University of Western Australia Press, 1974)

Santamaria, B. A., *Santamaria, A Memoir* (OUP, 1997)

Sawer, Geoffrey, *Australian Federal Politics and the Law 1929-1949* (MUP, 1963)

Scott, Natalie, *Woman in Question*, ABC TV (1978)

Southwood, W. T., *A Prayer Calendar of Deceased Priests in Australia* (self published/no date)

Shedvin, C. B., *Australia and the Great Depression* (Sydney University Press, 1970)

Starr, Graeme, *The Liberal Party of Australia - A Documentary History* (Drummond/Heinemann, 1980)

Stevens, B. S. B., 'J. A. Lyons', *Australian Quarterly*, Vol. II, No. 2, June 1939

Townsley, W. A. *The Government of Tasmania* (University of Queensland Press, 1976)

Turner Naomi, *Catholics in Australia* (CollinsDove, 1992)

Weller, Patrick, *Cabinet Government in Australia, 1901-2006* (UNSW Press, 2007)

Were, J. B. & Son, *The House of Were* (1954)

White, Kate, *A Political Love Story - Joe and Enid Lyons* (Penguin, 1987)

Younger, R. M., *Keith Murdoch - Founder of a Media Empire* (HarperCollins, 2003)

Zwar, Desmond, *In Search of Keith Murdoch* (Macmillan, 1980)

INDEX

Notes: EB: Enid Burnell, EL: Enid Lyons,
JL: Joe Lyons

achondroplasia, 136

Ada (home help at Devonport), 111, 113

Adelaide (South Australia), visit by EL &
JL, 167

Advisory War Council, 290

All For Australia League (New South
Wales), 155

Allison, Norm, 63, 83

annuities controversy, 260-63, 283

Anthony, Doug, 291, 303, 338, 339, 346

Anthony, Larry, 291-2, 303, 309, 337

Apps, John, 27

Apps, Kathleen, 31

Apps family, 27

Ashbolt, Sir Alfred, 110

Astor, Lady, vii, 225

Augustus Wilhelm, Prince, 216

Austin, Enid (née Lyons)
    at EL's National Library interview,
        257
    encouragement to EL, 276
    at Frankston, 308
    at 'Home Hill,' 275
    negotiates payments for EL's
        journalism, 313
    return from Washington, 305

Austin, Lt Maurice, 272, 305

Australia
    links with Britain, 226
    US relations, 229–30
    as viewed by US, 228–9

Australian ambassador to
    Washington, 229

Australian Broadcasting Commission
    (ABC)
    board of, 309-10
    Launceston radio station, 320
    radio broadcasts, 234, 280, 294, 316
    radio broadcasts by EL, 267
    television programs, 320-2

*Australian Catholics – the Contribution of
    Catholics to the Development of Australian
    Society* (Campion), 319

Australian Council of Trade Unions
    (ACTU), 297

Australian delegation to Britain (1935),
    216

Australian Labor Party (ALP), 161
    breakaway group, 157
    economic priorities, 156
    image of, 101-2
    'Labor rat' tag for JL, 157, 171
    in Tasmania, 102, 150

Australian Women's National League
    (AWNL), 184, 296

Australian Women's Weekly (magazine), 51,
    261

Australian Worker, The (AWU journal), 150

Australians abroad, 317

Baldwin, Mrs Lucy, 241, 243

Baldwin, Stanley, 226, 239, 241

Bank Nationalisation Bill, 287, 302

basic wage, 207, 285

Beck, Mr (boarder), 39

353

beef exports, 207

Bell, Sir George, 275

Belton, James, 81, 88

Berkery, Mrs (landlady), 126

Bjelke-Petersen, Joh, 159

Bourne family, 143

Boyer, Richard, 320-21

Brady, Frank, 305, 307

Brady, Moira (née Lyons), 305, 307, 313

Britain (1931), 165

Broinowski, Leo, 149-50

Bruce, Ethel, 178, 221

Bruce, Stanley, 140

    advice to EL, 194

    Australian High Commissioner to Britain, 193, 216, 240

    meet EL & JL on arrival in Britain, 221

    on 1929 election, 141

    prime ministerial candidate, 193-4

    re-nominates for seat, 172

    relationship with JL, 127

    residence at 'The Lodge', 178

    resignation, 137-8, 193-4

    return to Australia, 181

Bugg, Bill, 40

Burnell, Annie, 16, 20, 44, 64, 182

Burnell, Bertram, 16, 20, 46, 48, 97-8, 266

Burnell, Charles, 15, 37, 46, 120

Burnell, Eliza (née Taggett), ix, 9

    accounts of and attributes, 16–17, 41, 97

    appearance, 48–9

    in Burnie society, 105

    at Burringbar, 16

    candidate in 1925 Tas. election, 115, 117, 119

    Cooee land 'purchase,' 32-34

    cottage at 'Home Hill', 265

    death, 30, 272-3

    dinner-table discussions, 50

    Fabian attitudes, 40, 49

    health, 47-48, 265

    horror of alcohol, 12–13

    income from 'boarders,' 39-40

    independent and adapatable, 17–18

    intolerance of conceit, 56

    Justice of the Peace, 113

    'loan' and income, 20, 32-4

    local involvement, 48

    married life, 16–17

    Methodism, 12–13, 44

    to northern Tasmania, 16

    political awareness, 48–9, 70, 117

    pride in children's achievements, 44, 182

    relationship with Aloysius Joyce (jun.), 25–27

    relationship with JL, 74–5

    religious beliefs, 16

    self-improvement and education, 18–19, 26, 36, 39, 49

    sets boundaries for children, 41

    spiritualism, 18

    values education for daughters, 43–4

    visits Tas. state parliament, 59–61

    work, 22

    and Workers Political League, 49

    WPL membership, 70-71

Burnell, Elizabeth, 14–15, 46

Burnell, Enid Muriel

see also Lyons, Enid

Muriel; Lyons, Enid Muriel (née
    Burnell)
wedding plans, 75–77
welcomed to Canberra, 178–9
as wife of Tas. premier, 109-110
wins federal seat Darwin, 275–7
on women's role, 206–8, 213–4
workload, 183, 300
writing style, 54, 323–4
Burnell, Frank, 15, 46
Burnell, Nellie
    see also Glover, Nellie (née Burnell)
    birth, 16
    engagement, 58, 60, 62
    marriage to Hubert Glover, 58,
        104–5
    studious, 42
    at Teachers Training College, 51
    teaching, 54
Burnell, William
    accounts of, 15, 16–17, 105
    Aloysius Joyce affair, 25–7
    at Burringbar (NSW), 16
    childhood, 14
    consents to EB's marriage, 73-4
    cottage at 'Home Hill,' 265
    dance hall management, 42, 45
    death, 300-01
    employment, 21–2
    fidelity suspected, 25
    marriage, 15–6
    migration to Australia, 14
    no religous beliefs, 17
    to northern Tasmania, 16

paternity of Enid, 21–2, 25–7, 31
pride in JL as PM, 182
sawyer, 9, 14, 27
unemployment, 54
Burnell family
    appearance, 31
    close contact, 22
    at Cooee, 45–7
    at Emu Bay district, 32
    finances, 55–56
    to Lees Mill, Duck River, 28
    residences, 21–22
    to Stowport (Tas.), 38
Burnie (Tas.), social environment, 39
Bush, Elsie, 180, 188
by-elections
    1931, East Sydney, 162
    1941, Bass, 84

Cadman, Lady, 223
Calwell, Arthur, 295–6
Cameron, Archie, 291
Canberra (ACT), 144–5, 177–6
Carmody, Sister, 181, 197
Carroll, Catherine, 67
Carroll, Dennis, 67
Carroll, Ellen, 67, 68, 73
Carroll, Etty, 67, 79
Carroll, John (jun.), 67
Carroll, John (sen.), 67
Carroll, Mary, 67, 79, 181
Carroll, Molly, 209
Casey, Maie, 197, 260
Casey, Richard
    assistant treasurer, 193

generosity after JL's death, 260

JL's funeral arrangements, 254

ministerial position, 304

at William Burnell's funeral, 300-1

Catholic 'Authority', 79

Catholic benefactors, 26, 27

Catholic press, criticism of JL, 209

Catholic voters, 160–1, 319–20

Catholic Women's Guild, 270

Catholics, bigotry against, 223–4

Chamberlain, Anne, 242, 316, 342

Chamberlain, Neville, 316

    death, 272

    EL & JL meet, 225

    Munich Agreement, 4, 212

    Mussolini–Hitler discussions, 245–46

    political skills, 242

    prime minister, 241-2

Charlton, Michael, 321

Chesterton, GK, 318

Chifley, Ben, 161, 282

Chifley, Elizabeth, 180

Chifley government, 301-2

childbirth, 212-3

choir practice, 106–7

Churchill, Winston, 217, 273

Cilento, Lady Phyllis, 294

Citizens League (South Australia), 155

Citizens League (Victoria), 155

citizens leagues, 155, 166

Clare, Sister Blanche, 180-1

Clark, Dr Colin, 294

Clark, Manning, 248, 324–5

Cockburn, Stewart, 298

Cole, Hedley, 335

Colorgravure Publications, 308

Commonwealth funding to states, 137–8

Commonwealth Grants Commission, 193

communication

    see also under letters

    shipboard wireless, 219

    telephone, 124, 143, 145, 235

conscription for war service, 85

Conway, Mrs (housekeeper), 79

Copland, Prof. Douglas, 147

coronation of Queen Elizabeth II, 317

Costello, Peter, 237

Couchman, Dame Elizabeth (May), 184, 296

Country Hour (ABC radio program), 320

Country Party, 156, 164, 172, 248, 274, 291, 296, 299, 302, 303

Cowan, Edith, 117

Craig, Hazel, 183

Craigavon, Lord (James Craig), 223-4

Curr, Edward, 66

Curtin, Elsie, x, 180, 263, 283

Curtin, John

    annuities issue, x, 283

    and Australia–US links, 207–8

    death, 283

    Labor prime minister, 145, 235, 274

    relationship with EL, 282–3

Curtis, Harry, 123

Czech crisis, 245

Dardanelles campaign, 81

Darwin (federal electorate in Tas.), 274–5

Dawson, Geoffrey, 225

De Valera, Éamon, 239

Deakin, Alfred, 18, 315

Denning, Warren, 148

Desborough, Lady, 226

Dickson, Charlie, 40

Diethelm, Dr Oscar, 7, 255

Dominion League (WA secessionist group), 202

Donohue, Jack, 266

Douglas, Irvine, 218, 240

Dublin Castle, 225

Earle, John, 49, 64, 84, 85, 93

Edward VIII, King of Britain, 238

    abdication crisis, 237–9

Edwards, Dorothy, 322

Edwards, Frank, 276, 277

Edwards, Madge, 277

election campaigns

    1931, 174–5

    1934, 189ff

elections, see by-elections; federal elections; Tasmanian state elections

Elliott, John, 159

Emily Hotel (later Union Hotel, Stanley, Tas.), 67

Evatt, HV, 147

Everett, Bridget, 323

Fadden, Arthur, 274, 275, 292

Fairbairn, James, 273

federal elections

    1931, 156, 170–3

    1940, 273

    1943, 275, 279

    1946, 296

    1949, 299–300

Fenton, James (Jim), 144, 147, 148, 150, 154, 156, 157, 166, 172, 173, 175

Ferguson, Vera, 99

Findlay, AP, 267-8

Fisher, Andrew, 6, 80, 84

Fisher, Margaret, 86

Flynn, Errol, 57, 223

Flynn, Prof. Theodore, 223

Francis, Eliza, see Taggett, Eliza

Francis, Henry, 12

Fraser, Malcolm, 280, 333

Fraser, Tamara, 200, 333

Fulton, Mr (clerk), 123

Gabb, Joel (Moses), 157, 161

Game, Sir Philip, 146

George V, King of Britain, 22, 238, 284

    Silver Jubilee year, 216, 228

George VI, King of Britain, 232, 241, 314

Giblin, Lyndhurst F, 110, 147

Gibson, Sir Robert, 146

Gillard, Julia, 283

Gilmore, Mary, 247-48

Gloucester, Duke of, 196

Glover, Hubert, 56, 72, 104, 182, 318, 332

Glover, Marion, 254

Glover, Nellie (née Burnell), 58, 104, 182, 187, 332

Gordon, Gilbert, 292

Gordon, Kathleen (née Lyons), 292, 314

Gorton, John, 263, 324

governors-general, 147

government borrowings, 146

Gowrie, Lady Zara, 197, 260, 274

Gowrie, Lord, 260, 281, 295

Gray, Dwyer, 96

Green, Albert, 149

Green, Frank, 250

Gregory, Clara, *see* Joyce, Clara

Groom, Lady, 197

Groom, Ray, 337-38

Grosvenor, Marjorie (Marge), 218

'the Group' (conservative political group), 151, 163, 169, 195, 236

Guild of St Joan (Catholic feminist group), 221

Guilfoyle, Senator Margaret, 334

Gullett, Penny, 197, 211, 218, 226, 270

Gullett, Sir Henry, 164, 197, 212, 216, 246-7, 273

Guy, James (Allan), 126, 130, 140, 157, 163, 259, 292, 298

Haire, Dr Norman, 294

Hare-Clarke voting system, 70, 116, 134

Hawke, Hazel, 200

Hawker, Charles, 244

Hawson, Nurse, 111

Haydon, Fr Patrick, 189

Hayes, Fr Pat, 27, 81

Haywood, Ivy, 58, 76

Heinemann Australia (book publishers), 322

Henderson, Kingsley, 151, 236. 266

Herald Broadcasting Stations (3DB), 268

Herald Gravure (magazine publisher), 312

Hetherington, John, 322

Higgins, Sir John, 151

Hilda (staff member at 'The Lodge'), 180, 196

Hitler, Adolf, 4, 212-3, 216, 217, 242-5

Hodgman, Michael, 280-1

Holman, Ada, 87

Holt, Harold, 199, 291, 298, 320

Holt, Zara, 196

home help, 99-100, 112, 143, 179-80, 208

'Home Hill' (Devonport home of Lyons family)

    building of house, 1, 90

    cottage for Burnells, 265

    extensions to, 130, 249-50

    garden, 137

    holidays, 176

    home for adult children, 313-4

    National Trust museum, 341-2

    owned by EL, 250

    purchase from Jensen family, 130

    returns to, 98, 145, 256, 264–5

    sale (1920), 99

    setting, 132

    visitors to, 179, 321

Horner, HG, 267

household budgeting, 295-96

Housewives Association (Canberra), 178

Howard, Janette, 236

Howard, John, 236, 302

Howroyd, Charles, 93

Hudson, Fr, 7

Hughes, Dame Mary, 197, 290

Hughes, William Morris (Billy), xii, 4, 84, 92, 107, 138, 249, 286, 290

Hutchinson, Bill, 294

hydro-electricity, 132

Imperial Conference (London, 1937), 240

Inglis, Ken, 310, 320

Irish Catholics, 68

Isaacs, Sir Isaac, 147, 177, 183, 282

Jensen, Eveline and Carl, 130

Joyce, Agnes, 21, 26, 27

Joyce, Aloysius James (sen.), 21
    agreement with William Burnell, 26
    Branxholm school, 69
    Catholic benefactor, 27
    intolerance, 77
    land holdings, 24
    obligations to 'granddaughter,' 32-3

Joyce, Aloysius (jnr)
    appearance, 26
    birth, 24
    to Boer War, 28
    to Canadian gold rush, 28
    death, 29
    and Eliza Burnell, 25–7
    farm work, 25
    follows EL's progress, 34-5
    to Kalgoorlie, 28
    marriage to Elizabeth Borradale, 28
    meeting with EL, 34-35, 274
    miner, 24
    naming of children, 24, 27

Joyce, Clara, 24

Joyce, Eileen Natal, 21
    arranges Enid–Aloysius meeting, 34
    integrity, 29
    memory of mother, 24
    overhears William Burnell's
        accusation, 25, 26, 29–30

Joyce, Eileen, 277

Joyce, Henry, 22

Joyce, Joseph, 27

Joyce, Joseph (later Clarence), 27

Joyce, Mary, 27

Joyce, Mary (later Grace), 27

Joyce, Mary (née Poole), 22

Joyce, William James, 28–9

Jubilee balls at Buckingham Palace, 222

Jubilee day at Smithton, 311

Keating, Annita, 200

Keating, Paul, 237

Keller, Helen, 299-300

Kent, Ivy, 310

Kingsmill, Sen. Walter, 203

Korean War, 306

Labor League, 53

Lampe, Frederick, 296

Lane, Frances, 299, 313, 314

Lang, John Thomas (Jack), 145-6, 148,
    162, 165, 171, 192-4

Langoulant, Allan, 323

Lanyon, Capt. HT, 163

Latham, John, 154, 159, 161, 164, 166,
    168-9, 181, 193

Leary, John, 277

Lee, Robert, 57

Lee, Sir Walter, 107

Leech, George, 40

Leesville, Duck River (now Smithton,
    Tas.), 9

Lenihan, Eileen, 240, 259

letters
    condolence, 57-58

EB to JL during engagement, 71, 75

EL to Menzies, 324-26

JL to EB

    on Catholic wedding, 77-8

    on engagement, 75-6

    on Hobart teaching position, 72–3

    on separation and longing, 73, 78

    on wedding plans, 75

JL to EL

    on care of children, 196

    on family finances, 250

    loving, 196, 250

    mixed tone, 64-6

    on swearing in as PM, 176

    on teaching bond, 59

Lewis, Sir Elliot, 110

Liberal Party of Australia, 201, 296

loan conversion campaign, 151–3

Lockhart, John, 239

'The Lodge' (prime minister's residence, Canberra), 322

    dining room, 163-4

    domestic arrangements at, 180-1

    family life at, 232-3

    invitations to, 197

    Lyons family arrives at, 177

    Lyons family leaves, 259

    Lyons family life at, 177, 188–9, 196

    renovations, 176

    too small for Lyons family, 175–6

Lowndes, Arthur, 321

Luck, Aubrey, 307

Lyons, Adeline, 44, 50, 67, 70

Lyons, Barry, 177, 191

achondroplasia, 3, 136, 191, 218, 250

birth, 3, 136, 180

education, 264

on EL in ministry, 303

at 'Home Hill,' 304–5

independence, 136, 332

on Menzies government, 244

singing, 196

at 'The Lodge', 177, 196

Lyons, Brendan

    birth, 126, 128

    education, 264

    at 'Home Hill,' 304–5

    loving nature, 196

    at 'The Lodge', 177, 195

Lyons, Carmel, 130, 132, 177, 182, 232, 245

Lyons, Ellen (née Carroll), 67, 68, 73

Lyons, Enid and Joe

    affection and longing, 64–5

    ancestor-hunting, 225

    assist others find employment, 184–85

    British public interest in, 221–2

    Catholicism, 101, 209, 318–9

    at 'Chequers', 225

    companionship on board ship, 219–21

    courtship, 63–5

    dining with Lady Astor, 225

    donations to charity, 184

    faith in divine providence, 123

    family life, 102, 107, 113–14, 134, 135

    finances, 250

    gifts given/received, 242

holidays, 114

honeymoon, 86

love of conversation, 265

marriage, 81

meeting with Chamberlains, 225, 242

meeting with Pope Pius XI, 228

modern marriage, 196

partnership style, 186

personality cult, 165-6, 190

public support in UK, 240–1

relationship, 246

religious beliefs, 79

return to Devonport, 129-30, 133

separations, 75, 93–4

travel

    Canada (1935), 232

    Europe (1935), 215–27

    Ireland (1935), 225

    London (1935), 221

    London (coronation, 1937), 239-40

    northern Tasmania (1932), 181

    Queensland (1933), 206

    Rome (1935), 217, 228

    US (1935), 207-08, 231

    Western Australia (1933), 202-3

    Windsor Castle (1935), 226–8

wedding plans, 75–7

Lyons, Enid (later Enid Austin), 257

after JL's death, 253

birth, 98

care of younger siblings, 188–9, 195, 259

education, 170, 188

housekeeping, 249

in Launceston, 126

marriage, 272

Lyons, Enid Muriel (née Burnell)

see also Burnell, Enid Muriel; letters; Lyons, Enid and Joe; policies and beliefs of EL

ABC commissioner, 309–10, 320–1

ability to move an audience, xiii, 167

anecdotes about teaching, 56

annuity from parliament, 260, 261–2, 308–9

birth, 9, 16

Cabinet position without portfolio, 302-3

campaigning, 277–8, 301

candidate in 1925 Tas. election, 116-30

car accident, 300

Catholic baptism, 80

ceased public engagements, 272

challenge to her election, 282-3

child raising methods, 170

childbirth, 94, 97, 99, 104, 111, 126, 136, 137, 170, 181, 191, 195

church choir, 107, 114–5

community-spirited, 57

condolence letters received, 57–8

confidence, 54–55, 289–90

conversion to Catholicism, 77-78, 114

cooking skill, 136

craving for babies, 94

criticism by cynics, 210

Dame Grand Cross of the Order of the British Empire, 241

on death of children, 122

debating style, 118-19

defence of JL's reputation, 324-5

on 'dominant male' persona, 290

donates JL's letters to National
Library, 65

drama performances, 44, 57

driving, 131, 335

education, 41

efficiency, 143

electoral assistance to JL, 103, 134

electorate supporters, 277

empathy, 213

employment after JL's death, 261

engagement ring, 76

engagement to JL, 63-4

female perspective, 103-4

first woman member in House of
Representatives, 279

fortune telling, 18–9

hate mail about annuity, 262, 283

in high society, 197

homemaking and housework, 56, 88

hysterectomy, 235-6

illness and nervous exhaustion, 100,
120, 128, 133, 191, 196, 233-4,
258, 269, 298, 301, 306

income after JL's death, 260, 309

at JL's funeral, 255–6

journalism, 222-3, 240, 261, 308-12

'A Prime Minister's Wife on The Joys
of a Large Family,' 223

account of coronation, 317

columns for *Sun,* 316

The Old Haggis (collection of
columns), 323

royalties for writing, 323

learns parliamentary procedure, 288

lecture tour to US proposed, 271

Liberal Party policy committee, 296

maiden speech in federal parliament,
281, 283-6

at Maribyrnong meeting, 172–3

meeting with Aloysius Joyce, 34

meeting with Indigenous Australians,
329

memoirs, 271, 322-23

So We Take Comfort, 346

Among the Carrion Crows (2nd
installment), 324

My Life, 308-9

on Menzies' election as PM, 255, 289

miscarriages, 88–9, 120,   123, 126

on 'natural mothering,' 212-13

on Nazi Germany, 245–7

'night under the pines,' 314

pacifism, 211-12, 240, 244, 286

popularity, 167-8, 201-2, 206, 211

on principles of conduct, 214

public vs private life, 100

rejection of contraception, 100

reaction to Menzies' death, 357

reaction to her mother's death, 272

shipboard life, 217–20

Silver Jubilee Sir John Morris
Memorial Lecture, 327

speeches, 293

on 'art of living,' 210

in Western Australia, 202–5

stands down from Darwin, 306

suspender incident, 292

swearing in to federal parliament,
282-3

at Teachers Training College, 51-2

television interviews, 316, 321

tributes on standing down from parliament, 307

'You Asked Me,' 312

Lyons, Garnet, 3, 11-13, 120-3, 128, 342

Lyons, Gerald Desmond

after JL's death, 253

birth, 93-95, 97, 99

boarding at St Virgil's, 126, 182

close to Aunt Nell, 187

education, 142, 170

as EL's electoral secretary. 299

intelligence, 114, 150, 235, 308

mathematics teacher, 308

photo with Menzies, 264

in RAAF, 274

university study, 188, 235

work, 249

Lyons, Gertrude, 67, 89

Lyons, Janice Mary, 195

birth, 179, 195

boarding school, impact of, 263-4

to Canberra, 305

coronation trip to UK and Europe, 316

education, 259, 305

on mother's need for privacy, 133, 179

Lyons, Joseph Aloysius (Joe), 71, 83

see also under letters

absences from family, 175, 186

acting treasurer, 144

administrative style, 202

anti-conscriptionist, 95

on Australia–British links, 226

birth and childhood, 67

burial in Devonport, 256

business backing, 163–4

Cabinet member in Tas. government, 71

campaign against conscription, 85

candidate for federal seat of Darwin, 98

candidate for Tas. elections, 115

car accident and recovery, 3, 120-3, 129

care of children, 196

common touch, 70

Commonwealth Grants Commission set up, 193

constitutional monarchist, 127

constraints of parliamentary office, 84

consultative style, 110

criticism of, 246-7

cultivation of the press, 125

death and impact of, 6–7, 171, 253

defection from Labor, 156–7, 161

defence by EL, 323–26

education, 68-69

election as Tas. Labor leader, 93

entry to Tas. parliament, 49-50

family involvement, 143, 196

financial policies, 146-50, 155

first meeting with Enid, 44-5

generosity, 262

German peace negotiations, 212

gift at birth of Garnet, 111-12

illness, 2, 5, 6–7, 236-7, 248

income support for family, 154

Labor allegiance, 161

Labor Member for Wilmot, 68

'Labor rat' tag, 171

love and longing for EL, 84-5, 95, 147–8, 176, 194, 251–2

meets 'the Group', 155

meeting with Indigenous Australians, 329

memorial service in Melbourne, 255

minister of education, 58

'moderate' (Catholic view), 150-1

monarchist, 150

monitor teacher, 52

mother's influence, 68

parliamentary income, 249-50

political ambitions, 102-3, 134

popularity, 108, 159

premier of Tasmania, 108, 127

pride in EL, 199-200, 205

prime minister, 177

Privy Councilor, 224

radio broadcast, 174

refused armchairs at Manuka church, 189

relationship with Menzies, 245-8, 257-6

resignation from federal Cabinet, 154

retirement, 250-1

salary as prime minister, 262

seeks permission to marry EB, 73-4

shift in political allegiance, 151

support for Chamberlain, 244-5

support from Scullin, 149

tour of SE states, 164-5

tributes to, 253-4, 257–8

UAP leadership, 160

voice, 91

wins federal seat of Wilmot, 137

work as a child, 67-8

WPL involvement, 68-9

Lyons, Kathleen
  birth, 99
  boarding school, 264
  car accident, 3, 134
  education, 114, 170, 187
  at JL's death, 7, 253
  in Launceston, 126
  marriage, 292
  in WAAAF, 275

Lyons, Kevin
  birth, 104
  childhood, 113
  education, 2, 170, 187, 260, 264
  at JL's death and funeral, 7, 253
  in RAAF, 274
  speaker, Tasmanian House of Assembly, 332
  state member for Darwin, 300, 308
  stays with Eliza Burnell, 126

Lyons, Libby, 258

Lyons, Lynette, 177, 182, 232

Lyons, Mary, 67, 89, 181

Lyons, Michael (grandfather), 66-7, 89

Lyons, Michael (father), 67, 89

Lyons, Moira
  after JL's death, 253, 255
  in AWAS, 275
  birth, 99, 111
  childhood, 111
  education, 170, 187
  marriage, 305
  stays with Eliza Burnell, 126

Lyons, Peter (Enid's son)
  birth, 170, 172, 181

comments on EL, 142, 335
    on Desmond, 299
    divorce, 332
    education, 259, 264
    living in Tasmania, 195
    "Nanny Brabham", 278
    overhears 'scandal' row, 30
    at 'The Lodge', 177
Lyons, Peter (Enid's grandson)
    comments on EL, 213, 252, 259, 290, 319
    at 'Home Hill,' with EL 334-5, 329
    on strong family personalities, 313
Lyons, Rev Patrick, 282
Lyons, Rosemary
    appearance, 196
    birth, 135-36
    boarding school, impact of, 264
    education, 171
    illness, 232
    journalist, 308
    marriage, 314
    musically gifted, 264, 332
    in Melbourne, 170
    party and 'night under the pines,' 314
    at 'The Lodge', 175, 192
Lyons, Sarah, 184
Lyons, Sheila (Lacey), viii, 304
    after JL's death, 253, 255
    as baby, 97
    backstop for Enid, 188
    in Canberra, 175, 236
    care of younger siblings, 186–7
    close to Aunt Nell, 187
    education, 99, 114, 170, 186-7, 236

'Faith in Australia' flight, 190-91
    feted, 264
    housekeeping, 249
    parties in PM's office, 198
    to London, 240-1
    marriage, 271
Lyons, Tom and Mavis
    care of EL & JL's children, xii, 114, 121, 124, 135, 182, 232
    New Town home, 105, 129-30
    telegram from JL, 183
Lyons family,
    accidents, 3
    Catholicism, 161
    children's living arrangements, 186-7
    Christmas presents very modest, 184, 265
    family discipline, 142
    golf, 186–7
    life in Canberra, 188-9
    photographs of, 189-90
    as reported in newspapers, 189-90
    Sunday routine in Canberra, 189
Lyons government (federal), 192-3, 194, 207, 248
Lyons homes, 94
    see also 'Home Hill' (Devonport home of Lyons family)
    150 Barkers Rd, Kew, 170, 173, 175
    309 Dandenong Rd, East St Kilda, 142
    115 Main Rd, New Town, Hobart, 122, 130
    11 Valley View Rd, East Malvern, 269
    Liverpool St, Hobart, 88
    67 Pedder St, New Town, Hobart, 106-07

MacDonald, Ishbel, 22-6, 241

MacDonald, Ramsay, 165, 170, 223, 225-6, 241

Macquarie Broadcasting Services, 269

Maher, Frank, 270

'Manila girls' affair, 295

Mannix, Abp Daniel, 160, 255

Maritime Industries Bill, 138

Martin, Allan, 151, 246

Martin, George, 57, 60

McCall, Robert, 270

McCoy, William, 81

McElwain, A, 312

McEwen, John, 292

McFie, Hector, 277

McGrath, David, 157

McGrath, Frank (Hookey), 314

McGrath, Mary (later Mary Pridmore), 169, 331

McGuire, Margaret, 319

McGuire, Paul, 319–20

McMahon, William, 324

McTiernan, EA, 147

Medley, Molly, 321

Medley, Prof. John, 321

Melba, Dame Nellie, 154

Melbourne Agreement, 146

Menzies, Heather, 188

Menzies, Pattie, 168, 176, 200, 249
 to Europe, 215

Menzies, Robert, 3–4
 Afternoon Light, 325
 on arrival in Britain, 220-1
 attorney general, 193
 blamed for JL's illness, 257
 to Britain, 273-4
 on Catholic vote, 319
 challenge to JL, 248
 on EL and ministry, 303
 on EL's public speaking, xi, 168
 on JL and EL's energy, 180
 to Europe, 215
 formation of UAP, 164
 leader of UAP, 258
 on marriage of Edward VIII, 239
 'overthrow JL' (theory), 246
 press clippings on JL's death to EL, 258–9
 relationship with JL, 245
 resignation from Cabinet, 249
 tribute to JL, 256–7
 Young Nationalists leadership, 151

Menzies government, 302

Mollison, Jack, 40

Moore, Alice, 57

Moore, Tess, 184

Moses, Charles, 322

Munich Agreement (1938), 4, 212, 228, 242, 246, 248

Murdoch, Elisabeth, 218, 244, 279-80, 346

Murdoch, Sir Keith
 arranges job for young Enid, 270-1
 conservative political grouping, 159-60
 EL's radio broadcasts, 268-9
 figurehead of 'the Group', 246
 'Heathfield' (Toorak home), 163
 meetings with JL, 236-7
 on Munich Agreement, 212
 publishes Enid's columns, vii

support for Menzies, 248

supports JL as treasurer, 153

Murdoch, Walter, 321

Murray, Tom, 253

Mussolini, Benito, 213-14, 217, 228, 238-9, 242- 8

National Civic Council, 320

National Council of Women of Australia, 210

National Insurance legislation, 249, 324, 326

'Nation's Forum of the Air' (ABC radio program), 294

Newman, Jocelyn, xiii, 338-39

Niemeyer, Sir Otto, 146

non-aggression pacts, 267

Norris, Charles, 151

O'Brien, Thomas, 27

O'Byrne, Mary (née Sullivan), 171

O'Callaghan, Jack, 107

O'Donnell, Fr Thomas (Tom), ix, 78-81, 85, 93

Ogilvie, Albert, 130-1, 267

O'Grady, Sir James, 125

O'Keefe, Mick, 115, 123-4

Okines, T A, 130

O'Malley, King, 50, 71

O'Neill, Esther, 231

Orchard, *see* Taggett, Louisa

Pacific Pact, 229

Page, Earle, 1, 6, 127, 164, 229, 244–5, 248-9, 253, 260, 262, 257, 288, 290, 304

Parkes, Edward, 124

Parkhill, Sir Archdale, 193, 244

Parliament of Australia
female MPs, 281, 283-4, 287
radio broadcast of, 288

Paul, Marian, 187, 345

Peacock, Sir Alexander, 86

Pearce, Sen. George, 204, 229

Persse, Michael Collins, vii, 317

Pioneer (Fabian-style journal), 40

Pithouse, Horace, 53

Pius XI, Pope, 228

policies and beliefs of EL, 278
Australian-made products, 118
child endowment, xi, 285, 297
Commonwealth–State relations, 294
dental clinics, 118
dignity of labour, 118
education, 118
health and medical, 296
housing, 280
international relations, 286
milk distribution, 118
mothers and families, 294
opposition to Powers Referendum, 293
returned servicemen, 285
slum clearance, 118
social justice, 280, 285
stevedoring industry, 291

Pratt, Ambrose, 151

Premiers' Plan, 146

Price, John, 157

protectionist policies, 205

radio broadcasts, 174, 191, 267–9

Rankin, Annabelle, 307

Rankin, Janet, 306

Rapke, Julia, 211

Reece, Eric, 279

Ricketson, Staniforth, 147, 151, 152, 155, 159, 163-4, 236

Riordan, David, 139

Rischbeith, Bessie, 204, 223

Robertson, Agnes, 307

Roosevelt, Eleanor, 169, 231, 253, 279, 313

Roosevelt, Franklin D, viii, 169, 228-9, 231, 294

Russell, Leonard, 57, 74

Ryan, Rupert, 197

Sambell, Theo, 322, 323

Santamaria, BA, 319, 320

Scott, Sir Ernest, 256

Scullin, Jim, 134–5, 139–40, 280, 315
    Catholicism, 157
    lived at Kurrajong Hotel, 176
    prime minister, 231
    support for JL, 145
    tribute to JL, 250

Scullin, Sarah, 140, 178

Scullin government, 141, 147–8

sectarianism, 75, 77, 101

Semmler, Clem, 321

Seton, Maj., 10

Simonds, Abp Dr Justin, 256

Simpson, Mrs Wallis, 238

slum clearance, 118

Smith, Sgt Issy, 173

social conventions and formality, 63–4, 87

Spanish influenza pandemic (1919), 97–8

Spender, Percy, 293

spiritualism, 18

St Brigid's Catholic Church (Wynyard, Tas.), 81

St Christopher's Catholic Church (Manaka), 189

St Francis' Church (Lonsdale St, Melbourne), 209

Stanley, Massey, 311

State Labor conference (1918), 96

State School Patriotic Fund, 89

Stevens, Bertram, 192–3

Stowport public school, 35, 41

Street, Geoffrey, 273

Street, Jessie, 259, 270, 294

suffrage, 37, 49

Sun column (newspaper), 311

Swanson, Jack, 186, 218, 240, 259

Swanston, Jack, 184

Swaythling, Lady, 219, 224, 241

Sydney Harbour Bridge, opening of, 194

Taggett, Eliza (daughter), 12–16
    see also Burnell, Eliza (née Taggett)

Taggett, Eliza (mother), 11, 12

Taggett, Elizabeth Jane, 12

Taggett, Harry (or Henry; 'Gentleman Harry'), 10–13

Taggett, Henry, 14

Taggett, Joseph, 14

Taggett, Lavinia, 11, 12

Taggett, Louisa, 12, 13, 14, 79, 85, 105, 114

Taggett, Mark, 14

Taggett, Matilda, 11, 14, 105

Taggett, Mrs, 10

Taggett, William Henry, 11

Taggett family, 10–14

Tangney, Dorothy, 279, 281, 287, 289, 310–11

Tasmanian politics
Ogilvie scandal, 130–1, 134

Tasmanian state elections
1916, 84, 89, 90
1922, 102
1925, 115, 119
1928, 129, 131
1948, 300
compulsory voting from 1928, 103, 134

Taylor, Albert, 184

telephones, 124, 145, 235

Temple, Shirley, 232

Theodore, Esther, 144

Theodore, Ted, 144, 146, 153–5

Thirmuthus (home help in Devonport), 969

'This I Believe' (radio series), 320

Thomas, Archer, 311

Thorby, Harold, 216

Thornton, Lyndall, 290

Threlfall, Martyn, 177, 179, 180, 182, 183, 185, 259

Tracey, Edward, 32–3

Tracey, Ray, 6, 186, 189

Truby King, Dr Frederick, 170

Truby King, Mary, 213

Truby King baby-care methods, 181, 212

'Tune in with Britain' catch-cry, 165

Tye, Jimmy, 40, 42

Tye, Tommy, 40, 42

Ulm, Charles, 190

union militancy, 137-8

United Australia Party (UAP), 4
alliances within, 237
coalition government, 248, 275
formation, 160, 169
JL's commitment to, 170–1
party leadership, 249-50
rally (July 1937), 243-4
wins government at 1931 election, 175

Van Diemen's Land Company, 38

Victoria League, 111

Vo Kong, Charlie, 42

Wales, Prince of (Edward, later Edward VIII), 227, 238, 243

Ward, Eddie, 162, 262

Warneke, George, 261

Wedgewood, Ivy, 307, 337

Wells, HG, 247–8

Western Australia visit, 202-6

White, Murray, 277

White, Vera, 315

White, Sir Thomas, 315

Whitlam, Gough, 202, 213, 235, 324, 334

Whitlam, Margaret, 199, 334

Whitsitt, Joshua, 71, 75, 81, 84

Wilde, Oscar, 318

Wingfield, Sir Charles, 228

Woman's Day and Home (magazine), 312

Woman's Day (magazine)
serial biography of EL, 308–9

women
achievements not recognised, 304

appointment to Olympic Games
organising committee, 305
civic rights of, 119
election candidates, 115
election to federal parliament, 279
financial skills, 167-68
involvement in public affairs, 206–7
and 'men's domain,' 119, 287
ministerial positions, 303–4
not men's equal at work, 211
pay levels, 303–4
political significance, 165
in politics, 116, 117–19
power of, 209
rights of, 214
sacrifice of, 293
Women's Suffrage League, 19
WorkChoices legislation, 302
Workers Political League (WPL), 44, 49,
50, 68–70
world peace, 211
World War I, 84, 91

Australian involvement, 84, 211
bigotry against German-origin
citizens, 91
conscription, 85, 92
embarkment for, 83
food prices, 91
fundraising events, 90
impact on home front, 88
volunteers, 90
World War II
fall of Singapore, 274
foreshadowed, 4, 243, 267
Pearl Harbour, 274
public disillusionment with, 274
Worrell, David, 268
Wright, John, 277

Yeats, WB (poetry), 323
York, Duchess of (Elizabeth), 125
York, Duke of (Prince Albert), 125
Young, Abp Guilford (Gilly), 319
Young Nationalists, 152